D0403268

REMARKABLE

REMARKABLE

PROVEN INSIGHTS TO
ACCELERATE YOUR CAREER

DAVID KRONFELD

Matt Holt Books
An Imprint of BenBella Books, Inc.
Dallas, TX

This book is designed to provide accurate and authoritative information about career and job searching and related personal development. Neither the author nor the publisher is engaged in rendering legal, accounting, or other professional services by publishing this book. If any such assistance is required, the services of a qualified financial professional should be sought. The author and publisher will not be responsible for any liability, loss, or risk incurred as a result of the use and application of any information contained in this book.

Remarkable copyright © 2021 by David Kronfeld

All rights reserved. No part of this book may be used or reproduced in any manner whatsoever without written permission of the publisher, except in the case of brief quotations embodied in critical articles or reviews.

Matt Holt Books is an imprint of BenBella Books, Inc.
10440 N. Central Expressway
Suite 800
Dallas, TX 75231
benbellabooks.com
Send feedback to feedback@benbellabooks.com

BenBella is a federally registered trademark. MATT HOLT and logo are trademarks of BenBella Books.

Printed in the United States of America
10 9 8 7 6 5 4 3 2 1

Library of Congress Control Number: 2021012415
ISBN 9781953295637
ebk ISBN 9781953295972

Editing by Brian Nicol
Copyediting by Michael Fedison
Proofreading by Marissa Wold Uhrina and Cape Cod Compositors, Inc.
Text design by Aaron Edmiston
Cover design by Paul McCarthy
Printed by Lake Book Manufacturing

Special discounts for bulk sales are available.
Please contact bulkorders@benbellabooks.com.

*To Colton and Aaron—may you always
remember how remarkable you can be*

CONTENTS

SECTION IV: SUCCESS THROUGH INFLUENCE

SECTION V: SUCCESSFUL NEGOTIATIONS

SECTION VI: INTERVIEWING WELL FOR A JOB

SECTION VII: A SOUND METHODOLOGY
FOR BUSINESS ANALYSES

PREFACE

I am a successful businessperson by any measure and have been rewarded financially with great prosperity, despite significant obstacles I had to overcome. When I emigrated from Israel to the United States, I could barely speak English. While studying to earn my engineering degree, I came to understand the language reasonably well, but I spoke it poorly. I also had a thick accent, which, combined with my crude English, made it troublesome for people to comprehend me. To make matters worse, my native country had a different culture and behavioral norms. Some of these norms were quite dissimilar and not very endearing to Americans, particularly not in the corporate world. Given all that, the odds of success were stacked against me, and most likely I would have had an average career, at best, had it not been for this one exonerating characteristic. I attribute *insight* as the single most important factor that allowed me to accelerate my career. In fact, if you were to ask people who know me best, they would acknowledge and affirm that I have proven to be quite insightful, and uniquely so. Even my most prosperous peers would concur.

Although insightfulness mostly reflects innate talent, I claim that I can *teach* you to become more insightful. This is my ultimate purpose in writing this book. **The primary objective of this book is to teach you how to become more insightful in business, make better decisions, and more quickly advance your career.** I don't do it by simply recounting my own career progression and experiences with the hope that you discover insights that you can emulate. Although imitation might be flattering, applying what you learn from my experiences and advice will yield much better results for you.

The genesis of this book originated with my daughter, Beth, who managed to do well in her own right. Over the years, as any involved father would do, I offered her advice and guidance. Beth maintains that my advice and insights were unique and meaningfully contributed to her success. She implored me to memorialize it in a book so that her children, grandchildren, and many others could benefit, too.

My first reaction was, "You were the beneficiary—you know exactly what helped. Why don't you put it in writing yourself?"

She responded, "I would not be able to explain it the way you can. On top of being insightful, you have an uncanny ability to explain everything in a way that is simple and yet powerful enough to leave a strong impression on people so that they actually adopt and put the wisdom to use." It was factual logic. So, I acquiesced. Sometime later, we decided to expand the premise of the book to allow more people to potentially benefit from my advice. And so the idea of publishing a book for general readership emerged.

I incorporate some personal stories into the book to provide real-life examples that illustrate many of the lessons and techniques the book teaches, thereby enhancing the reader's learning and comprehension. Some of the personal stories also serve to provide a more proper perspective of the sacrifices, obstacles, perseverance, and all the ups and downs on the road to success, as well as a fuller understanding of me as an individual.

Over my long career, I have been a management consultant dealing with the most critical strategic decisions companies face, a corporate executive, and a venture capitalist. I've had intimate exposure to the highest priority challenges facing hundreds of companies. I have seen strategies that flourished and plans that floundered. I have witnessed companies thrive and companies fail, managers who prospered and managers who suffered setbacks and even disgrace. Be it hiring or firing, I decided the fates of many managers at all levels, including CEOs. Through this book, I aspire to instill all the insight I've acquired so that you become wiser.

The odyssey of my success was an arduous one, in both my personal circumstances and business trajectory. As it turns out, less than favorable circumstances were part of my life from early childhood. I came from a poor background, and nothing was effortless for me in my formative years. I completely lacked appreciation for the value of education and had no awareness of the business opportunities that education may have provided me. No mentor or educated person was around to offer me a better perspective. Significant amounts of *resilience* and *perseverance* were required to overcome many obstacles. Throughout the book I share some selected personal experiences, not just to provide perspective on the **importance of resilience and perseverance for one's career success**, but also as way to help inspire the fortitude and motivation to persevere when your own hardships arise. In most cases, the personal stories enhance and elucidate the hard-core business observations as well.

The book's primary audience is professionals in the early stages of their careers (up to ten years of work experience) or those planning to have such careers. That being said, the guidance can be of substantive value to the more experienced and even seasoned executives, who can leverage the insightful perspectives. In addition, this book offers a special, added value to foreign students and foreigners in general who wish to pursue a career in the United States, particularly those who come from cultures different from the American culture. My personal stories and experiences should be quite illuminating to such foreigners and perhaps help them plow an easier path to success than the one I had to endure. Also, I include a short section for young adults to elevate the importance of a quality education with the hope of bolstering their inner drive and resolve to work hard and do well in school. It provides cogent logic that will be a complement to their parents' advice and guidance. As we all know, sometimes children are more open to advice given by others, even if it is the same as the parents'! Consider bringing this section to the attention of your own children or nieces and nephews.

I wrote this book in a conversational style to aid both comprehension and readability. My hope is that the relaxed and informal language creates the sense that you're sitting around a table discussing intriguing topics with friends or family. The book is organized around specific lessons, observations, loosely stated rules, and a list of dos and don'ts. I present observations with definitive justification and rationale to enable you to ascertain their value while retaining the flexibility of context so the learnings can be adapted to your particular circumstance.

There are ample observations and insights in this book. Some simple, others profound, and all variations in between. A single casual reading will not provide the reader with the full wisdom of the book, so one will benefit from revisiting it from time to time. The more often you visit these pages, the more you'll see. This is particularly so with the passage of time and as your own experience grows and your perspectives change. I would not hesitate to bet that each successive reading will find you reacting to different topics in different ways, multiplying your awareness and adoption of insightfulness.

At times, I express my ideas in a precise, more definitive manner. I use definitive language for a variety of reasons. Mostly, I have conviction regarding my ideas and believe that communicating in a succinct and direct way is the most effective, particularly in a teaching context. Black-and-white statements are easily understood when not burdened with too many qualifying ones. Whatever my reasons, be assured that it is not out of arrogance or overconfidence that "I know it all."

Along the same vein, I also make many observations about human behavioral traits and may use the same definitive language. Please keep in mind that I'm not trained in, nor do I claim to have, specific knowledge of behavioral science or its related fields. Whatever comments I make represent my personal perspectives and beliefs and are introduced to provide some potential rationale and context regarding the business-related observations and recommendations.

Finally, as I provide observations and rules, please bear in mind that there are exceptions to every rule, and an exception to every exception. **However, an exception doesn't create its own rule, nor does it invalidate one. A rule is only meant to give you the highest probability for an outcome.** Thus, just because you may be able to conceptualize an exception doesn't invalidate the rule or learning I am offering.

I hope you enjoy and benefit from reading this book. All the best and good luck in your endeavors.

DAVID KRONFELD

AUTHOR'S NOTE

This book focuses on a single dimension that I believe has the highest impact on one's career—*insightfulness*. The book addresses insightfulness at three levels, each with a specific objective or goal:

- **Level 1.** Sharing general *observations and recommendations*. Basically, a list of dos and don'ts, which are based on the insights I learned over my career. The objective here is to provide value-added knowledge and specific insightful rules that you can use to increase the probability of your own success.

- **Level 2.** Giving you *tools* that you can use to become more insightful yourself. The goal here is to teach you the art of how to become more insightful when analyzing situations and reaching business decisions.

- **Level 3.** Teaching you *advanced techniques* of how to become as insightful as your potential may allow.

In other words, and by analogy, let's say you want to be a basketball player and I'm an experienced coach. The first level means that I will give you pointers that will make you a better shooter, rebounder, defender, passer, and so on. At the second level, I'll teach you how to analyze rudimentary tactics, team plays, and the strengths and weaknesses of opponents so that you can apply tactics to win games. At the third level, I'll teach you the advanced techniques used by professionals at the top of their game.

Clearly, everybody can benefit from the first level of insightfulness. However, just how much one benefits from the second and third levels depends on two things. First, the way one thinks and uses their "brains"—I refer to it as "brainpower." Second, one's innate skills that dictate the limit of a person's potential, meaning I can teach you all the tactics and strategies of basketball, but how your brain works will determine just how good a tactician or strategist you'll become. In the same vein, I can teach you everything that Michael Jordan was taught, but how close you'll get to becoming a Michael Jordan will depend on your innate athletic skills.

As the basketball example demonstrates, in the case of sport competition, the success requirements are innate athletic ability and appropriate brainpower. In the context of this book, and from the perspective of business career advancements, there is only one variable—how you use your brainpower.

As you read the book, the sophistication of what it says, the degree of nuance presented, and the depth of discussion surrounding some theories and tools will vary, because they will reflect which level of teaching I'm addressing. If you have the inclination and the brainpower to enjoy the Level 3 readings, then you'll enjoy the whole book. If not, you might find some places a bit too "philosophical" for your taste, so you might choose to skim through those sections.

Please keep in mind that the main goal of the book is not to make you the next Michael Jordan in your chosen profession. Rather, it is to make you a better player. Anybody and everybody who **reads and puts to practice what the book teaches will most likely greatly increase their probability for success in business.** Just how much so will depend on you as an individual. Consider this: Michael Jordan was renowned for his long hours of practice. He truly believed that continued practice allowed him to reach and maintain his best potential. The same thing is true with insightfulness. The tools and techniques discussed in this book need to be studied and restudied, practiced and re-practiced, not just read once, to allow you to reach your highest potential as well.

The discerning reader may also observe that I have a secondary objective for the book. I mentioned that I substantiate my opinions and recommendations with detailed reasoning. The primary purpose of doing so is to give you, the reader, as much explanation as possible, so that you will be able to better judge the wisdom and value of

my advice as well as adjust my recommendations to your unique circumstances. The secondary objective is to demonstrate the granularity
of thinking that leads to superior analyses—a critical component in
reaching insightfulness. In other words, my secondary objective is to
demonstrate how to think more deeply and analytically in both business and in life in general. Although a secondary objective, it is not of
secondary value. In fact, insightfulness is achieved precisely because
of increased analytical skills. As a result, although the book's primary
audience is someone early in their career, the more experienced professional will benefit from the sections that dive deeply into the granularity of thought and analyses.

So please be patient with the sections you feel may be too philosophical and challenging and enjoy the sections you find helpful.

UNDERSTANDING INSIGHTFULNESS

1

"Insight" in the Context of Business and What Makes It Unique

I claim that *insight* is the single most important factor that allowed me to accelerate my career. I also claim that I can teach you to become more insightful yourself. However, I use the words "insight" and "insightfulness" in a somewhat unique way. It is specifically tailored to be applicable in the business world. Understanding the way I define it, and its nuances, is imperative.

"Insight" and "insightfulness" are words that describe a concept. Translating a concept into actions that can be taught and in turn used by someone is a challenging task. This is particularly so for concepts that appear clear and are well understood, yet in reality are overly general and somewhat amorphous. By way of analogy, let's take the word "astute." Everybody understands what the word means, but how does one actually become astute, or more astute than one already is? When we hear a statement that provides a perspective deeper or different from our own, we may characterize it as astute. It is easy for us to identify it. But what can we actually do to become more astute ourselves? Clearly, it is not an easy thing to understand and do, yet it is exactly the objective of this book—to teach you how to become more insightful in the context of the business world. To do this, I need to define "insight" and "insightfulness" in my own way, so please bear with me as I first discuss my definition. I believe that you will likely

3

discover some new "insights" (pun intended!) that will allow you not just to better appreciate what follows, but more importantly, to be better equipped to benefit from it.

Let's look first at the definition of "insight" from Dictionary.com:

insight. n
1) An instance of apprehending the true nature of a thing, especially through intuitive understanding.
2) Penetrating mental vision or discernment; faculty of seeing into inner character or underlying truth.

Note the strong reference to *intuitive understanding* and *mental vision*. You could conclude that insight is something dependent on innate capabilities we are born with and that it cannot be taught or learned. So, how can I make the claim that by reading this book the reader can become more insightful? The answer lies in looking at insight in a slightly different way.

Colloquially, the word "insight" is used in many ways that are not based on intuition or mental vision of one kind or another. For example, it is used to describe some information one has that is not immediately available to others (e.g., "He has some insight about what's going on in that country."). This reflects some knowledge that is not generally known. It is this kind of an insight that I am referring to in my experience and in this book.

How does one arrive at such insight?

I suggest that insightfulness comprises two separate dimensions. The first is a keen understanding that reflects the accumulated *knowledge* and *wisdom* one brings to bear in situations and circumstances that commonly occur with similar dynamics and reasonably predictable outcomes. It can come from one's own experience or observations and lessons imparted by others from their experience. These lessons teach us about how things "really work" and the dos and don'ts in such situations. The second reflects on one's *ability to conduct more discerning analyses* of unique business situations/challenges, leading to observations and conclusions that are uniquely different from what others may arrive at. I refer to the second one as *specific situational analyses.* This ability to reach insightful specific situational analyses is heavily driven by distinct tools and techniques. This book addresses both aspects. It offers specific observations and lessons as well as the various tools and techniques that lead to more insightful situational analyses. To this end, I define *insight* and *insightfulness* in a unique way. Both the definition of insight is unique, and so is the conceptual difference between insight and insightfulness. It may seem at first to be a minor nuance, but it is not. It captures the essence of this book.

Insight: An ability to observe situations, evaluate all relevant information, discern the *true* nature of things, and attain a perspective that helps reach and/or influence a correct evaluation and decision in support of a desired outcome.

Note that my definition represents an ideal of utmost perfection in that it implies that we observe all or everything there is to observe, and discern all the truth there is to be discerned. Clearly, rarely can such perfection be attained. In reality there are varying degrees of insights, kind of "partial" insights, which are much more likely. It means that only some of the analyses are conducted insightfully, while others may not be. Or that only some greater "truth" had been discovered, but not necessarily the "whole truth" and "nothing but the truth." However, this fact doesn't take away from the value I attribute in this book to insight, be it partial or full perfection. First, we all strive for full perfection, and second, any partial insightfulness will still result in superior outcomes relative to analyses performed without any insights, or with lesser insights. Thus, henceforth, whenever I refer to insight, it includes both partial and total perfection.

I believe that everything attributed to me as having a unique insightful talent is meant in the way I just defined it. No sixth sense or extraordinary degree of intuition, instincts, or mental capability; only the ability *to observe* all of the relevant information and *analyze it correctly*, so that you may discern the *true* nature of things, which will result in a *correct* evaluation and a *correct* decision.

Note that my definition clearly implies that in any given situation one can't be wrong and still be insightful. And conversely, one can't be insightful and be wrong. Thus, if you learn to become more insightful, you have learned to be more correct. **That is why learning how to become more insightful will allow you to make correct decisions and accelerate your career.**

Not only can the above definition of insight be taught and learned, but as importantly, it is most relevant in business. I refer to it in a simple way as **the ability to "see the forest for the trees," yet still see the "trees in the forest," combined with "thinking out of the box," and driven by pure, simple logic and correct data,** which often represent a big challenge in business situations and can be important and, at times, critical.

As you look closely at my definition of *insight*, you may notice a seemingly interesting paradox. Notice that in my definition I use the phrase "an ability to observe situations." Well, if it is only the ability to *observe*, it means that *it is there for all to see*. If one *discerns* from that the true nature of things, then *many others could as well*. If it leads to *correct decision making*, then it implies that *most agree*, which means it must be logical and consistent with what people already know or understand. So, how can something be there for all to see, be logical, make a lot of sense, and that most agree with, yet be considered insightful? This appears to contradict the very definition of insightfulness. After all, insightfulness refers to *a unique* observation or capability that is *not apparent* to everybody.

An interesting paradox, but only conceptually. The reality is that even though all can observe and see the same things, only a few are able to see beyond the "obvious." It is the "obvious" that all can see and observe. Often, the less obvious appears to be a nuance, something that appears to be of no importance or significance, and therefore is frequently ignored. Indeed, many times, the nuance is not all that important. However, in some situations it may hold the key to correct understanding. It is in those situations that insightfulness can come into play. It just requires someone to be aware of a fact or an element that has escaped everyone else. As you continue to read the book, pay attention in the stories and examples to how what appears to be an unimportant nuance turns into an insightful observation that completely changes the analyses and conclusions.

We all possess the ability to be insightful. We all exhibit it, on and off, to one degree or another; there is nothing terribly unique about that. However, I would like to introduce a small nuance to differentiate between what all of us can do and what only a few of us can.

Insightfulness Is a Unique Capability

So far, I have intermingled insight, insightful, and insightfulness. I would separate and define the word "insightfulness" to mean something different from the other two. I'll define *insightfulness* in a way that applies to only a very few. Thus, I define *insightfulness* to represent a *unique capability*.

I define *insightfulness* or an *insightful person* as having **the ability to be insightful with a high degree of consistency.**

In other words, **it is not the occasional display of brilliance or insight that matters much. It is doing so consistently.** As such, one has a distinguishable talent, and uniquely so, that others will notice. Expanding your innate ability to be insightful and enabling you to do so more consistently is what I can teach you in this book. You will then become an *insightful person*.

My hope is that you will gain many new perspectives that will enable you to consistently reach better decisions and, by extension, be more successful. Much of the "art of insight" reflects a "different way of thinking," which requires paying attention to nuances, framing issues differently and uniquely, seeing beyond the obvious, and so on. It would be of value for you as you read this book to try to always ask yourself whether you would have indeed thought about each of the observations I make in the same way yourself. Better yet, try to second-guess me on each of my observations before you proceed to read my analyses and conclusions. It will help you realize that the perspective I have taken in many cases is different and indeed insightful.

One more thing: "Insight," "insightful," and "insightfulness" are conceptual words, which are not necessarily easy to measure. It would be useful for the purpose of this book to use some simplistic attributes that allow some characterization of how to differentiate and characterize the insightful person from the non-insightful, and the degree of insightfulness. I've already suggested that the answer lies in the difference between seeing the "obvious" from the "non-obvious" and the nuances in between. I will therefore use the following terms to loosely differentiate the insightful from the non-insightful: "Deep/ Refined Thinker" versus "Shallow Thinker" and correspondingly a continuum of "deep" (i.e., deep, deeper, deepest and shallow, shallower, shallowest) to differentiate between the relative degrees of insightfulness.

2

Arriving at Insightfulness

B ecause insightfulness is a concept, it is impossible to give a formula or recipe as to how to achieve it. There is no list of specific activities that will assure one attains it. However, there is a way of thinking and an approach to analyzing and dissecting situations that will increase the probability of getting there. I refer to it as the overall conceptual methodology for achieving insightfulness. It is a theoretical four-step process, which, when carried out properly, will significantly increase the likelihood of attaining insightfulness. As you study the methodology, try to understand what the objectives of each of the steps are. Understanding what you are after will help in doing it better.

The Four-Step Methodology for Achieving Insightfulness

Step 1: Define *precisely* the *correct* challenge that needs to be overcome.

The word "correct" is emphasized here because clearly if one doesn't identify correctly the challenge/problem that needs to be solved, then a correct solution will not likely be discovered. The word "precisely" is emphasized to ensure that people don't misinterpret the intentions behind the challenge to be overcome.

In most situations, the challenge or problem to be overcome is not defined very precisely and thus could be interpreted in various ways

9

and with significantly different implications. By definition, a situation like this is not precisely, and therefore, not correctly described. This generally happens because the challenge or problem is defined in a way that may at face value appear well understood, but in reality may have many nuanced implications.

For example, assume you were appointed to launch a new company in a new country. Your boss said the following: "Your main objective is to become the number one competitor in that country. We want everybody in that country to recognize our brand." Is it precisely clear as to what that challenge actually requires? What does it mean to become the number one competitor, and how will it be measured? If measured by the size (sales and market share), then would it be okay to sacrifice margins and profits, or even be unprofitable, to attain the goal and get more sales? What does it mean to have "everybody in the country recognize our brand"? Does it mean that as a result of becoming number one, our brand will therefore be better known? Or could we spend a substantial amount of money on marketing and advertisements to accomplish it? If so, could we do it even if we are not profitable, thus making the financial performance even worse?

Here is another example. Your boss tells you, "It is very important to finish the development and launch the new product as soon as possible. Get it done!" What does "as soon as possible" mean? Can you spend as much money and resources as you would like to make it happen, or is it subject to a budgetary constraint? If there are budgetary constraints, how much money can you spend? What does "as soon as possible" mean, and what kind of a delay would be unacceptable? Is it measured in days, weeks, or months? If the product has some minor flaws, would it be okay to release it sooner and then correct the minor flaws over time? If one feature of the product is difficult to complete and introduces delays, would it be okay to cancel that feature and introduce the product without it?

See how many questions and potential implications arise when challenges are not precisely defined?

Thus, given the above, a precise and correct definition of the challenge is imperative so as to lead to the right solutions. To arrive at the right definition, ask a simple question: **Does the problem/challenge** you have identified allow you to correctly define the actions/steps that will help overcome the problem/challenge and achieve the goal you desire? You will see many examples in this book of how easy it is to err, and conversely, how difficult it may be to "see the forest for the trees," while still "seeing the trees in the forest" when implementing this step.

Step 2: Break down the main challenge/problem identified in step 1 into "directional" subcategories that embody the full list of all the options/actions that should be addressed to reach a solution.

The objective here is to redefine the main challenge/problem from a conceptual level into elements that provide more directional specificity that would identify all the actions that need to be taken in order to achieve the desired end result. The subcategories can be stated in terms of other sub-goals, and/or questions, and/or tasks.

By way of an example, assume you live in an oasis in the desert. The well that supplies the inhabitants with water has begun to run dry. You need to do something about it or perish. Per step 1, the pressing challenge/problem is to increase the water supply. The subcategorization required by step 2 could be the following: (i) Can the well be modified to yield more water? (ii) Are there ways to reduce current water consumption? (iii) Are there ways to find new sources of water?

Step 3: Continue to break down each of the subcategories into their own subcategories.

Each such subcategory should be defined in a way that gives greater "directional" guidance/clarity into what actions/tasks might be necessary to accomplish it. By way of our example, the above subcategory (iii)—find new sources of water supply—could be broken down into (a) find new wells or (b) import water.

Step 4: Start a reiterative process and repeat step 3 until you bring it down to enough specificity to translate each of the subcategories into more definitive actions/tasks.

For example, the subcategory (b) of step 3 above—import water—can be broken down into (i) via a pipeline, (ii) via camels, and (iii) via trucks.

Follow the above conceptual methodology and make sure it yields a complete and correct list, as is required by my definition of insightfulness. Do so properly, and you'll be well on your way to insightfulness. There are many examples and tips in this book that demonstrate how this methodology is applied in practical terms.

3

The Art of Insightfulness in Practice: How to Write a Great Resume

It would be appropriate, at this point, to pause and go through an all-encompassing example that will demonstrate exactly how the concept of insightfulness is realized and achieved in practical terms. I will do so through a detailed, step-by-step description of a personal example. I will ask you to think alongside me yet to form your own thoughts and conclusions before I reveal mine. This way you'll be able to compare what you would have done under the same circumstances to what I did. This will give you a greater sense of how easy it is not to see the obvious, and how nuances turn into critical observations. It will also demonstrate the corollary: just how easy it is to become more insightful—it is nothing but using pure, simple logic.

The example involves the art of resume writing, where I was instrumental in changing a long-standing practice and "common wisdoms," which led to a new trend that spread like wildfire (although I'll never be given credit for it, since nobody ever knew how it all started). In addition, you will also learn how to write a great resume.

Before we walk through the example, let's recap the key elements of being insightful:

An ability *to observe* situations, evaluate all the *relevant* information, *discern* the *true* nature of things, and attain a perspective that helps

reach and/or influence a *correct* evaluation and decision, and do so in a *consistent* manner.

The definition clearly suggests that insightfulness refers to *a process* that requires deeper, more refined thinking to help discern the true nature of things. It requires us to look beyond the obvious and pay attention to the *subtleties* and *nuances*. It is done through collecting the right information, framing more precisely the desired outcome, and drawing the correct conclusions. It is an *iterative process*, not a flash of brilliance.

Before we take a deep dive into the example, I'd like to point out another rule for insightfulness, which will play an important role in getting the most out of this example. The rule has two parts:

1. The best insight can be achieved when one *correctly* understands the "what," "why," and "how" of a situation—all three!

2. Complete understanding is accomplished through an iterative process of constantly refining and narrowing the focus of the three questions above.

Again, the first rule may appear obvious and self-evident, but it is not. You would be surprised at how often people fail to do so. People understand one or two aspects in the first rule, but generally don't always understand all three. Many times, when they think they do, their understanding is incorrect. To me, the above rule reflects on *how deep or shallow* one's thinking is, which also reflects on the conclusions one reaches. The understanding-it-*correctly* part generally reflects on the *accuracy of the data* one uses. Keep this rule in mind when going over the following example.

I graduated from the Wharton School of Business with an MBA in 1977. I had to write a resume to submit to prospective employers for an intern summer position after the first year, and for full-time employment upon graduation.

To preface this example, I need to explain the state of technology in those days. There were no personal computers, no networks, and no word processing software. Documents and letters were typed on a typewriter, and there were no special fonts. Typos or changes, if minor, were corrected by using a white paste called Wite-Out and retyped over. More major changes required a retyping of the document.

Resumes at the time had a "standard" format. They provided the reader with detail of one's work and education history, and some noteworthy personal things, like hobbies, military service, distinctions, honors, and so on. The most common length was between two and four densely typed pages, depending on the length of one's experience. The content was organized into four categories: Objective, Work Experience, Education, and Personal. If one didn't have much work experience, like graduating students, then Education was displayed first. Below is what my first resume looked like at the time:

DAVID KRONFELD
1310 Spruce Street, Apt. 224
Philadelphia, Pennsylvania 19104

OBJECTIVE: A fulfilling job that utilizes my MBA skills. I would like to work in Strategic Planning, Marketing, or Finance for a company that can offer strong career advancement. My goal is to reach executive level management, over time.

WORK HISTORY:
(9/1974 – 4/1975)   Sammons Enterprises, Dallas, Texas
                               Title: Vice President of Systems

Responsibilities: As Vice President I was responsible for 12 System Analysts and 35 Programmers. I was responsible for all the development and maintenance of Sammons' data processing systems. As such I worked with the Presidents and General Managers of 8 different business divisions that comprised Sammons Enterprises. In this capacity I learned to understand all the workflows in their respective companies and departments; helped identify which data needed to be recorded and which management reports they needed; and developed such automated capabilities into our computers.

Accomplishments: When I joined the company, Data Processing had a terrible reputation. The computer that ran at night failed at least a few times a week, failing to have the necessary management and department reports ready for workers in the morning, causing significant productivity issues companywide. Additionally, any request for changes in reports or new reports took months and months to deliver, which was completely unacceptable to our "clients." After only a short period of time I was able to correct both problems to the complete satisfaction of all our clients, companywide.

(8/1973 – 9/1974)   **Electronic Data Systems Corporation**, Dallas, Texas
Title: Senior System Analyst

Responsibilities: I was part of a team that was responsible for the development and maintenance of all Data Processing needs of clients. As such, I constantly interacted with the different departments in trying to understand what data recording and management reports they needed to better conduct their business. As part of my work, I was assigned to different teams at different times. I worked most heavily on accounting and payroll systems. My clients were Blue Cross & Blue Shield of Texas and Blue Cross & Blue Shield of New York. I interacted heavily with the heads of the accounting and payroll departments.

Accomplishments: I was recognized as an excellent worker by my management and twice called into the Vice President's office for accommodations and "special" bonus awards. One was an extra cash bonus; the other was a one-week all-expenses-paid vacation for me and my wife. I subsequently was promoted to be an instructor in the company's "school." The company was exclusively hiring long-term U.S. military officers, and over a period of six months these officers were taught Computer Programming and Systems Analysis.

EDUCATION:
(8/1975 – Present) The Wharton School of Business, Philadelphia, Pennsylvania
Major: Finance.
(8/1971 – 5/1973) Stevens Institute of Technology, Hoboken, New Jersey
Degree: Masters in Computer Science.
(8/1971 – 5/1973) Stevens Institute of Technology
Degree: BS in Electrical Engineering with high honors.

PERSONAL: Married, no children. Tau Beta Phi Honor Society. Military service in the Israeli Armed Forces from 1966 to 1969.

My resume and those of other students were collated in the Wharton resume book, which was made available, upon request, to potential employers. Companies would come on campus to interview students through the school's placement office. In advance of the interviews, the placement office provided resumes to companies for those students who had expressed a desire to be interviewed by them. The number of requests for interviews far exceeded the number of interviews that were made available to students, so the companies would narrow down the field of applicants. The companies also looked through the resume book to see if they would like to initiate an interview request with a student who didn't sign up for an interview with them. Students were waiting breathlessly to be selected and go through the interview process. About 10 percent to 20 percent were able to land a summer internship job, and over 90 percent found a permanent job upon graduation.

I had some previous experience in job interviews, but for engineering positions, not highly sought-after career positions. I must have gone through at least five iterations in writing my resume, with constructive comments from the placement office and several second-year students, before finalizing the above resume. I waited anxiously for the process to begin.

The interviewing process was an interesting and an eye-opening experience for me. I learned quite a bit from the process. There were many observations I made, but one specifically stood out in my mind regarding the resume. I decided to make appropriate adjustments to my resume the following year, upon graduating and seeking full-time employment.

The following year I submitted a nonstandard-looking resume to the director of the placement office. He looked at me with a strange expression and simply said, "No, it doesn't make sense!" We had about an hour of a very lively conversation where I challenged him with "Why not?" I was adamant about my intent to submit a nonstandard resume and would not accept no for an answer.

To his credit, despite his initial consternation he was reasonably patient with me and tried to answer my challenging questions and observations as best he could. The conversation continued over the following days. His objections centered around two concerns. The first was the departure from the standard format of the resume, which might not bode well for the school. The second was that he believed that deviating from the standard would reflect badly on me and significantly detract from the attractiveness of my candidacy. His logic was that anything different from the accepted standard would be subject to scrutiny and raise concerns that I might be looked upon as a "rebel," and as such the type of person who may be disinclined to follow the rules. In his opinion, those aspects would likely be fatal to my candidacy.

I explained why I still wanted to do it my way, and why I didn't believe the implications would be as dire. After several conversations, he relented, mostly because I semi-convinced him that it wouldn't be that much of a departure in substance from the standard information provided in resumes, and that I was perfectly willing to assume full responsibility for the outcome. It would be illuminating to share some of that conversation. But first a bit of a background story and why I wasn't all that concerned about his "expert" observations and the dire warning of how this might be interpreted by potential employers. I had lost confidence in just how wise his previous advice had been.

As part of our training and preparation, the placement office offered tutorial classes on how to write a resume and do well in the interviewing process. (Older students also shared their war stories and tips about being interviewed.) There wasn't much to be said about the writing of the resume—standard format and information, with very little opportunity for any deviation. Most of the observations and recommendations the tutors made were related to the interviewing process and the interviews themselves. These recommendations were logical and appeared reasonable to me. To sum it all up, employers were looking for the "best, smartest, and brightest," but not just in terms of "brainpower"; they also emphasized that other dimensions, such as our character, personality, leadership capability, and so on, were just as important, if not more so. The tutors revealed the kind of different techniques that were used in interviews to arrive at those conclusions. Most of those discussions were of value and provided insights we were not aware of.

However, there were two specific recommendations that the tutors emphasized and wanted us to follow:

- "Show that your interest in working for the company is very high." The reason given was that companies don't want to hire somebody who may later leave them. Thus, showing that we would be dedicated employees was critical. We were told that we needed to demonstrate it with actions, not just words, and that the interviewer may test us by asking simple questions to see whether we knew some basic things about the company. So, we were to learn all we could about the company ahead of the interview.

- "Study the company's financial statements and come up with some 'insightful' observations to impress the interviewer with how smart you are, and how you can take what you learned at Wharton and apply it in the real world." The tutors pointed out that it would also be a good way to further demonstrate the previous point above. They said that a great way to bring it up would be through a question, when we were given an opportunity during the interview to ask questions.

Now, look at the above observations and recommendations closely. They make a lot of sense, are very reasonable, and perfectly logical. Or are they? Can you form an opinion as to whether they are right and the advice I was given was solid? Take a couple of minutes to think about it and ask yourself whether it is the same advice you would pass on to others, now that it has been revealed to you.

I launched into the interview process with great enthusiasm and felt that I was well equipped to deal with anything and everything. I had many interviews and subsequently observed many things on my own. Most were consistent with what I was taught by the tutors, but some were not. There were two observations I made regarding the two important recommendations mentioned above. Almost none of my interviews were conducted in a way in which the interviewer specifically looked to substantiate any of the above two points, nor did I have a chance to bring them up myself. The two times I forced the issue, the response almost made me fall out of my chair.

I studied the financial statements of a large conglomerate—a well-known company with great name recognition and a great reputation, and one for which I would have really liked to work. I spent a lot of time studying the company. I went through the financial statements diligently. I applied ratios to the numbers, just as we were taught in class, and identified three pertinent questions to ask. So, in my first initial interview and subsequently on the following round of interviews, when asked whether I had questions, I said that I had and proceeded to the first question on my list. I said, "I studied the company's financial statements in detail and noticed that for its division X, revenues went down since last year by 8 percent, but the gross margins went down by even more, 12 percent. What accounted for it, and how is the company planning to address it?" Genius, eh?

The interviewer looked at me, puzzled and disapproving. "I have been with the company for only one year and am working in a completely different division. How do you expect me to know the answer to your question?" I am a quick learner and took note of it. I was smarter in the second interview.

During the second interview, I asked a different question—this time about the overall margin deterioration for the whole company, not a mere division. The response was less dramatic, but I felt just as stupid. The answer was, "Well, to tell you the truth, I work for the marketing department, and this question may be more appropriate to ask of somebody in the finance department." I began to lose all confidence in the placement office. I decided to find out on my own how the interviewing process really works and what was important.

In all subsequent interviews, whenever I had an opportunity, I asked in subtle ways questions about the process to learn as much insight on my own. Some of the interviews were over lunch or dinner, which permitted more informal time to explore the topic in more depth. I came up with an effective line as to why I was asking those questions, without, in my view, coming across as presumptuous or seeking positive feedback. I first asked, "Would you terribly mind if I asked you a couple of general questions about the interviewing process? I have no experience in the matter, and it would help me a great deal in my future search for a job to have a better understanding." Not a single person refused. They were all too happy to give me good advice. There was no question that would be inappropriate to ask, either negative or positive. What I learned caused me to decide to change my resume, to depart from the standard form and format.

Back to my discussions with the director of the placement office about changing the resume. I already told you that he objected on two grounds. The first was the departure from the standard resume, which might not bode well for the school. The second was that not using the standard form would raise concerns that I was going to be unruly.

I begged to differ. I was fully prepared to engage in a debate. I felt that I understood better the rule of insightfulness I mentioned earlier: the "what," "how," and "why"—all three!

I asked him to explain to me *what* purpose, in his mind, a resume served. He was shocked. "What do you mean?"

I said, "It is a very serious question; please give me an answer."

With a puzzled expression he gave an immediate response: "What do you mean? It is to give employers all the information about you!"

I continued, "And *why* does the employer need to have this information?" Now, he was frustrated. "How else would he be able to make a decision whether they want to hire you or not?" I got him!

I said, "Okay, if that is the case, then *why* does the employer have to spend hours with me, arranging for multiple people and multiple interviews in order to decide whether to hire me or not?"

He said, "What do you mean? They need to confirm everything."

I responded, "Absolutely, but then the resume is not used to decide whether to hire me or not. The interviewing process does!"

"What are you getting at?" he asked.

"Simple," I said. "The purpose of the resume is not to get you a job offer; **the purpose of the resume is, first and foremost, to get you an interview!** Without an interview, you never get an opportunity for a job offer."

"It's one and the same," he said. "What is the difference?"

I said, "Well, if it is to get an interview, then the best question to ask is *what kind of a resume will increase your probability of being invited on an interview*, and the answer may suggest a completely different resume."

He was pensive and asked me to point out the differences. I continued and explained everything in great detail and pointed out the differences.

"I don't know," he said at the end. "It sounds pretty compelling, but something just doesn't feel right." (This just goes to show how hard it is to change "common wisdoms," even with compelling logic!)

I pointed out to him that I was willing to assume the risk and overall that my resume "was not really that much different from the standard information provided—the formatting is just a little different." He agreed to accept the resume.

Have you paid attention to how the "what" and "why" changed here? *What* is the purpose of the resume changed from giving complete historical information to . . . something different (yet to be discussed). The *why* changed from giving all the information so that a potential employer could determine whether to make an offer, or even want to interview us, to simply increasing the probability of being asked on an interview. The *how* to do it will be discussed next. But, once we change the initial "what" and "why," it is easier to see which other questions and conclusions may follow. As suggested, it is an iterative process.

Back to the example. I'd like for the purpose of the exercise to place you in my position at the time. I'll provide all the relevant information I was able to get from my questions and my own observations of what took place during the various interviews. Subsequently, I'll ask you to see what conclusions you would draw from them, and then I'll give you mine, for comparison. This hopefully will give you the most out of this exercise.

Here are the observations, not necessarily in order of importance, and they may not be mutually exclusive and can be even contradictory to some degree. All the initial observations are applicable to entry-level positions, the type of position one is hired for upon graduation. Obviously, they may be different for non-entry positions. All the observations relate to how the interviewing process works and how the initial reviewer of the resume decides whether to grant an interview or invite one to an interview. The dynamics in the interview sessions themselves will follow.

- The initial screeners, who were responsible for deciding which candidates were to be interviewed, rarely read a resume in its entirety because of the sheer volume of resumes. If something catches their attention, or they want more clarity, they may read some parts more carefully than others.

- On average they spend between twenty to thirty seconds per resume on the initial pass. Perhaps another minute or so if they want to refocus on something on a second pass.

- They generally look for *proven* "brainpower," *proven* track record, and other traits that imply to them that the candidate will be a good addition to the company.

- They look at the overall reputation of the schools the candidate has attended and the grades they earned to determine proven brainpower. They look at how reputable the companies are that hired the person in the past. The interviewers assume that the better the reputation of the company, the smarter the candidate. They also look to the candidate's career promotions as proven ability to perform well at work.

- They look for any negatives or flaws. The most common mentioned were time gaps in employment and education, short-tenure jobs, job-hopping, and "anything else that jumps out at me," as they said. However, there was one fatal thing that would most likely generate immediate rejection—typos and grammatical errors. The logic was that if you didn't pay attention to them in something as important as your own resume, how could you be trusted with other things?

- When asked about how they decide whether to proceed with a specific candidate, they all said that they have some "standards," below which they will not move forward, and those who pass their "standards" are ranked along with other candidates, and only the "best" candidates would progress.

- The interviewers make their decisions about the candidate from what they observed in person during the interview. What is said in the resume itself becomes pretty moot at that point.

- Generally, multiple people interview a candidate, separately, in each round. At the end, they get together and rank the candidates they saw and decide which candidates should be invited to the next round.

- A different team is assigned for each round of interviews. Each team gets the resume of the candidate, but generally not any notes and perceptions from previous rounds.

- With each subsequent round of interviews, the list of candidates gets smaller, and more senior people get involved interviewing the candidates.

My observations were the product of asking multiple questions. Now, think as to whether you would have asked the questions and followed up with the kind of questions that would have yielded the same information.

I also thought that understanding what specifically they liked, or didn't, about me as a candidate was important, and so I asked those questions as well. Here, I had to be very careful, because people, in general, don't like to answer such questions. There was also a great risk that I might come across as an unconfident person seeking reassurance or, even worse, as an arrogant, presumptuous person who makes a habit of asking inappropriate questions in interviews. But I was careful as to how I framed my questions. Here are the observations I made; some were even a complete surprise to me.

- At the beginning of practically every interview, the interviewer took some time to skim through my resume and started to ask questions about some information that somehow caught their attention, just to break the ice. The information they focused on appeared to be somewhat random. I got the distinct impression that it was the first time the interviewer had read or at least attentively focused on my resume.

- After the initial questions, some interviewers continued to use the resume to guide the process, others did less so, and some never bothered to pay more attention to the resume. There was no apparent pattern and it was impossible to predict what questions and format the interviewer would take. I was frequently challenged with "case study analysis." Each interviewer devised their own case study. Some asked me to pick one from my past work experience or one that we studied in class, and we discussed it together.

- In general, interviewers were impressed with the fact that I was a student at Wharton and had two degrees in engineering. In their mind it proved that I was uniquely smart, capable, and offered great potential. Very few engineers pursued an MBA in those days. I was told that most MBA students came from non-quantitative backgrounds and were not very comfortable with "numbers." The business world requires substantial logic, analyses, and an analytical approach to problem solving. Obviously, those with engineering and other quantitative backgrounds, like math, physics, and so on, are much more adept with applying numbers. In fact, I was told that this quantitative analysis caused a real problem and presented real challenges for some MBAs.

- They liked that I attained and was promoted to a position of vice president, because it clearly indicated proven capability.

- They hadn't noticed initially that I earned two separate degrees with high honors, bachelor's and master's, at the same time. But when, during the interview, they realized this, they were immensely impressed. "You must be exceptionally smart," they said. (By the way, did you notice it?)

- They hadn't paid attention to it initially, but when during the interview they learned that Electronic Data Systems Corporation was actually EDS, a company widely considered successful, with one of the greatest reputations, they were very impressed. Everybody knew that EDS attracted and hired only the best talent.

- In general, the interviewers didn't go too deeply into my work experience and specific responsibilities. When I asked why not, I got a consistent answer: My past work experience would have little bearing on what I would be doing in the future, since I would be starting at an entry-level position and utilizing completely different skills.

- On the negative side, they were concerned about my short tenure at EDS and specifically at Sammons Enterprises, which was only six months. It made them nervous about whether I would be a long-term employee or a job-hopper.

Okay, you now have all the relevant information. What would you conclude from what you have read? More importantly, would any of my observations lead you to consider making changes to your resume? If so, what kind and specifically how? Lastly, again the same question, would you have initiated the kind of questions that would have given you the same observations I made? Please take some time to really think about it, and perhaps write them all down. Next, I'll share how I dissected all the above, for comparison.

Below I enumerate my reasoning and conclusions. The entire purpose of this example is to provide a "live" exercise to demonstrate what being insightful is, and how readily it is available to everybody. Part of insightfulness is to see "deeper" into facts, thereby drawing conclusions that may escape others. In my opinion, it is one dimension (of course, not the only one) that separates the more insightful person from the less insightful, as it pertains to the shallowness of the observations and conclusions. Clearly, some of being insightful reflects innate brainpower, but one doesn't need to be a genius to be more insightful; we are not talking about complicated scientific topics. Practically everybody can do it, if they are aware and willing to spend the extra time to think.

It's been my experience that people are lazy when it comes to making observations and drawing conclusions. Most people exposed to the same facts will tend to focus on what appears to them to be more relevant, perhaps the most obvious, and draw the "more important" conclusions and stop there. Others, the more insightful, less lazy thinkers, may expend the extra mental energy to seek deeper interpretations, to check whether other things may be important, as well. Often there might be nothing to see, but if there were, then insightfulness emerges.

As you read my analyses below, please pay attention to the granularity of the thought process and conclusions drawn. I'm bringing this point up not to boast about my capability, but rather to point out that insightfulness is not necessarily a flash of brilliance. Instead, it is a natural outcome of deeper, logical, step-by-step observations and analyses, or what commonly is referred to as analytical thinking. It is a process of constant analyses as one thought leads to another or raises a question, and the answer to that question leads to a conclusion, and so it continues, yielding a better, more complete understanding of the problem/challenge. This is the process of becoming more insightful!

The first observation that I made was that the interview process is divided into two phases. The initial phase is mostly the "elimination" phase, and the second phase transforms almost imperceptibly into a "selection" phase. The process of elimination starts with the initial decision of whom to accept for an interview and continues through the initial rounds of the interviews. This phase is characterized by more rudimentary "go, no-go" decisions and relies more on the interviewer's quick perception. During this phase, the candidates are vulnerable to the interviewer's quick judgments based on shallow and somewhat unsubstantiated, or uncorroborated, observations. With each round of interviews, however, more robust information is collected. But the main purpose is still to eliminate some candidates. This process works better in the earlier stages, since the difference between the better and worse candidates is more apparent. As the list narrows with attrition, the challenge becomes much greater, particularly among the candidates who are just above and below the cutoff line. As this process continues, the list gets narrower until it is brought down to a subset of desirable candidates who are considered worthy of a job offer. At that point the process changes minutely into the selection phase, which is a much tougher phase. Here the interviewers are much more probing and begin to apply a different logic to decide on the final candidate who will receive a job offer.

Can you think of what the importance is in this observation?

In my mind there are a couple of important observations. First, the resume plays a role at the very beginning of the process and much less so as the interviewing cycle progresses. Second, this substantiates what I stated in the previous paragraph. The process of elimination implies comparison to others, which further implies competition with others, which further implies that *differentiation* is the key. So, when looking at creating a resume, the most important factor is not to give the complete information that might be conventionally expected, but rather to give enough information that appears complete but focuses on how a candidate would like to differentiate themselves from other candidates. As I mentioned, I was told that the fact that I was a Wharton student was impressive, but the additional fact that I had an engineering background was a huge differentiating factor for me. Third, one needs to be mindful that the criteria used by the "judges" change from one phase of the interview to the next phase. (I will not elaborate on this point in this section. I devote a whole section to this specific topic later in the book.)

Back to my main observations. The people who read the resume mostly skim through it, which clearly implies that there is a probability that they may miss factors that the aspiring candidate feels would make them stand out. Conversely, the interviewer may pick up on information the candidate may think unfavorable. It may appear as a simple observation, but the implications are far more reaching.

One implication is simpler to understand; the other is much more nuanced but just as important. I'm pointing it out now because it will play a key role subsequently. The simpler implication to understand is that, at the beginning of the process, when resumes are used to decide on inviting a candidate to an interview, missing a positive differentiating aspect and/or focusing on a negative aspect is critical, as there is little room and opportunity for recovery. The other implication is more subtle but important.

I mentioned earlier that during interviews, some of the interviewers would look at the resume to pick the next topic of conversation. In those interviews, the above point becomes quite relevant. If the interviewer quickly looks at the resume and happens to notice a positive differentiating attribute and focuses the conversation in that direction, then that would be valuable. But what if the interviewer happens to pick a neutral fact, or worse, a slightly negative one? Then valuable time of a short interview is spent discussing things not to your advantage, decreasing your opportunity to differentiate yourself successfully. I refer to the second phenomenon as an *opportunity lost*. It is subtle, because it is not as apparent. It is subtle because one would rarely think about the fact that it could have been avoided. The same will work on the positive side; there could be an opportunity lost where a better outcome could have been created. This is another one of those terms that I'll keep mentioning throughout the book, because I believe it receives little recognition from many people and it can enhance one's ability to be insightful.

Back to the original point of observation, that only a small portion of the resume is read. Naturally, this raises a key question: Is there a way we can increase the probability that the reader will not miss what we want them to observe, and if so, how? As soon as one asks this question, a host of other observations, thoughts, and questions arise, thus yielding an iterative process.

Clearly, there are several ways by which we can address the above question:

- Make the resume as succinct as possible. The fewer the words, the less likely that important information will be overlooked. Different interviewers may look at different parts of the resume or seek different information from it. Also, the information sought may change as the interviewing process progresses, and other "secondary" things may be used in the process of elimination. Thus, although succinct, it should give reasonably complete information on one's background. But it clearly follows that a succinct resume has advantages.

    This raises another observation. If we only knew better what the reader would be looking for in the resume throughout the process, we could then be that much smarter about eliminating superfluous information from the resume. Thus, a new question arises: What are the things that really matter in a resume, because they would help differentiate us and increase the likelihood that the interviewers throughout the process will focus on the "right" topics? This question is a bit conceptual, and I'll re-word it and break it up into two separate questions to give clearer directions as to what one may need to actually do to find answers: (i) What do the interviewers really look for throughout the process?; and (ii) What else, if anything, would we like them to see or notice? Answer these questions and your resume will end up being much more effective. I address this topic elsewhere in the book as well.

- Avoid, if possible, small, dense paragraphs, which are the toughest to quickly skim through.

- A single page is easier to skim through than multiple pages. In reality, second and third pages get the most cursory look, if any at all.

Thus, the first conclusion I drew was to **reduce my resume to a single page, no matter what.** This could be accomplished by only giving the most important and revealing information and eliminating completely the information that is given for the sake of completeness. In other words, **the resume need not have all the information about you, but rather only the important information that is necessary and used throughout the process**—maybe a nuance, but a substantial departure from the common wisdom!

Okay, let's continue with the analysis. If one quickly scans a document, one will tend to do it from the top-left side of the page and move down to the bottom, which means: (i) Whatever is written on the top left will be given most attention and focus and therefore will likely be most noticed; and (ii) As the reader moves down the page, the reader reads less, and the eyes begin to scan more. Thus, there is a greater probability not to notice things as you go down the page. I drew two conclusions from this observation. First, put the more differentiating aspects at the top, if possible, and place *the most important information on the top left.*

The third aspect was the extra credibility and credit I got for being "bright" when the interviewers learned that I had earned two degrees in parallel, which they initially missed. All of the interviewers' comments were rooted in my education. So, I decided to switch the order in my resume and start with the education at the top, as opposed to the work experience, another departure from the standard format and common wisdom. In the same vein, I bolded **Wharton** so that it jumped off the page. I created a separate line under the "Distinction" to emphasize that both degrees were earned at the same time. Additionally, and in accordance with the above logic, I moved the dates to the right side as they were comparatively trivial, another departure from the standard.

Next, I asked myself whether there was anything else I could manipulate on the page that would immediately draw a reader's eye. I decided that I would use physical techniques to highlight different parts of the resume, through using different fonts, bold-typing, bullet points, spacing, and so on. None was possible with a standard typewriter and therefore would require going to a printing house with typesetting capabilities, as done with books. This would be a very expensive proposition, but I believed it would end up being a great investment for my job search.

Next, I asked what in my resume was negative. I was told that my short tenure at work—particularly the six months at Sammons Enterprises—was viewed somewhat negatively. I decided to address it in three ways. First, the dates went from the left side to the right side. Second, I used light-shaded font as opposed to the standard font, so it caught less attention. Third, I changed the format and eliminated giving the months of work experience throughout the resume, thereby giving the impression that two years are involved whenever the year changes. In addition, instead of the end date for Sammons Enterprises I inserted the words "Until admission to Wharton," which everybody accepted as a good, valid reason to leave employment—another departure from standard!

See the following page for the revised resume.

David Kronfeld
1310 Spruce Street, Apt. 224
Philadelphia, Pennsylvania 19104
Tel. (555) 555-5555

Objective: A fulfilling and challenging job in the area of Strategic Planning, Finance, and Marketing.

Education:
The Wharton School of Business   *Philadelphia, Pennsylvania (1975–Present)*
Degree: **MBA**, Finance
Stevens Institute of Technology   *Hoboken, New Jersey (1970–1973)*
Degrees: (1) **Masters,** Computer Science
                    (2) **BS,** Electrical Engineering—*High Honors*
Distinctions: **Both degrees earned in same 3-year period.**
                Tau Beta Phi, an honor society in recognition of highest academic achievements.

Experience:
Sammons Enterprises   Dallas, Texas *(1974–until admission to Wharton)*
Title: **Vice President, Systems**
Responsibilities: Responsible for 12 System Analysts and 35 Programmers. I was responsible for all development and maintenance of Sammons' Data Processing systems. As such, I worked with the Presidents and General Managers of 8 different business divisions that comprised Sammons Enterprises. In this capacity, I learned to understand all the workflows in the respective companies and departments, and helped identify which data needed to be recorded and which management reports clients needed, and developed such automated capabilities in our computer systems.

EDS (Electronic Data Systems Corporation)   Dallas, Texas *(1973–1974)*
Title: **Senior System Analyst**
Responsibilities: I was part of a team that was responsible for the development and maintenance of all Data Processing needs of clients. As such, I constantly interacted with the different departments in trying to understand what data recording and management reports clients needed to better conduct their business. I was subsequently promoted to be an instructor in the company's "school." The company was exclusively hiring long-term U.S. military officers, and over a period of six months these veterans were taught Computer Programming and System Analysis.

Personal: Military service in the Israeli Armed Forces.   *(1966–1969)*

The resume ended up being a huge success. I was never passed over for an interview I wanted. Many companies that came to Wharton to interview students, and which I didn't sign up with, called the placement office and asked to see if I'd be willing to interview with them, a fact that didn't escape the placement office. The biggest bonus was somewhat indirect. Many interviewers commented on the nonstandard look of the resume. I said, "Well, it's not random; there is some good logic to it." They all asked me to explain what I meant, whether from being polite, curious, or truly wanting to understand. I took the opportunity to go over all the thought processes from beginning to end, which took a good five to ten minutes. Every interviewer was impressed with the insightful logic and analytical thinking. It allowed me to start my interview with a tremendous, unexpected positive differentiation. The rest of the conversation focused on exactly the things I was hoping would catch the interviewer's attention. Mission accomplished!

I believe that the logic that was behind designing my resume left such a strong impression that, in two cases, I was introduced to a top executive who was ready to make me an offer.

I ended up having the most interviews on campus and received the most job offers. I was asked to interview with the local TV station about Wharton students' success in getting great job opportunities. Needless to say, from that year on, a one-page resume, with bullet points, became the format recommended by the placement office.

As stated earlier, the new ideas and conclusions I brought forth have spread like wildfire and have since become the new standards imparted by placement offices and throughout the business world at large. As you have probably discerned by now, although the primary purpose of this example was to demonstrate how insightfulness is arrived at, I also used this specific example with a secondary objective in mind—providing you with the full original thinking and a more granular explanation and reasoning behind writing an effective resume, so that you will now be able to apply better, more refined judgment when you write your own resume. With this secondary objective in mind, I would like to point out two key observations.

First, the advent of Microsoft Word has made the task of writing a resume that addresses the visual parts of my observations easy to accomplish. At the same time, as stated, many of my conclusions have since become the new standard when writing resumes. So, a key question arises: How can one achieve "differentiation" when currently everybody may receive the same advice? The answer is quite simple. If the visual techniques no longer afford unique differentiation, then it follows that **the differentiation can only be achieved by the actual content of the resume—what and how you include, or don't include, in the resume.** There is ample opportunity to achieve effective differentiation via the content and unique attributes, since everybody has a different background, experiences, and accomplishments.

Second, new "common wisdom" has emerged regarding the "content" of resumes, particularly for people with previous work experience and managers at all levels. In my opinion, some of the currently prevailing common wisdom regarding the content is flawed. I address this issue later, in section III, chapter eight, titled: "Nothing Is More Powerful Than to Prove a 'Common Wisdom' Wrong!" It provides additional observations and logic regarding resume writing for the more experienced professionals and managers at all levels, but would also be applicable to students with limited experience.

SECTION II
UNDERSTANDING THE WORK ENVIRONMENT

4

The Good News: You Don't Need to Be a Genius to Do Exceptionally Well in Business!

How do we measure being "smart"? How do we decide if we are smart or not, or at least smart enough to advance our careers? As we grow older, we learn that "smart" is not so easy to define. There are many different "smarts," and one can be smart in some ways, but not in others. Nevertheless, most will look to one's intelligence quotient (IQ) to determine just how smart one is.

We accept as truth that the higher a person's IQ, the more likely the person would excel in school and business, and the corollary, that the lower the IQ, the less likely the person would do well in both school and business. We accept that as truth at an early age when our point of reference is distorted. At an early age, we can only perceive "smarts" from the perspective of being successful in school, where indeed the higher the IQ, the more likely the success. It is most apparent at the extreme ranges. In many cases it appears to us that those who have a very high IQ are so much more successful in school than those with a lower IQ. Not just more successful, but it appears that achieving high grades comes so much easier to them—there is just no way we could compete with such intelligent people. In my opinion, while that may be the case for excelling in school, it is not the case in the workplace.

Unfortunately, many of us may not realize it. Worse yet, believing in an absolute equation between success and IQ, particularly in our formative years, may have long-lasting and damaging implications that place people at a significant disadvantage over time and particularly in the corporate business world. It is time to correct that belief!

I am not suggesting that people with a high IQ may not have an inherent advantage at potentially excelling both in school and work. What I am suggesting, though, from interacting with and observing many high-IQ people, is that it is not necessarily so. We have all heard the differentiation between "book smart" and "street smart." You may have even heard it said, "They are very smart but wouldn't be able to find their way out of a paper bag." I do believe that a higher IQ does give one an inherent advantage in the work environment for sure, as we use our brains constantly at work. So, it stands to reason that the higher the IQ, the more of an advantage one may have. However, this advantage of IQ would likely be more evident at the lower levels of a career path, at the first, second, or maybe even third management levels. This advantage diminishes at higher management levels.

To summarize, in my opinion, a higher IQ may be one of the more important determinants in one's ability to excel in an academic environment, but not necessarily when it comes to excelling in business. It takes a different kind of "smarts" to excel in business. Where is the difference? What kind of "smarts" are needed to succeed in business? Why is it not necessarily the same as for school? I have my own perception regarding these questions.

To excel in school and academia, one is required to quickly and constantly absorb new, complicated, and interrelated facts, theorems, and theories—think physics, math, chemistry, and so on. Grasping new concepts and facts in subsequent lessons relies heavily on understanding the prior lessons. It is a never-ending cycle, where new, more complicated topics are introduced at a fast pace. At the same time, the amount of information one needs to comprehend and integrate grows in complexity over the years and is practically infinite in quantity. In addition, one needs to memorize it all and recall it for subsequent use. In this kind of an environment, one's IQ may indeed be a predictor for success: The higher the IQ, the more successful one may become.

The business world is completely different. First and foremost, there is no single predominant skill or set of skills that yields success. This is particularly so as one advances into higher management levels. To succeed in business, one must be skilled in many different dimensions, where each dimension represents many different unique skills. Think interpersonal skills, communication skills, articulation skills, motivational skills, execution skills, psychological skills, judgment skills, leadership skills, character skills (like commitment, perseverance, dedication), selling skills (oneself and concepts), skills that represent experience and knowledge, intuition, creativity, and on and on. Also, such skills all must come together over a longer period, throughout a career path that is measured in years, not semesters. Thus, simply stated, in school and academia a *single skill*—higher IQ—may offer an advantage in mastering a practically *infinite amount of information* that needs to be integrated. In contrast, business requires a practically *"infinite" amount of skills*, not just one, that need to be well integrated for a *single success*—career advancement. See the difference? Almost the reverse!

Additionally, what one learns in school is always new, complex, and continuous. Business, on the other hand, represents the reverse; what one learns is somewhat relatively limited in quantity and not very complicated, relative to years of academic studies. And once learned, it is applied over and over, making someone an "expert" strictly due to experience and the passage of time. Thus, a high IQ is not as predictive of success. To state it in a simpler way: One doesn't need to be a genius to do well in business. Most of what one needs to learn, including how to analyze problems and produce solutions, can be acquired, understood, and utilized by practically everybody.

Also, problems and solutions in school, particularly in science topics, generally have a single black-and-white solution. A solution is either right or wrong, and can be proven so. In contrast, the business world deals with situational problems and challenges that almost never have a proven, single solution. Rather, there are thousands of shades of gray, with many solutions differentiated more by "better" or "worse" and the risk/reward trade-off involved. It can rarely be proven in advance, and the proof almost always comes in retrospect!

Notwithstanding the above, there are some "smarts" related to one's brainpower that could play a very important role in business success, namely, one's **ability to analyze, dissect, apply judgment, and draw pragmatic conclusions.** In my opinion, one's ability to do these well can singularly tilt one's probability for success. So what does it take to do it well? This topic and the answer are so important that I devote a full section to them later in the book.

Allow me to complete this chapter by pointing out another personal opinion regarding an observation I made earlier about the long-lasting damage that may be inflicted on some of us in our formative years when we learn to believe that high IQ is key to one's success, or at least that it would be very difficult to compete successfully with people with high IQ.

I believe that in our formative years, through our school experience, the only thing we can observe and are exposed to is what it takes to do well in school. When we are in school, the main measures of success are academic (e.g., grades and test scores). The people who do well are thought to be smart and those who don't are believed not to be as smart. Schoolchildren absorb these opinions of themselves and their fellow students almost osmotically. So each student forms a view as to their smartness during their school years. Additionally, as a result of poorer academic performance, some may be guided away from professional business aspirations. So if you do well in school, you benefit because you believe that you can outperform others and solve all challenges that come your way. As you progress through school, you begin to develop a high level of self-confidence and taste the fruits of success. The taste of success is great, and it pushes you to want to continue it. Therefore, over time, you apply yourself harder and harder with greater commitment and sacrifice to continue your momentum of success. Self-confidence and hard work are traits that are important for success in business as well. So, someone who has done well in school develops a built-in early advantage. Just as importantly, they learn that they can overcome problems others find difficult to solve.

Unfortunately, the opposite may well occur to the people who experience performance difficulties in school. They may draw the opposite conclusions: they are not as smart and don't do as well. So, they may grow up believing that they have very little chance to do well. Their self-confidence may therefore be lacking—a major disadvantage. Also, as a result, many of them may not even try to pursue the kind of career that could yield greater business success, and those who do may lack confidence and have more modest aspirations.

5

Competing Successfully Is at the Center of Career Advancement

Success is a result of successfully competing! You might be asking, Why is David stating the obvious? You guessed it; it is not as obvious as one would believe. In my opinion, this is one of the most fundamental observations that at first blush may appear obvious but is not. It is particularly true when one expands this statement and asks oneself, "How do I compete successfully?" Here the answer is not so clear-cut and has many subtle nuances. We rarely take time to think about them. Why should we? Isn't competing just going out there doing the best we can and trying to do it better than others? Isn't it completely instinctive to everybody? Yes, kind of—but no, not really.

It is common wisdom in business that thinking ahead is the most important ingredient for a company's success. Do it well and you measurably increase the probability of success. Do it poorly and the business/company is most likely to fail. Yet few give any serious thought to the fact that the same applies to success in one's career. Ask successful people to give you the formula for career advancement and you are very likely to hear, "Be competent, be a good worker, and do your best—these are the most critical ingredients for one's success." This is the common wisdom imparted from the "wise" to the "less wise," from parents to children, from teachers to students, from successful people to as yet unsuccessful people, from bosses to subordinates.

It is not that it is bad advice. It is just that, by itself, it is not complete advice, and therefore is perhaps even "poor" advice. Although it appears to be a minor and subtle semantic difference, it is not. It embodies a logical flaw with major implications. This logical flaw is referred to again and again throughout the book. It comprises situations where the facts provided to support some logic and conclusions are perceived to be correct, but, in fact, are incomplete and missing some important additional elements. As such, the conclusions drawn may be insufficient, faulty, or even erroneous to some extent.

The critical logical "flaw" lies in the subtle observation that the elements of the statement are correct, but together they do not guarantee the outcome. In other words, you could follow this advice in a superb way, but still will not have assurances that the outcome will be achieved. In math it is referred to as **"necessary, but not sufficient."** The paradox regarding this advice and the lack of a guaranteed outcome reflects the fact that one is given the most important aspects of the advice, which generally are those aspects that if not accomplished will deny success; however, other things might be needed to increase the probability that the expected outcome will more likely follow. **Both aspects are needed to change the "necessary, but not sufficient" into what in math is referred to as "necessary *and* sufficient."**

Outside of the above discrepancy in logic, there are additional complexities. The advice mentioned earlier to be competent and do your best uses conceptual words that provide no specifics to help one decide how to best put it into practice. What does it mean to be competent? How does one achieve competence? When does one know if one has reached it? The same questions apply to being a good worker and doing one's best. To make things worse, one can think of a zillion specific ways to do things that are consistent with the original advice. A zillion ways to interpret and implement advice is as good as getting no advice at all! This is analogous to thinking about how to be successful in marriage or a successful parent. Ask for advice on what that means, and how to do it well, and you'll get zillions of different specific opinions. How does one go about deciding which opinions are more, or less, important? It begins with perspective.

The Process of "Necessary and Sufficient" Starts with a Correct Perspective

Okay, back to the main topic: What are the "necessary and sufficient" conditions to succeed in one's career? Let's first begin with a conceptual understanding, and then go into the details that give specific information about how to implement it.

Let us follow the four-step "methodology" for insightfulness I introduced earlier. As a first step, we need to identify the correct challenge we must overcome. I suggest that the key conceptual observation is the realization that one must *compete successfully* to succeed. Think about it: For every single career advancement—from getting the job in the first place through all of the promotions—multiple candidates are evaluated and only one is selected. One constantly competes with others at every step of one's career. Thus, successful competition is the most critical factor in one's success. In other words, the best advice one can give you about how to best advance your career is to tell you that you must successfully compete. A subtle difference, but profound.

Note, in one set of advice you are the center of it all, and the focus is completely on what you do. In the other interpretation, you are no longer the center; other people and the actions they take are just as critical. What you do is only meaningful and relevant when compared to what others do. Thus, the new challenge has shifted from a focus on doing your best to a focus on doing better than others (i.e., effectively competing). Directionally, this implies substantially different things. So, now we know what the central objective is and how we need to shift our mindset. (Can you see how insightfulness can lead to an obvious observation that can lead to a different approach to a challenge, and increase the chances for success?)

Now that we conceptually understand better what we are trying to accomplish, we can focus and devise ways to get there. The word "compete" conveys a concept only; it lacks the specificity of how to do it well. So, per the insightfulness methodology, we need to translate the word "compete" into a more directional, task-oriented list of subcategories. In fact, please take a moment and ask yourself what specifically one needs to do and accomplish to compete successfully.

Make a list of the traits and action steps. I'll bet you'll have a hard time wrapping your thoughts around it. You could probably identify a great many specific things, but how are you able to prioritize them and have enough clarity as to how to practically put them to use? How can you tell that, even with a long list of ideas, you haven't missed anything important? Rather than give you an answer, I will use this opportunity to welcome you to the first step in becoming insightful.

Correct Perspectives Are Driven by an All-Encompassing Thought Process

The first question that comes to mind is, obviously, what does it mean to compete successfully? Can you think of the different conceptual categories that will lead you to the desired outcome?

Let me give you a list that is implied in doing it successfully. Clearly, the first is to have an opportunity to compete. Second, you must be noticed by those who decide whether you are better, or worse, than other competitors. If you are not noticed, you will never be better, nor worse. Third, being noticed is not enough. You had best be noticed for things you are doing better than others, not worse. Fourth, being noticed is "necessary, but not sufficient." So, what are the critical things that influence the perceptions of those making a judgment? Only by answering this last question correctly will you know what you need to do better. You can also avoid wasting energy on all the trivial things that you might do better but will yield nothing of value relative to what you need to accomplish at the end.

Fifth, avoid major potential mistakes on the path to promotion. Remember, **bad mistakes are more costly than great successes** (at least in the shorter term). How many times have you heard people say that only a few of the thousands of good deeds one does in their lifetime are remembered, but every single bad deed is? You may think of another question or two, but I think that for the first-level categorization, these are pretty much the primary questions; the rest may come up in the iterative nature of the process. So, let's stop here and take a tally. To compete successfully, we need to accomplish four things:

1. **Have an opportunity to compete.**

2. **Be noticed.** This can be accomplished in three separate ways. I purposely enumerate them in reverse order of importance, just because I want to emphasize the process of thinking and how to make sure it is thorough and more complete. You will be noticed because you:

   o   have something, wear something, or do something (unrelated to the quality of your work) that will make you different, thereby be noticed.

   o   do something "stupid" or make a stupid mistake.

   o   do measurably better in some or all of the things that are being observed.

3. Be noticed for the **critical** things that **matter the most for those who make the final judgments**.

4. **Avoid major mistakes.**

Okay, now you have a complete set of directional, conceptual things that you need to accomplish. I look at the list above and can bring it down to a simple, more elegant, and accurate way to say it all, and in the process use terms that are widely understood in the context of competition: **To compete successfully, one must have a *differentiation* that gives them a *competitive advantage* and *avoid* making *major mistakes*.**

Now I can go to the next step and expand each of the above concepts in the same manner into subcategories in an iterative way, until I get to much more specific tasks that I can focus on.

Avoid Superficiality: Thoroughness Is the Key

One last comment about the process/methodology. Note that to accomplish the third item above—be noticed for the **critical** things that **matter the most**—you must correctly know the things that will be important to those who will be involved in the decision to give you the promotion. So, you now must understand what the people who decide on promoting somebody look at when making such a decision. Clearly, here you need to look at what they will view *positively* and what they will view *negatively*. Get it right and you have just come up with exactly what you need to pay attention to if you want to get promoted. All you will need to do now is execute it well. You may or may not know exactly how your manager decides on promotions, or all that goes into their decision. So, it is appropriate to **seek counsel**, talk to people who promoted others, and ask them. **But make sure you get more than the obvious,** or just the **most important** factors, because there will be other "competitors" who will possess those as well. Thus, seek to **understand the "secondary" things** that will go into the final selection from the group that will pass the primary criteria. Note the importance of the secondary list; it will become critical at the time when a final differentiation is made of those who passed the initial list. In other words, when you have gotten to understand the decision-making process of those people, you'll have the real insight of exactly how the final decision for promotion is made!

See the logical progression of how to think about getting your answers? Apply this kind of logical progression and use it throughout your life in all situations, and you will put yourself on a solid path to becoming more insightful.

6

The 80-20 Rule

This chapter is presented as background information for a concept that will be utilized throughout the book. As such, other than explaining the rule, there will be little in the way of insightful implications drawn here. However, in my opinion, the concept represents a powerful set of observations that I will subsequently refer to many times.

If you have business experience, then you must have heard this famous rule on many occasions. It is used in many different ways, but conceptually represents the same loosely defined thought—20 percent of any group is responsible for 80 percent of the outcomes from that group. It started a while back after some consultants did work for multi-product companies and discovered, quite consistently, that 20 percent of the products were responsible for 80 percent of the profits for the company. It became known as the 80-20 Rule.

It has since been expanded to describe any group in which a minority is responsible for the majority of that group's output. Neither the nature of the group itself, nor what the output is, is relevant. For example, 20 percent of the divisions are responsible for 80 percent of the profits (or sales) of the company; 20 percent of a work team is responsible for 80 percent of the output; 20 percent of the population is responsible for 80 percent of the taxes collected; 20 percent of the world owns 80 percent of the wealth; and so on, and so on. As I said, it represents more of a conceptual reality; the actual numbers and ratios are not the point.

I believe it is a rule that describes reality in practically all situations in life. You may use this rule to guide your thoughts, analyses, and conclusions whenever appropriate. You probably will not go wrong with starting with this rule as a basic assumption. However, this is not why I bring it to your attention—it would have been interesting, but not insightful with important consequences.

I redefined and expanded this rule for my own purposes, and it is this redefined rule that leads to meaningful and insightful implications, which I plan to share with you throughout the book. I am explaining the rule now to spare the reader from unnecessary digressions later on.

First, I narrowed the **content** of the rule to refer only to people's understanding, wisdom, insightfulness, perceptiveness, judgment, foresight, discernment, acuteness, astuteness, ingenuity, and so on. In other words, all things related to *brainpower* and how *insightfully* it is used. Second, I expanded the rule to become **iterative** (e.g., take any group of people in any category, and the 80-20 Rule will continue to apply to the subgroups).

In other words, let's take a profession, say, lawyers. The rule will say that 20 percent of the lawyers have the brainpower as I defined it, and the remaining 80 percent do not, or will be of average brainpower relative to the group selected. You may take the subgroup of the 20 percent above and apply the rule again. The selected subset of the 20 percent group can also be differentiated within themselves with the 80-20 Rule, and so on. However, just keep in mind that the rule may apply, but the measuring scale must change.

For example, let's start with a random group of all students in the country. The measuring scale relative to how insightful they all are will include the full range of cognitive words:

Not Insightful / Poor Insight / Weak / Less than Average / Average / Somewhat Above Average / Above Average / High / Very High / Highest

This measuring scale will be appropriate and would adequately represent the distribution in the group. However, if you apply the iterative process and select only the 20 percent as a subgroup, then the measuring scale obviously changes to only the high-end portion of the scale. In fact, the scale will represent less of absolute terms, like in the widest group, and more of a "relative-to-each-other" scale. In other words, to apply the 80-20 Rule, you must have an appropriate scale to properly show how the group is separated along a continuum. It generally can reflect absolute terms or relative-to-each-other differentiation.

The final and the most profound observation I would like to leave you with regarding the categorization of people based on brainpower or insightfulness (understanding, wisdom, perceptiveness, judgment, foresight, discernment, acuteness, astuteness, ingenuity, etc.) is that **the separation between the 20 percent and the 80 percent of any subgroup is not closely correlated to how successful one is, or what a great experience, background, or resume one brings. In other words, great success, long experience, impressive resume, etc. are not necessarily an indication of whether one falls in the 20 or the 80 group.** As I said earlier in the book, one's success is influenced by many factors, whereas my definition of brainpower reflects a singular talent and capability, which may, or may not, be correlated with the degree of one's success—particularly not in business.

At first glance, the above observation may appear to contradict the main premise of the book—that insightfulness leads to career success. If my main premise is true, then how can I now suggest that great success may not correlate with whether one falls in the 20 or 80 percent group from an insightfulness standpoint? Note the subtlety of why this is not a contradiction: Insightfulness may and most likely does correlate with success, but success does not guarantee the presence of insightfulness because success may be driven by other factors. In math it is stated as: if A leads to B, it doesn't follow that B also leads to A. A simple example: If every practicing lawyer (A) must receive a lawyer's license (B), it doesn't imply that everybody with a lawyer's license (B) is a practicing lawyer (A).

7

Business Is Full of "Mediocrity": Don't Get Angry; Rejoice!

It may appear counterintuitive (particularly to people with limited business experience), but the statement that business is full of mediocrity at all levels is actually true. We accept that government bureaucracies may display much mediocrity, but business is touted to be the exact opposite. After all, how could economies and companies have advanced if mediocrity was in evidence everywhere? It may appear contradictory, but it really isn't. The implication of my statement doesn't reflect on the overall quality and the progress that an entity can achieve. Rather, it reflects more on the various competencies at the individual level and therefore the opportunity for an individual to advance their career. I suggest that three principal factors contribute to mediocrity in business: (i) lack of motivation, (ii) the Peter Principle, and (iii) the 80-20 Rule.

Lack of Motivation

Just think about the broader set where mediocrity is prevalent. Think about all the possible jobs performed out there in the world. Millions and millions of workers go to work every day and perform their work duties. I'm including here all possible jobs, large corporations, small companies, factory workers, hospital workers, farmers, plumbers, store salespeople, waitresses, clerks everywhere, private sector, government sector—every job that pays.

For the majority of workers, work doesn't represent the highest priority in their lives. Work is mostly viewed as a necessary evil to get through life. Most do not have a significant opportunity for career advancement, and only a very small percentage will be presented with such opportunities. Most probably dislike their jobs and would quit without hesitation if they won a lottery. So, I would dare say that the majority of the workers around the world view their jobs mostly with indifference. One doesn't find widespread mediocrity because of lack of motivation in today's corporate world, at least not in the United States. If there is any of that, it would be at the very lowest levels of the corporate hierarchies, and not widely spread.

So, for those who view their careers as an important priority and a way to substantially improve the quality of their lives, lack of motivation and drive is anathema.

The Peter Principle

You may know, or may have heard about, the Peter Principle. The Peter Principle implies that the majority of management positions are occupied by managers who lack the competency to perform their job well. The principle is named after the Canadian researcher Dr. Laurence J. Peter, who popularized this observation in his 1969 book, *The Peter Principle*. In the book he made the observation that "the tendency in most organizational hierarchies, such as that of a corporation, is for every employee to rise in the hierarchy through promotion until they reach a level of respective incompetence." In other words, the majority of management positions may be performed at a relatively suboptimal or even an incompetent level. **Note that this doesn't mean the managers are incompetent or incapable. Nor does it mean the managers are not smart, educated, or motivated.** It actually means the opposite. These managers are very good at what they do, and as a result they were continually rewarded with promotion. As I stated before in this book, different management levels require different skills, and so sooner or later these managers will be promoted to a level where they do not possess the skills to perform well. At that point they will not get promoted again, but will also not get demoted, and thus they will occupy a position in which their performance level is not optimal.

I would be remiss if I didn't point out another implied conclusion from the Peter Principle, which I'm confident didn't jump to your mind. I'm bringing it up not just because it is an important observation in its own right, but because this book is about teaching you how to think insightfully. Always look for the different nuances, conclusions, and perspectives. If you don't look for them, you'll rarely find them.

The other conclusion that can be implied from the Peter Principle is that **the higher you go in the corporate hierarchy, the less prevalent is mediocrity**. Mediocrity is really a relative concept. It is relative to the level of competence one would expect, on average, from smart, competent, and motivated people. Once you reach the higher management levels of larger corporations, you will be dealing with high performers who possess way-above-average smarts, or else they wouldn't have gotten promoted to those levels. They may have reached their competence level with their latest promotion, per the Peter Principle, but it may be at such a level that is significantly beyond even the best of us—way above what you and I might be able to achieve, which means they are quite competent in absolute terms!

The 80-20 Rule

This was discussed earlier. I will just say here that the Peter Principle may partially contribute to the 80-20 Rule, although the 80-20 Rule is much broader and more encompassing.

Dealing with Mediocrity

So, mediocrity is everywhere. Let's talk about how we react to it and what we should do about it. I can best do this by describing how, over the course of many years, I learned to understand and deal with mediocrity.

Personally, I could never understand mediocrity. From the time I was a child, I didn't deal well with it. I never understood it to be a function of motivation or capability. To me it always indicated "stupidity and ignorance" and a perceived "lack of logic." And my response to that was always my Achilles' heel.

As a child, I didn't really comprehend that different people may have different brainpower abilities. Actually, I never gave it any thought. I never thought of myself as being smart. I was just an average kid, with average smarts. I did well in grade school; however, I didn't attribute it to being smarter than others. I always believed that it was because I just knew how to cram and study well for exams. The fact that I miserably failed my freshman year in high school in all the quantitative subjects—algebra, geometry, and physics—didn't help much in this matter. It just served to exacerbate this misguided notion that I wasn't very smart; I just knew how to study to do well on exams in the less challenging, non-quantitative subjects.

As I grew older, I started performing well in school. People and teachers kept telling me that I was very smart, but I never believed it. In my mind, I was always a very good "bullshit artist," able to make people believe that I was smart. As for receiving superb grades, I continued to attribute it purely to my talent for knowing how and what to study in order to do well on exams. In fact, as hard as it may be to comprehend, I believed it completely, until the age of thirty—when something really strange happened. The proverbial light bulb went on, and I began to accept that perhaps I was smarter than I gave myself credit for. I'll come back to this later in the book.

As I look back on it, after the light bulb went on, I realized that there was another reason for underestimating my own brainpower. I happened to have been one of those unfortunate students who consistently had a classmate who was a genius, and I mean a real Mensa kind. Over the years, as I compared myself to my genius classmates, it was obvious to me that I was not nearly as smart. So it didn't just corroborate my belief that I wasn't as smart as people thought I was; it unfortunately did the exact opposite at the same time. It corroborated in my own mind just how good I was at "bullshitting," since I was able to make everybody believe otherwise.

As a child, I grew up with a very strong work ethic. I attribute this to the fact that my native country, Israel, was still a young, independent nation. Everybody was poor and jobs were scarce, and all worked hard to make ends meet. There was no room for stupidity and ignorance; there was always somebody else waiting in the wings to take your job if you came up short. Not doing your best was not an option.

I didn't understand that people worked hard because they had to, and that if they didn't work hard, they would lose their jobs. I believed that you worked hard because you were paid to do your best. I started working at the age of thirteen. I always tried to do my best. It never occurred to me to do otherwise. I never saw anybody around me who was less committed. On the very few occasions when someone did something stupid or claimed ignorance, they were immediately admonished, not only by their managers, but more so by their families, who didn't want them to lose their jobs. All I witnessed was that everybody got angry with those people and kept saying to them, "How stupid and ignorant can you be?"

I was too young to understand the real reasons for the anger. To me it meant that when you see somebody not doing their best, it is because they are stupid and ignorant. You also get angry, admonish them, and force them to correct their ways.

As I grew older, I continued to attribute mediocrity to stupidity. At the same time, since I didn't consider myself to be overly smart, I believed that if I could assess a mediocre performance, everybody else should see it, too, including the culprit. I also realized that it wouldn't have taken all that much effort on the part of those people to do their jobs much better. So, if they didn't, it meant to me that they absolutely didn't care—they were just "stupid and ignorant." That always brought out the anger in me, as old habits die hard.

In daily life, everybody gets angry with incompetence when they are on the receiving end of it. It leads to arguments, raised voices, insults, and displeasure. Some people may be inclined to ignore incompetence because the emotional upset isn't worth it. Not me. I was brought up in a different culture that publicly identified incompetence for what it was. It was deeply engrained in my psyche; I just couldn't help myself. I would always get angry and try to make the incompetent person aware of their shortcomings. I believed I was helping them by doing so. As you would suspect, my reaction was never appreciated. Over time, I learned not to react in this way, despite the instinctive impulse to correct things.

I now realize that I was much more insightful and logical than the average person. So, I often saw faulty reasoning in what others presented and better ways to do things. At the same time, in those days, I didn't see shades of gray. It was either good or bad, right or wrong. I didn't realize that it was rarely an issue of being completely right or completely wrong. As I mentioned earlier, in business generally, a different scale applies—a more relative scale:

Superb / Much Better / A Little Better / Better / A Little Worse /
Somewhat Bad / Bad / Very Bad

It never dawned on me that I might see mediocrity where others didn't. Because I didn't consider myself to be overly smart, I always assumed that if others didn't see mediocrity, it meant that they really didn't care all that much. That would trigger my impulse to make people aware of their inadequate ways and push them to correct the situation.

As you can imagine, this created problems for me. In retrospect, I was a real idiot, and I mean an IDIOT! I truly never saw just how damaging my reactions were to my work relationships and career. I now know that the only reason I survived it, and thrived in spite of it, was purely because I was exceptional in other important skills. As a result, all were willing to live with my idiosyncrasies. In addition, I believe that they recognized, after a while, that I was doing it not out of maliciousness, but truly trying to help them and the company with the purest of motivations.

Two Examples: How Long It Took Me to Change Perspective on Mediocrity

The first time I became aware that something might be wrong was when I was at Booz Allen. As a neophyte consultant, I was given a single assignment only. My first assignment was a very large and complicated one. It had two senior partners, one junior partner, three very experienced job managers, and a host of consultants. I was fortunate to develop a very strong reputation on that job, and subsequently, the junior partner made sure that I was constantly reassigned to his projects. He had me working for him for almost three years continuously. I got promoted to job manager after one and a half years, which was very fast at the time. As a job manager I managed two to four assignments at a time. I worked for other partners, too, but this junior partner always found a way to get me on his jobs. He was an exceptionally smart and creative thinker—sharp as a surgeon's knife, very insightful. He became a great mentor to me. He taught me a lot. I owe much of my current wisdom to him.

About a year and a half into my tenure, I noticed a pattern. People with whom I started working, either within the firm or with client companies, initially didn't like me much. At the conclusion of the assignments, they were generous with their praise. However, I noticed that coworkers were often immediately liked by their clients from the outset.

I didn't speak English all that well at the time. I had a thick accent and I always sounded choppy, as if I were barking commands. I assumed that it had played some role in my observation as to how clients reacted to me initially. After a while, it really began to bother me. I went to my mentor and mentioned my observation to him and asked him for his opinion as to what he thought was going on. He looked at me and with a great smile said, "Don't worry about it; to know David is to love David." That was not a good enough answer for me. I said, "Yes, but why do I have to start with people disliking me and have to fight an uphill battle to have them like me, when everybody else is liked right away? If they make a mistake, they'll be forgiven; if I make one, I'm done for!"

He looked at me pensively and said, "You may have an interesting point there," and proceeded to tell me that I appeared to "correct" people all the time, and tended to argue with them when they disagreed. When I argued, I became loud and this made me appear to be angry. I also did not have a grasp of the nuances of the English language. I could not be subtle. Add to this a pushy Israeli mentality that seeks immediate resolution, and I ended up making everybody initially uncomfortable. "However," he continued, "they all learn over time that you turn out to be right most of the time, that you don't mean to insult them and are just trying to help everyone and the team. In the end, they realize that your positions and insights made the final product much better, and that everybody is better off for it. And then, they get to love you. So, don't worry too much about it. If you can, try to relax more when you disagree—that would help in the future." It was easier said than done. For me, it was a habit that I almost couldn't control. It was in my blood. Old habits die hard!

The second time I became aware of it was about five years later. I started working as an executive for Ameritech upon the breakup of the AT&T monopoly. I had people working for me, and I interacted with many executives in other departments, divisions, and companies under the corporate umbrella. They were important to me and I was important to them, as we were dependent on each other to get things done. All of the executives I dealt with were part of the original AT&T monopoly who suddenly found themselves in a competitive marketplace. They knew almost nothing about competitive dynamics. On the other hand, by that time, I was well trained and sophisticated in understanding how to perform well in a competitive environment. You can imagine how often I had to "help" and "correct" everybody else. I also knew that top management loved the results and what I was able to accomplish, and so quickly, too. I knew I had their total support.

One day about six months into my tenure, the president I reported to invited me to lunch. As soon as we sat down, he said in a very friendly tone, "David, I'd like to tell you something and I want you to listen to me very carefully, and really think about it afterwards."

"Sure," I said. He was a very wise, low-key person. He really liked me and had total trust in my abilities. He gave me a free hand to implement everything however I saw fit.

He continued, "David, you are one of the smartest people I've seen. You can help us achieve great things, but you need to be aware of a couple of things." He proceeded with an analogy that made me really understand that **being right and getting results are not the only things that count,** but that there are other important things as well.

He continued, "David, you are like a real thoroughbred racing horse. You were bred to race and to win. However, you are put in the same stable as all the other regular horses. You have all that pent-up energy inside you. You can't wait until the next race. You are impatient and restless. You move, you snort, and you kick the walls like a thoroughbred horse does. The problem is that, as a result, you make all the other horses extremely nervous, and that is not a very healthy situation. You need to find a way to calm down, to relax more, and to realize that you are surrounded by regular horses."

I understood the analogy, but my logic still only saw black and white. I replied, "I understand, but how else could I make changes without pushing others into it?"

As I said, he was a wise man. He smiled and said, "Yes, I figured that this is what motivates you and how you would reply. You are a very task-oriented person. Results are all you are concerned with. I was thinking about how to make you understand something that may be totally foreign to you and your mentality. I think I found a way." He then looked at me and with a serious voice said, "David, do you understand that if they all came to me and said, 'Unless he goes, we do,' I couldn't afford to let them all go and that I'd have to fire you?" I was stunned!

However, I perfectly understood what he was trying to tell me. "I understand what you are saying. I'll change," I said.

"There is more," he continued. "I described something conceptual to you, so I need to give you something more specific, so you will know exactly how you must change." He paused and pensively looked at me for a couple of seconds. "We've had a long-standing saying in this company that everybody is aware of: 'Don't spoil someone else's soup; it is the quickest way to lose your job.' If it is not your soup, leave it alone."

I understood what he was trying to tell me. I became aware of a whole different dimension, which I was never aware of before. I became determined to change. I gave it a lot of thought in the ensuing days, weeks, and months. I had to get to a point where I really owned it. Suddenly, I realized something very profound that changed me forever. I rarely became angry with mediocrity again. I realized that there was no right or wrong, good or bad—it is all relative, with the words "better" or "not as good" capturing the essence of everything. What hit me was the realization of two fundamental truths:

- Although mediocrity is everywhere, it is not the end of the world! With all the mediocrity around, the world has still managed, in spite of it, to do pretty well, over time. Somehow, things got done well, after all, even without me. Maybe they could have been better, but they are not bad, and are still significantly better than things were. I recognized that I was seeing things in black and white, and the world in reality had thousands of shades of gray, most leading to positive outcomes (perhaps not efficiently, but mostly in a positive direction).

- I should be thankful and not angry with all the mediocrity I see around me. If it were not for the mediocrity, if everybody were as smart, insightful, invested, and motivated as I was, I would have never been able to achieve as much as I had. I did so well precisely because others were not as capable or determined. I should thank them all for my career advancement and the quality of life I had achieved. I should not be angry; I should rejoice!

I worked very hard at changing. I never reached a point where I became great at it, but I became much better. I mellowed over time. I can also tell you, unequivocally, that as a result of this shift, I subsequently became much more effective, too.

Neither should you be angry. You, too, should rejoice. With mediocrity everywhere around us comes a great opportunity to excel!

LESSONS AND RULES

8

Nothing Is More Powerful Than to Prove a "Common Wisdom" Wrong!

I use "common wisdom" to mean anything that is widely accepted as truth, and as such, common wisdom is rarely challenged. Business is rife with common wisdom. Some such "wisdoms" are generic, some situational, and some specific.

Common wisdom is expressed as a belief that may reflect reality and may indeed be true, but likewise it may not completely reflect current reality, or may even be false. In either case, a common wisdom is rooted in experiences that are passed on as "wisdom" from one person to another, from one generation to another, as true observations and conclusions. While a common wisdom may have started out as true, over the years things may change and some of those "truths" could change as well, and in subtle ways. Although somewhat transfigured, the "common wisdoms" may continue to be passed on as still being wise and true. Few challenge a common wisdom as something that may be somewhat flawed.

As I mentioned in the previous section, I was a business consultant with a premier strategic consulting firm, Booz Allen. Our job was to evaluate competitive situations, analyze market dynamics, and recommend strategies for companies to compete successfully. Needless to say, our work and our success were contingent on correctly analyzing and understanding what was really happening in the marketplace and what our clients' competitors were up to. It was during those years that I was exposed to most of what I learned about insight. Our analyses were thorough and based only on facts. We utilized state-of-the-art techniques to arrive at sound conclusions. We spent an immense amount of energy focused on methods that led to truthful conclusions for our clients. As a result, we invariably ended up gaining knowledge and perspectives that were not so obvious to our clients, and oftentimes contradicted what the clients believed to be true. In other words, we consistently showed them new and different perspectives—new insights. The more insightful the analyses and conclusions, the more pleased the clients were. In fact, the differentiation of the premier consulting firms rested with their reputation for insightfulness. We were trained to evaluate things differently and look for a higher degree of understanding and perspective (aka insights). However, first and foremost, our perceptions had to be based on what was true in the marketplace, and something we could prove beyond any doubt. Our reputation and success were based on our ability to find those insights, prove them to be correct, draw the correct conclusions, and present them to the client, who hopefully said, "Wow, these are great, insightful analyses and recommendations."

It was early on during my tenure with Booz Allen that a senior partner gave me great advice. He explained to me what a "common wisdom" was and said, "Always check the common wisdoms. You'll be the greatest consultant if you can prove a common wisdom to be wrong, since that would come as the greatest revelation to clients, and the greatest insight you'll be able to come up with." I took it to heart and have never since accepted any common wisdom without first convincing myself that it still held true. It has proven to be a great asset throughout my career. I will discuss this topic later in the book in more detail, and will try to teach you the thought processes, creativity, comprehensiveness, and techniques necessary to enable you to do the same.

Meanwhile, I'll conclude this chapter with an example that will vividly demonstrate, even to the inexperienced person, just how widespread flawed common wisdoms can be. It addresses the topic of resume writing and thus should also be considered a complement to what was already presented in chapter three, "The Art of Insightfulness in Practice: How to Write a Great Resume." In addition, the example serves to offer another glimpse into how insightfulness is achieved through observing nuances, thinking out of the box, and using simple logic to draw different conclusions.

Example: How Not to Impress with a Resume!

About thirty years ago, a new common wisdom emerged regarding writing good resumes. The genesis was an observation that employers are looking for successful managers who can effectively and creatively manage employees to deliver real results and who are individuals of high morals and character. So, three conclusions emerged: (i) Make sure that you don't just give your employment history in your resume, but focus on your accomplishments; (ii) Make sure to emphasize that you are a person of "action," who possesses all the qualities required from a leader and a higher-level manager to effectively manage others and deliver superior results; and (iii) Show that you are a "good citizen" and involved in community affairs.

I would like to pause here to ask you to reflect on the above logic and conclusions. Do you agree or disagree with them? Will you use it yourself should you need to write a resume?

Obviously, the logic is reasonably compelling. We also know that it represents a long-standing, widely accepted common wisdom. Both argue that it therefore must also be true, no? My response: There is a difference between common logic and common wisdom, and insightful logic and insightful wisdom. Hopefully, this example will convince you of that.

On the following pages are a cover letter and resume, which I received over the transom and which is similar to thousands of other resumes I have seen over the last thirty years. Please read both and think about the positives and negatives (if any) you observe in them, and how you might revise them, if at all. Then I'll give you my observations for comparison.

From:	▮▮▮▮▮▮▮▮▮▮▮▮▮▮
To:	David Kronfeld
Subject:	Referral from ▮▮▮▮▮▮▮▮▮	COO	GM: ▮▮▮▮▮
Date:	Friday, June 12, 2020 2:36:26 PM
Attachments:	▮▮▮▮▮ Resume.pdf

Dear David:

If you are seeking an accomplished COO with Sales, Marketing, and Operations expertise within one of your portfolio companies, you may be interested in ▮▮▮▮▮▮▮ background and capabilities. ▮▮▮ brings authentic and invigorating leadership while developing high performing teams. He is known for maximizing value creation across diversified industries through revenue generation, M&A, organic growth, and accelerated profitability.

Currently, as GM for a mid-cap company, a leader in its industry, ▮▮▮ has successfully grown sales more than 25% to $440 million and increased net income 30% by focusing on enviable margin business. With seamless execution and savvy in his understanding of business levers and scalability, ▮▮▮ transforms status quo businesses into world-class, winning cultures. His effective start-up to mid-cap go-to-market strategies, food, e-commerce, digital media, consumer cleantech, SaaS, and social responsibility, round out his "best athlete" profile.

▮▮▮▮ customers find him to be passionate about the consumer experience. Throughout his career, he has developed exceptional relationships and has carefully cultivated these into trusted partnerships. ▮▮▮ is a forward-thinking and highly engaged leader. He effectively mentors, stretches, and empowers his teams to deliver extraordinary results.

Being intellectually agile, ▮▮▮ can quickly have an impact, respond to transformational business opportunities as an intentional response to pandemic challenges as most businesses need to revitalize their marketplace positions, while keeping their team safe and healthy.

I know that you will find him equally dynamic, intuitive, and dependable. FYI, ▮▮▮ is conducting a discreet search. Please feel free to reach out to ▮▮ directly at ▮▮▮▮▮▮▮ or ▮▮▮▮▮▮@gmail.com (www.linkedin.com/in▮▮▮▮▮▮

Thank you for your consideration.

Best regards,

▮▮▮▮▮▮▮▮▮▮▮▮▮▮▮
President & CEO, ▮▮▮▮▮▮▮▮▮ Inc.

▮▮▮▮▮▮▮▮▮▮▮▮▮▮▮▮▮▮▮

▮▮▮▮▮▮▮▮▮▮▮▮

38 years as a Global Executive Coaching and Leadership Development Consultancy. ▮▮ **effectively coaches, develops, and transitions executives.** Visit our website and Executive Blog: www▮▮▮▮▮▮▮▮▮▮

Unsubscribe

███████████   Los Angeles, CA
█████████ @gmail.com   www.linkedin.com/in█████████

CEO | COO | GM

Accomplished executive with a proven track record in Sales, Marketing, and Operations. Diversified experience in food, e-commerce, consumer cleantech, rewards & loyalty, Fintech, and digital media. Demonstrated startup DNA, hard-wired to accelerate revenue growth, profitability, and market share. Highly skilled in negotiations. Develop world-class leaders and teams that exceed expectations by modelling innovative leadership through greater collaboration and cross-functional synergies.

EXPERIENCE

███████ FOODS Los Angeles, CA   2016 – Present
A $440 million industry leader and global supplier of 125 million pounds of fresh and frozen seafood. (*U.S. Family Owned & Operated*)

General Manager   2017 – Present
P&L responsibility for managing National Sales, Sales Support, Non-Food Sourcing, Imports, Logistics, Packaging, Marketing, and Corporate Social Responsibility teams. Report to the CEO.

- Grew sales from $329 million to $440 million (+25%) and net income +30% through M&A and organic growth.

- Manage $10 million in annual spend and successfully negotiated $500,000+ in savings.

- Generated $25 million in incremental sales by elevating the national sales team's capabilities to be more consultative and responsive.

- Established key performance metrics, sales management processes, and coached sales talent to accelerate relationships with buyers and salesforce.

- Brought new products to market working across business lines while creating collaborative and innovative solutions.

- Manage marketing efforts, including new packaging design, interactive product catalog, website development, social media channels, and plan and execute our annual Seafood Expo North America.

Corporate Development & Strategy   2016 – 2017
Concurrently performed M&A due diligence, negotiated costs, and managed relationships with distributors. Integral role in assimilating two acquisitions into the parent company.

- Negotiated $1.9 million in annual cost savings with packaging distributors, cold storage warehouses, corrugated box manufacturers, import broker, information technology support, and freight providers.

- Delivered M&A due diligence, and in 2017 integrated two companies with combined revenues of $100 million and an expanded workforce of 60 employees.

- Prepared and presented sales reports, expense summaries, and P&L analysis.

████████ Los Angeles, CA   2013 – 2015
Delivered limited edition packages curated by influencers four times a year.
(*A* ██ *Ventures,* ████████ *Fund,* ███ *TechFund, and* ██ *Angel portfolio company*)

Chief Revenue Officer
Responsible for growing recurring revenue, hiring and managing sales, marketing, and PR teams. Coached account managers to increase package profitability and enabled and negotiated new fulfillment center deal terms.

- Increased annual revenue from $1.8 million to $5.5 million while spending minimal marketing budget that enhanced the organization's capability and services.

███████████ New York, NY　　　　　　　　　　　　　　2012 – 2013
A mobile app and virtual bank designed for kids and their parents to learn about fiscal responsibility.
(A ████████████████████ *company)*

SVP　Sales and Business Development
Provided the strategic national sales direction and identified key verticals and brands.

- Developed the go-to-market SaaS sales strategy, discovered decision-makers and influencers, cold-called, created demand for a new product, and sold the company's first $50,000 deal.

███████████ New York, NY　　　　　　　　　　　　　　2007 – 2012
████████ created a more sustainable future by rewarding people for taking green actions with discounts and deals from local and national businesses. *(A Kleiner Perkins portfolio company)*

VP　Advertising Sales
Trained new sales team hires and coached account managers to maximize existing account revenue while developing high-trust relationships with C-Level marketing executives at Honda, Kimberly-Clark, Albertsons, and Henkel.

- Sold $3.8 million in sponsorships to all new accounts.

████████████████ Los Angeles, CA　　　　　　　　　　　2004 – 2007
A leading media and internet company with more than 150 brands and products.

Director　Advertising Sales
Managed advertising sales and account management teams of 8 direct reports. Responsible for goal setting, territory alignment, hiring, training, and managing out underperformers.

- Generated $10 million in annual advertising revenue from Fortune 500 companies.

EDUCATION

BA Journalism　Minor in Spanish ████████████ ██████████ 1997

International Studies ██████████████████ ██████████ 1996

ADVISORY & VOLUNTEER WORK

Advisor
Los Angeles Cleantech Incubator　Los Angeles, CA　　　　　2012 – 2015

Advisor
Standard Razors (Acquired)　Los Angeles, CA　　　　　2015 – 2016

Advisor
Social Junction　Los Angeles, CA　　　　　2015 – 2018

Volunteer
Toastmasters International　Los Angeles, CA　　　　　2010 – 2012

Guest Lecturer
San Diego State University　San Diego, CA　　　　　Present

I would assume that most will view the cover letter and resume as being reasonably well constructed and effective. I would also not be surprised if most wouldn't find many flaws in either, or discover only minor flaws. I'm not sure if you noticed, but from the third-party reference in the cover letter you can surmise that it was actually written by a professional service firm specializing in representing candidates. So, you would definitely expect the cover letter and resume to be of a high standard. Indeed, I can confirm that in my opinion the cover letter and resume are of a higher level of quality than many I've seen written by individuals without the help of professional service providers. However, a positive first impression cannot hide the flaws in these documents, some of which may even be fatal.

You may remember that I concluded in chapter three that the purpose of a resume is to effectuate an invitation for an interview. However, unlike a resume collated in a student resume book, here we have an additional complexity. This resume was sent blind and not in response to an advertised position. This presents other key challenges, which I didn't address in chapter three, with respect to how over-the-transom resumes are dealt with.

First, the recipient of a blind resume is likely an HR manager/department head or a high-level manager, like the chairman, CEO, COO, president, CFO, vice president, and so on. There are a number of implications. One is a trivial observation; unlike in a student resume book, any resume sent via mail or email does require an "introductory" cover letter, which was indeed present in our example. Next, let's remember that an HR person or any higher-level manager is the likeliest addressee for all over-the-transom resumes. Thus, we can conclude that they constantly receive many resumes, probably in the tens and sometimes in the hundreds each month, depending on the size of the company. So, now let's put ourselves in their shoes to understand their reactions.

We can safely assume that the HR manager and the high-level executives are aware of current job openings. It would also be fair to assume that they will not bother to read resumes that cross their desk (with the possible exception of an HR manager), unless a current opening exists. For the sake of the example, let's assume that an opening does exist for a higher-level management position and thus they will indeed look at resumes for a potential fit. We already discussed in chapter three that few people, if any, will thoroughly read resumes. Instead, they quickly scan them to decide whether it should be of interest or not. So, the key question is: What might they be looking for in a quick scan of the resume in our specific situation? Please take a minute to think about the top three or four things they will most likely look for in order to decide whether to discard a resume or give it consideration.

I claim that the following list represents the elements they would scan for:

1. Is the level/title of the candidate a fit with the level/title of the position at hand? Meaning, if the open position is for a CEO, does the resume represent someone who has been a CEO or is ready to be promoted into a CEO position, i.e., a COO or president? Or, if the open position is for a COO, then does the resume state that the applicant currently holds a COO position, or is at a vice-president level and is ready to be promoted? Or, if the position is for a vice president, then does the resume represent someone who has served in that position or is a director-level manager ready to be promoted? In other words, the first thing they will want to see is the candidate's current title. Assuming a match, then:

2. Is the title in the appropriate functionality? Meaning, if the position is in the marketing department, the HR manager or senior executive will want to see experience in marketing. If in finance, they'll want to see a finance background, and so on. Obviously, for the CEO and COO positions, this question is less relevant. Assuming a match, then:

3. Is it in the same or a closely related industry? Clearly, each industry has its own competitive dynamics and special expertise and experiences, so the right title but in a different industry is not likely to offer a compelling match. Assuming a match, then:

4. Is the title and experience from a large and/or reputable company, or a small company? Clearly, a vice president in a small company

may not be perceived to be qualified for the same title in a large company. The opposite is not true and actually, in general, experience in a larger corporation is highly valued by smaller companies. This is because the larger companies are generally perceived to have greater, more sophisticated systems and procedures, and more depth of experience, than smaller companies.

If all four questions above produce a match, then the resume will receive another look; otherwise, it would be discarded. I doubt that anybody would disagree with the above list of questions and the resultant conclusions. So now, we only need to resolve whether the cover letter and resume are conducive to "help" easily find answers to the four questions above, and then evaluate whether the cover letter and resume in our example are well written and do justice to the candidate. I didn't address the cover letter in chapter three, so let me first share my primary observations regarding cover letters.

Cover Letters for Resumes

Most cover letters I've seen over the years have in my opinion been poorly written. The primary "mistakes" are that **they are too long** and **not cognizant of what the real objective of a cover letter should be.**

Just like with the resume, cover letters are not likely to be thoroughly read. Instead, they will be quickly scanned for pertinent information to determine whether to give the candidate additional attention or to discard the letter. So, the longer the cover letter, the greater the likelihood that the reader will lose patience. Also, the longer the letter, the less likely the reader will notice the more critical information they seek to glean from a quick scan. Thus, just like in a resume, **the more succinct the writing, the better.** Not only will the candidate reduce the risk of the reader prematurely discarding their resume due to loss of patience, but they will also increase the probability that the reader will indeed read what the candidate would like them to notice.

It appears to me that the biggest reason for lengthy cover letters is an attempt by the candidate to enumerate as many positive attributes as they believe could influence interest in them. Many times, the cover letter almost summarizes the resume itself, and/or adds qualitative elaborations about the candidate's experiences, positive traits, talents, and presumed accomplishments, thereby making it longer.

Clearly, just as with the resume, to write an effective cover letter, one must first define the real objective of the cover letter. In my opinion it is **not the same objective as the resume.** So, providing a summary and repeating in the cover letter what is captured in the resume makes no sense to me. Not just because it makes it longer, but more importantly, it creates a situation whereby the reader believes that they got the high-lights of the candidate's resume and as a result the resume will not even be looked at—the one document that the candidate labored so much over to ensure the most effective and compelling display of their background and experience.

From my perspective, **the real objective of the cover letter is to "incentivize" the reader to look at the resume.** Therefore, it follows that the real question to answer is: **What can be written in a cover letter that will maximize the inclination of a reader to look at the resume, while being as succinct as possible to avoid loss of patience and prematurely discarding the resume?**

In my opinion, the following guidelines will yield the most effective cover letter:

- **Be as succinct as possible.** But not in the same way as with the resume. In chapter three, I recommended that the resume "need not have all the information about you, but rather only the important information that is necessary and used throughout the process." Here, though, I literally mean succinct, without the burden of needing to be reasonably complete in providing all the necessary history about yourself. I recommend no more than one paragraph of substance (not including trivial contact information, confidentiality statement, referring person, etc.). If any past accomplishments and experiences are mentioned, they should not be an extensive list of all of them. Rather, select the top one, or two at most, and weave them as part of the single paragraph, mostly for the purpose of highlighting the accomplishments, rather than fully explaining them.

- **Don't summarize the resume.** Make sure it does not provide anything that resembles a summary of the resume itself.

- **Provide only the most critical differentiating factors.** Focus here on the real *impressive* and *differentiating* facts, as opposed to facts that many other candidates may be able to claim as well.

- **Be humble with self-compliments.** Strongly worded self-compliments are not well received. (I address this issue later in this chapter.)

- **Address a specific person and/or title, if possible.** The more "personal" the cover letter appears, the more attention it is likely to receive. Try to avoid "To whom it may concern." (Do some advance research if need be. Only use that phrase if there is no other way.)

- **Invoke a reference, if possible.** Referring to a specific person (either by name or title) who will be recognized by the addressee will add credibility and increase the inclination to pay more attention, rather than less.

Having said the above, there is another alternative that would be reasonable and even more effective at times: **Interchange the role of the resume with the cover letter.** That is, use the cover letter to promote your factual accomplishments as if it were the resume, and use the resume to provide a more complete historical biography. **This alternative would be more appropriate to consider if your resume would be too long otherwise.** This way, you take the best parts of what would normally be in your resume and push it up front to the cover letter, and the resume becomes just a "filler" to make sure you provided your full background. Obviously, with this alternative, you don't really care if the reader ever reads the resume itself because you have captured in the cover letter all the information you wanted the reader to glean. Should you choose this alternative approach, make sure that the resume is indeed simplistic and not a repetition of what was captured in the cover letter.

We can now go back and evaluate the cover letter and the resume in our example. Hopefully, it will give you additional insights about writing yours.

Let's look first at the content of the cover letter. Imagine that you are the CEO or the HR manager receiving the resume. Would you truly believe all the ambiguous and generic self-promoting claims in the cover letter, such as:

- "He brings authentic and invigorating leadership while developing high performing teams."

- "He is known for maximizing value creation."

- "He transforms status quo businesses into world-class, winning cultures."

- "His effective, start-up strategies, food, e-commerce . . . round out his 'best athlete' profile."

- "Customers find him to be passionate about the consumer experience"—and on and on?

Of course not. Nobody would! These claims quickly would be discounted, or completely discarded. If you think so, too, then one should ask why anybody (the candidate, or a professional service presenting them) would even make such claims. They are just a waste of space that makes scanning the resume for the more important aspects much more difficult, thereby increasing the temptation to discard the resume.

Worse yet, **any self-promotion is not looked upon favorably in the corporate world**. At a minimum, it reflects immaturity and naivete, because the inference is that the candidate is not even cognizant of how self-promotion of this kind is perceived. Worse, it connotes that the candidate lacks good judgment for thinking that it is appropriate to make such egotistical claims in a cover letter (or resume). I can tell you that I always react negatively to such asinine self-promotion, regardless of whether it was written by the candidates themselves or a professional agent representing them.

There are, however, aspects of self-promotion that are acceptable and desirable in a cover letter or resume. These would be specific and actual claims that are impressive, but also factual and provable. For example: "I outperformed expectations and grew the company at a 50 percent annual rate"; "I was the team leader"; "I was awarded a certificate of excellence"; "I was selected from a large group of candidates to . . .", and so on.

On the positive side, note that the first sentence of the second paragraph in the cover letter addresses well what I enumerated to be the four most important questions a reader may be scanning for. I also like the reference to the large size of the company the candidate managed and the factual, impressive growth and profitability figures. Otherwise, from my perspective, these are the only sentences of substance and interest to the reviewer. Had the cover letter only addressed those aspects, it would have been great. As it stands, the remainder added no value, and most likely only detracted from the attractiveness of the candidate and increased the probability that the reader would discard the resume prematurely.

Now we can look at the resume itself. What are your observations? Do you like it? Do you believe it is effective? Would you make any changes? Below are my observations.

What is first immediately apparent from an overall visual inspection is that the resume spans two pages, which I am not a fan of, as I described in chapter three. (Although it may be difficult to condense a longer career, particularly of a higher-level manager, into a single page, so in that case, two pages could be appropriate. However, I would try to keep the resume to a single page, if at all possible.) The second observation is that, visually, the resume looks very good, and is concise and well organized. It is also easy to scan.

As I read the content of the resume, a different picture emerges. The resume has some positive attributes, but for the most part, it is suboptimal. (Although it is consistent with the common wisdom and thus, perhaps, many others may not make the same observations I made.) Below are my observations:

- The introductory paragraph (where normally one states the "Objectives") comprises five lines that are nothing but generic self-promotion. As I stated earlier, these claims would be discounted, and they potentially present a risk of leaving the impression that the candidate lacks maturity and judgment. Additionally, allocating so much space to such claims necessitates the need for a two-page resume. Worse, this is the very first thing the reader gets to read!

- I like the mention of the $440 million in the company's description and in the first bullet point under the General Manager title. It points out that the company is of a decent size. I also like the mention of the growth both in revenue and profits; they are factual, meaningful, and suggestive. (Had it been a small company, I would have recommended not mentioning the exact size.)

- The second bullet point is a comedown. The previous reference to $440 million in revenues would lead one to infer that the candidate was exposed to a commensurate depth, breadth, and sophistication of experiences. The inference opens the possibility that the candidate might be qualified to be considered for an equivalent position in a larger company, even a billion-dollar firm. Unfortunately, the subsequent second bullet point dispels any such consideration. A $10 million annual spend is a very insignificant amount for a large corporation. Worse, $500,000 in savings is an insignificant amount relative to the expected results from a CEO/COO of any decent-sized corporation, and immediately leaves an impression that this candidate is a "small-time operator" and not really ready for the "big leagues." I would have excluded this bullet point altogether.

- The same observation is true about the third bullet point. Twenty-five million dollars in incremental sales is "little league" relative to expectation of a $400 to $500 million company, let alone any larger corporation. This point confirms the limited scale and experience the candidate brings. Worse, following it up with the fact that it was accomplished by "elevating the national sales team's capabilities to be more consultative and responsive" only serves to diminish the candidate's business maturity. All COOs are expected to achieve results using all the tools and strategies available to them. The way one gets there is mostly trivial; only that the results are accomplished. Mentioning specifically a single dimension as a reason is diminutive and reflects a lack of maturity for that level (unless it is actually unique and uncommon). I would do away with this bullet point, too.

- The same observation is true about the fourth bullet point. Highlighting the most obvious and basic steps that every successful manager implements as a matter of routine, as if it were a new discovery, is even more diminutive then the previous bullet point. Definitely out!

- I have the same observations for the fifth and sixth bullet points, as well as the bullet points under the Corporate Development & Strategy heading.

- One can see the exact same pattern in the remainder of the candidate's workplaces.

- Additionally, since the candidate is looking for a high-level position (GM, COO, or CEO), only the experiences that speak to his qualifications for that level are of significance. What the candidate may have done in the early years of his career is irrelevant. Thus, there is no need to elaborate on such early experiences, and deleting this text would allow for a resume of a single page. (I would make an exception only if there was something uniquely impressive in those early years that would create favorable impressions and some differentiation. For example, having worked and showing career progression with larger corporations of strong reputation would imply that the candidate had been highly sought after earlier in his career and done well under demanding circumstances.)

- The Education category is another disaster. The candidate fails to understand how COO-level experience is perceived and should be presented. At that level, any comment regarding past education is of little significance. Only the most recent work experience and achievements influence the decision to hire for such senior levels. (However, education could be used as an important secondary differentiating factor, when multiple candidates were found to be attractive. At that point, good schools, good grades, and any significant academic awards may give one a differentiating advantage. Commentary that offers no special distinction is irrelevant.) With this perspective in mind, let's look at the resume. Why would an experienced businessperson, particularly at a CEO/ COO level, even mention what their minor in college was? Who cares? What importance does it have? If it was added for the sake of completeness or meant to show that the candidate may be fluent in Spanish, why would anybody even believe that it would be a factor in getting a job offer? Moreover, even if it may be of value, then it would be more appropriate to mention at the end of the resume under the Personal category at the end of the resume, where one conventionally expects to find such information.

There is another problem. The candidate's degree is in journalism, which is not exactly the kind of major one would have expected of an ambitious and accomplished business professional. This fact by itself would not be problematic at the CEO/COO level, since, again, educational background plays a minor role in the decision to hire someone. However, in this particular case, where the candidate may have already left a perception of a lack of business maturity and perhaps being a small operator, indicating an unusual degree suggests the candidate never intended to be a high-level executive.

There is another problem—notice the dates for the candidate's education. The dates give the impression that the BA degree had been earned in two years, which is a questionable achievement. If the dates signal the graduation dates only, then the resume should have made it clear. If it is a typo, then it's a pretty bad reflection on the candidate. Typos can be fatal!

The last observation is about the final section, Advisory and Volunteer Work. Note how much space it takes! It may follow the directives of the common wisdom, which advises demonstrating good citizenship and involvement in community affairs, but it is counterproductive in our case. It substantiates and compounds the "immature" perception. Which "mature" CEO/COO would even think that those activities listed in the resume would rise to the point that might affect a decision to hire at that level? I would have not mentioned them at all (unless they were impressive organizations where the candidate had a key role, and where such involvement and contacts would be helpful to the job at hand).

Here is how I would have changed (and improved) the cover letter and resume:

Cover Letter

Dear David:

If you are seeking an accomplished COO/CEO with Sales, Marketing, and Operational expertise within one of your portfolio companies, you may be interested in (full name)'s background and capabilities.

Currently, as GM for a mid-cap company and a leader in the industry, (first name) has successfully grown sales more than 25 percent to $440 million, while increasing profits by 30 percent.

The attached resume provides (first name)'s full background. Please feel free to contact (first name) directly at (phone number). Please be advised that (first name) is conducting a discreet search.

Thank you,

Etc.

Resume

(full name)
(Phone number)   (Home address)
(Email)   (LinkedIn)

Objective: A CEO, COO, GM position commensurate with my background and experience.

Experience:

 FOODS   *Los Angeles, CA 2016–Present*

A $440-million industry leader and global supplier of 125 million pounds of fresh and frozen seafood.

General Manager   *2017–Present*

Major accomplishment: Introduced new products and grew sales from $329 million to $440 million (+25 percent) and net income +30 percent.

Corporate Development & Strategy   *2016–2017*

Major accomplishment: Acquired and integrated two companies with combined revenues of $100 million.

████████████ **CO.**   *Los Angeles, CA 2013–2015*

A venture capital-backed start-up company (████ Ventures, ████████████ Fund, ████ TechFund, and ██ Angel Portfolio) delivering limited edition packages.*

Chief Revenue Officer

Major accomplishment: Was able to quickly reach $5.5 million in revenues with minimal budget.

████████████ **CO.**   *New York, NY 2012–2013*
████████████ **CO.**   *New York, NY 2007–2012*
████████████ **CO.**   *Los Angeles, CA 2004–2007*

Education: BA, University of Missouri, Columbia, MO—graduated 1997.

Personal: Fluent in Spanish. Involved with various community affair activities.

*Author's note: I left it here because being backed by venture capitalists adds significant credibility.

I hope I convinced you that the rather typical resume in our example was not a very effective one, and that the changes to the cover letter and resume I offered would have made it better. This exercise again demonstrates that common wisdoms are not immune to flaws. I also hope that it served to illustrate how the small nuances, thinking out of the box, and pure, simple logic lead to insightful observations. Additionally, I hope that in the process you also gained a deeper understanding that complements your knowledge of how to write a great resume. However, before I conclude this chapter, I'd like to bring an additional observation to your attention.

You may be somewhat bewildered by the fact that common wisdoms remain prevalent and are well practiced, in spite of all the negative observations I've just pointed out. They are so simple and rudimentary and should therefore be obvious to the experts who write and read resumes. So, how come the experts haven't wised up to it by now? How is it even possible that such common wisdoms could survive for so long?

My answer is that as unbelievable and unexplainable as it may appear, it happens all the time. It is reality. I have my own explanation as to why. The primary reason is the fact that, from an overall perspective, the basic hypotheses behind the common wisdoms appear to be correct, but although appearing to be logical, the conclusions might not be. As a result, most accept the connection without further scrutiny.

In our example, the genesis for the common wisdom is correct. Employers do look for successful managers who can effectively and creatively manage employees to deliver real results and who are people of high morals and character. Ask any high-level manager whether these variables play a major role, and the answer will most likely be in the affirmative. However, **although correct, they are not determinative.** This means that, although it is true that those traits are important, and without them one may not get a job offer, it doesn't follow that they are the primary criteria for receiving a job offer. In other words, there are other, more important factors without which an offer will not be forthcoming no matter how strongly one demonstrates the above. In simple terms, and as mentioned earlier in the book (see chapter five), these conditions fit the "necessary but not sufficient" criterion. It takes more nuanced and deeper thinking to recognize such a flaw in logic, and so the common wisdom continues to survive.

At the same time, since everybody writes their resume in a manner consistent with the common wisdom, then all resumes embody the same flaws, so these flaws are ignored and are not particularly damaging. In situations like these, the damage reflects only an opportunity lost, which is much more difficult to ascertain. Meaning, there is no *obvious* damage in following the common wisdom, because many do so. However, if one is wiser, one can write a better, smarter resume that avoids negative inferences, thereby increasing, rather than decreasing, the probability of being invited for an in-person interview.

In summary: **Don't be afraid to look for potential flaws in common wisdoms, and don't be surprised when you easily find them. All you need to do is pay attention to the details and nuances, think out of the box, and make sure you accurately identify the correct challenges/objectives that need to be reached.**

9

Listen Carefully to People, but Make an Independent Judgment as to the Validity of What They Say

When I say "listen carefully," I don't mean listen without interruptions (although that probably is good advice in its own right). I mean, "*Listen* carefully; don't just *hear* what is being said." Pay close attention to what people mean to say. There are six related messages that I'd like to leave with you. Each on its own is of value and, in combination, they are invaluable.

1. **Listen not to what people say, but rather to what they *mean* to say.** This is a common adage and full of wisdom. Often, people are not as careful with their choice of words and articulation as they should be. So, if you want to understand a person you must listen carefully and try to understand the full context and perspective of the speaker. Don't let your own bias and what you might like to hear, or believe that you are likely to hear, interfere with focusing on what they really mean to say. I can assure you that it is easier said than done, so you need to always keep it in mind. Over time, as you practice this, it gets easier and easier, and it becomes second nature when you master it.

2. **Don't just listen to first-level logic. Learn to listen to all the nuances, and/or seek them out.** Often, once we hear the most important part, we tend to listen less carefully, because we think we understand what the other person is saying. This is true whether we agree or disagree with the person. Over many years of experience, I have learned that I enrich my knowledge and ability to exercise good judgment when I seek to understand all the nuances in a person's message or thinking, and I always ask questions to better understand those nuances.

3. **Don't dismiss inarticulation or an explanation that at first may not make sense to you. Always seek to understand without any ambiguity what a person means to say and their *reasoning* behind it.** Oftentimes, we will dismiss what a person says because they are not articulating their message well, so it appears to be unclear or incoherent. This point has some overlap with the previous one, but I am trying to raise awareness of poor articulation as opposed to poor logic. I would argue that this bias is more prevalent among more articulate and successful people. Poor articulation connotes to them a less intelligent person and someone undeserving of their full attention. I've seen it throughout my career, but early on learned to guard against it. I learned that people, regardless of smarts, may come up with some great observations, even if not articulated well. **Look beyond poor articulation; ask for the reasons behind what people say**, so that you can truly understand what they mean to express.

4. **Do not allow for misinterpretations.** The most common miscommunication I've experienced is the one arising from people who hear someone's words but understand them to mean something very different from what was intended. For example, assume you hear the CEO say, "This is unacceptable. We need to correct it." Are the CEO's marching orders clear? Is the CEO demanding that the issue be corrected immediately, or can it wait a while? Are we sure that the CEO fully understood the implications or the consequences before making the statement? What if the cost of correcting the situation would be prohibitive—would the CEO still have recommended doing so? Also, what does "unacceptable"

really mean? Does it mean that it is absolutely not acceptable, or may there be some room for adjustments, if appropriate? Do you see how many nuances and potential misinterpretations can arise? My advice is never to be timid or afraid to ask all the necessary follow-up questions until you are convinced that there is no room for misinterpreting what had been said. There is a secondary benefit to this advice; the questions may clarify the statement in the mind of the speaker and cause them to modify it significantly as a result. Follow this rule yourself when you speak to others. Ask if your message is clear and be patient with questions.

5. **Whenever possible, ask for the "insight" of situations.** Here I mean that you should ask to understand, whenever possible, not just the important outcome, but what took place behind the scenes: all the twists and turns, all the debates, all the motivations. In other words, look for the "what," "why," and "how" of a situation for context of a decision. Over time, you'll gain insight that will prove to be exceptionally valuable, as you will be better able to understand and anticipate the true dynamics in future similar circumstances.

6. **Listen carefully to everyone, regardless of how smart they may appear to be.** Many people pay more attention to those whom they consider intelligent and knowledgeable, and tend to ignore those they deem to be less so. **My advice is to not be one of these people!** Practically everybody possesses the ability to be insightful, on and off. This is true regardless of intelligence. You never know when someone will say something to you that will add value to your thinking or understanding. This value can come in one of two ways—as a flash of insight for a new idea or solution, or as something that may trigger a thought that leads you in a direction you otherwise may not have gone. The second is more likely, but I've personally experienced enough of both categories that I have learned to truly appreciate people's ability, regardless of intelligence, to be insightful and say something really smart.

Perhaps you might benefit from an approach I devised earlier in my career in order to make sure that my subordinates and I adhered to the same advice I've just given.

A Personal Approach to Listening Carefully: Understand the Real Justification for a Position

When I was a professional consultant with Booz Allen, the majority of what we learned came from interviews with people who possessed company- or industry-specific expertise that could help us. We called it "picking their brains." At the end of the study, we wrote a report with our observations and recommendations and presented it to our clients. We wanted to make sure that there would be no surprises at the final presentation to the CEO or the board of directors, and if any of the management disagreed with any part of the report, we wanted to be prepared to respond.

So, we made it a point to visit all the relevant management levels and share our observations and conclusions, hoping that they would concur. If they did not concur, we needed to understand why and be prepared with a response when the time came. I've learned the hard way to always listen very carefully, particularly when disagreements emerged.

I learned that **the best way to try to understand inarticulate people is to understand the logical reasons that they use to justify their position.** When I became a manager, I was always extra careful whenever my team alerted me to a potential disagreement that was summarily dismissed by the team. I always asked them to explain why they dismissed the disagreement. Invariably, the most common answer, predictably so, was, "They don't know what they are talking about. Their argument is based on some nonsense." This reaction is a classic response to someone who has an objection or question but is unable to articulate it well. One immediately assumes that "unconvincing" logic and poor articulation equal an illogical reason and therefore can be dismissed. Beware of reacting this way and dismissing someone outright.

I devised a way to get rid of this bias on my team. I told them, "Don't underestimate an executive who disagrees with you, just because they are not articulate enough to use MBA lingo to convince you. Don't even dismiss offhand reasons that appear illogical to you. All executives possess valuable experience, and if they appear to disagree, it may be something instinctive. Something in the back of their mind that they may find difficult to articulate. Don't assume that poor articulation means poor reasons. They didn't get promoted to their position for being stupid."

I always sent them back and asked them to find out the reasons for a disagreement. I told my team they **always have to start with the assumption that the disagreeing person is indeed right, and to find the right reasons in any way they could,** including using leading questions that might help sharpen the response. Only after they approached it with that assumption and still were unable to find a good reason would I accept that the disagreement had no merit.

Note that there are two interrelated messages in the above example. One is simple and obvious, while the other is more nuanced, but still important. The first and more obvious is to **never discount someone's opinion because they are unable to express it well enough to convince you.** *Try to understand what they mean to say and why.* **They may actually have something of value to offer, even if they themselves are inarticulate.** The second is actually more profound and you would do well to remember it throughout your career: **Only when you understand the true reasons why somebody believes a point of view are you in a position to make your own judgment as to the validity of such an opinion.** I have adhered to those rules, and over time they have paid significant dividends.

10

Treat Everyone Respectfully. Never Look Down on Anybody, Regardless of Socioeconomic Status

I discussed in the previous chapter that you should listen carefully and respectfully to all. Never be dismissive of what others say and always assume they may have something of value to say. Only after careful listening and reflection may you elect to be dismissive of their opinion, should it still not make any sense to you.

This is the very next extension of that advice. Never be disrespectful or dismissive of anybody. Never look down upon anybody. Let me state the corollary, just to emphasize the point: **Always treat people with respect and never look down on anybody, regardless of socioeconomic status!** This is not meant to be advice just for the business environment. This is meant to be an all-encompassing piece of advice for life in general.

It is proven by scholars such as Malcolm Gladwell that we harbor biases for others if they don't measure up to some "standards" we have set for interacting in society. Naturally, we may disrespect some, not like some, hate some, don't want to be associated with some, or whatever. I'm not suggesting that you shouldn't feel the way you do or should associate with people you might not want to. What I'm advising is different: **Never openly insult, be disrespectful to, or be dismissive** of anybody, regardless of how you may feel. More importantly: **Don't use socioeconomic or educational background as a basis upon which to have a lower opinion about people. Treat everyone as you would like to be treated.**

This is the way I have led my life. I didn't do it just to be nice, but because I wholeheartedly believe in it. I hope you do, too!

I served three years in the Israeli Army in a time of war. The army teaches you that your life depends on the person next to you and vice versa. You accept that as a given. You know it is true. It is the way it works.

I've seen people at their worst and at their best and can tell you unequivocally that socioeconomic and educational backgrounds are not predictive of a person's capability or character. The person who may come to your aid when you need help; the person who will jump through fire to save you; the person who will share their water with you in the desert; the person who will show you real and true kindness when you need it most; the person who will risk their life to save yours is not driven by any socioeconomic or educational level. I have many friends, and some of my dearest, whom I respect most, are in fact blue-collar, working-class people. And I don't say this to suggest I am something they are not. I mean that I never looked at them as being anything but equals. Perhaps a personal story about my father, which I heard as a child, will serve as an example.

My father lived in Poland when the Nazis stormed his homeland. He was the only Holocaust survivor from a family of nine. He survived by recognizing early on that the Nazi atrocities would only get worse with time. So he decided to escape into Russia.

The trip to the border would take weeks and was exceptionally hazardous. The Nazis would kill anybody caught outside their hometown. He faced anti-Semitism, harm, and betrayal. It was in the middle of winter, and food, water, and shelter would be a real challenge. The final hurdle was crossing the border itself, which meant crossing a large river. Anyone attempting to cross the river would be shot as a spy by either the Germans or the Russians—only a spy would attempt to make a dangerous crossing of a river and a border in the winter in a time of war.

My father talked to his brothers, but only one, an older brother, decided to join him. They used back roads to avoid military personnel. Every day was a touch-and-go situation for them, but they persevered. They met many kind people on their way, and some who treated them badly. They had some close calls but managed to reach the river. They had to wait until nightfall to try to cross the river. My father attributed their success in reaching the river to the fact that neither he nor his brother looked "Jewish" and that my father spoke Polish like a "real Polack."

While waiting for nightfall, the older brother got overwhelmed with the risks that they were about to face trying to cross the river. He decided to not go through with their plan, and tried to talk my father out of it as well. My father didn't yield—he was determined. The older brother wished him good luck and turned to go back home. He never made it.

My father was unable to cross the river for another three days. At a deserted location, he started crossing the river at dusk. It was dark enough to not be easily seen, but there was sufficient light for him to find his way across. He made it and headed downriver on the Russian side of the border. Unfortunately, he ran right into a small outpost of Russian soldiers and was captured.

They were sure he was a German spy and interrogated him for hours on end. It continued the following morning. After about three hours, the Russian soldiers took him outside and undressed him. They told him that if he wouldn't confess, they'd let him freeze to death. My father denied he was a spy. The soldiers poured cold water on him and told him that he would soon freeze to death. They waited for him to "break." My father was sure that he was about to die.

Then a jeep containing a driver and officer drove into the outpost. The officer inquired about what was happening and then approached my father and asked him who he was. My father told him that he was a Jew who was trying to escape the Nazis, just as he had told the others. The officer ordered the soldiers to dry my father off and let him in the cabin. Inside, the officer took my father into a corner and quietly said in Yiddish—a unique Jewish language—that he was very lucky and that he, himself, was also Jewish. He told my father that there was little chance he would be able to leave the front and reach a town or village without help. He then sat down and wrote something on a military form, signed it, and told my father that whenever he was stopped or needed anything along the way, he was to show the form.

My father thanked him, and then he was told to leave. My father had no idea how high-ranking the officer was. The only thing he knew was that he was stopped often, and every time he showed the form, he was treated with respect and offered help. My father reached a train station and after displaying the form once again was permitted to travel to the interior of the country. In time he met my mother. They were married in Russia.

Life can be very random and unpredictable. You never know who your savior might be. Never disrespect anybody!

11

Always Seek Perspectives and Advice from People Who Know Best. But Remember the 80-20 Rule and Always "Own" the Final Judgment

As I mentioned in the introduction, this book is full of observations, rules, and recommendations. Some you may think trivial, others more profound, and the rest will fall somewhere in between. I suggest that this chapter is one that bears especially careful reflection. This advice has three important components, which I will discuss individually:

- Always seek perspectives and advice from those who know best—in other words, those with expertise in the field you seek to understand.

- Be careful with how you receive and what you do with the advice you get. Some may be excellent and some mediocre or even bad.

- Regardless of the above, make sure the final judgment is yours and yours alone.

Seek Expertise

As we move through life, we often find ourselves facing questions and dilemmas we know little, if anything, about. It is true in all matters of life, and it is also true in all aspects of business and career progression. We should necessarily seek advice to enlighten us and help us reach decisions and resolve situations beyond our depth of understanding. This is hardly a profound observation, but the point is that most do not do this properly.

Throughout my experience, I noticed that the people we approach for advice tend to be people in our immediate circle of acquaintances, who we believe may possess knowledge or a perspective that is superior to ours. Such people, of course, are easily accessible to us. We may start with our parents, friends, teachers, neighbors, and so on. They, in turn, may refer us to others who they believe could be even more helpful to us. I'll refer to these circles of acquaintances as networks. We have our own network, and others we communicate with have theirs. We may know people in common.

The quality of the advice we receive is therefore heavily dependent on the expertise available to the people within our immediate network or one step removed from it (the network of an acquaintance). These people may or may not be the best source for the best advice. Therefore, one runs a significant risk of getting mediocre, poor, or even bad advice, colloquially referred to as "the blind leading the blind."

Notice that in the title of this chapter, I didn't say to seek advice from people who know more than you; I said seek advice from the people who *know best*! And I mean the best, not those who may know a lot, or those who may have a great amount of experience. I literally mean those who know best.

Clearly, this advice places some burden on you and introduces three challenges: (i) identifying who the people are who know best; (ii) how to contact them; and (iii) how to get them to give you, possibly a stranger, some quality time from their busy schedule.

Now, these are not trivial challenges, but the process is actually very straightforward and achievable. First, you make an appeal to your network of acquaintances. Describe the knowledge you are seeking, and ask your acquaintances to identify the person whom they consider the best to help you out. Then, ask your acquaintance's permission to use their name as the referring person when you contact their referrals. You then call, set up some in-person time, and get the advice you seek. (Of course, it would be better if your acquaintance is willing to call on your behalf.) Before you end your session, ask them the same question that led you to them: "Who do you believe may be someone I would benefit from for advice in this matter?" I assure you, the name of the person you will be given will possess as much knowledge, or even more, than the individual you have interviewed. Then ask for their permission to use their name when you contact the next group of referrals. Keep repeating this process. With each additional referral, you'll get closer and closer to those who know best.

As I said, this is easily achievable. I don't know many people who actually don't like to give advice when asked, so long as it is for a good purpose and for a credible person. Evoking a friendly name, whom they know and respect, as a referral will automatically put you in that category. You shouldn't have a problem getting face-to-face time, so long as you assure them you plan to keep it very short. So now, the only question that remains is: When should you stop this iterative process?

The answer to that question is actually simple. When you get to a point where the information you obtain from interviews becomes repetitive (that is, when you stop learning anything new), then you probably have received as much information as you will get and so you may stop the process.

It goes without saying that the more successful, accomplished, and knowledgeable people your own network of friends comprises, particularly those who fall into the 20 percent group, the quicker and better access to good advice you will have. Thus, **it is of real value to spend as much energy as possible during your career to build and maintain relationships with people who could over time add such value to you.**

There is another challenge you'll face as you interview people, particularly when you seek advice (it is less consequential when you seek general information and observations not related to advice). The 80-20 Rule suggests that, of those you interview, 20 percent will give you valuable advice and 80 percent may provide mediocre or even bad advice. By extension, those who are part of the 20 percent group are much more likely to refer you to the "better" sources, while those in the 80 percent group are likely to refer you to "just as poor" sources. In reality, statistically, you are more likely to start the process with people who are part of the 80 percent group. At the same time, you have little knowledge of how to discern whether one falls in the 20 percent or the 80 percent. As a result, the advice you will receive will likely be all over the map. So, how do you put the advice to use?

Weigh the Advice You Get

There are many reasons for the discrepancy and variance in the advice experts give. However, in my experience, most fall into one of four categories. The actual categorization is not as relevant to this section, since my recommendation of how to deal with it doesn't require understanding the underlying reasons. However, in keeping with my promise, I plan to give you sufficient illuminating and detailed information and analyses so that you fully understand the logic involved, which in turn I hope will convince you of my observations, conclusions, and recommendations. This one, in particular, serves two more purposes. The first will become more relevant elsewhere in the book, but since it was brought up here, I might as well discuss it here. The second is that I hope it will serve as another example that demonstrates the process of insightful thinking, which also includes **one's ability to think deeper, frame, categorize, and simplify things, thereby allowing one to see the forest for the trees while also seeing the trees in the forest, and drawing conclusions that otherwise might not be apparent.**

The four categories of reasons for the variation in advice given to us include:

Articulation: As we have discussed, some people are more capable than others of articulating their knowledge and transferring such knowledge to the listener. Take the example of two high school physics teachers. They both know the subject matter equally well. However, one can frame the subject matter and teach it to a class in a way that is cogent and clear.

The other teacher does not have this gift, and comprehension is made difficult. We call the former a great teacher and the latter a terrible one.

Discernment and Perspectives: Different experts with the same degree of knowledge may have different perspectives, particularly in what I defined earlier as "cognitive ability": understanding, wisdom, insightfulness, perceptiveness, judgment, foresight, discernment, acuteness, astuteness, ingenuity, and so on. In other words, all things related to "brainpower" and how insightfully it is used.

Superficial vs. Analytical Thinking: Some people are just very shallow thinkers, who grasp at the first logical thing that appears reasonable to them and seems to address the problem from an immediate and singular point of view. The analytical thinker is a deeper, more rigorous thinker.

The superficial thinker tends to see problems in their most narrow definition and rarely sees nuances, exceptions, and interrelationships, and the impact their narrow solution may have on other variables or situations. The analytical thinker defines a problem with all its complexities, sees exceptions, nuances, and interrelationships to other issues, and incorporates those into their analyses and solutions. As a result, the solution of the more analytical thinker, as opposed to the more superficial thinker, tends to be more comprehensive and less error prone.

By way of an extreme example, science, philosophy, and psychology studies require more of an analytical mind. Politicians, on the other hand, whether they themselves are superficial thinkers or not, are generally prone to more superficial thinking, or just use it to convey positions so as to affect acceptance. Oftentimes, in their view, a problem is caused by a single variable and thus a solution can be had by fixing that one variable. This leads to dismissing the interrelationships to other things that might get affected in the process.

Top-of-the-Wave Advice Givers: This category doesn't reflect on how one thinks through or analyzes situations. Rather, it reflects on how one thinks when giving advice. When giving advice, they tend to focus on the most important variables and issues and will only bring those up. This way, the advice is generally short and appears to be very simple to accept and follow. Oftentimes, although for different reasons, their advice would be similar to the advice from a superficial thinker. This occurs because they don't think it is necessary to complicate matters when asked for what appears to be simple advice. Sometimes they may be too disinterested to engage in a deeper discussion when not called for.

How to Weigh Variations in Advice

The most interesting thing to take away from the above is not that advice will vary significantly from one expert to the next. Rather, notice the one thing common to practically all of them, regardless of the category. The difference in the advice comes from how their brain works, and how they communicate it to the advice seeker. It does not at all reflect on how much knowledge they actually possess. It may appear like a nuanced observation, but it is not. It is the key to how to deal with it. It basically says that whereas most experts may not be able to originate and articulate "quality" thoughts themselves, they remain capable of grasping the implications and agreeing or disagreeing with someone else's observations. Therefore, there are two ways to deal with it effectively and maximize for yourself the value of the advice you finally accept:

1. **Always ask the reasons for their observations and rationale.** The more you know the reasoning behind what they say, the more likely you are to put yourself in a position to intelligently accept or reject it. Don't forget to ask all the probing follow-up questions to make sure you truly understand their thinking and reasoning.

2. **Confirm, and reconfirm, what you hear with other experts.** Consult other experts to see how they react to what you have already been told. This will give you a great way to gauge the validity of what previous experts have told you. You will also hear different rationales and perspectives about the same observations, and thus

be better able to decide, at the end of the process, which are the more correct and complete observations and recommendations for your situation.

The last element of the overall advice in this section is for you to "own" the final judgment.

Always "Own" the Final Judgment

Since you can expect variance in the quality of the advice you'll get, don't rely on any unless you are convinced as to its merits. In other words, the burden is always on you to reach the final observations, conclusions, and recommendations that make the most sense to you. Should you ever find yourself in a situation where you absolutely have to rely on information that you were given but unable to verify, then ask yourself a simple question: "Where would I place the expert giving me the advice—in the 20 percent group or the 80 percent group?" If the expert falls into the 20 percent group, you may feel a bit more confident. Otherwise, exercise caution.

Be Sure to Properly Match Your Questions with the Expertise of Those You Interview

This point is best explained through an example. My daughter, Beth, had just graduated from college and started work as an analyst at a premier investment banking firm on Wall Street. By this time, I had already started my own venture capital fund, JK&B Capital, and just finished raising a $500 million fund. The venture industry, as a whole, was garnering a strong reputation and was in the beginning of an accelerated growth phase. A large number of initial public offerings (IPOs) of hi-tech start-ups was propelling the awareness about the venture industry. Venture capital became associated with "making lots of money."

As a result, out of nowhere, the venture capital industry had suddenly become an exceptionally sought-after career opportunity.

However, it was a small, close-knit group of professionals, comprised of about two hundred venture capitalists in total—a very small industry indeed. Not many outsiders fully understood the exact nature of the work involved, the competencies needed to do this work, and exactly how the economics of the industry worked.

I had a lunch scheduled with Beth. We used to schedule lunches and dinners far in advance so that she could give notice to her managers and avoid last-minute assignments. We were to lunch in a week's time, and so I called her to confirm that she would still be able to make it. She said that things still looked good and that her manager promised not to surprise her with an urgent assignment on that day. She then asked whether I would mind if she invited a coworker to join us. She said that she had befriended a coworker who was thinking about leaving investment banking and finding a job with a venture capital firm. He knew through Beth that I was a chairman of a large venture fund and asked her if she would do him a favor and arrange an hour with me, so that he could get some insights. She thought that our upcoming lunch could be a great opportunity for that.

The following week, we met at a restaurant close to her place of work. She introduced her coworker to me and explained why he had asked to meet with me. I acknowledged that I would be happy to help him with advice and insights. He thanked me profusely for allowing him to come to lunch and meet with me. He was visibly nervous, but I gave him a reassuring smile and asked, "Okay, how can I be of help?" From that point on, for the duration of lunch, the conversation centered on answering whatever questions he raised.

He started by telling me that, other than having heard the terms "venture capital" and "venture capitalist," he knew nothing about what it really meant. His first question was, "Can you explain to me what venture capital is?" I proceeded to do just that.

He then asked a series of questions regarding the difference between a regular technology company and a hi-tech start-up. Then he launched into a bunch of questions regarding the difference between a regular company's IPO, which his department specialized in, and a hi-tech start-up's IPO. He then wanted to understand why the venture capital industry offered the opportunity to make so much money and how come it was not the same with other, regular companies that invented new technologies. I was very patient and responded to all his questions as informatively as I could, without going into a level of detail that would confuse rather than help his understanding. An hour later, he departed, thanking me for my time and acknowledging that he wanted to allow Beth and me to have some family time over dessert.

Beth thanked me again for allowing her to bring him along. She confirmed that he had become a very good friend of hers at work. I asked her how she viewed the "interview" and whether she thought he got most of what he was hoping to get out of it. She said, "Of course. He was very happy and learned a lot about the industry. I think he now understands what venture capital really means."

I looked at her and said, "Beth, let's use this as another teaching moment [a common phrase I used every time I wanted to teach her something]. I thought the interview was terrible, practically on all fronts, and from both his perspective and mine."

She looked at me completely surprised and said, "How so? It looked to me to have had a lot of value, at least from his perspective." I proceeded to tell her why I disagreed. At the end she exclaimed, "Wow, I never looked at this like you just explained." I assured her that it was not unusual for someone of her experience not to see all those things. I continued to tell her that these kinds of observations and wisdom are developed over time, and all I'm doing is just trying to help her get on the learning curve faster. (Helping expedite *your* growth in experience and wisdom is why I wrote this book.)

I enumerated all the things that in my view went wrong in the interview. She asked, "Would everybody else observe the same things you did, or is it a David Kronfeld special skill?"

I responded, "Absolutely everybody would have! They may observe the same or different things. They may draw the same conclusions, or others. They may be more insightful with their observations, or less. But all will indeed make these kinds of observations. Also, the more senior the people, the more they are likely to observe and be more correct with their observations and conclusions." Here is what I told Beth at the time:

The most important thing to have noticed is that her coworker didn't get a single thing from the interview that accomplished his intended goal or objective for the interview. He specifically told Beth, and also stated to me, that he was considering changing his career from investment banking to venture capital. Yet he didn't ask a single question that reflected on it. All his questions aimed at getting me to teach him the basics about the industry. By the time he covered the basics, time had run out and he had no opportunity to ask the most important questions to help him draw intelligent conclusions about the wisdom and opportunity to change careers. In other words, he had a reasonably rare opportunity to meet with a senior person who could give him valuable information, and instead wasted it on some basic tutoring. He could have, and should have, read an article or two about the industry. He also could have called an associate in his firm who was part of the team that specialized in the IPOs of hi-tech start-ups, offered the associate a free lunch, and learned the same basic stuff he got from me.

Had he done his homework, he could have asked me questions about whether it was wise for him to look at a career change and the difference between the two careers. He could have asked questions about what it took to be a successful professional venture capitalist, to better understand whether it made sense for him to contemplate a career change. He could have asked about what venture fund managers looked for when hiring professionals, and see whether he could get some insight into how he may enhance the likelihood that he could find a way into the industry. Instead, he did none of that. He wasted the time to learn basic simple information, which he could have easily gotten from more junior sources.

Additionally, everybody looking for a job and getting face time with a senior person always hopes that they are able to leave a strong impression on the senior person, so that it perhaps might lead to a job offer. Her coworker accomplished the exact opposite. I was left completely unimpressed. The fact that he didn't come prepared to his meeting with me showed a lack of initiative and purposeful planning, or worse yet, intellectual laziness. The fact that he didn't understand and didn't get valuable information from me showed that he was not exceptionally strong at conceptualizing important things he needed to accomplish and distinguishing them from the less important. The fact that he allowed the full hour to be wasted on the basics showed that he was not a person who knew how to manage interactions and information exchange in an efficient and productive way. The worst was the fact that he didn't understand that asking a senior person to teach you the basics is an absolute no-no. It meant to me that he lacked common sense and street smarts.

I wasn't only left unimpressed with him for the above reasons. I didn't only feel that he wasted a valuable opportunity given to him. Worse, I left feeling that he got trivial information, thereby wasting *my time*, too! As a result, I would not give him any leads to other people who could have been of further help. I wouldn't want to have other people have disappointing interactions with anybody I would recommend they meet and help.

Now, to be fair, he was young and inexperienced. He might have not known any better. Most people probably would have not known either. As I mentioned to Beth, this wisdom comes with time and experience. So naturally, a question comes to mind: Why did I "penalize" him so harshly for something I would have expected most people to do? Simple, and here is my takeaway for you as you think about your own career: **Senior managers don't care much for what 80 percent of the people will do in any given circumstance. They seek to find the extraordinary people who fall into the top 20 percent, those who have unique talents and abilities above and beyond most people.** So, if you want to impress a senior person, you must leave an impression that you are one of the top 20 percent with extraordinary understanding, brainpower, initiative, focus, and all else that may be appropriate under the circumstances, which are well ahead of your peers. Being one of the 80 percent will not buy very much in terms of career opportunities and career progressions. You must become one of the 20 percent.

So, specifically to the reason why I wrote this chapter: **Always understand what your objectives are from an interview, and always match the level of your questions to the level of the people you will be seeking advice from.**

12

Don't Try to Show How Smart You Are; Seek Little Credit; Give Lots of Credit; and Never, Ever Compete with Your Boss

Those with a successful career track likely know this sentiment already. So, the advice captured in the title of this chapter is probably more relevant for the younger, less-experienced worker. There are four aspects of behavior captured in this advice. I've seen them all at play, at various times, in one way or another. Sometimes, it is out there for all to see. Other times, it is there in more subtle ways. They do play an important role in one's career and are definitely worth a discussion. I'll address each individually and try to provide a unique perspective, which you might not have been aware of before.

Showing How "Smart" We Are

We all would like others to view us in a positive way, with our brainpower as a key positive attribute. There is nothing wrong with that. The question is: What is it that we can do to help influence how others view us in that regard?

Here, people tend to utilize two approaches. One approach is to be sure to *show* others just how smart and intelligent they are. The other is to have others *notice* it. It may sound merely like a semantic nuance, but it is not.

To "show" implies a proactive approach by you, where you are putting your smarts on display to make sure that others will indeed see how smart you are. The other, to "notice," implies a passive approach. You are not trying to actively show how smart you are, but rather hoping others will notice it. There is a world of difference in how people perceive and react to the two different approaches. One is viewed negatively, the other positively. One is an ineffective approach, the other much more effective.

My observation learned over many years, and I hope that you will always remember it, is that **people are very perceptive and notice much more than we give them credit for. It is true for all people, of all ages, from all walks of life, and from all backgrounds.**

It is exactly this observation that justifies the second approach of letting people notice, rather than needing to show it. One doesn't really need to show how smart one is; people will always notice, especially those in higher-level management.

Higher-level managers will always recognize how smart you are, even if you are modest and humble about it. To add a bonus here: **Be assured that not only will they notice it, they'll appreciate it more, like you more for it, and reward you more—you can't lose!** The reverse is true with the "showing" approach. It will invite a potentially strong and negative reaction, where one might be perceived as a show-off: arrogant, self-absorbed, and lacking self-confidence. That is where the damage to career advancement is done.

Seek Little Credit

Some of the same thoughts that lead people to try to show how smart they are also heighten their need to make sure that they "get the full credit they deserve" for a job well done. This behavior is mostly driven by our fear that people could take our great work for granted, or will not be fully aware of who contributed most to a successful outcome.

And if we don't receive the appropriate credit for our work, how will we ever be rewarded with career advancement? This need becomes even stronger when we feel that somebody else may want to "claim" or try to "steal" the credit we deserve. The same observation I made above for trying to appear smart holds true here as well—it is best to not worry about it!

The negative reaction to trying to grab credit—either deserved, partially deserved, or not deserved at all—is even worse than trying to show how smart we are. First, the negative reactions are much more intense and the dislike of you will likely be much stronger. Additionally, you will most likely be penalized and thought of as not being a team player—one of the worst labels in business! So, as is the case with "showing-off," **my advice is to avoid trying to "make sure," either directly or subtly, that you get the credit you feel you deserve.** As I said, people (unless highly incompetent) will always notice your achievements, even if you might not be aware that you and your efforts are being noticed. And I repeat, be assured that not only will they notice it, they'll appreciate it more, like you more for it, and reward you more—you can't lose!

Give Lots of Credit

This deals with the opposite of trying to "grab" credit. Here I'm not just talking about giving credit to people who deserve it. I'm talking about giving credit to people who might not be as deserving. It is perfectly okay—give credit to everybody. Always spread credit around.

Don't ever worry about diffusing or detracting from your own credit by doing so. I will repeat for the third time now, with a little variation, what I said above: **Be assured that not only will your superiors know exactly to whom the credit really belongs, but they'll appreciate it more, like you more for it, and reward you more. Again, you can't lose!**

Additionally, here you will earn a very important bonus. You will be labeled as a great team player, which is definitely an important factor in one's career progression.

Never, Ever Compete with Your Boss

This predicament generally starts with a personal observation that our boss is just not as competent, knowledgeable, or smart as we are. Once we buy into this observation, dislike for our boss could set in. We question how the team is managed and view some work as unnecessary and unproductive. We then begin to question the boss's relevance. At that point we will likely face three dilemmas: (i) We somehow "notice" that our boss makes more frequent mistakes and begin to wonder how much to disagree with them; (ii) we are not sure about what to do when our boss takes undeserved credit for work we have done; and (iii) we begin to wonder whether we should let other people, particularly higher management, know of our boss's incompetence. In my opinion, you will then, in essence and de facto, be "competing" with your boss. I'm here to tell you that such thinking is unhelpful, unproductive, and corrosive. **You should avoid at all cost the temptation to compete with your boss in any way, shape, or form.**

Sometimes, we may not realize that our behavior rises to the level of competing with our boss. So beware that competing with your boss can manifest itself in a number of different ways. The most common is by disagreeing with your boss more often than is warranted, not in a sensible way, but rather in a more defiant way, and trying to prove that your boss is wrong and, by default, that you are right. The next escalation is when you do the same, but in front of others. The next level of escalation is when you feel that your boss has unjustly taken credit for your work without pointing out to others the important role you played, and then you confront your boss with that observation. The highest level of escalation is when you may have an opportunity to talk to senior management without your boss being present and somehow leave an impression that your boss is not competent or that you are a more skilled individual than your boss. My advice is that **competing with your boss in any form is ill-advised and will hurt your career.** Avoid it like the plague!

In addition: **Never, overtly or covertly, directly or subtly, disparage your boss with senior management, or somehow try to leave an impression that your boss is not competent or that you are better than your boss.**

Having advised you about what not to do regarding your boss, it would be appropriate to emphasize what you should do. I sum it up in a very succinct way: **Always consider your job's highest priority to be supportive of your boss, regardless of what you think and how you feel about them.** As I said, people are extremely perceptive. They notice all, and your boss will always find it out one way or another. Remember, no one wants to have a subordinate who is not supportive.

Regarding receiving credit for a job well done, let your boss get all the credit, even if not well deserved—the more the better. The only credit you should hope for is that your boss will give you your due credit. Nobody else matters. Remember, it is always your boss who gets you promoted; it is your boss who can create or kill opportunities for you. It is your boss who can keep you or get you terminated. In other words, whether you like it or not, your career progression at any given phase is completely and solely in the hands of your boss. Treat them with respect, help them the most you can, and support them. In fact, I will state it even more emphatically: **Your job is to make your boss look the best you possibly can. Credit given to you from anybody else is irrelevant.** You will wisely learn over time that your boss's opinion is always sought when you are considered for promotion. Also, many career advancements come our way when our bosses are promoted, and they bring us along or recommend us to others.

Before concluding this section, I would like to bring up, for the sake of completeness, two additional observations. The first is simply to point out that there are three lessons you should take away from this section when you yourself are a manager of people:

Lesson 1: Demand the utmost loyalty from your subordinates, as I suggest you show toward your boss. In fact, I would recommend you share what I discussed above with your subordinates, so that they are clear on your expectations.

Lesson 2: Give well-deserved credit to your subordinates. They will thrive on it.

Lesson 3: Don't be afraid to allow your subordinates to receive credit from others, including your own superiors. It will never take away from you and will be a great motivator for your subordinates. In fact, don't hesitate to do it yourself and give credit to a well-deserved subordinate in front of your superiors. It is always appreciated by everyone, including your superiors.

The second observation deals with the possibility that indeed your boss may not be the most competent manager, or that indeed you may be smarter than your boss. I only suggested that it is irrelevant. However, you could also be wrong.

You might think you are smarter or better, but in many cases you might be wrong. Remember, earlier in the book, I told you that as one moves up the managerial ranks, different skills become more important. At any point of your career, you are only able to evaluate a position from your perspective, which is limited to your level and below—rarely above, including your boss's level. So, you are ill-equipped to judge.

Also, your ability to do it better doesn't mean they are doing it poorly. Remember the 80-20 Rule. Your boss may be one of the 80 percent group and you might be a member of the 20 percent group, so you may be correct with your observation that you might be able to do it better. However, the world is run by the 80 percenters, and their level of performance is quite acceptable and considered competent, in most cases. Your ability to do it better doesn't infer that they are incompetent or do things poorly. It could mean that you might have a more accelerated career than they may have had. So, strictly follow the advice in this section and remember: **The way you will evaluate how competent or effective your boss is will rarely mirror how your boss is evaluated by their superiors.**

An interesting observation may give you a good perspective. It is very apropos to the topic discussed. Over the years, I've heard many competent and wise managers repeat what they thought managers should do relative to their subordinates. One perspective kept repeating itself, one piece of advice that I followed myself and that paid many dividends: **Always hire subordinates who are smarter than you are. It is the best way to accelerate your own career!**

One last obvious but very important recommendation regarding this chapter: The advice given in this section is true not only relative to your behavior in the work environment, but should also be adhered to outside of work, particularly with all your job interviews. Any whiff of straying will most likely stop the interview process for you.

13

Don't Be Afraid to Admit Mistakes or Show That You Don't Know

President Kennedy famously said, "Success has many fathers; failures are orphans." In the previous chapter we focused on the first part of the saying, and my advice to you was to spread credit around as much as you can. This section will deal with the second part of Kennedy's observation: "failures are orphans."

Admitting failures and mistakes is one of the toughest things to do. Rarely in life do people just accept and admit full responsibility. If they cannot outright deny responsibility, they will urgently provide reasons as to why the mistake isn't their fault, or the mistake is minor, or was entirely beyond their control. Generally, denial is driven by two reasons. The first and most prevalent is that we believe we will be punished for a failure or mistake. The second has to do with our ego. We all want to be perceived as being smart, and admitting to a mistake may hurt our image.

I believe admitting to mistakes is even tougher for the smarter people and those who are quick on their feet and able to come up with good excuses under fire. I was one of those people. I never made mistakes and never failed—not me, not with my innate ability to dissect complex problems and provide different perspectives and logic "on demand." Of course, I've had plenty of failures and made many mistakes, but was always able to explain them away successfully—or so I thought.

In military boot camp and the early years of military service, not committing a mistake became a "survival" necessity. Every military person will tell you that you should never volunteer for anything, nor admit fault for anything. My "excusing away" skills became sharper and better honed during those years—the necessity was greater and required it.

The first time I learned differently happened in what I thought was a very innocent way. I didn't even actually fail or make a mistake that needed to be excused away in my view. It happened at Booz Allen when I started my consulting career.

On one of my first projects, I was responsible for collecting some specific data and doing some analyses. In one of the progress report sessions with the client, I presented my analyses and conclusions. The client asked whether I looked at something. I hadn't and immediately explained why I hadn't, and why the investigation would have not yielded a different conclusion. The client was a senior executive, very wise and polished. He looked at me and said, "Oh, okay, but do me a favor: Take a look at it, just to be on the safe side."

After the meeting was over, when we got back to the office, the senior partner on the engagement called me into his office. As soon as I sat down, he said, "You did a nice job at the client's today, but never try to cover up a mistake again."

"What do you mean?" I asked. "I didn't make a mistake; the analyses were correct and so were the conclusions. Didn't everybody agree with them?"

"Yes, but that's not what I'm talking about," he said. "I'm talking about your answer to his question about whether you did the analysis he asked you about."

I was shocked. *How did he notice?* I thought to myself.

He continued, "Never, ever cover up for anything. You make a mistake, you admit it! You miss something, you admit it! You forget something, you admit it! You don't know an answer, don't make one up. Admit it! Otherwise, you'll lose all credibility, and this is unacceptable at Booz Allen." His tone of voice was not one of anger or disappointment. It was a tone a teacher would use to teach a student about right from wrong.

He then said, "The best way to deal with the various mishaps is to say, depending on the mishap, 'I'm sorry; I'm not sure I know the answer. Let me get back to you,' or 'No, I didn't do it. Let me get back to you,' or 'I see your point. I may have been wrong. I'll make the necessary corrections; thank you for pointing it out.'"

Two major things stuck with me from this experience. I couldn't get over the fact that he noticed. I was so smooth about it, and my logic was so compelling. Not to mention the fact that the client accepted it completely. It was beside the point that he wanted me, as a favor, to look at it, just in case. The second thing was even more astonishing to me. I did it to make sure that the client didn't think I had made a mistake, or was stupid, yet the senior partner told me that I lost credibility. Talk about day-and-night difference in outcomes. I never made the same mistake again!

At Booz Allen, it was a pretty standard rule that was taught to all: There is nothing wrong with making a mistake or being wrong. But it is absolutely unacceptable to ever try to cover it up or not own up to it. The credibility of the individual and the firm was at stake. Over the years, I've learned how much wisdom was embodied in those words and directives. I never again tried to deflect or excuse away anything. As I progressed with my own career and had many people report to me, I can tell you with certainty that there is nothing wrong with admitting mistakes or failures. We all make them. If fully owned up to, they'll be forgiven by superiors. **But never attempt to deflect, excuse, or cover up a mistake or failure. Your credibility will be compromised.**

14

Business Is a Team Sport:
Everybody Is Worthy of Being Respected

This book was written with one objective in mind: to impart observations and lessons I've learned over the years, and the logic behind decisions I reached, to help create awareness for all of the dimensions that I believe could, over time, give you a competitive advantage so as to help you advance your career.

To adhere to my objective and singular purpose, I have offered a blunt and pragmatic picture of the state of the business world as I see it. I suggested that mediocrity reigns; the 80-20 Rule always applies; and pedestrian thinkers, incompetence, superficial thinking, and much more afflict business and are widespread.

I stand by all I have said, but please understand the context. My perspective is a pure, logical assessment of the talents and capabilities you will find out there, completely devoid of any other considerations. I said nothing about the quality of the people as individuals and as team players. I said nothing about their contributions in many other aspects to the quality of what is accomplished out there, day in and day out. I said nothing about the interpersonal dynamics that are part of it all, and the important role they play. I said nothing about it, because it wasn't as relevant in the context of this book's objective. However, I do not wish to overlook a very important observation: **Although mediocrity is widespread, it is a relative term, and much competence does exist** in the workplace. Also, the human aspects, although not addressed in this book, are important. This should always stay front and center in your mind.

The way I have thought this through is analogous to that of a coach of a sports team. The coach's job is to logically assess, in an unbiased way, all the strengths and weaknesses of the team as well as of the opponent. When the coach prepares a game plan, they will certainly focus on the weaknesses of the other team and how to take advantage of those weaknesses in order to win the game. It is a singularly, logically driven perspective. That doesn't mean the opponent is lacking in skill or that the skills they possess are unimportant. They are just not the purpose of the immediate conversation.

By way of example, take a basketball team. The coach may call out a player on the opposing team who is physically short and how that may be taken advantage of. However, that player may be a consummate leader, one who binds his team together. He may motivate the team and raise its performance. Yet, the coach will not mention a single thing about the player's positive aspects in the game plan, but rather just focus on the player's weaknesses. The focus may appear to be one-sided and negative. It doesn't mean that the coach doesn't have a great deal of respect for this player. So please consider all I have said in this book from the perspective of having a game-plan discussion before a game.

I said earlier never to look down at anybody. Everybody has something to offer. Respect and listen carefully to everybody. Most importantly, keep in mind that the short basketball player in our example may bring some weaknesses and will definitely need some tall teammates to win games. But it takes a team to win. No single individual can win the game. A single individual who doesn't know how to leverage the team will not consistently win games, regardless of their talent—not even Michael Jordan, one of the greatest basketball players ever to play the game.

Remember: **The business world is a team effort. No single individual is indispensable, and no single individual can do well without a team. You must know how to be an effective team player and how to leverage the team. It starts with respect for them. It starts by** recognizing that you are one of them. It starts by believing that you are equal to them, not better. Perhaps your role may be more important or less important, but that doesn't make you better and definitely not more important than the team as a whole.

There is one other point that is worth mentioning in this context. It is not a requirement that the coach has to be a former all-star player; in fact, he could have been a mediocre player. How he played may not necessarily correlate to how well he can teach, or coach. There is a difference between the power to observe and guide versus the power to execute.

There are many out there in the business world who will fall into this category. **They may not be able to effectively execute, but they can have a great power of observation and a great ability to guide. They can be very helpful in many different ways.** This particularly may apply to your boss.

Your boss may not be able to execute as well as you can, but they may be able to guide you and give you great advice. Many of my mentors who contributed to my understanding, insightfulness, knowledge, and guidance might not have been as capable as me in some respects. But I wouldn't have succeeded in business without them.

Additionally, and a completely different point, many people at work may not be as capable as you, but many could be great people in their own right. I would rather have them as friends than some of the more talented ones. Many such people come to mind, but two specifically stand out as great examples to demonstrate it all.

Early on in my career, when it appeared that I was on a sure path to significant success, a great hardship befell me. I lost my job and all my money within a single week. I was looking for a job and couldn't find any for two years. There was a recession and jobs were nowhere to be found. I was desperate and despondent. I saw my career and future success evaporate. I was helpless. I had reached bottom.

One of the senior partners at Booz Allen, who liked me a lot and was my mentor, coincidentally left the firm and joined one of the largest executive search firms, Korn Ferry International. He became a senior partner at the firm and headed up its Chicago office. I had lunch with him one day, and when he learned about my situation, he made me an offer to join his firm as an executive search person. I thought he was just trying to help me with my unfortunate financial distress. I appreciated his kind gesture very much. But with my heavy accent, lack of fluency in English, and somewhat poor interpersonal skills, I didn't think I could be effective and repay his kindness with worthwhile performance. I told him so. He surprised me with a wonderfully sensitive and thoughtful response.

He said that he was not offering me a job out of kindness. He believed that I would make a great executive search person, and that I may want to consider it as a career option. I asked him how I could possibly compete with others, those who were fluent in English and were much more polished with stronger interpersonal skills. He said to me, "None has your experience and knowledge. None can evaluate candidates for competency the way you can. You can also help companies truly understand what their business challenges and needs are, and direct them to the kind of talent they could benefit from. David, you'll be a superstar in this business. You'll make a lot of money, since we work on commissions." He encouraged me to give it a try.

I had nothing to lose, so I accepted. But I told him that I may leave his firm upon finding another attractive opportunity. He agreed, and I became an executive search professional. He was absolutely right. We won practically every proposal we submitted. Our clients came to understand that I could deeply and accurately assess a candidate's competencies and provide a service superior to our competitors, who offered a surface assessment of a candidate based on resume details and interview performance. I became exceptionally successful at it, in spite of my language barrier. I worked for the firm for about nine months before I found a different opportunity that changed my life. I owe this opportunity to another very special person.

As I mentioned previously, the massive AT&T monopoly was broken up and seven Baby Bells became fully operational companies overnight. The Baby Bell in the Midwest was called Ameritech. Before the breakup, all the personnel who subsequently comprised Ameritech were only responsible for running the communications networks in the Midwest for AT&T. They operated mostly as network engineers and plant managers, but suddenly they were transformed into a fully operational company—Ameritech. The managers' responsibilities changed along with it. They were no longer plant managers, but rather top executives of a very large corporation, which needed to compete effectively in a new marketplace. None of them had the requisite experience or qualifications. They would need to learn on the job.

Ameritech created a new group that would be responsible for making venture investments in start-up communication companies. An internal team comprised of lower- to middle-level managers was assembled, and this team was put in charge of this new activity. The team knew the technology aspects extremely well, but knew nothing of competitive dynamics and would have a hard time evaluating whether a new start-up had the wherewithal to become successful in a competitive marketplace. So, some hiring was done from outside the company to bring in lower- to mid-level managers with a strong understanding of competitive dynamics. That's when somebody referred me to Jim, the president.

I met Jim and loved what he had to say about the opportunity and playing a role in venture investments. I had hoped to get into the emerging venture capital field but couldn't find an opportunity for various reasons. After my interview, Jim said that although they were looking to hire lower- to mid-level professionals, he would be willing to offer me the title of a vice president, given my experience and background. I was ready to accept the job on the spot. He asked me for my current salary. I told him. He went completely pale.

Jim proceeded to tell me that, under the AT&T monopoly, benefits were great, but salaries were very low. There was no way he could even come close to matching what I made at the time. He noted that even the chairman of the company didn't make that kind of money.

I told him that I didn't care much about the salary. He told me what the salary would be. The salary was identical to the offer I had received at Booz Allen when I started there, seven years earlier. I was making more than six times that amount at the time. I made a quick assessment of the situation. I may have found an opportunity to enter an emerging industry, which I somehow was unable to do before. I understood that, in the longer term, the venture capital industry presented the best fit with my profile and my strengths and weaknesses. My strengths would serve me very well, while my weaknesses wouldn't be a factor any longer. I understood that if I, as a venture capitalist, would hand out money, nobody would care about my lack of fluency in English, imperfect interpersonal skills, or any other weaknesses. They would only care about whether I was able to make wise investments. I decided to accept the offer for the salary he was able to pay. Jim said that he needed to think about it.

He called me the next day and told me he decided against extending the offer. I was devastated. I asked him why. His response was, "You are a senior, experienced person who is worth a lot of money in the marketplace. I can't, in good faith, offer you such a low salary, so I decided against making the offer." I told him that I didn't mind at all, that the salary was not that important to me. He said, "I understand your motivation. I know that this might be a good way for you to enter the venture industry. You will leave us as soon as you find a more lucrative replacement. It would not serve me all that well."

I told him, "Jim, I'll make a promise to you that I will keep. I will stay at least three years with your company. I'll help set up the group, hire the right people, and train them. Three years is more than plenty for that. You'll get the full benefits of hiring me before I will ever consider leaving you." Jim promised to think about it some more, but said that he still felt very uncomfortable because it was not a fair offer from his perspective.

Over the next two months, I must have had at least six conversations with him. He was still unable to overcome his sense of extending an unfair offer, in spite of me pointing out the obvious—that it was for me to decide whether it was fair or not. It wasn't his responsibility to worry about it. He was just a very decent human being who felt that he might be taking advantage of me, and felt very uncomfortable doing so.

I kept trying. I called him regularly to try to convince him. I sensed that he truly liked me and my experience, but somehow was unable to internally resolve the issue of the unfair offer. During one conversation, he told me that he had another vice president who was managing the group and that he wanted me to meet with him. I'm sure he offered it just to relieve the pressure on himself. I called the vice president, and we agreed to meet for lunch. I met the most wonderful person anyone could ever meet.

His name was John, a longtime employee of AT&T, a mid-level manager who was offered a vice president's title to acknowledge he would help head up this group. We talked for almost three hours. He was very attentive and wanted to hear all about my experience and how I could help them. We had a productive conversation. He asked me about the salary issue. I repeated my feelings about the irrelevancy of the salary. He told me that Jim had real misgivings about it. I explained that he shouldn't.

I will never forget what he told me before we parted. In fact, tears are coming into my eyes now as I'm recalling this incident. He said, "David, you are one of the most impressive people I've met. You can help us a lot. It would be stupid not to hire you. I plan to tell Jim that he would be an idiot not to hire you immediately."

It wasn't lost on me that he decided to make a recommendation to bring somebody on board to be at the same level he was—to be a competitor of his. Very few people would have done so, particularly if they could easily avoid it. Jim called the next day to offer me the job. I was ecstatic. I told him that it was the best birthday present he could have given me. (It actually was my birthday.)

Within six months, I caught the attention of all the senior executives of Ameritech. I had knowledge about competitive dynamics that none of them had. I was an experienced consultant; I knew how to counsel them. I became known in the organization as the most influential person with the top management team. I helped in many ways, many more than my responsibilities called for. I became an informal personal advisor to the chairman. I got his full confidence. I was running high. Within six months, I was running my group. John, who was presumably more senior to me when I joined, was now informally reporting to me. Three months later, there was a formal organizational change, and I became his boss. About a month before I formally became his boss, we sat down for a heart-to-heart talk at my request.

I told him that we needed to replace some of the people working in our group. They were not of the caliber we needed if we wanted to do well. He said he had no issue with it. I then had one of the toughest messages I've ever had to deliver to a coworker. I told him that we would need to increase the pay scale of everybody in our group, and substantially so, in order to attract the necessary experience and quality of people. It would be equivalent in salary to some of the more senior executives at Ameritech.

I said I believed I would be able to convince the chairman to authorize it by explaining that we were investing tens and potentially hundreds of millions of dollars and needed the best talent and experience money could buy. We were in need of ex-consultants, who are expensive to bring onboard. Their salaries would pale, however, relative to the money we stood to lose without them, or could gain with them. I then told him that I had only one problem that stood in my way. I would not immediately be able to have the chairman authorize that kind of a salary increase for John or any other ex-AT&T employee within our group, though I told him that over time I was fairly certain I could.

I felt terrible; I was concerned that he would get insulted and view my explanation as a way to benefit myself at his expense. But he looked at me and very calmly said, "David, I don't mind; go ahead and give it a try. I will not subsequently mind if you are unable to increase my salary. Your plan makes a lot of sense to me. It is best for the company. I am all for it." John agreed with much style, grace, class, and integrity—no bitterness whatsoever.

The chairman approved my plan. I started hiring and my team grew from six people to over twenty. I was assigned additional responsibilities. I became responsible not just for venture investments, but for all business transactions, mergers and acquisitions, and partnerships on behalf of Ameritech. Two months later, organizational changes formalized it. I became the Vice President of Merger, Acquisitions, and Venture Investments. Within exactly one year from my starting with Ameritech, my salary was adjusted to reflect market value. I was back on top of the world, doing superbly well. Six months later, John received the first in a series of raises to his salary. Two years later, he was making four times the salary he had when I had the heart-to-heart talk with him. We both benefited immensely. But that is not the end of the story.

About a year later, the CFO of Ameritech somehow learned that John was making a lot of money. He thought of John as a mid-level manager. He was suddenly making as much money as top-level managers in other parts of the company, including presidents of some of the divisions. He relayed this to the chairman. I was called to the chairman's office.

The chairman told me that the situation with John's salary was unacceptable and would demoralize other executives. He told me to fire John. I told him that I understood the dilemma, and would do so, but in good time. This was not a good time for my organization to let John go. We hired great consultants who knew how to evaluate companies and competitive dynamics. But they didn't possess the technical knowledge required in the communications industry. John was used as a resource for that. He was invaluable in that role and at that juncture. I said I would fire him when that situation changed, and his value became less critical. The chairman looked at me and said, "Okay, but make it sooner rather than later." I nodded my head in assent, but I had no intention of firing John. I owed him that much.

Over the next couple of years, the chairman asked me at least ten times if I had fired John. My answer was the same. *I will, but the time is not right.* About two years from the initial request, the chairman asked me yet again, and my answer was the same. The chairman looked at me and asked, "David, do you ever intend to do so?" I replied, "Not really." He looked at me and said, "I just finally figured it out." He never brought the topic up again. John learned from indirect sources what I had done for him for the previous two years. He came to my office, acknowledged what he learned, and thanked me profusely. I got up from my chair, walked over to him, hugged him, and said, "No, I need to thank you. Without you and your class act, I would never be here now."

Don't let success get too much to your head. Never, ever look down on people. Never, ever disrespect people. None of us is indispensable. We are all dependent on each other!

15

Right Versus Wrong Is Rarely the Issue. Learn to Be Patient with Conflicts

I already mentioned many times that in the business world, from a strategic/competitive standpoint, there is rarely black and white, right and wrong. To some extent, the same is true in life, too. There is one aspect that is worth pointing out, which is both significant and insightful. It will prove helpful in many conflict situations, whether business related or personal.

From the time we are children, we are taught right from wrong. Everything revolves around right and wrong. I have no issues with that. That's the way it should be, but with a caveat. When a situation involves a conflict with another person, often the situation cannot be reduced to an absolute right versus wrong. Each person has their own version of the event or situation, and there are many shades of gray. It may not be a situation where one person is completely right and the other completely wrong. It is in these situations that what we learned as children does not serve us well.

In situations like these, we tend to resort to trying to decipher who is more right and who is more wrong—who is more at fault and therefore more to blame. We use this logic to justify blaming or punishing the person who is more in the wrong and vice versa. Over the years, therefore, we are logically conditioned to use those measurements to justify our actions. Think about many of the arguments you may have had. I'll bet the majority of the arguments centered around the discussion of who was right and who was wrong; who was to blame; who started it all; who should bear more responsibility; and so on.

Once we have decided that we are in the right and the other person is in the wrong, we demand that they take the necessary corrective action to make it right again. After all, it was their fault, so they now have the responsibility to fix it. This is the way, over the years, we have been conditioned to think. This is the yardstick by which we measure our response and our expectations from the other party in a conflict. The problem is this: Right or wrong isn't helpful for finding solutions to conflicts. How does one find a solution where both sides feel that they are right and the other party is wrong? Both sides are equally conditioned to require concessions from the other side because the other side is at fault!

Often, a third party is called in to place judgment on which party is more right and which is more wrong. Again, the assignment of right and wrong becomes the guide to the resolution of the conflict. The irony is that in many situations a resolution is not likely to happen as long as the right from wrong is used as a measurement scale. To find a resolution, both sides must reject this notion. Rather, **both sides must ask themselves how much they are willing to compromise in order to resolve the conflict.** In other words, **draw redlines based on the consequences of the conflict at hand, rather than the right or wrong.** Stating it more simply, right or wrong should not be an issue.

It should not be an issue not just because it would be easier to resolve conflicts if it weren't. It should not be an issue because many times there is no right or wrong. It is in the eye of the beholder. An extreme example will vividly demonstrate this point. People could kill others because they could believe they are justified to do so based on being in the right. They would even be willing to die for this belief. The problem is that the other side feels exactly the same; they would be willing to kill and die for a cause, believing they are on the side of right. How can there be right or wrong when both sides are willing to die in the belief that they are right? There is no right or wrong in situations like these. Being right or wrong is almost irrelevant!

I am not suggesting that one side couldn't indeed be right and the other be completely wrong, from an outside-looking-in perspective, or some absolute measurement of right versus wrong. All I'm saying is that when both sides believe that they are more in the right, who actually is more in the right is almost irrelevant. The conflict can only be resolved amicably if the issue of right and wrong is off the table. I learned this lesson in the most unexpected way, and it stuck with me.

A Personal Approach: How I Discovered the Irrelevancy of Right vs. Wrong

My wife and I were married in Israel, and we were both quite young. I was twenty-one years old at the time. Ten years later, when we were living in the United States, she informed me that she wanted a divorce. Culturally, the idea of divorce didn't sit well with me. In Israel, where I grew up, a divorce was granted only in extreme cases. It was also considered to be a symbol of failure in life, an act of running away from problems. It was not the case in the United States, where divorce was more commonplace.

I probably would have initially resisted her request, but would have given in quickly. However, this happened just a few months after our daughter, Beth, was born. At that point, I would have never accepted a divorce. Besides the stigma of what a divorce connoted in my mind, I was suddenly also about to lose my only daughter. I wasn't going to let that happen. I also didn't believe that my wife had the right to singularly decide to separate my daughter from me. She was the mother, but I was the father. Neither one of us had the right to take her away from the other. I knew that the law here was different. But to me, this was not an issue of what the law allowed. It was an issue of right versus wrong.

In addition, the timing and the whole concept made no sense to me from anybody's perspective: not from mine; not from hers; and definitely not from Beth's (who had no say in the matter). It was unquestionably an overall lose-lose-lose situation for all three people involved. It just made no logical sense to me.

I tried to talk my wife out of proceeding with a divorce, but she wouldn't budge. The more I tried, the more determined she appeared to become. I used all the logic I could muster, but to no avail. She didn't have any logical reasons for her actions, only an emotional stubbornness. I always had a hard time dealing with poor logic or lack of logic to begin with—imagine how I felt when it came to a topic as important as divorce. With time, the situation worsened and the interactions between us became more difficult. It took quite a toll on me.

A friend at Booz Allen suggested that my wife and I should visit a marriage counselor. I didn't think that anybody who was on the outside could help me. My friend said that she knew this person, a psychologist, very well. She assured me that I would like him. Besides, she asked me, what had I to lose? I agreed. I thought to myself that maybe, just maybe, he would be able to talk some sense into my wife. Initially, my wife refused to go, insisting that there was no way anybody, or anything, would change her mind about the divorce. However, she eventually agreed.

We went to see the psychologist. He asked to talk to us individually. He first spoke with my wife for about twenty minutes. He then asked me into his office and asked for my thoughts and perspective about the situation. I spent almost ten minutes explaining my perspective. He didn't ask a single question or make a comment while I talked. At the end, he looked at me in a strange way, somewhat puzzled, somewhat confused. He seemed to be at a loss for words. He finally said, "I don't know exactly what to say. I have never heard such compelling logic and arguments, ever! Your logic is impeccable. I cannot find a single thing wrong with it. It is so clear that I don't even have a single question." I was encouraged; finally, someone with some brains!

He then continued, drawing a circle with his hand, and said, "You have a circle here, and inside that circle you placed perfectly interwoven logic; not a single flaw, not even a minor one. However, there is only one problem. The whole circle, as perfect as it may be, doesn't apply here. It doesn't belong here." I had no idea what he was talking about, and told him so. He said, "Your logic is irrelevant here. Being right is irrelevant here. Your wife is seeking a divorce for completely different reasons, completely unrelated to your logic. So, all the logic in the world will not change her mind. The real question is whether you, your wife, and your daughter are better off working it out and staying married, or not. Being right or wrong doesn't apply here."

I kind of understood what he was saying, but not fully. He continued, "I heard you and I heard your wife. I normally spend more time with couples before I render advice. But in this case, it is easy for me to decide. My observation is that both of you will be better off divorced. You are two completely different people. Marriage would not be a happy one for either of you. It would be the least fair to your daughter. She should not be exposed to unhappy parents. In my opinion, everybody would be better off with a divorce." I was shocked, but understood what he said. I accepted the unthinkable. I realized that it was inevitable. This was the first time I became aware of the irrelevancy of right versus wrong. It was a wise lesson that I learned the hard way.

Even more surprisingly, after I indicated that I understood, he said something completely unexpected. He wanted to see me again. He said, "You are a fascinating person; I want to discuss another matter with you, which I believe will help you a lot with your job and career. Please come back for one more visit; trust me." I agreed. I learned another very important lesson on the following visit. I will come back to it later in the book.

Meanwhile, as related to this section, my advice to you is simple: **Whenever in a conflict situation, the concept of right versus wrong is mostly irrelevant. Resolution of the conflict should be based on how much the parties are willing to compromise based on the consequences of the conflict continuing or stopping.** You cannot make other people think the same. But in many cases, as soon as you start thinking like this, you may be able to influence a resolution of conflicts strictly based on what you are willing to compromise.

I also believe that in many conflict situations, finding a solution is more relevant than assigning blame. This is particularly true in business, where assigning blame without a resolution of a conflict is a reason, albeit perhaps justified, for not having reached an agreement. **But reaching an agreement is an *accomplishment*, and accomplishments are more rewarded than reasons.**

16

"And the Truth Shall Set You Free"— A Unique Management Style!

There is a plethora of different management styles, perhaps as many as there are managers. Each manager brings their own personality traits intertwined with what they have learned about managing or believe to be the best way to manage those who report to them. Some of the various styles reflect more generic philosophical approaches and theories, while others reflect the huge variance of personal traits and interpersonal skills of the individual manager and how they interact with subordinates.

In my opinion, there is no one management style that can be conclusively argued to be the best or most effective. Nor can one claim that one style has a clear advantage over another. In the majority of cases, it is in the eye of the beholder. I do not intend to add my own opinion regarding the different management styles. However, consistent with the purpose of this book, I would like to bring to your attention one unique management approach that is rarely practiced, yet it is one I have used exclusively over my career because I believe it offers substantial value. It is not an easy style to practice. It requires commitment, self-discipline, self-control, and avoidance of any emotional reactions. However, it could easily be adopted by anyone once they decide to commit to its goal. But be forewarned, this style can't be partially practiced or practiced on and off, depending on mood and circumstances.

It has to be adhered to totally and completely, all the time and at all times, with no exceptions. Any deviation will likely completely and permanently negate the inherent value offered by this approach.

This style is based on the philosophy that **mistakes by subordinates are never to be punished in any form, regardless of the severity of the mistake and ensuing damage caused.** I define "mistake" here in the broadest possible way: the classic type of mistakes made by erroneous actions; mistakes made through the mishandling of situations of all kinds; verbal/communication mistakes; proactive or passive mistakes; inclusion or omission mistakes; as well as mistakes in business judgments of all kinds.

However, there are some conditions that accompany this management style that are required for it to prove valuable. It is these conditions that make this approach one of significant value to the manager, the department, and the company. Before elaborating on the approach and the necessary conditions, please allow me first to explain the reasoning and rationale behind this management philosophy. The underpinning of this approach relies on five straightforward observations:

1. **Mistakes are unavoidable.** Mistakes can be made by any employee regardless of how good and competent that employee may be. Obviously, managers and organizations need to put in the effort to minimize the occurrence of mistakes. Despite best efforts, some mistakes will continue to be made.

2. **Mistakes have consequences.** By definition, mistakes mean that something unintended that shouldn't have occurred has indeed occurred. Thus, the end result is much more likely to be less than optimal or certainly fall below expectations. Some mistakes may be simple and trivial with only minimal implications and ramifications. Others may be more severe with significantly greater implications and ramifications. Yet others may be grave with major damage and consequences.

3. **Corrective actions must always be taken to undo the negative consequences of mistakes.** Clearly, since mistakes have consequences that lead to less than optimal outcomes, corrective

actions are always necessary to counter the negative impact that has occurred or may occur. Additional corrective actions will also most likely be needed to restore the original expected path to the desired optimal outcome. As stated above, some mistakes are easy to correct, while others may be more complicated. Still others may be impossible to recover from.

4. **All corrective actions require analyses.** Proper situational assessment is necessary to understand all the potential implications and ramifications of a mistake. Subsequent analyses are also needed to help determine the proper damage control and required corrective actions. Some of the assessments/analyses, depending on the mistake, could be simple and obvious, but others may not be and may require more energy and deeper evaluation.

5. **The quality and value of the assessments/analyses, and thus the subsequent corrective actions taken, are directly correlated to how accurately all factors and circumstances related to the mistakes are understood.** This is an obvious statement: the better the understanding of all variables and factors, the better the corrective actions. Conversely, the less accurate the understanding, the less effective the corrective actions will be.

There is a simple and straightforward conclusion that can be drawn from the above observations. To avoid damages that may be caused by mistakes, it is optimal **to minimize the occurrence of mistakes, but should mistakes occur, it is the best analyses that will lead to the best corrective actions.**

As stated, the avoidance of mistakes is an important goal for managers and organizations. There are many ways used by organizations and individual managers to attempt to reach this goal. I don't have much to add on this specific topic; I haven't discovered any specific insights different from the common ways that are currently practiced. All I can say is to again emphasize that this goal is indeed critically important to address in the most effective way. It deserves focus and the time, energy, and commitment on the part of both individual managers and the organization at large. I can also tell you that, although everybody agrees that minimizing mistakes should always be a critical goal, in practice it is rarely implemented with the importance and attention it deserves. So, whereas I have no insight to impart to you on how to minimize mistakes, I can strongly recommend and encourage you to do all you can in whichever way you deem appropriate to attain this goal. It definitely will impact your career advancement over time.

However, it is the second part of the above overall conclusion—**it is the best analyses that will lead to the best corrective actions**—that I'd like to address. It is this dimension that led me to adopt my unique management style. To explain this, I will digress a bit.

The first digression involves a small nuance, which is the intermingling of the classic or conventional type of mistakes made by negligence of one kind or another versus judgments made that were subsequently proven to be wrong, and therefore a mistake. In general, classic mistakes are dealt with and treated quite differently from mistakes in judgment. **Classic mistakes should be avoided at all costs and are unacceptable. But errors in judgment are unavoidable, will always occur, are to be expected, and, therefore, are completely acceptable.** The business world requires constant analyses, assumptions, and judgment calls. Judgments are made based on the best information available at the time the judgments are rendered. Such judgments are all vulnerable and understood to embody inherent risks of not materializing as predicted. Also, and as a result, it is only in retrospect that judgment calls are proven to be mistakes. They are unavoidable, and since no one can tell the future, we are all likely to make them. These mistakes are generally not looked upon with the same scorn as making errors and classic mistakes. So, you might ask, why have I included judgment mistakes in my definition, and why do I treat them the same way as the classic mistakes, which occur because of negligence and errors?

My response is that, once identified, both categories require corrective actions. In both cases, best corrective actions are arrived at through the best analyses. Also, since the management style I am advocating is completely devoid of punishment, and since the subsequent analyses and corrective actions follow the same process, then it is irrelevant whether I deal with them as a single group of mistakes or separately. Had my management style not called for avoidance of punishment, then the two categories of mistakes should not be treated as if they are the same—judgment mistakes would have been treated with more understanding and leniency, and the classic mistakes with much greater severity.

The second digression involves the understanding of human behavior when it comes to mistakes. There are two categories of reactions: (i) the reaction of the people who made the mistakes, and (ii) the reaction of their superiors. Let's start with the reaction of the superiors.

We are taught throughout our upbringing that mistakes are bad and punishment is sure to follow, although forgiveness may be warranted on occasion. We differentiate between various severities and consequences of mistakes, and punish those who make them accordingly. This is true in all aspects of life. Without punishment, mistakes would be difficult to control. I agree with this philosophy, so why do I advocate for an absence of punishment in the workplace?

To understand the reason, let's shift attention to the reaction of the person who makes the mistake. The reaction is quite predictable. Rarely will one volunteer that they have made a mistake, if there is a good chance that it wouldn't be caught. When caught, the mistake maker rarely owns up to it with the *truth, the whole truth, and nothing but the truth*. They will most likely minimize the severity as much as they can, minimize the role they played in it, and minimize the blame they deserve by distorting the facts that led to the mistake. They will do all they can to deflect or influence the severity of the punishment that they believe is sure to follow, as well as the scorn and embarrassment they know will befall them. This is all quite predictable for most.

Let's move to a situation where a mistake has been made and requires corrective action to address the potential damage. As stated above, once a mistake has happened, it is the best analyses that will lead to the best corrective action. Common sense suggests that the most critical element of the best analyses always depends on the quality of the information and understanding of all the factors involved. So, if people making mistakes rarely own up to the truth, the whole truth, and nothing but the truth, then we will most likely not have the best understanding of all the variables and factors involved and therefore rarely have the best analyses, and as a result not have the best corrective actions. In other words, the end result is that the damage will not likely be fully and properly addressed and corrected.

Thus, it follows that the team/department/company will end up with suboptimal results. Therefore, if one wants to get the best corrective actions to negate a mistake, one must ensure that subsequent to a mistake one gets the truth, the whole truth, and nothing but the truth. The only way to do so is to make sure that everybody understands, in advance, that regardless of their severity, mistakes will never be punished. This lack of punishment is only the case that will produce the truth, the whole truth, and nothing but the truth.

That being said, some employees may still wonder whether their superiors will indeed honor the commitment not to punish. Therefore, they may initially be tempted not to offer the truth, the whole truth, and nothing but the truth to see if they can get away with it. Others may feel so badly about having made a mistake that if not caught might not bring it to their manager's attention. There are also other situations where mistakes were not necessarily made, but analyses are conducted and still require the whole truth. For these reasons, I incorporated into my approach an element of punishment. I let all staff know in advance the following rule:

Mistakes will not be punished if one completely owns up to them and tells the truth, the whole truth, and nothing but the truth. At the same time, any deviation from the truth, the whole truth, and nothing but the truth, or any other form of lying and misleading, will be harshly punished.

As stated, I almost never come across a manager or company practicing this management style to the fullest extent. On the other hand, the idea of making truth-telling one of the most important aspects of a manager's philosophy is not necessarily new. It is adamantly practiced, for example, in the military. In fact, I was first exposed to it when I joined the military service in Israel. This was the first thing that was drilled into our heads and throughout our service, and for the exact same reasons. There is an added element, because in the military the damages and consequences of not telling the truth could be dire: People may lose their lives; battles could be won or lost. However, I added my own twist to this "never lie" rule from my military days. I knew that to have this outcome of the whole truth, I needed to eliminate the strongest motivation as to why someone may lie or distort the truth. In the military, mistakes are never tolerated and almost always severely punished. Thus, I needed to eliminate any reason to avoid telling the truth and thereby substantially increase the likelihood of utmost compliance.

There are other conditions that must be applied to ensure overall effective implementation of this management philosophy. They are more secondary in nature and perhaps not as evident, and thus not practiced well. Nevertheless, in my mind, they are important and require just as much attention and adherence.

The first deals with the recognition that scorn, ridicule, display of anger or dissatisfaction, embarrassment, criticism, loss of face, finger-pointing, repetitively referencing mistakes, and even teasing will be considered by many as forms of punishment, and therefore, motivators for someone to distort and lie. Thus, as part of this management style, it must be clear that none of the above happens. As a supervisor, you have to make sure that neither you nor anybody on your team resorts in any way to any of the above. I used to state it forcefully to my subordinates, but put a positive spin on it: "Once a mistake is made, the most critical thing to do is to properly analyze the consequences and take corrective actions. Thus, all our energy and focus need to be future oriented. After collecting the facts, dwelling on what happened (beyond just trying to analyze for the purpose of learning from the mistake to avoid future mistakes) and why it happened becomes unproductive and just creates a team environment that is less than optimal to determine the best corrective actions." In meetings, I would openly admonish and immediately cut off any deviation from this approach. I made sure that there truly was no punishment or perceived experience of punishment of any kind for mistakes.

The second deals with how fully employees accept the key premise that no punishment will befall them. Here, we need to understand that not punishing mistakes is counterintuitive to our upbringing and our culture at large. As such, the first reaction from employees would be doubt and distrust. They'll put it down as another of the thousands of promises we all hear during our lifetime to entice us to behave in a certain way, but then are rarely adhered to. It is for this reason that I said there could never be a deviation from this rule. This is easier said than practiced.

For example, imagine a mistake comes to your attention that has major consequences and was made out of complete stupidity. Could you resist the impulse to become angry and ask the rhetorical question, "How stupid are you?" Instead, using my method, you now must maintain a neutral expression and calm demeanor. The reality is that even a single deviation could give rise to the natural doubt and apprehension we all have toward promises that are counterintuitive in nature. It is the practice of adhering to it over time, without any deviation, that will serve to convince employees that this set of rules will indeed be followed.

I am positive that by now the counterintuitive aspect of not punishing mistakes in any form has raised in your own mind a doubt of credibility. I would be surprised if you haven't questioned the wisdom of this. Even a generous nature will not forever tolerate employees who make serial mistakes. Yet you might point out that my management style will not permit someone being fired. Well, not really!

Although I advocate that making a mistake should not be punished, I actually do endorse the concept that repetitive mistakes can and should lead to punishment and even dismissal. However, to me it doesn't contradict anything I said above. Notice that my sentence differentiated between a singular "mistake" versus the plural "mistakes." To me, a mistake should not be punished. However, someone who persists in making serial mistakes falls into an entirely different category, one that reflects on an employee's competence. In such cases, the punishment is not for making mistakes, but rather it is for being an incompetent employee.

Okay, I gave you my logic and now you can make up your own mind as to whether this management style could be effective and whether you might want to adopt it. If you do, just remember that it is not easy to practice and requires full commitment without any deviation. If you still are willing to do the hard work internally that it requires to keep a calm and level head, then good luck to you. I expect you will soon see the rewards of having your employees come to you when problems are small as opposed to when mistakes or a cover-up have gotten out of hand.

17

"No Risk, No Reward!" "No Guts, No Glory!" Pragmatism Is the Key

These are proverbs that attempt to teach us what it takes to reach success. The conclusions they inspire may appear to be even more relevant since we know that, to succeed, we need to compete, and we all know that in any competition, with sports a perfect example, risk taking is an important element in outperforming your competitors. A similar proverb that emphasizes the same concept and is worded more appropriately for business is "nothing ventured, nothing gained." All these proverbs are true to a large extent in business, but a word of caution here. Although the proverbs impart valuable wisdom, like most proverbs, they are also laden with potential misapplications.

The most obvious potential fallacy of this proverb is simple. Even if it were always true, which it is not, it does not say that if one takes risks, one is guaranteed success. Again, the "necessary, but not sufficient" phenomenon. I have seen many times over the years, both in business and life situations, where this proverb gets abused. It is important to recognize that not all risks are the same. Some risks don't make much sense to undertake; others are perfectly okay to forgo, even if the "glory" might therefore not follow.

Clearly, taking risks may have its rewards, but the key is to understand **the probability of success and the potential cost of failure.** How to deal with risk and when to take a risk are important subjects and deserve in-depth assessment. The best results are achieved when you have an accurate assessment, which stems from good and sufficient data and analyses, combined with a strong dose of pragmatism. **Pragmatism here is the most critical element.** A personal example comes to mind that illustrates how pragmatism was not applied well.

I was asked by an acquaintance who didn't know much about the business world to meet with a young woman, a friend of hers who was seeking some advice. Her friend was ready to make a career change and hoped to become a consultant with one of the four top strategic consulting firms. These consulting firms had a reputation for hiring only the best talent and consequently paying exceptionally high salaries. She was ready to quit her job and pursue this new direction and career.

As I have related, I joined one of these firms, Booz Allen, after graduating from the Wharton School of Business with an MBA. I had left the firm about three years earlier, after a reasonably long career there. My acquaintance knew that I had worked for Booz Allen and thought that I could offer her friend good advice on how to get a job offer and succeed as a professional at the firm.

Her friend told me she was working for a small family company that had about thirty employees. She completed two years of college and was hired as a secretary to the owner ten years earlier when the company had just started operations. In the subsequent five years, the company grew, and as new employees were hired, she was assigned the added responsibility of dealing with the human resources aspects of the business. After two years in this role, she was promoted to vice president of HR and received a nice salary bump.

At this point the son of the owner of the company took over the day-to-day operations. She didn't think he was all that smart and hated working for him. She wanted to leave the company and after some research found out that the premier consulting firms, like Booz Allen, paid substantially higher salaries to professionals who consulted clients on human resources issues. She believed she had learned, as she stated it to me, "everything there is to know about human resources" as she was the only person in the company who performed those duties. She was hoping that I could give her more details about working at Booz Allen and how to do well there after she was hired.

At this point, and for the purpose of this example, I would just say that practically every student from the top MBA schools would have loved to work for any of the premier strategic consulting firms, but getting a job offer was exceptionally difficult. These firms indeed paid extraordinarily high salaries; however, they hire nothing but those whom they consider to be "the best of the best," and mostly from the top MBA business schools. I knew that the woman who sat in front of me, who believed that experience in a thirty-employee company made her an expert, had quite a distorted view of what real expertise in the field of human resources entailed. Worse yet, she would have no chance of being hired as a consultant with a premier consulting firm, especially without an advanced degree.

I asked her whether she had already given termination of employment notice to her current company. She answered that she hadn't. I then decided to give her the best advice she would benefit from. I told her that she had done very well for herself, so far. I then gently proceeded to tell her that landing a job with any of the premier consulting firms would be exceptionally difficult. I explained to her that the expertise in human resources required to consult large corporations, like those serviced by these firms, is much different and much more complicated than the expertise one might gain from working in a small thirty-employee company. I knew that she was fortunate to have been promoted to her position, but it would be unusual to have a vice president title anywhere else without a full college degree, and probably not even the title of a manager. I encouraged her to stay at her current job if it was at all possible. I told her, "You are not likely to find a better salary or a vice president title with any other company. In fact, you may not even be able to replace what you currently have."

I received a very angry call the following day from my acquaintance who had set up the meeting with this woman. She was angry because her friend left the meeting with me quite upset with what I had told her. I asked her why her friend was upset. After all, I gave her the best advice anybody could have given her. Her response was illuminating. She said, "When somebody wants to take a risk and try for something better, you are supposed to be supportive and encouraging, not negative and discouraging." I replied, "But you wanted me to give her good advice, and that's exactly what I did. It would be the worst decision if she indeed followed through with her plan and left her current job. She will not likely even find a new job to replace what she had, let alone find something better."

My acquaintance didn't buy that and said that it is more important to be supportive under such circumstances than to "kill and destroy a person's dream." I come from a different culture and upbringing. I come from a culture where if you ask for advice you get advice, not encouragement and sympathy.

About two years later, I had an opportunity to talk to my acquaintance and asked about this person. She told me that she left her job, as she had planned to do, not long after she and I had met. She still had not found employment. As I stated, "no risk, no reward," but **one must be very pragmatic in assessing the probability of success before undertaking any undue risk.**

Back to the topic at hand. I would expand on the proverb "no risk, no reward," but reword it and offer five separate observations to help with better assessing its appropriateness:

- Most successful people have taken risks and experienced failures.

- Some risk taking is wise, some is not. Carefully analyze risks and rewards so as to avoid unwise risks.

- Unwise risks are the risks such that the cost of failure has consequences you are unwilling to take or whose potential outcomes you would rather not encounter.

- One must obtain accurate and complete information, and be exceptionally pragmatic, to help avoid unwise risks.

- Never avoid risks because of the fear of failure and how people might view it. Remember, "no risk, no reward"; "no guts, no glory."

I wish to make a separate observation regarding the last point. I have seen some people who fear failure so much that they would rather not take any risk to avoid feeling humiliated should they fail. It is for those people that I bring the following observation. Follow my expanded definition of the wisdom of taking risks, and never fear failure. I'll share with you an observation I made over the years, which I believe to be universally true: **People rarely look down at trying and failing; we are the ones who assume they do!**

18

Advice on Risking
Your Hard-Earned Money

As a venture capitalist, my advice is often solicited regarding ideas for starting a business or investment opportunities. Any advice that might be of benefit must consider the unique circumstances surrounding that opportunity. However, over the years I have found that I keep repeating some observations I make to people, regardless of the unique circumstances of the specific opportunity. I thought that I would share this generic advice, should you ever find yourself tempted by the lure of making "big" money.

Underscoring all advice is this fundamental tenet: **Understand the difference in business between taking a risk and gambling.** People willing to invest in a business opportunity never think in terms of gambling, but rather in terms of risk. They get even more excited when the investment opportunity is in a start-up company, particularly a hi-tech one. They are all aware of the fact that venture capitalists can make a fortune investing in high-risk companies and are very tempted to personally benefit by doing the same. This is a common wisdom that has a fallacy.

Let me dispel this common perception about venture capitalists and the venture capital industry. It is generally believed that a venture capitalist is in the business of taking high risks in order to benefit from high returns. Many venture capitalists may even agree with that statement.

I would consider those to be pedestrian thinkers. The deep and perceptive thinkers will immediately understand the fallacy. Although there is some truth to the fact that venture capitalists invest in high-risk situations in order to benefit from high returns, it is completely wrong to think they are in the business of doing so. Understanding this nuance is the key to benefiting from my advice.

Venture capitalists do not take high risks. They take risks that they believe they can manage and thereby mitigate. The nuance should be clear: Venture capitalists are not in the business of taking risks; rather, they are in the business of managing risk. The former I consider to be more akin to gambling, and the latter I believe falls into the camp of legitimate risk taking. The industry even coined a term for the former category: "dumb money."

The fundamental difference between the two lies in two aspects: (i) having the right knowledge and/or expertise to make a judgment on the magnitude of the risk and whether the risk is manageable, and (ii) having the ability to wisely and competently help manage the risk. Competent venture capitalists will not likely invest in other scenarios. If they do, they will fully understand that they are taking more of a gamble, even if they don't consciously think about it that way.

Keep in mind that even for the venture capitalist the risk of failure of any given investment, even the best ones, is very high. About 50 percent of individual deals fail, even for the best venture capitalist, and this is after the VC has applied their expert judgment to the opportunity, completed thorough due diligence, and consulted with their partners, convincing them of the merits and wisdom of making such an investment. Deals fail because it takes much, much more than just a great idea to end up with a successful business. There are many other factors involved, including a large dose of luck, both positive—being lucky—and negative—being unlucky.

Now that you understand the above, you will have a better appreciation of the rationale behind my observations and recommendations below regarding investing in a start-up if you are not an experienced venture capitalist:

- No matter how simple it may appear to be, there is no such thing as a no-brainer start-up—not even a restaurant, a retail store, or a hot dog stand.

- Never invest in a deal, including your own start-up, that falls more into my definition of gambling, meaning:

  o Where you don't completely possess the necessary expertise to make a competent judgment. Knowing a little bit about it doesn't count as expertise!

  o Where you don't have complete confidence that it is a situation where you can personally help manage and mitigate the risk.

- You may make an exception only on rare occasions, where you are making the investment based on someone's recommendation, someone whom you completely trust and who will be in a position with the right skills and influence to place the opportunity in the non-gambling category. However:

  o Never give this trust to anybody who is absolutely not very close to you, and who doesn't have a long, established, and proven track record that you can personally vouch for, from your own experience.

  o The person should not be just a decent friend whom you know.

  o The person should never be a stranger, or somebody you don't know extremely well.

- Don't ever invest in start-ups or early-stage companies based on the advice of stockbrokers or investment professionals, regardless of the reputation of the firm they work for.

- **Never invest money unless you absolutely also stand ready to lose it all**, without major consequences to you, and over which you will not lose any sleep. In other words, **never invest money you can't afford to lose or are unwilling to lose.**

- o   In fact, I always advise people before they make an investment to assume that it is all lost and just *hope* for a possible pleasant surprise in the future.

- You may ignore the above when:

  - o   the amount is inconsequential to you, and you are fully prepared and willing to lose it all.

  - o   you fully understand that you will be taking a gamble, with the same odds and expected outcomes you would expect from a pure gambling situation.

Never let greed blind you from following the above advice. That is exactly what the people who are trying to convince you to make the investment count on!

SECTION IV

SUCCESS THROUGH INFLUENCE

19

Influencing Outcomes, Not Others, Is the Single Most Significant Contributor to Success

Practically everything we do in life, throughout every single day and every single moment of our lives, is an attempt to influence others to act or think as we would like them to act or think. I make no judgment in this observation of human interaction—good or bad, right or wrong, should or shouldn't—it is just the way it is! Of course, everybody tries to influence everybody else for many ulterior motives, but that is not the point. The point is just stating the most obvious observation of them all: Often what we do or say is to influence the thoughts and actions of others.

We try to influence others in multiple ways. The two most common, non-nefarious ways include using interpersonal skills and psychological approaches and using logical arguments by communicating benefits versus the repercussions, should our position not be accepted. However, in the business world, and specifically as related to career advancement, there is another dimension that rarely gets its proper due. It is utilized on and off, but mostly haphazardly, or we stumble onto it. This section focuses on this single, underutilized influencing element, which in turn offers the greatest opportunity to differentiate oneself and allows one an accelerated career advancement. Whereas the other two more commonly used approaches center on *how to influence individuals or groups*, at the center of this underutilized approach is *how to influence **outcomes** as opposed to individuals*. Perhaps it may initially appear as a small conceptual nuance, since influencing an individual leads to influencing an outcome, but you will see that it actually is a fundamentally different approach that requires a completely different mindset. A number of examples will help explain the difference, the value, and how to put this approach to influencing outcomes into practice.

First, I'd like to set the stage so that you know what to look for as we work through this topic. Keep in mind that henceforth whenever I use the words "influence" or "influencing," I exclusively refer to the underutilized approach—the one that influences outcomes. There are three parts to the stage-setting: (i) introducing the concept of "owning" a solution, (ii) explaining how influencing and job responsibilities intersect, and (iii) explaining the relationship between "doing one's best" and influencing.

I have used the word "own" a number of times so far in this book. It is a favorite word of mine that I've used for years and to which I attribute a specific and special meaning. I plan to continue to use the word, and so allow me to better define what I mean.

I use "own" or "owning" to mean **a total acceptance of a position, followed by a full sense of responsibility and commitment to treat it with the utmost priority, and proactively take all necessary actions to implement it successfully.** The opposite of "owning" would be to do something haphazardly or without full commitment.

As stated, I attribute a special meaning to the word "influencing." To me it refers to influencing an outcome, which represents a higher level of duty when it comes to performing our job. Our principal job responsibility calls for us to competently do our best. "Influencing," on the other hand, as I define it, requires even more than that. This concept is well understood in the military and in the public safety sectors, such as police, firefighters, and so on. It is called "above and beyond the call of duty." It refers to the fact that the "call of duty" already requires one to do the best, most competent job they can, but going "above and beyond the call of duty" is a whole different performance level, one that yields the most recognition and rewards. The way I see it, the "call of duty" in business is to do one's best work while influencing outcomes requires you to go "above and beyond the call of duty." Let me elaborate to explain.

The Call of Duty in the Business World

We are taught to present things logically and prove that we are "right" in order to influence others to accept our position. In fact, perhaps all human interactions are based on this premise: that logic is the strongest driver of behavior and acceptance of position (in a civil world, without nefarious motivations). When we try to influence others, or resolve a conflict with others, we default to explaining the validity of our logic.

In reality there are five factors, which together influence us the most, and we use them as we try to influence one another. The five factors are:

1. Pointing out the benefits (advantages) vs. negative repercussions

2. Showing that our position is logical, whereas the opponent's is not

3. Showing that we are more in the right

4. Pointing out that we are being fair vs. unfair

5. Achieving a moral outcome (i.e., good vs. bad)

In other words, we have become conditioned to believe that compelling logic and being right should always prevail, and thus we need only to prove it to others to have them accept our position. To prove this point, just imagine any argument or conflict that needs to be resolved in a civil way. The first things that are pointed out are the benefits (advantages) offered should the position be accepted, and the reverse—the negative repercussions that might befall us if we don't. Next on the priority list is pointing out the compelling logic of our position, particularly in trying to prove that we are more in the right than the other side. If that is not convincing enough, we'll fall back to point out the fairness of our position, versus being unfair. The other side is trying to do the same.

We reach agreement through a compromise, which means taking the other side's position into account. Our final judgment will most likely represent what we consider to be a fair solution that reflects a degree of validity in each party's logic. It is this reality that gave rise to the famous adage "in business you get not what you deserve, but what you negotiate." It basically means that if one is better at presenting their logic, they are much more likely to get a better outcome than the other party. Or, stated more simply, the more compelling the logic, the more likely one is to get their preferred resolution.

Notice that the above explanation is silent on how behavioral inter-actions and feelings may affect the resolution of a conflict situation. We all know they do. We all know that they are in direct conflict with the "logical" way of resolving conflict situations. We refer to them as "irrational" reactions, while the logical way is the "rational" behavior. In the business world, everybody kind of understands that rationality needs to prevail, and so the likelihood of being irrational and introduc-ing behavioral considerations and feelings is minimized.

A problem arises when one side concludes that the other side's posi-tion reflects biased, incomplete facts or faulty logic and poor judgment. Once a party believes the other party is rejecting its position despite "fair and valid" reasons, then upset and intransigence set in. The situa-tion could even lead to some anger and irritation, and the probability of reaching a fair compromise is significantly reduced.

Given the above, the "call of duty" requires us to originate the best logic, present it in the most compelling way, and reach the best resolu-tion for us and our company, without allowing emotions to affect us. At a minimum, we and the company expect that any compromise posi-tion will reflect the "fairest" one and be good for the business. Should a fair compromise not be possible, then we are expected to walk away. Do that and we have performed our job well—our call of duty.

Let me point out an important observation. Walking away from an unfair resolution of a conflict is perfectly acceptable and is part of our job. In other words, not getting the result we were initially looking for is perfectly acceptable, **so long as it was not within our control and doing otherwise would have been unfair and bad for the business.**

Here's an interesting thought, however: There is minimal burden placed on us to help minimize the irrational behavior of the other party, or the unreasonable, unwise, invalid, unsound position they adhere to, which ultimately denied successfully achieving an outcome. In many cases, we just accept this reality. After all, it's not our fault. How the other side ultimately behaves is out of our control, so what are we to do? But what if there was a way, and we could influence the other side's behavior? If indeed we could, then the payoff would be substantially better. Instead of justifiably walking away, we successfully achieved an outcome we desired. Now you are venturing into the "above and beyond the call of duty."

This, in my mind, is the difference between doing your job well and influencing others.

Above and Beyond the Call of Duty

In the example above, we legitimately walked away from resolving a conflict because of the irrationality of the other side. We feel we did our best, and our superiors would recognize our effort as excellent work. This is a predictable outcome in the business world. But what if we could have changed that outcome? What if we had some way to influence the other party in such a manner that success on both sides could be achieved? If it would have taken extra time and energy commitment on our part to make that happen, would it be worth doing so? What if we changed our mindset not to be satisfied with a "walking away" outcome, even though our superiors would have given us all the credit, regardless? If you decided to do so, then you would own a different philosophy regarding your job. You would view your job differently from one where you are just doing your best. You would define it within the context of how effective you are in influencing outcomes.

My advice is for you to do so. I can tell you from my experience that the answers to the above questions are definitely in the affirmative, perhaps not in all cases, but in enough cases to make your performance stand out above and beyond that of your coworkers.

So now you understand conceptually what the nuanced difference of viewing your job as influencing others is. Also, I suggested that it could yield positive results that otherwise might not have happened. We are now ready to look at the examples that will demonstrate that it does indeed work!

Example 1: The Philosophy of Influencing Outcomes at Booz Allen

This example will help make the case that influencing outcomes is not just a concept, but an independent factor in its own right in achieving success. It clearly demonstrates that a change in mindset is not just a conceptual change. Rather, if you own it, you make real changes in work processes that significantly improve the probability of achieving the outcome you seek.

As I have said, Booz Allen is one of the premier consulting firms. I joined its strategy group right after graduating from Wharton. The group I joined provided strategic and competitive analyses at the CEO and board of directors' level. The other three top consulting firms at the time were McKinsey & Company, Boston Consulting Group (BCG), and Bain & Company. These firms were our direct competitors. It was at Booz Allen where I first learned that my job was not to do the best analyses and come up with the best recommendations possible. Booz Allen had a philosophy: Unless the client implemented our recommendations, we provided little value to that client. So, our job as individuals and as a firm was not just to present what we deemed as the best solutions for a client, but rather to influence a client to own and implement the recommendations.

The firm dedicated its systems and processes to increasing the probability that the influence would indeed yield results. It added about one-third extra effort, time, and cost to us. It was a massive effort on the firm's part, and it was a massive extra burden on us as individuals. It included many different components, and I'll just quickly mention a few to show how the mindset was translated into real work and effort.

There were two major things that we did, with a substantially different effort and commitment level than our competitors. We knew it to be true because our clients told us so many times, and we had personally witnessed the difference as over time we had opportunities to assess each other's work, albeit of course for different projects.

The difference was not in the quality of the analyses done or in the recommendations given. The four firms had an equally great reputation on that front. The difference lay in the extra work that was involved in influencing the clients and how much time and effort was spent on that. Booz Allen spent the most. As I said, at Booz Allen, one-third of our time was dedicated to it. Another firm, which I got to know very well, spent almost no time worrying about it. A third firm was more sensitive to the issue, but didn't spend an inordinate amount of time and energy on it. The fourth firm, which happened to have been Bain & Co., made it part of its practice as well, and would only do work for clients where they were also involved in the actual implementation of the recommendations.

I can't tell you with certainty whether the difference I am highlighting indeed translated into a difference in financial performance for the consulting firms. Even with the extra time, energy, and effort that went into it, it may, nevertheless, have made no difference at all. But I can tell you that the implementation rate of the recommendations was significantly different among the firms and directly correlated to the effort spent on the influence dimension.

Once Booz Allen decided to own the issue of the implementation rate, with a target of 100 percent, the company embarked on an effort to understand how it could pragmatically reach it. Clearly, to do that well, the firm needed to first understand the reasons that hinder the implementation rate. Then, once those reasons were identified, come up with the actions that would minimize the obstacles.

Booz Allen's own research revealed two key reasons why implementation is hindered:

1. There is no complete buy-in of the recommendations on the part of the executive(s) who would subsequently be responsible for some of the implementation in their departments/organizations. There were three general reasons why that happened:

   A. The board and/or CEO forced a decision, and the executive team was not part of the deliberation process.

   B. The executive team was part of the deliberation process, but never fully agreed with the recommendations reached by the board/CEO, so the executive team didn't really own the decision, even though the executive team endorsed it in the final vote.

   C. Self-serving, ulterior motives.

2. The executive level was fine with the recommendations, but the next layer of managers found a thousand ways either to slow the process down or halt it altogether.

When digging into why the next layer of managers did so, the same three general reasons that pertained to the executives emerged, with one notable important addition. In most cases, the next layer of managers never understood the logic behind the implementation. Further research suggested that the key reason was simply because their executives didn't take the necessary time to explain the analyses used to arrive at the recommendations. All the executives did was to drop off the final consultant's presentation and say, "Read the recommendations and tell me if you have any issues and make sure to implement them."

The presentation that was left behind by the consultants generally consisted of bullet points and key words. Nobody could understand them without hearing the presenter, who gave it the proper context and rationale. This wasn't much of an issue with the executive team that was present at the consultant's presentation. However, it surely would never be well understood by those who were given the presentation deck only. They would get the overall messages or conclusions, but very little understanding of the underlying analyses and all the intricacies that justified those conclusions. Thus, the next layer of managers never owned the analyses and conclusions, and therefore the recommendations.

Once the reasons were fully understood, Booz Allen then sought potential solutions that would address them as much as possible, thereby increasing the probability of avoiding them. As a result, two key decisions were made, each placing substantially extra effort on the working team. These became the standard operating procedures that were passed on from one generation to the next. The decisions included the following:

- Our final reports would still be in bullet-point format, but each bullet point was to be logical, grammatically correct, and expressed in complete sentences. Sub-bullet points were used so that no long paragraphs were required. The guiding directive was that the report "has to be written in a way that anybody reading it will have the full AND SAME comprehension and understanding as those hearing it in the presentation itself."

- The team had to make sure that all the data we used, all the analyses we conducted, and all the conclusions we drew were run by all the managers who would be responsible for the implementation. Any disagreements or apprehension on any manager's part needed to be addressed and resolved. As a result, what we did was to make each one of those managers feel as if they were part of the team by involving them on an ongoing basis. We asked them to help with the data collection; we showed them the initial conclusions we drew from the analyses and asked for their feedback; and we took whatever they said very seriously, even when we thought it was nonsensical. Once we had buy-in on a subset of the analyses and conclusions, we would then run it by the executives for their comments and endorsement. This was an ongoing cycle. We never walked into the final presentation to the CEO and the board without knowing that all managers had fully endorsed our recommendations. If there were any disagreements, we fully understood the reasons and were prepared to refute them. However, it rarely happened.

You can surmise from the above how much extra time and effort went into this process. Needless to say, the team responsible for the work disliked putting in this extra effort. We already worked long hours and on weekends, and this increased the workload. But it yielded the proper results. I found out just how different the results were from other firms by happenstance.

A close acquaintance was a senior job manager at the Boston Consulting Group. He decided to leave the firm and wrote a resume to circulate. He asked me as a friend to look it over. I did so. One of the things that caught my attention was that he listed ten projects he had personally managed, in bullet-point format, with each bullet representing one project. However, the last bullet said, "Four of the projects were implemented by the client." I recommended that he remove this point. He asked why.

I said, "Why would you highlight something negative?"

"It's not a negative, it is a real positive," he replied.

I patiently responded, "But it tells everybody that 60 percent of your projects were not implemented, and that raises the question of how good your recommendations were, to have a 60 percent failure rate."

He replied, "What do you mean? Everybody knows that very few recommendations are actually fully implemented, because of organizational resistance. A 40 percent implementation ratio is a great success."

I asked what the firm's average ratio was, and he replied about 30 to 40 percent. He was very proud of his 40 percent achievement. I was dumbfounded. He asked me what the ratio was at Booz Allen; I told him it was close to 90 percent. I told him that I still thought that it would be safer to remove the 40 percent reference, thereby leaving the impression that perhaps the full 100 percent were implemented. He bought that logic and deleted the reference to the 40 percent success rate.

Example 2: An Example of Proactive Influencing

We at Booz Allen were involved with a study of a conglomerate that had enjoyed almost fifteen years of great success, but its performance over the last five years had deteriorated significantly. The company didn't understand why and needed help. For essential background information, this company had little competition in its markets. It was almost a monopoly. Then two major changes happened at the same time. New regulations were introduced that gave rise to significant competition, and a big recession impacted the markets. Two years went by, and the board believed that the main reason for the decline was that the company had not adjusted its operations to effectively address the new regulatory environment. They therefore concluded that a stronger legal background was needed at the CEO level. The CEO at the time had no legal background and was let go. The senior executive vice president of legal became the new CEO. Two years later, performance had deteriorated even further. The CEO called us to help him turn it around.

In our introductory meeting with the CEO, he described the overall performance problems, but specifically mentioned that he was completely at a loss, because his corporate-level vice presidents and division-level presidents were making quarterly adjustments to forecasts, and at times as often as monthly, but those forecasts just never materialized. He asked, "How is it possible to miss in a big way forecasts every single month, particularly on profit forecasts?"

I was the job manager for this project, and on the team were a consultant who worked directly for me, a junior partner, and a senior partner. It didn't take me long to grasp the problem. The monopoly had changed into a competitive marketplace. The company's managers at all levels had stayed the same. They were completely unequipped to be effective in a competitive marketplace, and the recession just made things worse. Everybody believed that all they needed was to change their "regulatory expertise" and that it would solve their problems. They had no concept of how to forecast with a proper methodology and did not have a control mechanism in place to adjust expenses in real time. The CEO actually only got reports at a consolidated overall corporate level. Nobody even kept track of how much was spent in each of the divisions, let alone looked at the numbers when they became available months later. So, whatever the managers budgeted to spend at the beginning of the year, based on the forecasts at the time, was actually spent during the year, regardless of any downward adjustment to revenue forecasts as the year progressed. This resulted in huge losses that could have been easily controlled. Most importantly, there was no penalty whatsoever for consistently missing forecasts, either on revenues or cash flow and losses.

We did all the necessary analyses to help formulate effective competitive strategies. But in addition, major organizational changes needed to occur. New management processes had to be put in place, the biggest of which was establishing methodology-based forecasts, including at the consolidated, overall company level as well as the divisional level. It then had to have all the necessary tracking and control mechanisms that allowed for quick and timely adjustments to expenses, should expected revenues not materialize. The centerpiece of the forecasts and control processes was a penalty system that was meaningful enough to ensure accuracy, which included dismissal for continuing to be substantially off the readjusted shorter-term revenue forecasts and the management of expenses.

We wrote a full presentation report that went through a number of iterations, because we were very sensitive to how potentially damning to the CEO all the findings might appear to the board. After all, he'd been there for two years already and hadn't assessed the need for these changes.

The evening before the presentation to the CEO, the senior partner called the team to a meeting. When the team assembled, he pensively pointed out a big dilemma that he anticipated might arise. The centerpiece of our recommendation was full accountability (dismissal) for continued deviation from forecasts. This would place the CEO himself at risk vis-à-vis his board, should that pattern of failing to meet forecasts not be corrected. Would the CEO, then, choose not to implement the recommendations because they would place him at risk? Might he not allow us to make our presentation to the board, which we expected to happen at the conclusion of our assignment?

The discussion that followed focused on what we should do if the CEO canceled the presentation to the board. We debated who our client really was—the CEO who hired us or the board of directors. The senior partner decided that our ultimate responsibility was to the board. So, if the CEO decided to kill the project because it increased his personal risk exposure, we would go over his head and contact the board to share our observations and recommendations. Obviously, this was the last thing we wanted to happen.

Since Booz Allen's mindset was influence-oriented, the conversation quickly focused on the best way to mitigate this potential possibility. The conclusion was obvious: Get the CEO to enthusiastically endorse everything we were recommending, but how? What could we do or say to make it happen? The senior partner then raised a single question and asked each of the team members to answer it in order of seniority—the consultant first, then me, and then the junior partner. He gave us a minute to think about it. The question was, "What do I tell the CEO at the very beginning of the presentation to get him into a mindset that would be so welcoming of our recommendations that he would move forward with them despite the fact that he may place himself at a greater personal risk?" The responses were exceptionally revealing to me.

The consultant replied, "The company has had massive losses, and they can be stopped. Our recommendations can accomplish just that."

I was next. My answer was, "Market dynamics have changed quickly and dramatically over the last five years and have had a lot of turbulence. The company needs to dramatically change, to make it more competitive in the marketplace. The good news is that we believe it can be done quickly, particularly with immediate substantial improvement to the company's bottom line, but it will require some bold actions and potentially be less forgiving to division-level presidents."

The junior partner said, "I would tell the CEO that there are good reasons to explain why the deteriorated performance occurred. We can help you with a presentation to the board that will highlight all that has happened. It also gives pragmatic recommendations that will quickly help you cure everything. We would like you to know that Booz Allen has a high degree of confidence that the recommendations, when fully implemented, will correct the situation quickly. We also believe that within one year you can change from losing money to becoming profitable."

Just from our responses you should see that influencing doesn't just happen. A correct mindset is a prerequisite, but spending the time and energy and proactively thinking about it is also required. Also, notice how the responses varied, even though we were all aware of the issue and were trained to think about how to influence an outcome. You probably noticed the purposely inserted little nuances and how each attempted to solve what the team perceived to be the challenge they were trying to influence. I'll point them out just to show that the actual solution can be more art than science. But thinking ahead and identifying the correct potential obstacle is a prerequisite step to influencing.

The consultant used pure logic, emphasizing the benefits/rewards in the "scariest" and most factual way as to allay the potential concern of the CEO. He basically said, your company is dying and we can help resuscitate it. If you don't implement our recommendations, the company is doomed (and, therefore, so are you). Powerful, logical, and an emotional motivator based on a fear factor.

I introduced the idea that we would ascribe the company's deteriorating performance to market dynamics, thereby implying that it was not the CEO's fault. It follows that the company must change substantially to respond to those dynamics, thus preconditioning the CEO's thinking that substantial changes were the appropriate response. Then we would tell the CEO that we could confidently deal with the situation quickly. I then shifted the personal risk embodied in our recommendations to the division presidents so that the CEO's personal risk was minimized and the CEO would retain the rewards.

The junior partner used the exact same reasoning I had, but used simpler and more concise phrasing, leaving nothing to the CEO's interpretation. [As a side note, I learned over the years that if you can talk about the expected outcomes by using powerful influencing key words or concepts, it is much more effective than trying to describe and focus on the different factors that imply the same outcome. In other words, the first communicates the outcome directly, while the latter communicates factors that directly and obviously lead to the same outcome. For example, "Doing this will successfully reduce the costs and improve your margins" vs. "Doing this will improve your profitability." Note the first is indirectly implying what the second states directly and explicitly, with a key influencing word—"profits"—which is most sensitive to the CEO.] Note another subtle difference in his response versus mine. Like me, he explained that the deteriorating performance was due to market factors (by implications, not the CEO's fault) and suggested directly that we could present these facts to the board to help them understand it. This would lead the CEO to consider that our presentation to the board would help him personally.

The senior partner pensively looked at us and said, "I don't know, let me sleep on it," and the meeting concluded. I can assure you that he was still struggling with the best way to address it.

I couldn't wait to hear what the senior partner would say the very next morning. I intuitively understood that I had just found myself in the center of something very nuanced, but very important, which I needed to make an integral part of my own thinking in the future.

We assembled in the CEO's office the next morning. The senior partner took a completely different approach. As soon as the meeting started, he said, "Jim, thank you for the opportunity to help you with a very perplexing situation and the challenges you are facing. You told us, earlier on, that the biggest source of frustration for you is being so wrong with forecasts, so often, and almost monthly, am I correct?"

Jim replied with a neutral tone and expression. "Yes."

"Jim," said the senior partner, "how would you like to be able to stand in front of your board and give them forecasts knowing with confidence that they will not change on you?"

Jim's face lit up. "Are you serious? That would be the greatest thing. Is it possible?"

I was blown away. I learned a lifelong lesson. You, the readers, are now the beneficiaries. The CEO was ecstatic when he understood that our recommendations were focused on solving his greatest frustration. As soon as he understood our rationale and why our recommendations would work, he was completely sold. There wasn't even a question about not taking it to the board.

Example 3: How Influence Solved a Roadblock at Ameritech

This example demonstrates that a correct mindset, with a proactive influence mentality, may indeed lead to actions that otherwise might not occur. I was responsible for all venture investments on behalf of Ameritech. We were looking to invest in start-up companies whose technology and products could enhance our competitive position. It happened immediately after the breakup of AT&T's nationwide monopoly.

The breakup of AT&T split the long-distance telephone operations and their networks from the local telephone businesses. The local telephone networks were managed separately in each of the states and were generally called the "Bell" companies, such as Illinois Bell, Indiana Bell, Ohio Bell, and so on. All the corporate functions, such as strategic planning, product planning, technology developments, financing, and so on were conducted at the corporate AT&T level. The breakup of AT&T resulted in eight separate telephone companies. The long-distance business remained at AT&T, but state telephone operations were consolidated into seven "Baby Bells," and Ameritech was one of them.

Upon the split-up, all the Baby Bells, on day one, looked identical in their technological capabilities, products, and services offerings. Each, however, was located in a different geographical market. Ameritech was the entity under AT&T that served much of the Midwest—Michigan, Ohio, Illinois, Indiana, and Wisconsin. There were no restrictions placed on the Baby Bell companies to expand into each other's territories. All knew that they would shortly start competing with each other in earnest. Everybody expected a wave of start-up companies that would introduce new technologies and service capabilities that the Bell companies could implement to differentiate themselves from one another. The idea behind our venture investments at Ameritech was that if we invest with start-up companies early on, we can influence the development of the technology and be the first to market with it, thereby improving our competitive position.

I had a dedicated staff of six professionals looking for investment opportunities. There were two lower- to mid-level managers from the old AT&T organization who worked in the engineering and marketing groups and understood the specific technologies, products, and services offered by Ameritech. Their job was to help identify whether the technology of the start-up companies would fit Ameritech's needs, and subsequently work with the various organizations within Ameritech to help with our in-depth due diligence requirements. The rest were hired from the outside; one was a brilliant PhD in electrical engineering with specialization in semiconductor science.

Final investment decisions had to be approved by my board committee, which was composed of Ameritech's chairman and CEO; CFO; president; executive vice president, legal counsel; executive vice president, corporate strategy; and executive vice president, Ameritech Engineering (the group responsible for all the networks and integration of new technologies). There was one stipulation in my charter from my board committee, whose approval I needed to make investments. On top of convincing the committee that the investment would lead to attractive returns, I also needed to show a strategic synergy with Ameritech's needs. My large approval committee spanned all the different areas, thereby allowing us to make a decision with a single meeting.

We looked for opportunities to invest equity capital in appropriate start-ups. There was no shortage of them. We had about eight potential investment opportunities for which we eagerly started doing the necessary market and competitive due diligence, and had asked the engineering organization to assign a team to evaluate whether Ameritech would benefit from those technologies.

It took about two to three months for a technology start-up to close on raising its capital from the venture capital community. We had to make a final decision within that time frame. The response we got from the various engineers assigned to us was very slow, and at times they didn't even return calls.

I placed a call to the VP of engineering and explained my issue. He was a very nice guy and sympathetic to my problem, but said that there was not much he could do except try to prod them. The engineers had their primary responsibilities that took precedence, and he couldn't force them to change their priorities. I told my staff to try harder. Two weeks later, we reconvened. There was no progress on the issue. We discussed what we could do to change this reality and concluded that there was nothing we could do to get the due diligence we needed on a timely basis. However, with my influencing mentality, I refused to accept that there was nothing we could do.

I met again with the vice president to explore how everything worked in his organization. Again, he was very responsive to all my questions, but continued to state that he couldn't force his staff to shift focus away from their primary responsibilities; they would have to do so voluntarily. However, I didn't just accept the inevitable. I did see a solution that was unorthodox, but one that could potentially work under the circumstances.

I went back to my office and called in Ray, the brilliant PhD. I told him that I had a solution for our problem and that he was the focal point of it. I told him what I expected him to do and he just looked at me and said, "Are you serious?" I said, "Absolutely!" Ray then replied, "Okay, you are the boss. It is your call."

I basically told him that there was no way to shift the priorities of the supporting engineers to do any due diligence work for us in the time frame we needed. But technically, we as an organization didn't need their due diligence capability, because we could do the due diligence ourselves. Instead, all we really needed was for them to state that the technology had potential synergies with Ameritech's networks and future technology needs. He asked, "How can we get them to do so without them doing their own homework about a new technology they know nothing about, let alone how it would evolve and could be used in the telecommunications networks?" I said, "That's a great question and here is what I want you to do. You do it well and I will guarantee to double your salary once you make it work well for us."

I then proceeded to tell him that I wanted him to become a student again and do what he did when he was a full-time student. I told him to focus his full attention on studying everything about telecommunications networks from a technology standpoint. And since he was more scientifically qualified than the engineers, I expected that at the end of his self-study he would know more about their technologies than they knew themselves. This way he would conduct the due diligence we otherwise would have had to rely on the engineers to do. Then we would only need to meet them and convince them why and how the technology should and could be integrated into "their network." At that point, all they would have to do is buy in on what we presented to them and say that they agreed with our conclusions. There were five such key managers working for the VP, so Ray also needed to develop friendly relationships with them. I told him that I had secured permission from the VP to allow him unlimited access to their restricted areas and that the VP would make the proper introductions to the managers. "The rest is up to you," I said.

Within two months Ray became accepted by the engineers as if he were part of their organization, since he was seen there so often, and I made sure that the VP invited him to some staff meetings every once in a while, when technology issues were discussed. Ray showed the engineers the benefits of new technologies we wanted to invest in, and I made sure that he offered them the opportunity to "champion" the concept internally so they would get the credit for it.

It worked better than I ever imagined. Ray was very effective, and we would get their approval on a timely basis. It also added value to the VP himself, because we brought to his attention new technologies and potential capabilities that would help his organization and enhance his own position, effectiveness, and workload as related to future technology planning. He then started to work more closely with Ray and my organization. In fact, the VP recognized the brilliance and outside perspective that Ray brought to him. He asked my permission to have Ray more involved with him personally to help with his own future plans for the network, even when not related to any specific investment opportunities for my organization. A while later, I asked the VP if I could use his name for approving the synergy of technologies I was required to show, instead of using his managers' names. He agreed. He then voluntarily offered to come to every meeting I had with my board (which included his direct boss) and attest to the potential synergies and attractiveness of the technology. He was thought of highly by senior management. Nobody would challenge his conclusions, so investments I recommended were approved with little further discussion.

The VP and I developed a close relationship over the years. He would ask me to look for specific technologies that he would like for us to get close to, which I was glad to do. Our appreciation for each other's professional capabilities grew. After I left Ameritech to join a venture capital independent group, I constantly used his technical help and advice. Just as a reference, he had a superb nationwide reputation. He was one of the original six engineers who developed the cellular technology. When I started my own firm and raised my second and very large fund, I invited him to join me as a partner, which he did. We worked together until his retirement.

Example 4: Beth and the Music Icon

As you now know, Beth is my daughter. When she was a junior in high school, she was involved with the TV production club at school. The club produced various TV programs for the consumption of fellow students. Once a year, some of the better programs were submitted for local, regional, and then state competition. Beth undertook to cover a charismatic individual who worked at a toll collection booth. He was always cheerful and funny, and found a way to be endearing to all those who passed through his tollbooth. Over the years, practically everybody who lived in the vicinity knew him and thought fondly of him. Beth decided to do a short TV segment about him.

She went to the collection booth and interviewed him and some of the drivers of cars that passed through. It was an entertaining and high-quality segment. Even I was quite impressed when I saw the clip. A very creative part of the clip was the background music she selected. The name of the tollbooth collector was Jack. She selected the song "Hit the Road Jack" for the background music.

Beth's piece won many awards at the local, regional, and state competitions. At a national competition, sixteen clips were selected as finalists. Hers was one of them. Those sixteen clips were submitted to CNN, which scheduled a two-hour program on a Sunday morning four weeks later to select and award prizes to the top three winners.

The school received the notification that Beth's clip was selected to compete at the finals. Beth received a telephone call from CNN, notifying her that she was selected, but they had a big issue with the clip, and unless she could resolve it in time, they would not be able to enter her clip for the final competition.

The problem was the background song. Unless Beth had a license to use the song from the copyright owner, CNN would not be able to play the clip, as it would be an infringement of copyright. CNN also indicated to her that, absent a license, the next best thing she could have was permission from the copyright holder to play the song on TV.

A teacher was assigned to help Beth through the process of trying to secure a letter of consent from the copyright holder. The teacher wrote a letter on behalf of the school and Beth asking for his approval, so that CNN's requirement could be satisfied. With a copy of that letter in hand, Beth approached me and asked for my opinion. She filled me in on all the details up to that point, and told me that she had already spoken on the phone with the assistant of the copyright holder and confirmed that the person indeed held the copyright for the song. Beth said the assistant was very sympathetic to her request, but the copyright holder would not give his approval. The assistant said she had been with him for ten years, and that they received hundreds of such requests every year. Even in the face of noble and compelling reasons, he had never granted a single one. She concluded, "You can try, but I don't want you to get disappointed. I'm telling you that there is no way he will give his approval. He doesn't care about the reasons. His answer is always no!"

Below is a synopsis of the letter the teacher wrote, which Beth showed me for my comments:

Dear Mr. [Name]:

My name is [____] and I am Beth Kronfeld's teacher at [____] High School. Beth is a junior and is one of the top students here. Besides being a top student, Beth is a wonderful person, liked by all, who volunteers for many extracurricular activities to help the needy. She is giving so much of herself to help others and now she needs your help with a simple act of generosity.

Beth produced a wonderful TV clip about a very colorful and beloved individual who works at a toll collection booth on a major toll road. He has worked there for many years, and is always cheerful and funny. Every driver that lives in the vicinity knows him well, and all are very fond of him. Beth's clip was so well done that it was submitted to compete nationally as part of a CNN-sponsored competition. Beth's clip was selected as one of the top sixteen finalists. CNN plans to have a two-hour airing of the productions of the sixteen finalists and award prizes to the top three.

However, because the clip was about a beloved toll collector at the highway, Beth selected the song "Hit the Road Jack" as the background music for the clip, which was so appropriate for the subject matter. CNN notified the school that they might be risking infringement on your copyright of the song, and unless they get specific approval from the copyright holder, they will not enter Beth's clip into the final competition. They gave us two weeks to secure such permission, before finalizing the competing clips.

Beth, I and the whole school hope that you will be magnanimous and give such permission. It would mean so much to everybody at school, and even more so to Beth, who always gives so much of herself to help others.

We all thank you in advance,
God bless you,
Sincerely,
[etc.]

Let's pause here for a minute. Place yourself in my position and assess the letter. Would you make any changes?

At this point, I could give you my recommendations to Beth, but for the sake of illustration, I prefer to share the thought process that led to the recommendations. Thus, I will walk you step by step through my conversation with Beth.

My first response was, "I am extremely impressed! How the heck did you find so quickly the name and phone number of the person who owns the copyright for the song?" Now, keep in mind that this was in a different era—no internet, no Google, no anything! I would have suspected that it would have taken months and months to uncover that, and yet, she did it in two days! She gave me an answer, which I actually don't recall now. But I remember being superbly impressed that a sixteen-year-old could have done it!

My second question was, "His assistant told you that there is no way that he will grant such permission, so why are you sending such a letter?"

Her response was, "There is nothing to lose, is there?"

"No," I said, "but if you're already trying against the odds, why not do something differently from everything that was unsuccessfully tried before?"

"What do you mean, Dad?" she replied.

I said, "Look at your proposed letter. Is there anything in this letter that you believe is unique enough, or that hasn't been tried and said before?"

"I don't know. How would I know what others wrote?" asked Beth.

"Well," I said, "just try to put yourself in everybody else's position and what they would likely use in their letter. Do you think that they will take a different approach? Or do you think they will all do exactly what you are doing in your letter?"

She reflected a minute and said, "I see your point. It would probably be the same kind of a letter, because it is *the best logical approach that can work*!" She emphasized the words "best logical approach" with a smile on her face, believing that she had outsmarted me.

"Correct," I said, "and it would be the best approach under *normal circumstances*, but I'm not sure it would be here."

"Why, what's the difference?" she asked.

I replied, "The difference is very simple, and you fell into the same trap that everybody else would have likely fallen into. Under normal circumstances, you would have no insights whatsoever, and so going with the 'best logical approach' would make the most sense. But, is it the same in your case?"

She was completely puzzled. "What do you mean?" she asked. "What insight do I have?"

Now I put on a big smile and said, "The biggest insight there is! His assistant who has worked for him for the last ten years has told you, in no uncertain terms, that hundreds of such letters have never worked. So, why do you think that writing the same letter, or doing the same thing, would work now for you?"

"I didn't think of that," she said. "You have an interesting point."

"Yes," I said. "Most would have not thought of it."

She said, "Okay, so what can I do? Is there anything that can be done? On second thought, if the 'best logical approach' didn't work, then anything else would be a second choice, which, by definition, would be less preferable to the 'best approach.' So, how could a lesser-than-best approach work better than the best approach?" Good question. I was impressed with her logic, and not just because she was my daughter. Years of trying to teach her how to dissect situations and logic seemed to be paying off.

Okay, let's pause again, and let me ask you the reader to reflect on the above. Was your original approach different? If not, do you agree with the above observations? Do you have any thoughts on how to proceed?

Back to my conversation with Beth. I said, "Well, whatever the approach is, it can't be second to the best. It will have to be better than the best. Otherwise, as you stated, it would be an inferior approach and not likely work."

Again perplexed, she said, "Dad, are you trying to confuse me? If we agree that the letter my teacher wrote was the best approach, how could there be a better than best? If there was a better than best, it means the best was not really the best!"

Again, I was impressed with how she caught on to the nuance. I was actually very proud. "Well," I said, "by completely changing your perspective!"

"What do you mean, Dad?" she asked.

I replied, "Let's look at the situation in front of us. There are two assumptions we can make, based on what the assistant told us. The first and most logical, which I expect everybody will take away from what she said, would be that the copyright holder has no compassion or magnanimity whatsoever. Otherwise, there would have been some exceptions that he would have made over the years for special cases. But she specifically emphasized that no matter what the reasons were, none was approved.

"The second assumption we can make is that perhaps the person may be magnanimous, but there are other reasons that lead him to outright reject all requests. If the first assumption is the real truth, then, tough luck, you will not be getting it either. But what if the second assumption is the correct one?"

"What other reasons can there be?" she asked.

"Well, to see if there might be other reasons, you'll have to put yourself in his shoes and try to see if you might be able to think like he does. If you are able to do so, then you'll know why he turned all the previous requests down and approach him in a way that addresses his real concerns. If you do that, you'll have a much better chance. Do you see the logic and approach here?" I asked. "So, let's start by putting ourselves in his shoes.

"If he is a considerate and magnanimous person, then we can conclude that he would have loved to accommodate such requests, but he doesn't, ever! It means that he must have some very compelling reasons for not doing what otherwise he might have easily been willing to do. Can you think of what his biggest concern might be when faced with granting permission to play the song on TV?"

Beth was unable to think of anything. The few wild guesses she took made no sense.

I said, "I see three major factors; each is enough in its own right to justify turning down automatically any and all requests. More importantly, I believe that these are the true reasons, and that if we find a way to address them, you will stand a much better chance at getting an approval."

"Really, you could think of three and I couldn't have thought of a single one!" she exclaimed.

"Don't feel badly," I said. "You are in the majority. But I've been trying to teach you all these years to try and think differently, but always apply discerning logic. In this specific case, your experience is very limited, so there is no way you could have generated it on your own. Nevertheless, it is a great example and exercise for you to try and do it together with me now."

I started by telling Beth that the first thing to understand is how the copyright holder makes money. "He gets royalties from the song. To get royalties, he needs to give approval and, in exchange, he receives royalties every time the song is played. These are not simple license-royalty agreements; they are complicated. An agreement not only needs to specify the terms and the payments, but it also will have to go into many aspects of defining specific terms and whatever the parties agreed to. For example, the length of time for which the license is granted. How royalty prices will change over time. To whom and how royalty payments be submitted. Are there any cancellation rights or penalties? Such agreements define what recourse the copyright holder has should royalties not be paid. See how complicated a little concept becomes when legal documents must be drafted to capture what was agreed to? It will be pages and pages of documentation that unquestionably requires a lawyer's review. So we can be assured that the copyright holder will never sign anything related to his copyright without having his lawyer draft the documentation.

"So it is now quite obvious why he might never grant requests. Even if he wanted to, it will have to go to a lawyer to draft a legally binding agreement. That costs money, every single time, let alone for hundreds of them a year. There is only one solution to this: Never grant permission."

Beth was quick to see this. "I see where you are going. What if I offered in the letter to pay for the costs?"

"Now you are talking," I said. "But, unfortunately, you don't have enough time to go through the whole process. Let's keep thinking and see if we can find a good solution to all the issues he might have."

I then explained that the second reason reflects the concern that anybody granting a license for anything would have, which is that they could face potential "abuse" by the recipient. I explained that from a legal standpoint, if an entity doesn't have any authorization, it is clear that they are infringing on a copyright and actions to stop them can be immediate. However, once any kind of authorization is granted, then if they break the signed contract and start infringing on it, any attempt to stop it is not immediate. Ceasing such use requires a court proceeding, which might be lengthy and costly. Once the authorization is signed, the person with malicious intent can claim that they have the right to continue. They can make up whatever reasons they want. Under these kinds of circumstances, one will need a court order and lawyers to debate the legitimacy of the claims of each party.

Also, in the original contract, there most likely is a section dealing with potential infringements, and it specifies that if the copyright holder is forced to go to court to enforce their rights, then the infringer is liable for all the legal costs of the copyright holder—that is, assuming that the copyright holder wins the case. If the infringer is a company, then the copyright holder knows that if they file a lawsuit, they will ultimately be able to recoup the legal costs. However, if the infringer is an individual, it would be exceptionally difficult to collect any costs from individuals. So, this fear of potential abuse, by itself, is enough to never sign any authorization with any entity that would not enable an easy and apparent way to enforce infringement judgments.

The third reason is the inconvenience and the "trouble" factor. Assuming that the first two reasons would have not been real concerns and the copyright holder was willing to sign a document that he didn't have to pass by a lawyer, think about what he would have to do then to actually accommodate the request. He would need to dictate a letter, explaining exactly what he is, and is not, authorizing. An assistant then needs to type it up. He'll need to proof it before signing. Then it must be sent in the mail. Well, it might not be much, but still, it is a pain in the butt, which most people would rather avoid, and particularly if it happens a lot and makes no money.

"So," I told Beth, "if there is a solution, it has to address all three of the above issues." I continued, "I would write a completely different letter, based on the conversation so far. Additionally, it must be something that he will feel safe to sign, without needing to forward it to his lawyer. But there is one additional problem that I can't predict, nor control, nor influence much, on such short notice. However, you might be able to, and that would be your part. If you can make it happen, then the probability will increase substantially; otherwise, I'm not so sure it will work, particularly given the short time constraint."

"What is it I need to do?" she asked.

I explained, "The letter could be perfect, *but not if he doesn't get to read it.* I also must assume that, given the hundreds of requests a year that he never responds to, he most likely stopped reading such letters and tosses them as soon as he realizes what they are. Worse yet, he may have already given instructions to his assistant to never pass them on to him."

"So, what can I do?" Beth asked.

I replied, "You have already initiated a phone conversation with his assistant, and it seems like she responded well to you, since in my opinion, she was very patient and gave you quite a bit of her time in a sympathetic way. So, what you need to do is call her again. Be nice and plead and appeal to her to do you one small favor. Be sure to tell her that you fully understand that it might not yield results. But all you are imploring her to do is to put the letter in front of him and tell him that you sounded like a real nice and smart girl, and that is why she brings the letter to his attention. At that point, tell her, 'You would have done all I'm begging of you to do, and I'll be forever grateful.'

"So, as you see," I said, "from this point on, the biggest responsibility is yours. If you succeed, we stand a good chance. If not, well, it was a good try."

We then started composing the letter that I recommended she send. I told her to make sure to send it via FedEx with a returned paid-up FedEx envelope, so the only thing the copyright holder would need to do is to sign the letter and put it in the envelope. Beth seemed to have been quite happy when she left.

The next day she called and told me that she talked to the assistant and that the assistant promised to do what she had asked. "But," said Beth, "I spoke to my teacher and showed her your letter. She thought it was a bad idea and didn't recommend it at all. I'm not sure I explained the reasoning all that well. She insisted that the letter she drafted was a much better approach. Dad, what should I do?"

I asked, "Which letter do you think would be better?" She replied, "I don't know. You are my father, but she is my teacher and I'm confused."

I said, "Beth, for years I told you to seek advice, but I always emphasized that the final judgment must be yours and yours alone. So, think logically, reassess the situation, decide which approach you believe to be a better one, and go with that decision. Good luck to you!"

I can imagine how difficult a decision it must have been for her. At that age, many teenagers believe that their teachers know everything better than the rest of the world, so how do you decide? Ultimately, Beth decided to go with my recommendation. The letter she sent was a two-page letter. The first page was designed to be long enough to make sure that it conveyed all the information to catch his attention and sympathy, but not too long so as to minimize the probability that he'd get impatient in the middle of reading it and just toss it away. The first page was:

[Name]
[Address]
[Date]

Subject: "Hit the Road Jack"—Royalties*

Dear Mr. [Name]:

My name is Beth Kronfeld and I'm a junior at [____] High School. I produced a documentary TV clip about a wonderful human being who works as a collector at a toll booth. The person has worked there for over 20 years. He makes the experience joyous for drivers who pass his booth. He is absolutely beloved by everybody who lives in the vicinity. My segment has won awards in local, regional and state-wide competitions, and recently was selected in a nation-wide competition as one of the 16 finalists. CNN is planning to broadcast live, in three weeks, the selection of the top three. However, I can't proceed to the next level without your kind consideration.

Because it was a segment about a beloved toll booth collector named Jack, I used in the background the song "Hit the Road Jack."

CNN informed me that they will not be willing to accept my clip for the final live competition, unless I obtained a specific permission from the copyright holder of the song. I know that generally it is a complicated contract that requires lawyers. However, please see on the following page a simple release paragraph that grants a one-time

* Author's note: Subject was put here purposefully to suggest a legitimate inquiry for a royalty arrangement.

use, limited to 30 days. It is a special and specific authorization, to use the song only in conjunction with CNN's program related to this competition. It is also worded in a very definitive way to ensure that there is no possibility of any kind of misunderstandings, misinterpretations, or any kind of a potential for "abuse."

I would be extremely thankful for your consideration. Please, read the release paragraph on the following page, and if you are convinced that I presented the release language in an accurate way, I would appreciate your magnanimity.

Thank you so much, for your consideration,
Beth Kronfeld

Page two was as follows:

A limited one-time, special purpose release for the song "Hit the Road Jack"

I [name] am the holder of the copyrighted song "Hit the Road Jack." I hereby grant a special thirty-day permission, from [date to date], to CNN to broadcast, without fee, Beth Kronfeld's TV clip, which plays the above song in the background.

This permission is granted specifically for the above-mentioned clip only. No other broadcasting of any kind is permissible under this release. This release is in no way subject to any time extensions. It will automatically expire on [date].

CNN implicitly agrees, and Beth Kronfeld explicitly agrees, by her signature, that this release cannot be used in any way to claim that the granting of this release implies other agreements or intentions, or understandings, or any other rights, or claims, that are not specifically written in this release.

Signature _____   Signature _____
Name _____   Name <u>Beth Kronfeld</u>
Date _____   Date _____

Beth sent the letter via FedEx. Four days later, I received a call from her. She didn't say, "Hi, Dad," which she normally does. The first thing I heard was, "Dad, you are a genius!" She got the signature; she was excited to no end. At the finals, aired on CNN as planned, she won second place and got to see her creation being played over and over again. She was ecstatic.

In summary, I hope you got a good sense from the four examples in this section of what influencing really entails. I believe that the examples clearly illustrate that the word "influencing" is conceptually easy to understand, but the execution is not so trivial, nor easy. At the end, it all follows simple logic. Practically everything is based on logic and experience. However, please be mindful of what I stated at the beginning of the book, when I defined what insightfulness requires. I emphasized two key words—*correct* and *complete* understanding and analyses. As the last example of the music icon demonstrated so vividly, it may appear simple, but it is not. **Beware, logic oftentimes appears sound and compelling but, unbeknownst to the person, may not always be correct or complete.**

Also, for the sake of completeness, allow me to double-check that I don't leave you with the wrong impression regarding what influencing really means. The examples demonstrated how influencing came into play at the most critical junctures when trying to affect the most important challenge and/or outcome. However, please don't draw the conclusion that influencing is limited to single challenges, outcomes, or events. Although influencing the most important outcome is the crown jewel and the ultimate prize, in practicality, it never happens in isolation. In the same way that a complex piece of machinery will fail when even the most insignificant screw is misaligned, so it is also the case with influencing. **Influencing refers to influencing a process, to the daily ongoing activities that attempt to anticipate and influence nearly every single step (important as well as trivial) along the path of achieving a goal from the very beginning to the very last step.** Some may have a greater effect on the final outcome, while others may be trivial and perhaps even inconsequential. But just like the insignificant screw in the machinery, all have to be tended to and oiled appropriately, at the right time, and with as much care as possible. In other words: **Influencing is a process. It is a constant effort that needs to be applied continuously, from the very beginning to the very end of the process of overcoming a challenge and achieving an objective.**

20

To Learn How to Influence Well, Assume Everything That Goes Wrong Is Your Fault

This advice may sound strange, but it will serve you well. The overall logic for this observation is quite simple. If you believe in the idea that your main goal is to proactively influence outcomes, then by definition any undesired outcome means that you weren't "smart" enough to "avoid" it through influence. Thus, the blame rests with you.

This is true not only for what you unsuccessfully tried to influence, but can be expanded to undesired situations in general, even including things that happen to you without your doing anything, or that were outside of your own control. This may sound like stretching it a bit, but my logic here is that you weren't smart enough to anticipate, recognize, or avoid it, so it is your fault as well.

Now, I'm not suggesting that indeed you are always at fault. You may not be, and you will not be able to influence everything around you. What I'm suggesting is that if you want to develop the art of influencing, you must start with the assumption that you are always at fault for any undesired outcome, regardless. Only when you start with this assumption will you reevaluate every situation and ask yourself how you might have been able to avoid a poor outcome. Did you anticipate everything? Should you have? Did you read all the signs properly? Over time, these introspective analyses will train your mind to anticipate much more and look at many more possible scenarios, beforehand. You will actually be amazed at how much better you will become at proactively influencing outcomes around you. I have experienced it myself.

When I was younger, I first noticed that practically everybody's first instinct for all undesirable outcomes that involved themselves, both in business and personal life, was to blame other people or circumstances. Somehow, it always ended up being the fault of others and never theirs. I'm sure you have seen it yourself, to one degree or another, many times. The next thing I observed, and which took time for me to notice, was that because of blaming others, people learned very little from their mistakes. Clearly, if something is not your fault to begin with, it is not your mistake, thus there is no need for retrospection and reevaluation. I've seen this pattern repeat itself, over and over again. With time and perspective, I also began to see just how damaging this behavior was to a person's own personal growth and career progression. What I didn't see for the longest time was that I, too, was guilty of externalizing blame.

I actually believed that I was different and didn't do what everybody else did. I believed I was much smarter (in terms of being more "right") than the average person I interacted with. So, whenever we reached a disagreement of sorts, it was indeed the other person's fault. They were the "stupid" ones, so it wasn't my mistake, and therefore there was nothing to learn from. It was even worse—I was amazed, bewildered, and just couldn't understand how they never cared to learn from their own mistakes, even after I explained so logically to them where they were wrong in their thought processes.

Truth be told, oftentimes logic may have been on my side. But that is not the point. What I didn't understand at the time was that by focusing on right and wrong, logical or illogical, I was completely blind to the art of influencing. Only when that changed and when I stopped evaluating everything from the perspective of logically right and wrong did I recognize that the issue was not right versus wrong. The issue was that an outcome wasn't achieved, regardless of fault. When the outcome takes precedence over fault or right versus wrong, only then did I put myself in a position to ask the most basic question of them all: Could I have achieved the desired outcome in any other way? That's when and how the art of influencing began for me.

It began first by dissecting outcomes I desired and was unable to achieve. The questions I started asking were, What could I have done better, or differently? Then it followed with anticipating potential conflict situations and proactively trying to influence the outcome. With time, I became better and better at it. However, only much later in life did I expand the definition to assume responsibility for all undesirable situations, including those I had little, if any, control over. I assumed full responsibility and adopted for myself the same advice I am giving you in this chapter. That was the last stage of my learning and becoming more effective at influencing.

There were some extra side benefits to this philosophy of never blaming anybody else but yourself for all undesirable outcomes. Whenever a person believes that they are not at fault, they also tend to become more defensive and confrontational with the people they perceive to be at fault. This brings about two potential problems. First, it is almost impossible to effectively influence when portraying a defensive and confrontational attitude. So, the situation at hand may not get corrected and the desired outcome not likely to be achieved. Second, defensiveness and confrontational attitudes are rarely viewed favorably in the business world. A person developing such a reputation will most likely slow down or even damage their career progression. Assume responsibility, per my recommendation, and you not only significantly increase the opportunity after the fact to correct an undesirable outcome, but you will also likely help your career progression.

21

The Art of Influencing Through Questions

As I mentioned in the previous section, my definition of "influencing" did not embody any interpersonal skills, behavioral science, or other psychological techniques and methods. Clearly, those could be complementary and can be effective in helping influence people and, as a result, outcomes. So, educating yourself on those could prove to be beneficial and indeed likely to enhance your ability to influence. Also, as I mentioned, I have no expertise in behavioral science, and my interpersonal skills are actually quite poor compared to my peers. However, there is one aspect that relates to communication skills that I can address with confidence and that I believe would help you substantially when interacting with other people where there might be potential for tension, resistance, and conflict. It specifically deals with how to minimize these reactions in situations where you communicate a different position from someone else, or somewhat "correct" someone else. It is effective in a one-on-one conversation or in group discussions.

One need not be a behavioral scientist to know that most people instinctively react internally somewhat negatively and defensively when faced with disagreements. The question is how much of this instinctive internal reaction comes out to the surface and becomes apparent with a real defensive behavior. This reaction becomes even more intense when a person has first communicated a rationale for their position, only to have it undermined by more compelling logic by someone else.

There are probably many reasons for such a negative/defensive reaction. In my opinion, it mostly stems from being challenged in the first place, or being made to feel stupid. An opinion the presenter believes significant doesn't seem to matter much and is summarily dismissed. In our mind, somebody has just told us, "I disagree with your assessment and logic. I think that you are completely wrong, and you don't know what you are talking about. Let me tell you why I think so, and then I'll give you the right solution." So, any communication, verbal and otherwise, that gives rise to such interpretations will elicit defensiveness. On the other hand, any communication that can mitigate such an interpretation can help eliminate defensiveness.

Obviously, any defensiveness and resistance potentially stand in the way of effectively influencing another person. So, a question arises as to whether there are ways by which to reduce such an instinctively negative response when communicating a dissenting view. Clearly there are, and most are related to psychological and behavioral science factors. Understanding them and perhaps utilizing them is definitely something I would recommend. However, I'd like to suggest to you a simple and always applicable technique that I believe is one of the more effective ways to avert a likely negative reaction when the need arises to disagree with someone's perspective or solution. This technique involves the use of questions. Anybody can do it effectively. It always works, and works well.

Understanding the trigger points for such defensive and negative reactions will help better define the remedies. In my opinion, there are two important factors that are most likely to affect the severity of the negative and defensive reactions: general demeanor and the articulation used by the disagreeing party. I'll address them separately.

General Demeanor

We always react to the demeanor we face. We tend to become more aggressive, argumentative, and closed-minded when faced with an aggressive demeanor, and more relaxed and open-minded when facing a relaxed and friendly one. Thus, the first step in avoiding a negative reaction is to understand what may contribute to a perception of an aggressive demeanor versus a relaxed, more friendly one. The following is a partial list of the most common postures or gestures that evoke a reaction on the part of a listener. In general, the more intense the gesture, the more severe the negative and defensive reaction and vice versa.

Aggressive Gestures	Friendly Gestures
Tense, combative body posture	Relaxed posture
Serious countenance	Smiling countenance
Intense look	Casual, "normal" eye contact, with a smile
Display of anger, irritation, or disapproval	Expression of empathy and understanding
Loud or raised voice	Quiet, soft-spoken voice
Quick cadence of the voice	Slower cadence
Restlessness, or impatient demeanor	Calm, patient demeanor
Exaggerated/dramatic hand gestures	Gesture of approval, like nodding the head
Pointing the index finger	Patting listener's arm, when naturally done
Being stubborn and closed-minded	Being sympathetic and open-minded
Continually disagreeing	Continually demonstrating agreements
Standing too close to the listener	Respecting personal space
Interrupting the other person	Being fully present to the other person

Articulation

How we articulate our position, and specifically with respect to disagreements, is an important element in the reaction we evoke from a listener. There are two aspects to articulation that matter most in situations like this: "preemptive/disarming" statements and the actual articulation of the specific disagreement. The preemptive/disarming articulation aims to communicate positive gestures to evoke a positive state of mind before communicating the negative disagreement, thereby counterbalancing or reducing from the severity of the defensiveness that might follow when articulating the disagreement.

In the disarming phase, we aim to preemptively address the potential negative interpretation by stating up front that the other person is not being challenged and that their opinion is always respected. There are many ways to articulate and accomplish the preemptive part. Some are more effective than others, but any is better than none.

In the second phase, when articulating disagreements, we need to recognize that the exact words and phrasing we use will evoke either positive or negative reactions and affect the intensity level of such reactions. So, being wise with how we articulate our disagreement is the key to getting the outcome we desire.

Below, for demonstration purposes, are some examples of phrases and words that elicit different degrees of intensity and reaction. They are presented in the order of the least sensitive (most offensive) to the most sensitive (least offensive), or those that evoke the most intense defensive reactions to those that disarm the best. I selected these examples to illustrate the wide range and many nuances involved, just to conceptually illustrate how it might work. The list also points out that even a small variation can be impactful. Avoid using the words and phrases in the beginning of the list, as they are the most offensive. Rather, always try to use the concepts demonstrated toward the end of the list, and you will go a long way toward disarming defensiveness.

- "You are wrong!"

- "I completely disagree!"

- "What you said doesn't make sense!"

- "I disagree."

- "What you said is incorrect."

- "What you said is not logical."

- "What you said may not be completely logical."

- "You are not right."

- "What you said is not completely right."

- "What you said may not be completely right."

- "I understand what you said, but it may not be completely accurate."

- "What you said is interesting, but it might not be as applicable in our situation."

- "What you said made sense, but it is not applicable in this situation."

- "What you said made sense, but it might not be as applicable in this specific case."

- "What you said made sense; however, our case may be different."

- "What you said made sense; however, there might be additional considerations that need to be addressed."

- "What you said makes a lot of sense and I agree with much of it; however, I believe that there are some mitigating factors that also need to be considered."

- "What you said makes a lot of sense and I agree with much of it; however, I believe that we also need to consider some additional factors."

- "What you said makes a lot of sense and I agree with much of it; however, I wonder whether we need to consider some additional factors."

- "What you said made a lot of sense, but I'm not sure if I'm completely convinced. Here is my concern."

However, there is one approach that is the most effective in not only disarming defensiveness, but that will also prepare the other party to accept the rationale for your position. It is this approach that I'm recommending you use as often as you can. It is done through raising "guiding" questions, rather than stating an absolute position and rationale. You point out through "innocent" questions the flaws in the logic you heard, while at the same time raising the potential solution, and then you ask the listener for their opinion. Since there was no disagreement, per se, and since the listener responded to questions and ended up "formulating" the final solution, they therefore "own" it. After all, it is their solution and they will accept it wholeheartedly, even though it was different from their initial position. This is the art of influencing through questions at work!

Although very easy in concept, most will find this approach hard in practice. The biggest reason is that this approach denies you the instinctive desire and opportunity to show just how smart you are. This is so because asking the questions does not imply that you also know the solution or answer, even though you do. Instead, you allow the listener to come up with the right conclusion, and thus they will receive credit for it. Worse yet, as far as you are concerned, the person who got the credit didn't even deserve it, because the solution they proposed was incorrect and without your guidance they would not have arrived at the right one.

The best advice I can give you regarding the above trade-off is *to do it regardless*! First, and most importantly, is the fact that this is the best way to "influence," and per the advice offered in the previous section, the best way in the long haul to advance your own career is to lose the occasional battle but to win the war.

However, the most illuminating observation I would like to leave with you is that **the perception that you may deny yourself credit with this approach is wrong!** You may perceive it this way, but everybody else will have understood exactly what you have done and that you must have known the answer to raise the questions in the first place. So, in reality, you will not only be able to influence in the best way, but you will also be getting the full credit for your smarts. Better yet, you'll get additional credit for being a team player with wise interpersonal skills—a win-win-win situation overall.

The only thing left to conclude this chapter is to give you some examples to illustrate how to apply this questions approach. Clearly, to have a good "guiding" question, it must also incorporate some of the correct response. Otherwise, you may run a risk of not arriving at the right outcome. This will become apparent shortly.

There are many ways by which questions could be stated. There can be more questions, each "guiding" in small increments, or fewer questions, each "guiding" with more complete observations, or even a single question with the full solution embedded in the question. It really doesn't matter which approach you use, because they all work well. The fewer the questions, the more of the solution needs to be embodied in each of the questions.

Different situations and circumstances may call for different approaches, and of course you may mix and match, as you feel appropriate. Keep in mind that I'm referring here to real questions, where you expect the listener to respond, and not to rhetorical questions where you don't expect an answer.

The following example will demonstrate the questions approach. I will use the debate I had with the placement director at Wharton regarding resume writing and job interviews as the framework. I offer various levels of response to illustrate how this method works.

Placement director's claim: "You should always study the financial statements of the company you will be interviewing with. Discover some performance-related issues the financial statements reveal and bring them up with the interviewer. You'll benefit in two ways: First, you will show the interviewer that you are smart and can use what you learned at Wharton to the practical benefit of the company; and second, you will show the interviewer that you have a very strong interest in working for the company, as demonstrated by the fact that you took the necessary time to study and prepare in advance of the interview. As everybody knows, showing strong interest in a company is very important, since no company will extend a job offer to a candidate who didn't display interest, excitement, and enthusiasm for potentially working there."

Response 1: Unconditionally Critical
(most offensive—doesn't use the questions approach)

Candidate: "I completely disagree with you on both observations. Let's start with your first reason. I tried it and I was laughed off. In reality, the interviewer became angry. In one case, I raised an issue with the performance of one of the divisions and the response I got was, 'I work for a different division; how would you expect me to know the answer?' On another occasion, I asked about the performance of the corporation in an attempt to avoid the previous awkward situation from happening, but it didn't help much. The response was, 'I have no idea; I work for the marketing department. Your question would be best addressed to somebody in the finance department.' So, you see, your recommendation is faulty and may result in a candidate being dismissed outright.

"Regarding your second reason, I find it hard to believe and completely illogical that a company will offhandedly reject an otherwise great candidate just because they didn't advertise that they had dedicated extra time to studying the company's financial statements in advance of the interview. Everybody knows that all students look at alternatives and that, in the end, the company will need to 'sell' itself and convince the candidate that they present an attractive opportunity for the candidate. So, whether a student knows more or less about a company's financial statements in the interview is not all that critical. The qualifications of the candidate and how they perform during the interview are the most critical factors. However, I will partially agree with what you said about showing interest. Indeed, no company will extend a job offer unless they believe that the candidate is highly interested and is excited about working there. But this would be important at the end of the interviewing process, not the very beginning, which often is conducted by a lower-level employee whose real aim is to provide an initial go/no-go screening of all the potential candidates. Besides, there are much better, more direct, and more effective ways to communicate interest in, excitement about, and enthusiasm for potentially working at a company than using a surrogate like spending the time to study the financial statements in advance of the interview. So, although it couldn't hurt to study the financial statements of a company in advance of an interview, I would not characterize it as being imperative."

Response 2: Conditionally Critical
(less offensive—no questions used)

Candidate: "Your recommendations make a lot of sense, but I wonder if there might be some potential pitfalls that need to be considered. The pitfalls stem from the possibility that the interviewer may not know the answer to the questions/issues raised. For example, the questions are financially related, yet the interviewer may work in a completely different department. Or if the interviewer works in the finance department, they may not have the level of experience to know how to respond. In such situations, the questions raised may backfire. The interviewer might conclude the candidate has little common sense for asking the wrong questions of the wrong person. There are other, more effective ways to show enthusiasm in an interview itself. So, in my mind, why take the risk?

"Regarding your second reason, indeed, you are correct; a company will not likely extend an offer to a candidate who hasn't shown excitement and enthusiasm for working at the firm. However, I wonder whether showing this kind of enthusiasm is imperative at the beginning of the interviewing process, or perhaps becomes imperative toward the end of the process. I find it hard to believe that a company will offhandedly reject an otherwise qualified candidate just because they didn't demonstrate they spent time studying the company's financial statements in advance of the interview. Everybody knows that students look at other options and that it is up to a company to 'sell' itself to the candidate. So, whether a student knows more or less about a company in the initial interview is not that critical. The qualifications of the candidate and how they perform during the interview are the most critical factors. Although it couldn't hurt to study the financial statements of a company in advance of an interview, I would not characterize it as being imperative. Besides, there are much better, more direct, and more effective ways to communicate interest in, excitement about, and enthusiasm for potentially working at a company than using a surrogate that might imply interest."

Response 3: Using the Questions Approach (with more questions, each with less guidance)

Candidate: "I understand what you are recommending. It is very logical and makes a lot of sense. I have a couple of questions on the two recommendations you made: What if I ask a question about some financial issues and for whatever reason the interviewer doesn't know the answer?"

Director: "Oh, of course you need to make sure that the interviewer is in a position to know the answer."

Candidate: "How would I do so?"

Director: "Ask the interviewer about their role in the firm before you ask your questions."

Candidate: "Wouldn't it be difficult to ascertain this in practical terms?"

Director: "Why would it?"

Candidate: "It appears to me that there are too many variables involved. Let's say I study the company in advance and find a financial performance issue with a division of the company. So, if the interviewer doesn't work for that division, then it follows that I should not ask the question, correct?"

Director: "Correct. You would be better off to find issues related to the corporate level and not divisions."

Candidate: "Yes, that makes a lot of sense. But what if I ask a corporate-level question and the interviewer doesn't work for the finance department? Would they know the answer? Would it not be a mistake, too?"

Director: "Of course it would. You need to make sure that they work for the finance department."

Candidate: "But what if they are a lower-level financial analyst and might not be aware of the issue or know the answer? Would it not be better to avoid asking them, too?"

Director: "Probably."

Candidate: "Do you believe that the benefit of asking the questions in the first place—to show one's smarts in finance—outweighs the potential risk of alienation that might happen because the question was asked of the wrong person?"

Director: "You know, you are bringing up an interesting point. On second thought, maybe we are better off not asking such questions in the first place."

Candidate: "Regarding your second point that it is important to show that the candidate is interested in working for a company, I wholeheartedly agree. However, I wonder, do you believe that if a company finds a very attractive candidate, they will dismiss him or her offhandedly just because they didn't show that they studied the company's financial statements in advance of the interview?"

Director: "Well, it is not the studying per se; rather, the candidate is illustrating their interest in the company."

Candidate: "I got it. Clearly, no company will make an offer to a candidate who doesn't show strong interest in working for it. But is it critical to show such interest in the beginning of the interviewing process, which is generally done with a lower-level employee, or toward the end of the process, right before the company is ready to extend an offer?"

Director: "You should do it throughout!"

Candidate: "Of course, it is better throughout, but the question is whether it is *imperative* to study the financial statements in advance of the interviews, and even at the beginning of the interviewing process?"

Director: "What do you mean by 'imperative'?"

Candidate: "Well, imperative means that by not doing so the candidate will most likely not advance to the next level of the process, even if otherwise they are most qualified and came across very impressively in the interview session itself."

Director: "Well, I wouldn't say that it is that imperative, but it doesn't cost much, and it does add value to do so, so why not?"

Candidate: "I understand this and it makes sense, but aren't there better, more direct, and more effective ways to communicate interest, excitement, and enthusiasm for the job and the company through appropriate body gestures and directly stating so face to face, as opposed to using a 'surrogate' that might imply the same?"

Director: "Yeah, it would be better."

Candidate: "So, what I hear you say is that although it couldn't hurt to study the financial statements of a company in advance of an interview, you would not characterize it as being imperative. You also believe that there are much better, more direct, and more effective ways to communicate interest, excitement, and enthusiasm in potentially working at a company. In other words, what you are saying is that although it couldn't hurt to study the financial statements of a company in advance of an interview, you would not characterize it as being imperative and would recommend caution in how to use the information you gleaned via questions."

Director: "That's exactly what I am saying."

Response 4: Using the Questions Approach (with fewer questions, each providing more guidance)

Candidate: "I understand what you are recommending. It is very logical and makes a lot of sense. I have a couple of questions on the two observations you made. I wonder whether there might be a potential pitfall in the event that the questions are raised with the wrong person who may not be able to answer them properly."

Director: "What do you mean?"

Candidate: "Let's say I discover a financial issue with one of the divisions, but the interviewer doesn't work in that division. How would they be able to respond to the question? Or, say I discover a corporate-level financial issue, but the interviewer doesn't work for the finance department. Or, say the interviewer works for the finance department, but is a lower-level employee with no knowledge of the issue I raise. Wouldn't they think that I demonstrated a lack of common sense by asking the wrong question of the wrong person? Wouldn't it diminish my standing somewhat?"

Director: "Yes, of course you need to make sure that you raise those questions only with the people who are in a position to respond to them appropriately."

Candidate: "Yes, that makes a lot of sense. Given that concern, do you believe that the benefit of asking the questions in the first place—to show one's interest in the company—outweighs the potential risk of alienation that might occur should the question be asked of the wrong person? Also, wouldn't it be better to communicate and articulate interest, excitement, and enthusiasm for a company through gestures and directly stating so during the interviews than through an implied interest?"

Director: "You know, you are bringing up an interesting point. Yes, it probably would be better."

Candidate: "So, what I hear you say is that although it couldn't hurt to study the financial statements of a company in advance of an interview, you would not characterize it as being imperative. You also believe that there are much better, more direct, and more effective ways to communicate interest, excitement, and enthusiasm and that candidates should keep that in mind during the interviewing process. Additionally, you are saying that although it couldn't hurt to study the financial statements of a company in advance of an interview, you would recommend caution in raising questions about them unless you are certain that the interviewer would know the answer."

Director: "That's exactly what I am saying."

Response 5: A Single Question (provides the full solution)

Candidate: "I understand what you are recommending. It is very logical and makes a lot of sense. I wonder whether there might be a potential pitfall in the event that the questions are raised with the wrong person, who may not be able to answer them properly. Let's say I discover a financial issue with one of the divisions, but the interviewer doesn't work in that division. How would they be able to respond to the question? Or, say I discover a corporate-level financial issue, but the interviewer doesn't work for the finance department. Or, say they work for the finance department, but at a lower level of responsibility and so they have no knowledge of the issue I raise. Wouldn't they think that I demonstrated a lack of common sense by asking the wrong question of the wrong person? Wouldn't it diminish my standing somewhat? It raises the question of whether the benefit of asking the questions in the first place, which are meant to show one's interest in the company, outweighs the potential risk of alienation that might happen because the question was asked of the wrong person. Also, wouldn't it be better to communicate and articulate interest, excitement, and enthusiasm for a company through gestures and directly stating so during the interviews instead of using the surrogate of studying the financial statements in advance of an interview, which, only at best, may imply interest?"

Director: "You know, you are bringing up an interesting point. Yes, it probably would be better."

Candidate: "So, what I hear you say is that although it couldn't hurt to study the financial statements of a company in advance of an interview, you would not characterize it as being imperative. There are much better, more direct, and more effective ways to communicate interest and enthusiasm in an interview. Additionally, you recommend using caution with bringing up questions about financial statements, because candidates must make sure to raise such questions only with interviewers who are sure to know the answer."

Director: "That's exactly what I am saying."

To summarize: **When communicating a disagreement, always first acknowledge that you heard the other person's rationale and that it has merit. Only then proceed with stating your position.**

When communicating a disagreement, always be sensitive to your body gestures and actual articulation. Be as sensitive as possible in such communication. The best way is through raising questions, rather than stating positions.

Finally, this approach works not just in direct face-to-face communications; it has just as much value in written ones. Also, it should be applied not just in a case where there are complete disagreements and where one is right and the other wrong. It is just as valuable in situations where there is a partial disagreement, or only minor corrections and adjustments to one's point of view.

SUCCESSFUL NEGOTIATIONS

22

Successful Negotiations: The Art of Compromising Without a Compromise

Successful negotiation is an intricate process. There are many factors that play a role in whether the outcome is successful or not. An entire book can be devoted to the intricacies behind successful negotiations. I do not intend to teach you how to become a better negotiator, but merely to bring a couple of nuanced observations to your attention, which I believe will significantly increase the probability of reaching successful outcomes. My observations apply to transactional business negotiations, although they may affect other situations as well.

Notice that I said "reaching successful outcomes" and not "out-negotiating the other party" or "winning over the other party." I didn't say "negotiating a good deal" or "how to avoid a bad deal." My focus is on how to avoid failures in reaching any agreement and walking away from a potential deal altogether, or the corollary, which is how to reach successful outcomes.

In my view, when two sides enter business negotiations and such negotiations do not produce a successful outcome, then both sides have lost! This is particularly so if there were ways to avoid an unsuccessful outcome. I am not suggesting that there are ways to ensure that failures never happen. What I can tell you is that, from my experience, a large number of failed negotiations could have been salvaged. It is those kinds of situations that I would like to make you aware of and to help you avoid. I believe that my suggestions will not only allow you to salvage an otherwise failed negotiation, but will also make you a much better overall negotiator as well.

I've negotiated business transactions for the better part of my career. I was responsible for all business transactions for a large corporation as the vice president of mergers, acquisitions, and investments. Subsequently, as a venture capitalist, as you may surmise, I have been involved in hundreds, if not thousands, of transactional business negotiations. I have experienced a lot, noticed a lot, and learned a lot. There are two specific nuances that I'd like to discuss in this section, and both are, in my view, rarely discussed in business literature and both could be critical to a successful outcome. The first observation is about the person who *really* makes the final decision to accept or reject a deal with the other side. It is not who you might assume it is. You might assume that the person with final say in a negotiation is the highest-level executive. Technically, you might be correct. Indeed, the buck stops with that executive. However, my intent was not to ask an obvious question; it was to raise a nuanced question, with a nuanced answer, but with a fundamental implication about how to avoid failed negotiations for reasons that could have been avoided. To ask the question properly and accurately, I should have asked instead, "Who may have veto power that even the top-level executives would be reluctant to overrule?"

I am not looking for some clever interpretation of my question. Neither am I looking for some obscure *éminence grise* in the organizational structure who may have the legitimate ability to formally veto the top executive. This is not a mysterious person. All are aware of this person, but few give it a second thought. This person is each of the lawyers assigned to the negotiation team, on both sides. (Just as an aside and for the purpose of completeness, when the deal involves technical issues, then the technical experts on the team will also have such a veto power, but this fact is not pertinent in the context of this chapter.)

Thus, the first nuanced observation is: **The lawyers advising the negotiating team, regardless of title, position, and importance in the organizational hierarchy, have an informal veto power that not even top-level executives will likely ignore.**

Legal advice is just that—advice. The giving of advice implies that a final decision rests with the person who receives the advice. This is true in most cases, but there may be exceptions. Legal advice is normally presented with various alternatives and their legal implications, according to the lawyer's expert opinion. The businessperson will weigh legal advice and the implied business trade-offs and make the call on which alternatives to accept and which to ignore or reject. However, there is a redline no businessperson, not even the top executive, will cross. The redline is drawn by the lawyers should they say, "I would definitely not recommend moving forward or accepting what is in front of us." Or even in more subtle ways, like, "I really don't like this option, or the alternative." Or, "The risk here appears too high." Even though technically it is just a recommendation, de facto it becomes a definitive position for the executive.

What makes the above so important from my perspective is the fact that most deals that fail do so for two overall reasons. The first one falls in the domain of the business team and its inability to reach proper compromise on the overall business terms. The second one falls in the domain of the lawyers and their inability to reach agreement on the myriad of the nitty-gritty details behind the business deal that need to be captured in the text of the final agreement. This is when the adage "the devil is in the details" truly comes to life.

In my experience, sometimes (perhaps even often) negotiations fail because the lawyers and their business teams have different styles of communication and approaches to negotiations. Thus, the key questions are: What is the difference? How does it lead to obstacles and potentially failed negotiations? And, more importantly, can it be averted?

The answer lies in understanding how lawyers think and behave, and how redlines are drawn by the negotiating team. Understand this and you are much more likely to come up with alternatives that will avoid bringing a negotiation to a premature close. Thus, by definition, you'll increase the rate of successful outcomes and reduce the rate of failed outcomes.

Lawyers are trained to see nuances and exceptions to practically everything. They are adept at dissecting sentences and finding words to alter a point so that it becomes acceptable to both sides. At the same time, practically every lawyer when writing up their first version of their draft will word it in a way that gives them the greatest "protection" and minimizes their own "legal exposure." Clearly, they understand that it would be unacceptable to the other side, since the other side would want the exact opposite. The lawyers understand this well, and expect further negotiations. It is just the way legal negotiations work.

However, while lawyers are very good and adept at slicing and dicing the language, defining and redefining, and allowing for exceptions, the businesspeople who do the actual negotiations are not as adept at doing the same.

A problem may arise when the business negotiation team gets the legal briefings and advice. The team is made aware of legally sensitive issues that they need to protect, or get as concessions from the other side. At this point, the lawyers do what they always do—they describe the legal position that needs to be maintained with the broadest protections possible. When the other side is not sensitive to an issue, they will yield to the broader protection. Conversely, if they see the broader protections as detrimental to their position, they will not accept them. However, unlike the lawyers, who can easily adjust the language to reach amicable compromises, businesspeople are not equipped to work with nuances of language to reach compromise, so they insist on maintaining the original language and guidance given to them by their lawyers. Thus, a potential for a deadlock exists.

A similar problem may arise not because of legal briefings, but for the exact same tendency. Businesspeople know what they will *not* compromise on, no matter what, which is their redline from a business negotiation standpoint. However, since they are not very adept at using language to refine the final definitions of the redlines, they define them in very broad terms. So, instead of fighting a "battle" for a narrowly defined position, they fight a broadly defined position—a whole "front." Clearly, the broader the definition, the more likely a conflict will arise, increasing the likelihood of irreconcilable differences. An example by way of a metaphor will help illustrate what I mean.

The Tale of Two Armies

Assume two armies have an informal truce. They are not in a state of war, but they do consider each other a potential threat. Neither side wants to escalate the situation on the ground. There is one area in the desert where a river flows within the territory of one army. Off the river, a small irrigation channel has been dug, which crosses over into the territory of the opposing army and is the main source of drinking water for them. The army controlling the territory of the river considers the river a strategically important barrier.

The distance from the front to the river is half a mile. The army that controls the river territory has little defensive capability should the river be breached. As a result, the top general issues a directive to all the units along the river to defend the front at all costs and not allow the other army to reach the river. The order says, "Fight to the death, if necessary."

Imagine that a captain responsible for the small but vital sector of the front, where the channel crosses into the territory of the other army, sees a large unit from the opposing army approaching his defensive line. The officer in charge of the approaching army unit approaches the captain under the protection of a white flag to deliver a message, with the hope of avoiding an all-out war. Below are a number of scenarios that together will help clearly demonstrate the point I'm trying to make. For the metaphor, assume that the top general at headquarters is a lawyer in the business world and the officers are the negotiation teams.

Scenario I: The officer with the approaching force tells the captain, "We must have access to the river. We are ready to die to do so. Allow us to get there and we can avoid a war." The captain sends the following message to his general: "Enemy approached us. They are ready to die if we don't let them get to the river. What should we do?" The response is predictable: "Are you crazy? You must not allow the enemy to reach the river. Fight to the death, if necessary." A war breaks out subsequently.

Scenario II: Same as scenario I, but the defending officer attempts to understand why the other army is ready to start a war over this. So, he asks the aggressor officer, "Why is it so important for you to reach the river?" The answer is, "I have no idea. My superior officer told me to get to the river and control the access to the river. He said fight to the death, if necessary." The captain sends the following message to his general: "Enemy approached us. They are ready to die if we don't let them control access to the river. What should we do?" The response is predictable: "Are you crazy? You must not allow the enemy any beachhead at the river. Fight to the death, if necessary." A war breaks out subsequently.

Scenario III: Same as scenario II, only this time the aggressor officer responds to the question asked in the following way: "The irrigation channel that flows into our territory was accidentally poisoned. We have no other source of drinking water. We will die from thirst unless we have access to the river. We have nothing to lose. We'll fight to the death to get access to the river, but I can assure you that we have no intention to cross the river and attack you."

The captain sends the following message to his general: "Enemy approached us. They told us that the irrigation channel was accidentally poisoned. They have no other source of drinking water. They face death unless they get access to our river. They promise that they will never attack us. They are ready to die otherwise. They will fight to the death. What should I do?"

The response is likely to be, "I feel sorry for them, and hate to see them die from thirst. But I don't trust them enough to place us in such a vulnerable position where they have a beachhead from which they may possibly one day decide to attack. You must not allow them any beachhead at the river. Fight to the death, if necessary." A war breaks out subsequently.

Scenario IV: Same as scenario III, but one or both of the officers is not a pedestrian thinker. So an additional conversation ensues, as follows: "Would you accept another option to get the water you need? Would you still demand a beachhead at the river?" The aggressor officer sends a message to his superior officer (assume the superior officer is a lawyer for the other side): "If we get all the water we need in another way, would we still need to fight to establish a beachhead?" The superior officer responds, "What is the other way of getting drinking water, and can you guarantee that we can get as much as we need?"

The conversation continues between the two officers who are trying to avoid a war. The captain says, "Let me explain our situation. We don't want, and will not try, to stop you from having drinking water. We also don't care all that much about that little narrow irrigation ditch that gives you access to drinking water. What we really care about is your potential ability to then cross the river and attack us. I will fight to the death to stop you from doing that. Keep in mind that this is exactly the reason why we established our front line half a mile past the river, giving us a safety zone. This guarantees that you don't have any access to the river and therefore will never be able to cross it. So, I can give you access, as long as I have a guarantee that you will not be in a position to attack us. A promise is not enough for us." Both officers then begin to think of ways by which the armies can get what they want, thereby avoiding a war. I can think of a number of different ways of accommodating the most essential sensitivities of both sides, without compromising anything important to either side, yet avoiding a war. Following is just one example.

Assume the following messages are written by each of the opposing officers. The captain sends the following message to his general: "Enemy approached us. They told us that the irrigation channel on their side was accidentally poisoned. They have no other source of drinking water. They face death unless they get access to drinking water. They will fight to the death if they don't. There is a way to avoid war, if we allow them, under our escort, to drive their water trucks each morning to the river to fill them up with water. Can I commit to this solution, or should I prepare for an all-out war?"

The other officer writes to his superior officer, "The enemy is ready to allow us as much access to drinking water as we need. However, they would like to do it in a different way that addresses their concerns. They will let our water trucks drive to the river to fill up, each and every single day. This will avoid war. Can I agree to these terms?"

Of course, both officers would get approval for this solution and so avoid a conflict. This situation happens all the time in business negotiations. Just substitute the word "war" with a terminated or failed negotiation.

As in this example, businesses have specific things they want to protect or achieve at all costs. These things become their redlines. To do so, either because of initial lawyers' briefings, or lazy thinking on the part of higher-level executives, the negotiators draw a wider circle around these specific points, thereby establishing a kind of safety zone. The circles then become the "front lines" for the negotiating team; as in our example, the front was half a mile from the river itself.

As I mentioned earlier, businesspeople are not adept at digging into the reasons behind the way the front is established to see if some adjustments are possible. Those who can do it generally find a way to avoid a hopeless conflict. All it takes is a little redefinition of the front without having to compromise on anything important. In most cases, they will have enough of a safety zone between the boundaries of a specific point and the broader circles drawn to allow for creative adjustments. Most negotiators are "pedestrian" thinkers who often don't think deeply enough to find creative alternatives. Or, like the officers at the front in some of the scenarios, they may not even know that it might be possible.

To avoid failures of this kind, first **make sure that the difference between the specific points and the safety zone of the other side is understood. Then, seek creative ways to find solutions, which will narrow or bend the safety zone circles, but still fully protect the real specific points of sensitivity.**

My experience has proven to me that, in most cases, it is absolutely possible to avert such "wars" in business negotiations. That is why I selected as the title of this chapter "Successful Negotiations: The Art of Compromising Without a Compromise." Below are a couple of real-life examples to further illustrate this point.

Defining Broad, Counterproductive Redlines

In the late 1990s, a large corporation developed a new technology in its research and development department. The company internally funded and launched a start-up company to bring the product to market. Typical of larger corporations, it overstaffed the start-up with new hires and layered it with a top-heavy bureaucracy (which venture capitalists would never allow at the very early stages of a start-up). Such staffing included internal lawyers, accountants to see that all of the corporate-required financial reporting was adhered to, human resources personnel, a full contingency of salespeople, numerous layers of management, and well-furnished offices.

The start-up didn't perform to expectations in the first couple of years, which is not surprising. However, the excessive (and unnecessary) overhead costs generated large losses for the corporation. The executive of the parent company decided to sell the start-up to avoid further and future losses. To avoid potential legal liabilities with the managers and employees of the start-up, the parent company resorted to a common practice in those days: It offered management the opportunity to buy the start-up and own it outright (a management buyout).

The management team and employees usually view very favorably such opportunities to become independent entrepreneurs. As such, they would end up personally owning 20 percent of the new company, which was a standard incentive offered by venture capital firms. All the management team needed to do was find a venture capital firm that would be willing to meet the parent company's purchase price and commit to fund the start-up's operations from that point on. That is how the start-up opportunity came to my firm's attention.

The management team gave us an impressive pitch. We assessed that the technology and product had great potential. We also saw ways to reduce overhead costs significantly. We told the management team that our interest was strong and initiated our intensive due diligence process, which took about four weeks. Then we told the management team that we were ready to proceed with the buyout. The management team was ecstatic.

We made a formal offer to the corporation (the parent company) that contained a summary of terms. Of course, it was subject to the final negotiations of the purchase agreement and additional due diligence by us. The corporation agreed to our term sheet, and we both signed it.

We immediately started working on the documentation of the final purchase agreement. As is typical in situations like this, the management team of the start-up was our negotiating team. A few days later, we got the first draft of the purchase agreement from the corporation's legal department.

As I read the draft, I came across a clause that both surprised me and gave me concern. I had never seen such a clause before in any buyout situation. The clause stated that both the start-up and the corporation would have ownership of the intellectual property (IP) for all the existing and future technology of the start-up. The practice almost always is that the purchaser of the start-up has outright ownership of all of the IP. I thought the clause had been inserted in error.

I called the CEO of the start-up, who was responsible for the negotiations with the corporation, and told him that this clause was inserted in error and to make sure it was removed. I never gave it another thought. Then he called a couple of hours later and told me that the corporation's lawyers refused to either remove or make any changes to the clause. The lawyers insisted that IP ownership was a condition for the buyout. Obviously, this would be crossing a redline for us.

I asked the CEO whether he was aware of this condition beforehand. He said yes. I was flabbergasted. I asked him why did he not make it clear to us earlier on, before we launched our due diligence process. His answer was that he didn't think it was such a big deal. After all, it allowed us to do whatever we wanted to do with the IP, *as if* we owned it solely. It didn't limit us in any way.

I explained to him that it may be as simple as that from his perspective, but it was not from ours. I proceeded to explain to him that the endgame for us was "exiting" the investment, either through taking the company public (IPO), thereby allowing all shareholders to "exit" and cash out by selling their shares on the stock market, or by outright acquisition—that is, selling the company to another company for cash. The clause regarding common IP ownership might not be much of a problem if we had an IPO, but it would be a showstopper for any exit through an acquisition. An acquiring company would want complete and untethered control over the IP. A shared ownership would not be acceptable. I asked the CEO to explain our position to the lawyers and have the clause removed.

The following day, he called and told me that the lawyers were adamant that the clause remain intact. However, the lawyers were willing to add language to the effect that the parent company would not build a competing product to ours. They believed that such a qualification should satisfy all of our concerns.

They were completely ignorant of our concern and perspective. Their response is analogous to the scenario where the approaching army said that it only needed a small beachhead and promised never to attack or cross the river. My response was exactly the same response of the general's, which is that nobody would be willing to assume the risk and trust the other side's stated intent. No potential buyer would accept that kind of a vulnerability. I again requested removal of the clause.

His next call made it clear the lawyers would not budge. Their response kept making absolutely no sense to me. If they never planned to use that technology to compete with us, why would they insist on owning it? I asked the CEO whether he knew of any reason that would cause them to be so unreasonable. He said he had no idea why the lawyers insisted on co-ownership. I notified him that we would not proceed with the deal and asked that he send it up the chain of command and out of the corporate legal department. I assumed that the lawyers may just be unreasonable, and that any higher-level executive would see our side of the issue. The CEO promised to do so.

A couple of days later, the CEO called back and told me that the president was notified, but the situation continued to remain a redline for them. I told him that there must be a reason as to why it was of such great importance to justify walking away from the deal. I also made a mental note that my CEO may not be the right person for our company. He never attempted to get all the necessary information in a proactive, anticipatory way. He was a pedestrian thinker who never exhibited a curiosity to comprehensively understand the situation.

Two days later, he called back with some information that shed light on the matter. Some of the corporation's products used elements of our technology. The parent corporation was concerned that it might expose them to a potential claim of IP infringement if it no longer had rights to the IP. I asked the CEO how important, from a technology standpoint, the "common technology" was to us. He replied that it was minor and completely inconsequential. However, I now understood why the company was so adamant about the common ownership clause. I also understood that, in a typical lawyerly way, the lawyers had created a front to protect a specific point. They were ready to "die" to protect their "river."

I asked the CEO to go back with a final proposition. We would be willing to have a common ownership of the specific technology that created their anxiety and potential liability. But they didn't really need to have common ownership on the rest. A day later, he came back and said they had agreed to that. A failed negotiation was averted—the **art of compromising without a compromise!**

As it turned out, there were additional problems and we became even more concerned about the CEO's capabilities, and so we decided not to consummate the deal, but it was our choice.

Starting a "War" Instead of Winning a "Battle"

A scientist invented a new technology around which he wanted to build a company. He approached various venture capital firms to raise the necessary money to launch a start-up. We listened to his pitch and liked what we heard. We told him that we would be interested in potentially proceeding with him.

From our experience, one of the greatest impediments for striking a deal with such scientists/founders is their exaggerated perception of the value of their newly founded company. In the venture capital world, this value is referred to as the "pre-money valuation" of the company. It is an important concept since it determines how much ownership the venture capitalist (VC) receives for its investment in a company. Conversely, it also determines how much ownership the founder will retain.

To determine the amount of ownership, the venture capitalist assigns a monetary value to what the founder created before the contemplated transaction, which is the "pre-money valuation." The pre-money refers to the value before our money goes in as an investment. Once that value is determined, the percent ownership is determined by a mathematical formula.

For example, let's assume that the VC assigns a value of $10 million to the company (that is, a $10 million pre-money valuation). Let's further assume that the VC will invest $5 million in cash. Thus, the total value of the enterprise after the $5 million infusion of cash from the VC is $15 million (i.e., the $10 million cash equivalent the founder brings to the party, plus the $5 million the VC brings to the party). The $15 million is referred to as "post-money valuation" (that is, the company is worth a combined cash and cash-equivalent value of $15 million). The VC contributes $5 million of the $15 million, or $5/$15 = 33.33 percent of the value. The founder brings $10 million of value, or $10/$15 = 66.66 percent of the value. These proportions thus represent the percent ownership of the company after the consummation of the deal. Clearly, every founder will try to negotiate the highest pre-money valuation for their company, since the higher the pre-money valuation, the higher will be their percent ownership.

As I mentioned, most founders have an exaggerated estimate of what their company is worth. They think their company will be worth billions of dollars in the future, ergo it must be worth hundreds of millions today. VCs look at it differently. Although the estimated potential may be realistically great, most companies never get there. "Exits" occur much earlier and at much lower valuations, reflecting real performance, not some exaggerated potential beliefs. VCs place a more realistic expectation on performance and potential exit values. The pre-money valuation the VC would be willing to offer is mathematically driven from that exit value.

Let's assume the VC places a $300 million exit valuation. The VC will then estimate how much money they will need to invest to make it happen. They require a certain multiple return for their investment. Thus, they know exactly how much of the company they need to own to get that multiple return. This in turn determines the pre-money valuation.

For example, assume that a VC requires at least a 5-times multiplier on investment upon exit. Assume that the VC estimates that they will need to invest $20 million in the company. Thus, they will need at the time of the exit $20 million × 5 = $100 million. The VC estimates that it will sell the company at exit for $300 million. At that exit price, the VC needs to own 33 percent of the company to receive the required $100 million return ($300 million × 33 percent = $100 million). To own 33 percent of the company with a $20 million investment, the pre-money valuation will need to be no more than $40 million ($40 million pre-money plus $20 million in cash equals $60 million post-money; $20/$60 = 33 percent). The point of this exercise is to alert you to the fact that a VC has a strict mathematical formula to determine the pre-money valuation of a potential investment.

Given the typical exaggerated estimate that founders have, the VC will bring up the pre-money valuation issue with a founder up front so as to avoid any disagreements over money in future negotiations. They will ask a founder in the very first meeting what their expectations are for the pre-money valuation. They will need to see that the founder has reasonable expectations; otherwise, they will not proceed with the deal and will not start any due diligence.

That was on my mind when the founder presented his business opportunity to us. He told us that he wanted a $40 million pre-money valuation, and wanted us to invest $15 million. Forty million dollars was an exaggerated estimate for the valuation of his company. I liked the deal and was willing to invest the time and resources to do in-depth due diligence, but I had to make sure that it wouldn't be in vain because of a disagreement on valuation. So I told him that his pre-money valuation would not be acceptable to us.

I told him that the pre-money valuation appeared to me to be more in the $20 million to $25 million range. I proceeded to tell him that if he didn't accept it, we would pass. I also told him that if our due diligence showed that our estimate of the pre-money valuation was overly punitive, we would increase the valuation. He contemplated this for a while. I'm sure that he had spoken to other VCs and probably got the same pre-money valuation range. He accepted our proposal. We drafted a nonbinding term sheet with that valuation along with other terms and conditions we normally require. He signed it a number of days later, and we proceeded with due diligence.

We liked what we found out in our due diligence. We were ready to proceed with the transaction. However, we thought the company would need to raise at least $25 million, instead of the founder's initial estimation of $15 million. We thought that his revenues would come in at a slower rate than he estimated, and therefore had to fund losses for a longer time. We gave him the final proposal. We were willing to invest and help raise $25 million, at a $20 million pre-money valuation. All other terms and conditions would remain unchanged from our initial term sheet.

I did not anticipate his response. He said that he would not accept a $20 million pre-money valuation. He said that the minimum valuation he would accept would be $30 million. I reminded him that he was made aware of this valuation in advance and agreed to it. His response was terse: "No, it is unacceptable; nothing less than $30 million." I told him that $30 million would be unacceptable to us, and asked him whether he would walk away from the deal. He answered, "Absolutely." I was sorry to lose this opportunity, as I really liked it. But I couldn't justify the higher pre-money valuation. The math would not justify it for us. I told him that I was disappointed and that we would pass.

By happenstance, I ran into him about a week later. He was very cordial, and we had some small talk. As part of the conversation, I asked him why he changed his mind about the valuation. He was a little evasive with his answer. I kept pushing the issue as best I could because I was curious. He kept being evasive. We went back and forth for a while, with him giving some benign responses, but never a convincing reason for why he changed his mind. I was a bit upset and kept pushing him for the real reason. Somewhere during these interactions, he snapped and said, "There is no way that I will not have majority control over my company."

I asked, "What do you mean?"

He responded, "This is my company and my life; I will not accept any situation where I don't own the majority of the company."

I now realized why he had turned the deal down. He lost the majority vote with the $20 million valuation and our insistence on raising $25 million. His objection, his "front," had nothing to do with the valuation, but it had everything to do with majority control over the company.

We, as venture capitalists, don't care how much of the company we own. It makes no difference to us whether we own a minority or majority position. Through separately written agreements, we acquire the controls we require, regardless of ownership. We are driven by the percent ownership, not the "controls."

I looked at him and asked, "How about if we take half of our position in non-voting shares? This way you'll still maintain the majority of the voting shares and have the same control you were trying to get through an increase in the pre-money valuation." He accepted it on the spot. Again, the **art of compromising without a compromise!**

SECTION VI

INTERVIEWING WELL FOR A JOB

23

How to Perform Well in a Job Interview

Interviewing for a job is obviously a very important topic in a book about insight and career advancement. An interview, by its nature, represents a high-risk hurdle, because it is a single, short exposure with a binary outcome. One either does well enough to pass on to the next stage, or one fails.

Many how-to books and articles have been written about interviews, presumably by those who know a lot about the subject. My intention is not to cover the same ground, but rather to cover aspects that provide you with additional insights—insights that I maintain are not passed on as common wisdom from experts and that I believe will help you get the job you want.

Preparing well for an interview involves understanding subtleties and nuances, and to do justice to the topic is to take you step-by-step through the logic, explanations, and examples. This in-depth process will not only serve you well in interviews, but will also serve you well throughout your entire career.

Clearly, an important element of a job search and the interviewing process is the resume. The topic of how to write a good resume was covered in chapter three and chapter eight. Chapter three also covered other things that relate to the interviewing process, and will not be repeated here. Please consider this section, "Interviewing Well for a Job," a complement to chapter three in that it focuses not on the interviewing process, but rather on specific interactions with the interviewers.

For the purposes of this section, I divide interviews into four categories:

1. Interviewing for a job upon graduating from school.

2. Interviewing for a job that seeks candidates with specific subject matter knowledge like finance, economics, human resources, strategy, marketing, and so on, as well as decent prior work experience in a specific area.

3. Interviewing for a job that seeks candidates with expertise in a specific subject matter and *extensive* work experience.

4. Interviewing for a higher-level management position.

This section pertains primarily to insights for the first two categories. Most observations and recommendations apply to both categories. I will point out whenever there are some notable differences that are important to understand. As I said, my goal in this section is to focus on topics I believe will allow you to gain an insightful perspective on interviews and enable you to perform well. I hope that you will indeed agree that this section discusses many insights, some of which may be illuminating even to experienced and knowledgeable professionals.

What Do Interviewers Look for in an Interview?

Although it seems like an obvious question to ask, this question seems to perplex people, including those who may consider themselves knowledgeable with the process and conduct of interviews. They may be nearly correct with their answers, but miss very important nuances. (I hope I've convinced you by now that what appears to be a small nuance could be quite important.) How can a candidate be most effective in an interview without knowing exactly what the interviewer is looking for? I believe that having a clear answer to this question is imperative.

Whenever asked for my advice, I start by asking people to enumerate and prioritize the top things that an interviewer seeks to learn about candidates. I then ask them to give examples of the kind of questions that the interviewers may ask to help them reach their conclusions. I generally get consistent answers, although expressed in different ways, and have collated the responses in the following Priority List:

1. **Subject expertise:** How competent is the candidate in the subject matter expertise the job requires? The interviewer will ask specific technical questions related to the subject matter to ascertain and reach a conclusion on this criterion.

2. **Smarts and brainpower:** How smart is the candidate? Interviewers ascertain this by presenting and discussing case studies with the interviewees.

3. **Enthusiasm for the job:** How passionate is a candidate for the potential job at hand? Interviewers have their different methods to discover a candidate's enthusiasm, and as such it is hard to predict specific questions they might ask.

4. **Communication skills:** How well can a candidate articulate their thoughts? Interviewers, for the most part, will be able to ascertain how well a candidate is able to articulate their thoughts from responses and dialogue during the interview itself.

5. **Interpersonal skills:** Can a candidate interact effectively from a social standpoint? Interviewers, for the most part, will be able to determine it from the interview itself. No special questions are warranted.

While these may be generally accepted notions of what interviewers attempt to discover in an interview, in my opinion the list does not accurately reflect what I believe are the most important aspects of the interviewing process. There are two critical observations to be pointed out in that regard.

First, the list is completely silent on an observation I made earlier in the book, which is that one always competes against others for job opportunities (or promotions). The above Priority List suggests that the candidate is at the center of the interviewing process, which is false!

At the center of the interviewing process are all other candidates and their positioning relative to one another. You may ask, "What is the difference from my perspective, since there is little I can do about other candidates?" You may also add the obvious, "I'll either measure well, or not, but it is not within my control. So, I can only do my best in an interview and hope to have done well." As I said, it may be a nuance, but an important nuance. Your observations, although logical, ignore another very important element I emphasize in this book—your ability to influence.

It is possible that you may be able to influence how the interviewer *will rank you relative to everybody else*, so that you are not completely passive about it. You may say, "Yes, sounds nice conceptually, but how can it be done in reality? It is completely out of my control." Maybe, but maybe not! Here, I will point to the central theme of this book: being insightful—having a different perspective that may lead to a different approach, and thus better potential results.

24

A Different Perspective on What Interviews Are All About

Can a different perspective lead to a different result, even though we approach an interview with the belief that we have no control over the outcome? Is it even reasonable to assume that we actually might be able to influence the outcome? My answer to these questions is yes. We may have more or less influence, but any influence is better than none, because it increases the probability of achieving the outcome we desire. Let me first try to convince you conceptually that it is doable.

Assume that all other interviewees you are competing against are as equally competent and as nice as you. All will also use the same Priority List provided in chapter twenty-three as a guide for the interview and will be given the same advice on answering the various questions. Now, it follows that all interviewees will respond to the interviewer's questions in much the same way. So, will your answers differ in any way?

The answer technically would be no, which means that everybody would be ranked somewhat equally. Thus, clearly everybody will be passively awaiting the final ranking by the interviewer. If all interviewees are reasonably equal in all aspects, the conclusion the interviewer draws will probably reflect some trivial, secondary observations, since the interviewer will use some kind of benchmark to lead to a final ranking. Drawing a conclusion may even be a random event (more on this topic below). One thing is certain: You can't expect a superior ranking if your answers are the same as everybody else's. But what if you gave answers that the interviewer perceives as different from the responses of other candidates? Would that not differentiate you from the rest? Of course it would! What if your answers were not just different, but also perceived to be "better," "smarter," more "mature," or anything else that would make the differentiation more positive for you? Would that not give you an edge? Of course it would!

So, for me, the real question regarding interviews becomes: **Is there a way to give the interviewer different answers from those of your competitors, which will help to differentiate your answers from others in a positive way?** The most important part is to think along those lines and challenge your mind to find answers. The whole purpose of this book is to get you to think this way and try to find unique answers. Do you see the nuance? If you think differently and find a different, more impressive way, then you would increase the probability of influencing the outcome.

The second critical observation about the Priority List relates to the highest priority item on the list—subject matter expertise. I don't agree with it, and I don't believe it is of a very high priority, if at all. It would be an important priority for the third category of jobs—those that require professionals with *extensive* expertise and work experience (which as I mentioned I do not address in this section), but not for the first two categories. It is almost of little significance for the first category, students seeking a job upon graduation. It is relevant for the second category, in which jobs seek some decent prior experience, but it is not of the highest importance, as the Priority List suggests. Obviously, some level of proficiency and competency in the subject matter is definitely required, but whether one is extremely proficient and competent, or reasonably so, is not as important. In other words, lack of proficiency and competence would be unacceptable and fatal, but proving greater proficiency and competence would not buy all that much in relative ranking. So, if probed during the interview, it is only to assure that one possesses an "acceptable" level of proficiency and not for the purpose of ranking the relative attractiveness of the different candidates.

This observation about the importance of the subject matter gives rise to an even more important hypothetical question. Assuming that

I'm right and subject matter level of competence (but not incompetence) is of minor consequence, how could you succeed in the interview above all others if you misjudge the interviewer's highest priority?

As long as one believes that demonstrating proficiency and competence in the subject matter is of the utmost importance, then one will tend to shape their answers to show how well they understand the subject matter. However, they might be better served focusing their attention and energy on something else that would be much more important to the interviewer and the relative ranking among the different candidates. Focusing on trying to show the greatest subject matter competence would place one at a disadvantage to somebody who may better address the real and most important concerns the interviewer is after. I have written this book to make sure that everybody else will be at a disadvantage to you, and not the other way around!

Back to the Priority List: To arrive at the right list, one needs to correctly understand how a job offer finally materializes, and just as importantly, why an otherwise very qualified candidate may be rejected. I suggest a different list, which specifies what I believe goes into the final decision either to make an offer or reject an otherwise qualified candidate. The list includes "Assets" vs. "Liabilities" criteria. The Assets are the things one positively must have, without which an offer will not be made. The Liabilities are the things that will eliminate a candidate, regardless of the Assets. Clearly, any item on such a list is a very critical element; any one of them can either make or break you. If you have such a list, then you know that you have indeed found the list of the highest priority, to you, the interviewer, and the opportunity for a job offer.

To get such a list, **one should shift the focus from the questions and topics that will be asked and discussed during the interviews to what observations the interviewer might take away from the answers and discussions in any given interview.** When I focus on the latter, I come up with a completely different kind of Priority List. It may even be a list whose items at first glance appear different to most experts. However, I am quite certain that it captures exactly the priorities of what they will most likely observe and react to at the end of the day. If you ever want to test whether I'm right, just ask any experienced interviewer the following question: "Would you offer a job to a candidate who didn't [state each of the items on my list]?" You'll find out that not very many will likely do so, thus validating the list.

The following is my Priority List of those attributes that will most positively or negatively impact whether or not you get a job offer. In each of the items, I categorize a positive perception by the interviewer as an Asset (**+++**), and if the interviewer believes you lack that quality, it becomes a Liability (**———**). The magnitude of the impact is captured by the relative length of the Asset or Liability.

- **The best brainpower:** Not just the smartest person from an IQ standpoint, but the kind of brainpower that will be most effective in dealing with the challenges that the job in question represents and will require. **++++++++++++**

- **A team player:** The degree to which the candidate will be a "team player." **++++** **———————**

- **The "fit" with other employees:** The degree to which the candidate will be able to integrate with other employees. **++** **————**

- **Intransigency disposition:** The degree to which the candidate will be easy or difficult to manage. **+++** **———————**

- **Energy level:** The degree to which a candidate can, and will, apply themselves to the job. **+++** **——**

- **General attitude:** Whether the candidate will bring a positive or negative attitude to work every day. **+++** **————**

- **Facility with basic math:** The candidate's level of competence and/or comfort with quantitative skills. [*This category doesn't apply to all situations, but rather to situations where the job requires comfort with manipulations and interpretations of "numbers," as well as some basic math skills and statistics.*] **+++** **————————**

You can see from this list that **judgment on your brainpower is the single most important thing for a job offer to materialize—nothing else comes close.** But be aware of the liabilities, because any single one is very likely to mean rejection.

25

How Interviewers Draw Conclusions About the Priority List Items

I t is here that I believe the biggest misconceptions exist on the part of the interviewees and advice they may receive. How can it be expected of an interviewer that they will in a half-hour, one-hour, or two-hour interview be able to obtain a definitive and accurate reading on a candidate? It is easier to see differences at the very beginning of the interviewing cycle when the candidates represent a wider range of talent and brainpower. However, as candidates meet expectations and progress through additional interviewing cycles, accurate differentiation becomes increasingly difficult.

With the exception of the very last category, "Comfort with basic math," there are no direct questions, or ways, by which one can accurately and definitively discern how a candidate "scores" on the various items on the list. During an interview, it is more of an art than a science. The most important thing to understand is that, absent any direct ways, all interviewers rely on "proxies" or "surrogates" to reach conclusions. This means that all interviewers infer from something they hear or see during the interview itself to project and reach conclusions.

This process of inferring and projecting is to a large extent a random process, because interviewers are different from each other: Some are smarter, some more perceptive, some deeper thinkers, some like/dislike different personality traits, and so on. In other words, **any one**

given interview is subject to being random in outcomes. We really have little control over that. Assume that ten interviewers are sitting in on the same interview with one candidate. It would not be unusual to get varying opinions regarding the initial observations about the candidate. As they discuss their observations, they are likely to reach a more persistent perspective. This suggests that although each interview session with any given interviewer may be subject to a level of "randomness," the overall process itself is likely to attenuate such randomness, which is the good news from the candidate's perspective.

The bad news is that this process doesn't work as well when a negative dissenting opinion comes from a higher-level manager, or if it were to happen at an earlier stage, where a single interviewer determines the outcome. There isn't really all that much one can do about it. One can only hope that their interviewers will fall more into the "average, more common" category, meaning that they are more likely to react in a rational and predictable way to what they see and hear in an interview, and are not likely to be outliers in how they react and infer things. The good news is that most experienced interviewers will tend to fall into the normal, predictable category. Keep in mind that it only means more predictable judgment and not necessarily more accurate judgment.

Clearly, then, the question becomes: How would the "normal, more common" interviewers draw conclusions from their inferences?

Here, in my opinion, the list is separated into two categories—the items on the Priority List that are likely to produce more accurate observations versus those that might be subject to a greater degree of variance and inaccuracy. The most important item on the list, brainpower, is more accurately discerned and falls in the first category. (Of course, the accuracy for the basic math category is very high, but the category is a minor one with secondary priority.) All others fall into the second category. This implies an important observation. On the positive side, the most important factor for a job offer would likely be ascertained reasonably well. On the negative side, the others are less accurately discernible, yet certain to yield a rejection. There is no real balance here; it is mostly an all-or-nothing proposition.

Another observation of significance is the fact that all the factors on the list are inferred from proxies. The proxies themselves are not made up of known and consistent elements. They can vary significantly. Worse yet, the same proxy may receive a positive observation with one interviewer, but a negative observation from another. For example, a candidate gives an opinion about an issue. The interviewer then raises a counterargument and asks for the candidate's response. The candidate counters with a logical premise. The interviewer responds with another counterpoint. The candidate rebuts with another logical counterpoint and in doing so maintains their original position. Assume further that the candidate's counterpoints have not been all that compelling to the interviewer, but nevertheless have been logical and not inferior responses.

It is then likely that the interviewer will draw one of two opposite conclusions. One, the candidate was quick on their feet and able to quickly adjust their original thinking, absorb new information, and respond in a logical way. The other, the candidate showed a tendency to be stubborn and argumentative, as evidenced by the fact that they kept holding on to their original position, in spite of the interviewer's logical counterpoints.

There is only one conclusion to draw from the above, outside of pointing to the randomness—that if one wants to maximize the outcome of a job interview, **one must demonstrate brainpower without overdoing it, so one doesn't give the impression of being arrogant. At the same time, one must avoid anything that might be viewed as a proxy for a critical liability.** I will attempt to elaborate and make proper recommendations to deal with it shortly, but before I do so, here are three personal examples that will demonstrate some of the discussion points about interviews.

Interviewing with Booz Allen: How Random Can It Be?

Between my first and second year at Wharton, I had an interview on campus for a summer internship with a partner from Booz Allen, who sought me out after consulting the resume book. He explained that he had selected me because it appeared I could be of value on a project that involved computer systems and information technology (IT). My prior experience at EDS would fit perfectly, he said. He told me that with my experience and understanding of computers and IT, I would be a major asset to the team and be paid full salary, which was a lot of money. I was salivating. The interview lasted for a number of hours, throughout which he reaffirmed my fit for the project.

My English at the time, as I mentioned earlier, was not very good. I had to really concentrate whenever I had to form sentences. When I concentrate, my countenance becomes very serious. During the interview, I also focused on trying to convince the interviewer that I was smart, since Booz Allen had a reputation for hiring very smart people. So my demeanor throughout the interview was serious. At the conclusion of the interview, the interviewer said, "David, you are very, very smart and a very impressive candidate, probably one of the best I've seen in years. Your knowledge of IT is superb. You would make a great addition to Booz Allen. But I'm not going to offer you the job with me for the summer. However, I will make sure that Booz Allen pursues you very aggressively for a full-time job next year following your graduation."

This was not the response I expected, and I asked him to explain why he decided against an offer after having repeated so often that I would be of great value to his team. He said, "You know, as consultants, team members spend hours upon hours with each other. We travel together, eat together, work together, and spend a tremendous amount of time together. You are a very serious person, nothing but business. I prefer someone who is fun to be with after work. Someone who has a sense of humor, who can crack a joke, and relax with the team. So, I decided not to offer you the job." Then he repeated again, "But I think Booz Allen should hire you, and I will make sure that they interview you next year, when you graduate."

I was devastated. First, a lucrative opportunity with a great firm had just dissipated in front of my eyes. Second, I didn't believe that he meant it when he said that he would advise Booz Allen to pursue me aggressively upon graduation. I was sure that he said it just to soften the blow. Third, I knew I came across very seriously, but to think that I didn't have a sense of humor?!

I stewed over what he said for the whole of the following week. I thought about it constantly. I was extremely upset with myself for having come across so seriously. Then I got even more upset with how I could have been so stupid not to have understood it in advance and been more relaxed and humorous during the interview. However, now that I understood it, I was determined to never repeat this mistake again.

Just to put things in perspective, the following year I went through five interviewing cycles with Booz Allen and accepted an attractive offer for a full-time job. After I had been at the firm for a while, I was curious as to whether my hiring was just part of the normal hiring process or if the partner had indeed followed up on what he told me. I went to the person in charge of the recruiting process, who had contacted me initially, and asked. The partner indeed had followed up on what he promised, writing a glowing letter to the head of the strategy group to make sure that they followed up with me. So, he didn't just use what he told me as an excuse; he actually meant everything he said.

Interviewing with Bain & Co.: How Random Can It Be?

Right before graduating and about nine months after my failed interview for the summer position with Booz Allen, I got a call from Bain & Co., ahead of the start of the recruiting season. You may remember the name, since I mentioned it in an earlier chapter. Bain & Co. was an up-and-coming consulting firm that was started by Bill Bain, who left the Boston Consulting Group (BCG) with a number of BCG partners to form their own firm. I was convinced that working for any of the top four consulting firms would offer a great career path.

In those days, the top four consulting firms were highly sought after by graduating students, and I tempered my expectations for succeeding in the interview process. Everybody knew how tough it was to receive an offer, and many did not even try. To be a successful consultant, one had to be articulate in spoken and written English. I questioned how well I would do, given my lack of proficiency in English.

I vividly remember a student who described to me exactly what those consulting firms were looking for. According to his father, who was the CEO of a large company, consulting firms look to hire only the best. But he went a step further. He said, "Let me give you an example of the kind of students they are looking to hire. They are looking for students who have already proven that they can walk on water, and now they want to see that they also could run on water."

Bain & Co. had decided to preempt the normal recruiting cycle. As soon as the Wharton students' resume book was released, Bain selected a number of students for early interviews. My resume caught their attention, which confirmed in my mind that I was right in my approach to restructuring the traditional resume. The initial interview on campus apparently went well, and I was invited to fly the very next week to Boston to interview at the company's headquarters. I interviewed with five professionals. I was called the following day and invited to attend another round of interviews. This time I met with a group of six different professionals, which resulted in being invited for a third round.

When I arrived for the third-round interview, I was greeted by the individual who first interviewed me on campus. He was a senior job manager at the firm and became my "handler" for the duration. He told me that I had done exceptionally well to that point, and that this time I would be interviewing with one of Bain's highest-level partners. I understood that this interview would be the final hurdle for me to cross. He then said to me, "Don't get nervous; you'll do well. You have done superbly well so far; I just don't see how you are not going to do well with this person." It was nice of him to say it. Indeed, it helped calm me down a bit.

I met with the senior partner. At the conclusion of the interview, I was asked to wait in a lobby. About half an hour passed and my handler came with the news that the firm was prepared to make an offer that very day. I was to have lunch with Bill Bain, the founder, who would formally extend the offer. I was elated.

I remembered my experience with the Booz Allen partner the year before, and I was determined not to repeat that same mistake. I wanted Bill Bain to see my light side, so I resorted to telling jokes over lunch so that he could see that I had a sense of humor. He seemed to have enjoyed the jokes and laughed quite a bit. But as we ordered dessert, an offer had not been made and I started to get nervous.

We finished dessert and still no offer was forthcoming. I thought that something must be wrong. I debated whether it would be wise for me to bring it up, but it seemed to me that once we concluded lunch and left the restaurant, I would not have another opportunity. I mustered my courage and asked Bain whether I could ask a sensitive question. He said, "Sure." I said, "I'm a bit confused. I was told that the firm was going to make an offer to me over lunch. Lunch is coming to an end. Did I misunderstand the situation?"

He responded, "Well, not exactly. A final decision had not been made."

I then asked, "What did I do wrong during lunch to lead you to decide against making a job offer?"

He said something polite but noncommittal, words I don't exactly recall. But I do remember every single word that followed.

I said, "Please, do me a favor. Please tell me what went wrong. I promise not to respond to your answer, no matter what."

He said, "Oh, nothing really. I just don't believe that we are ready to make the offer today."

I said, "Please, please, I know something went wrong. Please help me understand what it was, so that I don't make the same mistake again with somebody else. Please help me. I mean it; I promise not to say a single word in response."

He looked at me for a few seconds and said, "Okay, I'll tell you. Indeed, I took you out for lunch to make you an offer and try to convince you to accept it. But during lunch you didn't come across as a serious person. You kept telling all those jokes, and I don't know if we can trust you with the clients—we can't leave an impression that we are not serious professionals, so I decided not to make the offer."

I started laughing uncontrollably. I couldn't stop myself. He looked completely bewildered. After I had an opportunity to get ahold of myself, I said, "Thank you so much for telling me the truth. I really appreciate it. I know I told you that I would not respond to whatever answer you gave me, and I do not intend to do so. But let me tell you why I started laughing."

I told him about the previous experience with the Booz Allen partner and why I told the jokes. He shrugged his shoulders and said, "Well, that's the way the cookie crumbles." We got up and left the restaurant.

I am sharing these experiences not just for the entertainment value. They serve an important illustration of the overall points I'm trying to make. Before I start with specific recommendations, one more example may be in order. This example had nothing to do with interviews, but it does demonstrate how vulnerable we all are to inferences from proxies. This occurred when I started working at Sammons Enterprises as vice president of systems development.

Sammons Enterprises: Be Wary of Proxies, as They Are Not Irrelevant

As you will recall from my resume (chapter three), I was senior system analyst at Electronic Data Systems (EDS). I joined the company in 1973 after graduating with a master's degree in computer science. At the time, computers and systems development were experiencing rapid growth, and companies began to form their own IT departments, referred to as data processing (DP) departments. Knowledge and expertise in IT/DP were very sparse, and few companies knew how to manage this new practice well. It had become an expensive cost center with users constantly complaining about the poor quality of results and service.

EDS was an exception. It built its business by convincing its clients it could capably manage the IT/DP function with better performance and for a lesser cost than having the IT/DP function in-house. (This concept is nowadays referred to as "outsourcing.") The first clients they were able to procure were a number of Blue Cross Blue Shield companies. In the case of a company like Blue Cross Blue Shield, they did so for a predetermined fixed price per claim. EDS would also assume heavy penalties should the processing of the claims exceed a pre-agreed time period. The proposed fixed cost represented about 30 percent of Blue Cross Blue Shield's actual costs at that time. EDS also committed to improving the processing time of claims by 80 to 90 percent. EDS was so efficient, and its clients were so IT incompetent, that EDS was convinced that it would meet the new pricing with significant profit margins. EDS was indeed right, and their business started growing in leaps and bounds.

In 1974, I was recruited by Sammons Enterprises, a privately held conglomerate that owned eight different and independent companies. The owners wanted to launch a company that would emulate EDS's success. The first clients would be their eight captive companies, so that they could work out the bugs and create reference accounts. A year and a half later, there was nothing but problems. Performance was just terrible. No matter how hard they tried to fix it, it just didn't work. The client companies complained constantly.

Sammons's worst problem was that practically every single night, when the computers were supposed to process the day's business results and generate management reports for the following morning, they would crash. This meant that no management reports were available to the various client companies the following morning, because the computers had to be rebooted and the reason for the crash fixed. It took anywhere between one to three hours to do so, almost each and every morning. Finally, the owners decided to fire the management and brought in a new president to turn the situation around. The president was not an IT/DP person, and I have no idea why the owners thought he could help fix the problem. However, he was an experienced accounting professional and a very wise person. He asked an executive search firm to hire talent from EDS, and so I was contacted. For some odd reason, he believed that I was at a higher level than I really was, perhaps due to the recommendations I received. He contacted me, and after a number of interviews with the president, I was offered the position of vice president, with a large increase in salary. Two days into my job, I realized that the IT/DP company's processes were completely inadequate at the most basic of levels. I knew I could fix many of the problems with some simple procedural changes. I could stop the nightly computer crashes immediately. I informed the president and the owners that within a week the crashes would stop. They expressed disbelief, but I was certain!

The problem was relatively simple to fix. At EDS, we had two parallel systems. One was called the "production" system, and the other the "test" system. Whatever changes were needed were extensively tested with the test system. It is impossible to make changes to computer programs without encountering some mistakes. When a change was tested and failed, we needed to analyze it and figure out why it failed, make corrections, run the changes again, and so on, until all mistakes were rectified. This process could take days, weeks, or months, depending on the complexity of the changes. Only then did the manager give permission to migrate the changes to the production system. Thus, the production system rarely crashed.

Sammons Enterprises had no parallel test system. Every night, multiple programmers would make changes to the production system. Of course it crashed every single night! The answer was to copy the production system, thereby creating a test system, and not approve any updates to the production system until I was convinced a change had been extensively tested and the bugs worked out, just as we had done at EDS. A week later, I became a hero with the owners. The president became a good friend and mentor. He also gave me complete freedom to do whatever I wished from that point on. I actually did a great job for them. All their problems emanated from simple mistakes that were easy to correct.

About two months into the job, a group of four division presidents approached my president to discuss a project that had received considerable investment over the previous eighteen months, but its goals were not being achieved. The point had been reached where a decision had to be made to continue with the project or abort it. It involved building a new system, and these division presidents had heard about our IT/DP successes and wanted to know our opinion.

They described what the system was supposed to do and then asked me for my assessment. I knew exactly what needed to be done! I answered, "No problem. I can get it done within three weeks, fully running and completely implemented." They thanked me and then my president excused me.

About fifteen minutes later, the four division presidents left, and my president called me back into his office. As soon as I sat down, he said, "David, can you guess what the first thing was that they said to me as soon as you left?"

I figured that he was serious and expected a serious answer. I said, "Well, probably that I must be very smart, since I knew immediately the answer to their problem."

He laughed and said, "No, the first thing they said was, 'Can we trust that guy?'"

I was not proficient in formal English, let alone colloquial English. I interpreted words literally. So, I said, "Why would they have a problem with trusting me? They don't even know me."

He laughed again and said, "They didn't mean 'trusting you' in that way. They meant, 'Does he know what he is talking about?'"

Now I was completely surprised. I asked, "Why would they question if I know what I am talking about?"

He very patiently continued, "This is why I called you in. You are one of the smartest people I've ever met, and I know that you know exactly what you are talking about. I am also 100 percent certain that you can get done what you promised them within the next three weeks. But you have to look at it from the perspectives of other people. For them, it was a problem that nobody had been able to solve for the last eighteen months, in spite of many repeated promises. So, they believe that it is a difficult problem to solve and might even be impossible.

"They explained it for about twenty minutes to you. You heard it for the first time in your life. Yet, it took you no time at all to tell them that you can solve their problem—one that nobody has been able to solve. What else did you expect them to think?"

I looked at him and said, "But I know I'm right and they know that it is my job to know. If I didn't know, I would've told them so."

He laughed again and said, "David, you are missing the point. From now on, for the rest of your life, if you find yourself in the same situation, before you give an answer, just look at them and say, 'Hmmm, very interesting question or problem.' Take ten seconds to make them believe you are thinking about it, and then tell them in the following language: 'I believe it can be done, and I think I might be able to solve it.' Do it this way and nobody will ever question again whether they can trust you." **This was the first time I became aware of how important it is to think in terms of, and then put into words, an answer that relates to other people's perspectives.** Just in case you might be curious, I was able to meet the promise I had made. I was confident because I well knew that the challenge wasn't as complicated as it appeared to them, and that any reasonably competent professional could have easily accomplished the same.

In Conclusion: Be Aware and Beware of Proxies!

The above observations and examples clearly illustrate just how random an interview may be, and how easy it is to mischaracterize a candidate through inferences from proxies. However, don't draw the conclusion that as a result there is not much we can do about how we are perceived in an interview. On the contrary, there is!

First, the examples illustrate that in any one given interview the process may be random. At the same time, it is quite common for different interviewers to draw different inferences from the exact same interactions. That creates a real dilemma for a candidate with no ability to predict which interviewer may infer what in any given interview.

Thus, there is only one conclusion to draw if one wants to maximize the opportunity for a positive outcome from an interview: **Beware of proxies. Whether positive or negative, avoid them altogether!** Meaning, don't say anything that could be used to infer anything else, positive or negative. Of course, it is easier said than done. But I will provide you with a list of the most common and "damaging" proxies that you should know, and I hope this knowledge will help you.

To summarize, there are three critical observations worth repeating:

1. The brainpower criterion is an asset, without which an offer will not get extended.

2. Any single "negative proxy" may produce a liability that will most likely result in rejection.

3. Any single "positive proxy" will have a marginal impact on a final offer.

The last two points are why I said "avoid proxies altogether." The positive offers little benefit and the negative will kill you. The risk is just not balanced.

We are now ready to address the specific recommendations I believe will help you maximize the quality of your interviews. First, we turn to the brainpower criterion and then address how to deal with proxies.

26

The Brainpower Criterion

As I emphasized, brainpower is the most important and sole criterion for an affirmative decision for a job offer—nothing else matters as much! It is essential to understand exactly what it means. There are two different dimensions that define brainpower in the context of a business career: (i) Relative Reference Groups, and (ii) Specific Intellectual Ability.

Relative Reference Groups

In the business world, one's brainpower will always be a comparative measure. Your brainpower will be "measured" relative to others. In job interviews, there are two groups of people you will be compared to. You know of one group—the other candidates who are competing with you for the job. The ones ranked closer to the top will have the greatest advantage and opportunity for an offer.

However, you and all the other candidates will always be measured relative to the people already working for the company. When looking to hire, a company will have a profile that is representative of the brainpower resident within its employees. No candidate will be deemed acceptable unless they are thought to meet that representative level. The representative level varies widely depending on the job description, job title, group, department, company, nature of business, and so on. This is an obvious observation, but it serves to elucidate my earlier comment that one always competes against other candidates.

Specific Intellectual Ability

This refers to one's cognitive and intellectual abilities, those colloquially referred to as comprising a person's IQ level. I've already referred to it in the book using the word "smarts" and "brainpower." I will continue to use these words in a generic way to include all types of intelligence. In general, the levels are subjectively described as extremely smart, exceptionally smart, very smart, above-average smart, average smart, below-average smart, and so on.

I contend there are two different types of smarts, which are important in the business world. Each plays a decisive role in a person's career, but in different ways. The difference may appear to be a subtle one; however, the implications are not. One needs to understand the difference and subtlety to know how to best try to influence an interviewer's judgment. I find that most people confuse the two and as a result suboptimize the way they are perceived by interviewers.

The most prevalent misconception is the belief that command of subject expertise is how smarts are evaluated in job interviews. It is not. Others believe that their previous job performance (assuming it required a certain amount of brainpower) is proof enough. It is not. Yet others believe that their apparent higher IQ would suffice to prove smarts. It does not!

I refer to the two types of smarts as (i) raw cognitive smarts, and (ii) interpretive smarts. By way of a metaphor, imagine a powerful sports car. The car may be capable of reaching a speed in excess of 150 mph; however, only a slight amount of the power is utilized in daily, routine driving, particularly within city limits. At the same time, the driver need not be capable of intricate maneuvers at high speed. Instead, they simply must be able to find their way in the maze of city streets and alleys, drive defensively while constantly looking in the mirrors, back up and park in tight spaces, avoid traffic jams, and so on. I refer to the former as "raw potential" and the latter as "interpretive" power. The same concept applies to brainpower, particularly as related to business challenges. One's IQ is a measurement of raw cognitive smarts, while the "interpretive" smarts represent not the raw potential, but rather how brainpower is applied in unique situational analyses and specific applications.

The two may be correlated, but not necessarily act in tandem. One can expect that a person with a high IQ will also score reasonably high on the interpretive type scale, but it is not necessarily the case. In other words, someone with a genius IQ may or may not score at a high level on the interpretive smarts scale. In fact, in spite of the very high IQ, the interpretive ability may fall way down the scale, say, a smidgen above average. This may be an example of someone who is "book smart" in that they possess a very high IQ but not an impressive degree of brainpower otherwise. The same is true in reverse. A person who scores very high on the interpretive smarts scale may or may not score very high on the IQ scale—this may be an example of someone who has "street smarts." It is this subtle difference that captures the essence of the different role each type plays in interviews.

The real difference lies in the timing of when each of the two types plays a *more dominant* role. They both are critically influential, but at different times. The raw cognitive smarts play a dominant role in the initial screening that lands one an interview, and only a secondary role during the interview itself. The interpretive smarts play no role in the initial screening, but become the dominant factor during interviews.

There is another difference between the two types. Although both are inferred from proxies, the raw cognitive smarts are much more readily measured, and probably accurately so. Interpretive smarts are more difficult to measure, and accuracy is not guaranteed.

Raw, Cognitive Smarts

The most common proxy used to make a judgment on this category is a person's academic performance. One's grades and the reputation of the schools attended are the most determinative aspects. The better the reputation of the school and the higher the grades, the higher one will be perceived in this criterion. Grades are not viewed linearly; rather, they are lumped in categories: top 5 percent, top 10 percent, top quartile, second quartile, average, below average. Schools are ranked in similar categories. One gets the highest score in the raw cognitive smarts category if one achieves top grades at top schools. This will most likely greatly influence such a person's chances of being invited to an initial in-person interview. Such smarts also play an important role during the interviewing process itself. They are not dominant, but meaningful.

As soon as an interviewer scans the academic record of a candidate, a bias sets in based on the candidate's grades and schools attended. The bias could be positive, neutral, or negative. Bias tends to influence how the interviewers will react to what they see and hear during the interview session itself. Everything else being equal, the interviewers will more easily accept observations that confirm their bias, and will be more "forgiving" when observing what might contradict such bias, and vice versa. Although not dominant, it still is a meaningful advantage.

This is why a successful academic record is so important; it will open so many more doors into so many different opportunities over a person's career. The more the opportunities, the greater the likelihood for success. It is also nice to start any interviewing session with a strong positive bias.

There is another reason for the importance of past academic record. It plays a major role again in the third and fourth categories of interviews, which are those for very experienced professional and higher-level managers. I don't cover these categories in this book, but bring this dimension to your attention for the sake of completeness. For those categories of interviews, the most determinative factors are the candidate's expertise, work experience, and record of career advancement. Assuming one's factors are as attractive as those of the other candidates, the academic track record will then become the next greatest influencer on an interviewer's judgment, even though it might not even be discussed in the interview itself.

Interpretive Smarts

This category is the most highly regarded type of smarts in the business world, beginning with the interview process and throughout one's career. The business world, at all levels, is constantly facing changing opportunities and challenges. Therefore, the ability to anticipate them, analyze the implications, and draw the right conclusions becomes a highly sought-after skill. This ability is most commonly referred to as the *analytical skills* (as in the ability to analyze).

As I mentioned earlier in the book, those changing opportunities and challenges do not have black-and-white solutions. Rather, there is only a relative measurement scale, from better to worse. Each alternative for any recommended action will be measured relative to some other alternatives or benchmarks. The one deemed to be the better overall will likely be selected. Only after the fact is one able to tell to what degree a solution has been effective.

This has major implications for an employee. **Those employees who are deemed to contribute the most in this cycle of analyses, resolutions, and recommendations will likely be more highly rewarded.** There are three dimensions at play with the analytical skills: (i) one's brainpower, innate and developed through experience; (ii) the methodology used in the analyses—the thoroughness, techniques, and correctness of all the steps involved in the process of identifying, analyzing, drawing conclusions, and making recommendations; and (iii) creativity, or "thinking outside of the box."

One can measurably improve the first dimension, but clearly it is limited to the upper bounds of one's innate abilities. The second dimension is almost independent from the first. The methodology is something one can be taught and one can eventually master. Because of its importance, I dedicate an entire section (section VII: "A Sound Methodology for Business Analyses") to it. The third, creativity, is also an innate skill and also difficult to change much. However, one can sharpen their creative skills and apply them more effectively through observation, practice, and experience. Creative skill, like anything with brainpower, is not an all-or-nothing proposition. It is just a question of how much of it a person possesses, or doesn't, and how they use it.

At Booz Allen, we separated talent based on how creative they were. One could not do well without the first two capabilities—brainpower and methodology—but could succeed without the third, creativity. However, one with more highly developed creative skills, meaning one who was more able to think outside the box, stood a much greater chance of providing more inventive solutions to a client and being recognized for this within the company. We differentiated the two by referring to one as the "pedestrian thinker" and the output as "pedestrian analysis" versus the "creative thinker" and the output as "creative analysis."

Note that the distinction between pedestrian analysis and creative analysis is how different from the "obvious" the analysis and thinking are. The closer to the "obvious," the more pedestrian the analysis. The less obvious, therefore, becomes the product of the more creative thinker. **Notice the commonality between the creative thinker definition and how I defined "insightful" thinking—they are practically one and the same.**

Needless to say, if one is blessed with innate analytical brainpower and is competent at applying the proper methodology, one would be greatly rewarded over time. Add to it the third dimension, creativity (or insightfulness), and one has the greatest opportunity to stand out from the rest and enjoy an accelerated career.

27

Brainpower and the Interview Process

et's return to the interviewing process. Analytical skills are the most important, so therefore it is exactly those skills that the interviewer is looking for in a candidate during an interview. Unfortunately, some subjective judgment is involved and thus the outcome can vary with each interviewer. However, understanding how the interviewer is most likely to form a judgment will help mitigate such variability. The primary method used by interviewers is to **test a candidate's ability to reason.**

How Interviewers Deduce "Analytical" Skills

Testing a candidate's ability to reason is done by giving the candidate a problem to analyze and then to propose solutions. During this process, the interviewer will ask questions to see how well a candidate is able to adjust their thinking to different sets of conditions, and how broad or narrow their perspectives are. Each interviewer may have their own approach to determining the candidate's analytical skills, but most use case studies. Practically any two-way conversation about any topic could accomplish the same. Personally, I only use case studies toward the end of the interviewing process, when there are a few candidates with an equal shot at being hired. The case study analysis is probably the most challenging from the candidate's standpoint, and the most revealing from the interviewer's standpoint.

The case study approach places tremendous pressure on a candidate during the interview, and a candidate may suffer self-doubt for weeks afterward if they feel they did not do well. I think this happens a lot and is unnecessary.

Just how challenging case studies are is illustrated by an experience of a friend of mine. When I graduated from Wharton, this friend was interviewing with an up-and-coming technology company. The founder and CEO asked him the following question: "What would you do if I asked you to tell me how many manholes there are in the United States?" (Remember, there was no Google, internet, or any search technologies at the time.) He told me that the question took him by surprise, and he could not answer in a satisfactory way. He was not invited back. When I heard the question, I was also at a loss and couldn't think of a reasonable response, although now with more experience and knowledge, I can think of a number of ways one can answer such a question. I will come back to it later, when I discuss specific recommendations, as this example will serve well to illustrate some of what I plan to recommend.

You may have noticed that I have said nothing in my explanation of how the interview process works with regard to whether the answers, observations, or conclusions the candidates make are correct or not. Here we need to distinguish between category 1—interviews for graduating students—and category 2—interviews for a job with some specific prior experience. **It is my observation that for category 1—graduating students—the interviewer rarely cares about right from wrong, or whether an answer is correct or not, unless the interviewer's intention is that the candidate should reach a correct conclusion. In most cases, for nontechnical careers, the interviewer will ask difficult questions with no expectation that the candidate will be able to provide a correct answer.** The interviewer is focusing on how the candidate's mind assimilates and deals with complex, non-obvious scenarios. If all candidates are expected to reach correct answers and conclusions, then it would be difficult for the interviewer to differentiate between them, and the process would not be challenging enough to truly discern how a candidate's mind works. This subtle point has profound implications and is a key factor in how a candidate may be able to influence the interviewer's judgment. However, although the same observation is mostly true for category 2, there is a notable but important difference.

For category 2, in addition to the above, the interviewer would also try to ascertain just how much the candidate has been able to assimilate from their prior experience and how it has enriched their understanding and perspectives. The expectations are that the longer the experience, the more the candidate should be able to demonstrate a more complete and correct understanding and a broader perspective (together often referred to as "business maturity"). Here the interviewer will observe whether the candidate recognized most if not all the variables that need to be considered, and the soundness of the overall approach and methodology that the candidate utilized to arrive at potential conclusions. Just like in category 1, the accuracy of the conclusions themselves is not as important. **The overall approach and methodology are of much greater importance.**

Also, as mentioned earlier, there are some cases where the interviewer may test something different from the way a candidate "thinks" and intentionally expects correct answers. The very last category on the Priority List is such an example. For jobs that require comfort with basic math skills, the interviewer may present a "mini case study" in which specific numbers will be part of the input, and the interviewer expects some basic math manipulation to arrive at a correct answer. Consulting firms and financial and accounting jobs are examples of such positions. It is not a determinative dimension, but on the negative side it becomes a fatal flaw. (Note: Oftentimes, colloquially, quantitative skills may also be referred to as "analytical" skills. This book exclusively refers to *analytical* skills as the "way of thinking" and not as quantitative skills.)

Back to the more common case studies and measuring the candidate's analytical skill. I have my favorite method, too. This method was shared with me by a very smart and creative thinker early in my career. I would first ask the interviewee to come up with a familiar case they had personally worked on. It could be an example from their school exercises or work history, but I wanted to build a discussion around a topic they knew well and in detail. Following the initial description of the case study, I would ask for the conclusion or outcome. I then asked the candidate to take me through the logic they used to reach their conclusions. I learned a lot from just the above; however, that wasn't the real test.

I would then take the most important assumptions/facts the candidates used to arrive at their conclusions and change a factor or two. For example, I would ask the candidate to assume that one of those assumptions/facts showed exactly the opposite result from the one it showed in their study, and then ask them to tell me whether, and how, their recommendations would be affected. This method introduces a difficult mental challenge, because it takes something that the mind has accepted as valid and proven and then asks the mind to reject its validity.

This is even more difficult when the new assumption/fact I ask the candidate to assume appears to make no sense. For example, let's assume that the candidate says the challenge for the case study was how to turn around a company whose profitability is in decline. He then concludes that the best and easiest way to reverse the decline is by improving the margins for the product sold. He then describes very impressive analyses of the different ways margins could be affected, which of these ways would yield the best results, and which would be easiest to implement. Then he comes up with a trade-off between the different alternatives and recommends the one that optimizes the results.

I then ask the candidate to assume that improving margins would yield the exact opposite result and lead to an increase in losses, and to tell me how this scenario would change the conclusions that had been reached. Most candidates would have a hard time assimilating a conclusion that is counterintuitive and goes against common sense. How is it possible to have a situation where improving margins yields anything else but improved profits?

I have experienced a variety of responses from candidates. Some will suggest I'm illogical and that the way I have changed the scenario makes no sense. The smarter ones would try their best to create a completely different decision-tree in an attempt to answer the question. I only needed to see them attack the problem to be certain of their analytical skills. I built a reputation of being very good at evaluating a candidate's analytical skills.

You may wonder whether there is any satisfactory answer to the dilemma I posed in this example. As I said, there didn't have to be. To any candidate's response, I would have offered a new assumption in order to gauge their reactions and determine the soundness of their logic. I can also tell you that if someone would have tested me in the same manner, by using the same example, I'm not sure I would have come up with any good answer. Had anybody come up with a reasonable answer, I would have been exceptionally impressed. However, now, with all the experience I've gained, I can think of a number of responses. For example, the following response from a candidate would have astounded me:

> Now, it is counterintuitive to assume that increased margins will not yield improved profitability. You are asking me to make this assumption, regardless, correct? [Assume the interviewer agrees.] Okay! Clearly, there are multiple ways by which margins can be improved, such as by increasing the selling price of the product; reducing manufacturing costs; reducing overhead costs; redesigning the product with cheaper components; redesigning the whole product with fewer features, thereby reducing the overall cost; and any combinations thereof. As I described to you earlier, in this scenario, we evaluated eight different ways to improve margins and selected one of them for our final recommendation, because we viewed it to be the optimal one under the circumstances.
>
> Now, you have proposed that an increase in profit margin yields decreased profitability. This triggers the following question: Because margin improvement can be accomplished by changing a set of independent variables, it then gives rise to the question of which of the variables gives rise to reduced profitability. If I can find the right variable, then I can check which of the eight options we came up with don't rely on that variable. Those, therefore, may still prove to yield good recommendations. We then take those options and compare them to each other. The best of those remaining alternatives will then become the new recommended option.
>
> Now, if there is no such variable that causes the counterintuitive results, and I need to assume that any and all margin improvements

will result in decreased profitability per your scenario, then we need to eliminate all the alternatives we proposed and start from scratch.

The original challenge was to improve declining profits for the company. Margin is only one way to have done so, but is no longer an option now under the new scenario. So, we start looking at all the other ways that help improve profitability for the company without increasing product margins.

The most direct way is to increase sales. So, we'll need to evaluate the best way in which the company can aggressively increase sales. Another way is to reduce overhead costs for the company as a whole. Another way is to reduce all other costs, which are not part of the product margins.

Now, let me continue with an answer that is a bit on the humorous side. Generally, if an assumption (A) leads to an outcome (B), then the opposite of the assumption should lead to the opposite of the outcome: (Not A) leads to (Not B). This implies that if the assumption you gave me—that increasing margins leads to reduced profitability—then reducing margins should improve profitability! If that is so, I could find thousands of ways to throw away money, thereby reducing margins and thus, per your scenario, improving profitability. But somehow, I didn't think you would allow it as a valid assumption, so I didn't bring it up right away. ☺

The candidate would have completely thrown the logic right back at me, and I would have had to make up a different scenario. But I would be impressed as hell with the candidate and probably offered them a job on the spot.

Here's another example, but this time a real one:

While at Booz Allen, I was sent to Wharton to help screen a list of candidates and decide whom to invite for additional in-office interviews. Those who were invited could generally expect between two and four additional in-person interviewing rounds, with four to six interviewers in each round. The final round would likely be with a few top-level executives who would make the final decision as to whether to extend an offer. I was scheduled to meet with about eight candidates we had picked from the resume book. One of the candidates was a very unusual one. He was only twenty-one years old when he was about to graduate from Wharton MBA. His academic track record was perfect—the best schools and perfect grades. He was always the top student. He had perfect grades at Wharton as well.

I asked him to describe a case study he was very familiar with. He happened to have been part of a four-student team that with the help of their professor was involved with a semester-long consulting assignment for a local company. That became the case study we discussed in the interview. I asked probing questions, raised simple challenges, and listened to his responses. They were very good.

I then, little by little, increased the challenges and the pressure by pointing out flaws in their analyses and conclusions. I proceeded to give him different assumptions and scenarios, and rebutted his answers. I wanted to see how quickly his mind could adjust to new assumptions and the quality of thinking that followed.

He started to literally sweat in the interview, but I would not let up. I kept on challenging him. After a while, he realized and admitted that their recommendations to the company might have been wrong and that they really did not have enough information to definitively draw the conclusions they had reached. The interview lasted two hours, while it was scheduled for only one. When we parted, he was practically shaking. He looked at me and said, "I am so embarrassed. I can't believe how wrong I was and how many mistakes I have made."

When I returned to the office, I immediately went to a senior executive partner and told him that I came across an unbelievable candidate. I knew our competitors would make an offer, so I recommended that we fly this candidate to Chicago as soon as possible and let him interview with a team of eight people. I asked that at the conclusion of the interviews the head of the office talk to the team and be ready to extend an offer. I also recommended an unusually attractive offer, so that the candidate would be motivated to accept it and give no further consideration to any other alternatives. The managing partner of the Chicago office agreed.

I called the candidate that day and invited him to fly to Chicago the following week. He actually said that he was shocked that I even got back to him. He flew in the following week, interviewed with everybody, and at the end of the day the managing partner made him a very attractive offer, which he soon accepted.

I was his job manager for the first three assignments, which spanned about seven months. He was a superb talent. At the end of his second assignment, I gave him the customary performance appraisal. After I was done, he asked, "David, can I ask you a question that has been bothering me for a while?"

"Sure," I said.

He continued, "I did so badly on our first interview; I was wrong with practically every single answer. I never felt so stupid in my life. I was sure I'd blown the interview and would never hear back from Booz Allen. Yet, you called back, and now I'm here. How could it be possible?"

My answer was much longer than what I will state here, but in essence I told him that his answers were not wrong. I didn't care whether the answers were right or wrong. I wanted to understand how his mind worked and how analytical he was. He went on to have an impressive career at Booz Allen until his departure, at which point I lost track of his career progression.

How Interviewers Deduce "Liabilities"

Unlike the analytical skills, the liabilities are completely driven by proxies, which are random and hard to predict. Worse, they can be easily misinterpreted and viewed both in a positive or negative way, at the same time, and by different interviewers. Unlike the analytical skills, there are no methodologies or techniques that are somewhat common, and therefore easier to make you aware of them. The only way to help you avoid them is by listing the most common potential gaffes or blunders candidates innocently fall into during interviews.

The bad news is that an interviewer can easily incorrectly construe a candidate's comment or observation, however innocent. Worse, the interviewer may infer conclusions from a single statement that raises multiple liabilities at the same time. The good news is that interviewers have almost no ability to influence you. Thus, you have total control and can easily avoid making potential mistakes by being aware of the potential pitfalls.

Below is a list of the most generic mistakes interviewees make. I have seen interviewees, even experienced professionals and higher-level managers, make these mistakes while being interviewed:

- **Negative comments of any kind** about coworkers, managers, team members, departments, or the company overall will damage one's chances at having a successful outcome. *Examples*:

  "My coworkers were not as hardworking . . ." is a comment that may lead the interviewer to think that you:

  o   are potentially not a good team player.

  o   may be poor fit with employees.

  o   are apt to be overly critical and have a negative attitude.

  "I didn't agree with my boss . . ." is a comment that may lead the interviewer to think that you are potentially difficult to manage.

  "People working for that company are not very happy . . ." is a comment that may lead the interviewer to think that you:

  o   may be a difficult and unhappy employee.

  o   may have a negative attitude.

  "I was trying to tell them, but they didn't listen to me . . ." is a comment that may lead the interviewer to think that you:

  o   may not be a good team player.

  o   may potentially be difficult to manage.

  o   may be a person who is too sure of yourself.

  o   may be a person who has problems compromising.

o may not be capable of persuading coworkers when you actually have a better idea.

- **Using the word "I" too often** may lead the interviewer to think that you:

  o are not a team player.

  o are self-absorbed.

  o may be a poor fit with other employees.

- **Strongly maintaining an original opinion after being challenged by a question** from an interviewer can lead to a negative outcome. *Examples*:

  "I hear you, but I still think that I am right . . ." If the interviewer thinks you should have been open to a different perspective, then they may conclude that you:

  o have weak logic or analytical skills.

  o are stubborn, argumentative, closed-minded, and arrogant.

  o are likely not a team player.

  However, if the interviewer believes that you held your ground based on sound logical reasons, then some positive points may be given. Maintaining an original opinion even after the second challenge will trigger the same two potentially opposite responses, but with greater conviction.

- **Using extreme, definitive words** such as "I know," "I'm sure," "always," "never," "absolutely," "definitely," "there is no way," "the best," "the greatest," "the most," "the least," "the worst," and so on may suggest to the interviewer that you are closed-minded, arrogant, and too sure of yourself.

- **Trying to show that you are smart, even if subtle,** may suggest to the interviewer that you:

o   are immature.

o   are arrogant and a show-off.

o   are potentially an unproductive team player.

- **Obvious self-promotion or self-compliments of any kind**, without specifically being asked to give such comments during an interview, may suggest to the interviewer that you are a show-off and potentially a poor team player.

- **"Dropping names"** more than once may suggest to the interviewer that you are a show-off and immature.

28

Interview Dynamics

As mentioned throughout this section, the tone and/or style of any given interview session can vary widely. There is no significance to the tone or style. However, remember that **regardless of tone and style, the interviewers are focused on seeking information that will allow them to reach conclusions about the Priority List.**

Additionally, an inflection point typically occurs during an interview where the style and topics may change noticeably. By this I mean that the interview changes from inquiry-based to a more relaxed conversation. This occurs when the interviewer has reached a decision about the candidate and is not pressed for time.

At that point, the interviewer will extend an invitation to the candidate to ask questions. From my experience, the questions that candidates ask are not likely to influence the interviewer's overall judgement of the interview, with some exceptions. Most interviewees react in one of four ways:

1. Stating that they don't have any questions. This produces a neutral to a slightly negative reaction, but is not significant to the interviewer's overall assessment.

2. Coming up with some polite questions, believing that not asking any questions might reflect poorly on the candidate. This is a touch worse than the first, because the interviewer knows exactly what the

candidate is doing. However, it is so common that the interviewer will not exact a penalty, and asking polite questions will not influence the interviewer's overall assessment.

3. Asking questions about the company in order to impress the interviewer. Here, the candidate has done some research about the company with the expectation that showing interest in the company will be positively viewed by the interviewer. This is a common piece of advice given by schools to student-candidates, and then it becomes a habit for life, which is passed on from generation to generation of candidates.

    It is my belief that posing such questions will receive a poor reception. The interviewer may or may not be in a position to answer. I have mentioned this before, when I described my personal experience in the section dealing with writing a resume. Irritating the interviewer is exactly the reaction I got when I asked such questions.

    However, asking such questions is not likely to do much more than irritate the interviewer and will not influence the hiring decision.

4. Asking legitimate questions about the job and issues related to the job. **This would be viewed negatively in the early rounds of the interviewing cycle, but positively in later rounds, where it appears likely an offer will be extended. While such questions may be perceived as presumptuous at the early stage of an interview**, they can be reasonably expected in the latter stages. In either case, it is not likely, as in the previous three categories, to change the interviewer's overall assessment of the candidate.

The logical conclusion from the above is that, **unless you have to, or legitimately have some questions, politely decline the opportunity and don't ask any questions during early rounds of the interviewing cycle.** You may say, "Thank you for the opportunity to ask questions, but I don't really have anything that important at this point."

However, the above is not my overall recommendation. As I stated earlier, there are exceptions where I believe **a meaningful opportunity** does exist for candidates to set themselves apart through questions. This is so because most other candidates fall in one of the above-mentioned four categories, yet a *fifth* category does exist that mostly goes unrecognized. Just assume for argument's sake that there are some questions that would be viewed in a positive way by the interviewer, and that such questions would set you apart from the pack. Further assume that they are not just different but **would be viewed as smart, mature, or insightful questions, leading to meaningful, positive differentiation.** Wouldn't such questions give you a real opportunity to influence the interviewer's perception of you relative to other candidates? Of course they would. I'm here to tell you that there are such questions!

A list of these questions is provided at the end of this section (chapter thirty-two). They are different from what most candidates tend to ask and will be considered more mature, sound, and reasonable. They are also easy to answer, yet will be perceived as insightful, thereby generating a positive differentiation. However, keep in mind that it would be true only if you are viewed as a viable candidate by the interviewer.

You may ask any one or more of these questions as time allows. Be sensitive to how much time it takes. If you feel you don't have much time, ask only one or two. If there is more time, ask more questions. Use your judgment.

We have covered a lot of information so far in this section. With few exceptions, I mostly identified for you the issues and dynamics that take place in interviews. We are now ready to address the actual, specific recommendations that I believe will significantly increase your ability to influence interviewers.

As I have said, demonstrating analytical skills is the single most important factor in obtaining a job offer. There are three interrelated dimensions that together reflect on how one's analytical skills are evaluated and perceived. This is true not just in interviews, but in any short and condensed conversation about any topic. The three interrelated dimensions are:

1. the "way of thinking";

2. the way of articulating one's logic; and

3. methodologies that lead to sound analyses and recommendations.

The first and second dimensions, which I cover in this section, are the most important. However, they are based on innate talent that could be sharpened, but unfortunately there are no simple guidelines, instructions, or protocols to facilitate them. But I believe that one can become better at them, and I will give you my insights on how to improve yours. They are based on some subtleties that are easy to follow, once fully understood.

Fortunately, the third dimension is teachable, and you may be able to improve measurably your analytical skills. It involves a conceptual framework of how to properly analyze business conditions and opportunities. This is a more complicated topic to explain and will be discussed separately in great detail in a subsequent section (see section VII: "A Sound Methodology for Business Analyses").

Obviously, one will score the highest on the analytical skills when one is able to use effectively all the above three dimensions concurrently.

29

Dimension I: The "Way of Thinking"

People's perception of the "way one thinks" as related to analytical capabilities is driven by making observations about two questions: "How logical is the thought process?" and "What is the quality of reasoning behind the thought process?" People arrive at answers through inferences. They observe three key elements to help them separate the logical from the illogical and/or compelling reasoning from less compelling reasoning.

1. **"Deep" versus "Shallow"**—Deep thinkers build conclusions from the bottom up or conversely start at the top and drill down all the way to the bottom. Deep thinkers can take individual factors and see how they may be logically linked and combined to yield conclusions, and demonstrate how various conclusions can be combined to yield broader conclusions, and so on, until final conclusions are reached.

   Shallow thinkers are top-of-the-wave thinkers, in that they have a solution to offer that is based on shallow, incomplete logic and poor reasoning.

2. **"Thorough" versus "Scattered"**—Thorough thinkers give considerable thought to many factors that are relevant to the challenge at hand, and they will also reflect on the less relevant factors that may have a bearing on the analyses. They are able to differentiate the importance of the various factors, apply proper priorities to them,

and draw the right conclusions. Their logic properly supports the conclusions and recommendations.

Scattered thinkers rarely think of all the factors and draw conclusions based on partial logic and analyses. Often, they combine multiple separate observations to arrive at a single conclusion, but the observations used are only loosely coupled and not truly logical, nor directly supportive of the conclusion.

3. **"Broad perspectives" versus "Narrow perspectives"**—Broader thinkers can see and understand how one issue may affect other, seemingly unrelated issues. Narrow thinkers only see the one issue under consideration and draw conclusions based only on how that specific issue is impacted, without concern to how it might affect other issues.

Needless to say, perspectives that are deeper, more thoroughly logical, and broader are the most appreciated and will earn the highest score for analytical thinking. As I said, the way of thinking is an innate capability, but there are two quick ways to help improve it. One is a disciplined approach to asking yourself a number of questions before you reach final conclusions. The other involves what I will refer to as a "trick." It uses a combination of two factors: first, a unique perspective/understanding that will truly sharpen your analytical ability, and second, more of an articulation "trick," which will ensure that you receive the maximum credit for your analytical thinking. Following is a discussion of each.

The Disciplined Approach to Increasing Analytical Thinking

This approach utilizes a number of questions that will force you to proactively think in a way that yields better analytical results. Every time you articulate logic or draw conclusions, ask yourself:

1. Have I considered all the factors, relevant as well as less relevant, that affect the issue?

2. Is my statement supported by a bottom-up or top-down comprehensive logic? Are there any gaps in my logic? What are the counterarguments that might prove my logic wrong or weak?

3. Are there other seemingly unrelated areas that could be impacted? If so, how would that change my conclusions and recommendations?

Keep in mind that to do service to these questions, you will need to devote time to reflect on your logic and analyses, with a single focus of trying to find gaps and exceptions, and locating where your original analyses may not be complete or compelling. The good news is that when you ask these questions and take time to concentrate on them, the better your analyses will be. The best news is that with time you'll get better and better at it, and in the end it will happen automatically on your first iteration.

The "Trick" to Receiving Credit for Superior Analytical Thinking

I refer to it as a trick, but as you will see, it is not a real trick, per se. It is based on sound and insightful logic that works wonders on how people infer and draw conclusions regarding your analytical way of thinking. The "trick" emanates from a common mistake or logical flaw that people make, no matter how smart or analytical they are. By recognizing this flaw and pointing it out when appropriate, you will most likely stand out and be perceived as an insightful and analytical thinker, not just in an interview but in the workplace as well. The concept is a bit difficult to explain, but once you get the principle, it is relatively easy to put into practice.

The concept is based on the same principle as finding fallacy in common wisdom, but here it is somewhat different, and I call it a "mini common wisdom." It is not quite a common wisdom in magnitude and outcome, but it is also based on a logical fallacy that most don't pay attention to because it may appear to be flawless logic and/or has been passed on from one person to the next, and so people accept it as something true. I'll start with a conceptual graphical example of a logical decision-tree, and then follow with an actual example.

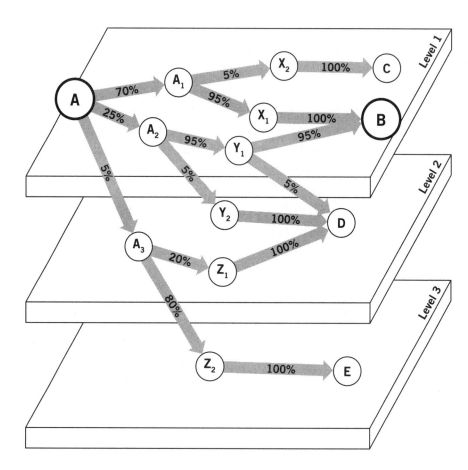

Fact (A) leads to three different scenarios: (A_1), (A_2), and (A_3). Each of these scenarios leads to two different scenarios: (A_1) to (X_1), (X_2); (A_2) to (Y_1), (Y_2); and (A_3) to (Z_1), (Z_2). (X_1) and (Y_1) lead to scenario (B), and the rest lead to other scenarios. The numbers on the branches of the decision-tree represent the probabilities of those branches to occurring.

Now, the probability that (A) will lead to (B) goes through two paths. (A) to (A_1) to (X_1) to (B), or (A) to (A_2) to (Y_1) to (B). Add up all the probabilities, and the probability of starting with (A) and ending up with (B) is over 90 percent, while the other scenarios have low probabilities as outcomes. Thus, in business, for the purpose of analyses, one will assume that (A) will lead to (B) and the conclusion would be perfectly acceptable, since this would be the preferred alternative. Obviously, as the decision-tree shows, there could be exceptions, but they are not very likely. Nevertheless, exceptions are possible, and thus there is a small logical flaw in assuming that (A) will lead to (B). This logical flaw is significant in two ways.

First, if you describe in the course of a conversation the real logical decision-tree, and show the different logical branches, concluding that the most logical outcome is that (A) will lead to (B), even if the final conclusion remains the same, which is that (A) leads to (B), you will impress everybody as to how logically deep and thorough you are. However, I can tell you unequivocally that in most situations there are exceptions. Just look for them and you'll find them. Should an exception you discover become key to solving a complex problem, you'll be looked upon as something of a hero.

The second point could actually be much more important. It deals with the "influencing" dimension. Each of the two branches represents different "rhymes and reasons" or different situations and different people and motivations. So, although they both lead to (B), the reasons, conditions, people, and motivations may be completely different. **If you want to influence, you will need to influence each of the branches.** Present such a logical decision-tree, show the different "branches" and the need to address them separately, and you will stand out from everybody else.

To summarize: **The "trick" is simply looking for the different paths (reasons) to an outcome and seeking commonalities and exceptions to the highest probability logic. Pointing out those exceptions and resolving them in whichever way may be appropriate will earn much credit for you. You will score the highest if, at the same time, you will show a better path to influence the outcome by following different logical branches.** Below are three examples of what I mean. The first is something I have already used earlier in the book. It is a simple, conceptual example that is easy to understand and clearly demonstrates how breaking a mini common wisdom into its components could lead to better, more insightful solutions. The other two provide real-life examples demonstrating that the "trick" is not limited to simple applications only, but rather has a much broader relevance in practically all situational analyses, whether in business or life.

A Simple Conceptual Example

In chapter eleven I discussed the topic of seeking advice. I guided you to seek advice from the "best" experts, but warned you to expect that the advice you are likely to receive could vary substantially. The simple initial solution was obvious: weigh the advice you get very carefully, and always own the final judgement.

Had I stopped there I would have imparted to you a mini common wisdom, which you would have likely accepted as solid, valued advice, but perhaps not seen as insightful, per se, and for sure not a detailed enough solution for how to deal with it.

I didn't just stop there, however. I used my "trick," as I have done many times in this book, and pointed out that there were four different component reasons for why significant variances in advice occur, and as a result, I was able to explain a key insight that led to more specific and powerful recommendations on how to deal with the variance. Just to refresh your memory, the four reasons for the variance included differences in articulation, discernment and perspectives, superficial and analytical thinking, and top-of-the-wave advice givers.

As soon as I broke it down into the various paths (reasons), an insightful observation emerged. As I wrote in chapter eleven: *The difference in the advice comes from how their brain works, and how they communicate it to the advice seeker. It does not at all reflect on how much knowledge they actually possess. It may appear like a nuanced observation, but it is not. It is the key to how to deal with it. It basically says that whereas most experts may not be able to originate and articulate "quality" thoughts themselves, they remain capable of grasping the implications and agreeing or disagreeing with someone else's observations. Therefore, there are two ways to deal with this nuance effectively and maximize for yourself the value of the advice you finally accept:*

1. **Always ask the reasons for their observations and rationale.** *The more you know the reasoning behind what they say, the more likely you are to put yourself in a position to intelligently accept or reject it. Don't forget to ask all the probing follow-up questions to make sure you truly understand their thinking and reasoning.*

2. **Confirm, and reconfirm, what you hear with other experts.** *Consult other experts to see how they react to what you have already been told. This will give you a great way to gauge the validity of what previous experts have told you. You will also hear different rationales and perspectives about the same observations, and thus be better able to decide, at the end of the process, which are the more correct and complete observations and recommendations for your situation.*

I hope you agree that the outcome I achieved by applying the "trick" yielded a much more insightful and powerful one.

The REAL MILK Example

While at Booz Allen I worked on an interesting case. The client was the Dairy Industry Association. It was the association that represented the milk-producing farmers in the United States as well as the companies involved in the dairy industry's supply chain, including manufacturers, distributors, and marketers of milk and dairy products. The study took place in the early 1980s. At the time, the U.S. government paid huge subsidies to the milk farmers by buying the milk they produced but could not sell. The price the government paid was based on the fat content per gallon of milk. The greater the percentage of fat, the higher the price paid. No surprise that all farmers were breeding and feeding cows to yield the highest-fat-content milk.

For about five years prior to my working on this case, the consumption of milk in the U.S. had declined precipitously. There were three main reasons. The first was the growing popularity, particularly among children, of soft drinks, which were offered in many flavors. The second was a huge trend in weight-loss programs and diets that advised avoiding high-calorie and high fat-content drinks. The third was the introduction of a product called a cheese substitute, which was much less expensive than the real thing and tasted like real cheese.

Although it was called a cheese substitute, it was still dairy based, but contained much less fat than natural cheese made from whole milk. Cheese and butter are made by extracting the fat content from milk. It takes a lot of milk to produce cheese and butter. The largest usage for cheese, in those days, was for making pizzas. The by-product from the milk, once the fat was extracted to make cheese and butter, was casein—milk without the fat content. Casein was dried and used to make powdered milk. Casein retained the protein, minerals, and vitamins originally in the milk. But there was little market for casein, and most of it was donated to countries in need.

Then a company "invented" a new type of cheese. They purchased casein at a very inexpensive price and added a small amount of real milk fat and some other ingredients to give the product the texture and look of real cheese. They introduced it to the market as "cheese with less fat and calories." The texture was almost the same as real cheese, and the taste was very good. After a few years, frozen pizza manufacturers substituted the much cheaper alternative cheese for the real cheese. The consumers didn't know the difference and perhaps would not have really cared. Not unexpectedly, many other food products that used milk as an ingredient began to use casein to reduce costs and calories in the product.

As a consequence, government subsidies increased at an alarming rate, making politicians very uncomfortable. They wanted to revisit the whole concept of subsidies. The Dairy Association was looking desperately at ways to increase consumer demand for milk in an attempt to avoid an increase in subsidies. Booz Allen was hired to look at the situation and make recommendations as to how to increase consumer demand for milk products.

By the time we entered the project, the association had devised a massive marketing campaign to alert the public to the fact that cheese-substitute products were not using real cheese, butter, and milk. This campaign would cost hundreds of millions of dollars over a five-year period. The association was betting on the fact that the consumer would no longer purchase cheese substitutes and other non-milk-based products once they knew the truth. The association would also print a seal on all milk-based products that would have the words "REAL MILK."

The association took a survey of its members to test whether the concept made sense, and whether the members would be willing to pay for the expensive advertising campaign. The results were astounding: 95 percent of their members thought the campaign was a great idea and were willing to pay money to implement such a program. It made a lot of sense to everyone, including the Booz Allen team, since in those days there was a general aversion to things that were not "real" and "natural." So, a mini common wisdom had just emerged into the light of day.

Coincidently, scientists discovered that the depletion of calcium during pregnancy and a subsequent lack of calcium in women's diets was a significant factor in osteoporosis, a condition that led to the loss of bone density, causing problematic brittle bones for older women in particular. Unfortunately, there are very few foods that contain calcium. Milk was an exception; it is a rich dietary source of calcium. The association's members believed that for this reason alone all women would now begin to drink milk to mitigate their calcium deficiency and help avoid longer-term osteoporosis issues. Everybody was convinced that this finding would contribute to reversing the trend and saving the industry. The Booz Allen team believed it, too.

So, as you can see, there were two (As) leading to a (B) solution for the industry. The first, the REAL MILK seal, had the expectation of alerting consumers to the "fake" alternative, and thereby they would purchase the "real" milk products. The second suggested that women would drink milk to avoid osteoporosis. The recommended daily consumption of milk to get the appropriate amount of calcium would be two glasses per day. Two glasses a day by women, by itself, would be enough to reverse the trend of milk consumption. Case closed! There was not a single person who didn't accept the above (A) led to (B).

I was the outlier. I had become aware of a new trend that no one else was yet aware of, which could logically counter the perceived (A) leads to (B). Additionally, by happenstance, I "discovered" another scenario in which (A) didn't necessarily lead to (B).

My father-in-law at the time suffered from a severe case of diabetes. He was taking insulin every day, which, over time, had a side effect of damaging his liver. He reached a point where his damaged liver became life threatening. My mother-in-law started to search for alternative ways to control his diabetic condition without resorting to insulin injections. This led her to seeking natural health alternatives. They became aware of claims that diabetes could be treated without insulin, strictly through "healthy" diet and food supplements.

For the next five years, my father-in-law never had to use insulin again, and his sugar level was in perfect balance. His diet was unpalatable, and I won't wish it on anybody—few would have the willpower to stick with it. But he did, and it worked.

Through that experience, I became aware of the emergence of a new industry—the health food industry—and the availability of extremely concentrated minerals and other food supplements in the form of powders and pills.

Hence, I saw the first possible exception to (A) leads to (B). If concentrated calcium were available in a pill form, with no calories, people would prefer to take it as a pill over consuming two glasses of milk a day. Under such a scenario, most likely (A) would not lead to (B), as everybody believed. I had found my first mini common wisdom fallacy.

My team did not accept my findings at first. Extracting minerals and converting foods into concentrated pills or powders was a foreign concept and somewhat defied logic at the time. I had to fight hard not to have the idea dismissed. I put a lot of time and effort into gathering enough information to present a compelling case to my team. The team eventually accepted the findings, which changed our entire thinking about what to recommend to our client. To this day I consider my contribution on this project to be one of the highlights of my consulting career.

The second case of (A) not leading to (B) happened luckily through one of the interviews I conducted as part of the project. As consultants, we interview a cross section of many different experts to gain knowledge and insights about a particular company, the industry, and its competitors. In a typical study, we may have in-person interviews with as many as twenty to fifty people, complemented by many more phone interviews.

In one of those interviews I met with a vice president of marketing for the largest manufacturer, distributor, and marketer of dairy products. This was a huge conglomerate with a well-known brand name. I was exploring with him the best way to launch the REAL MILK seal and advertising program. I must have spent almost three hours with him. During those three hours, I noticed that I kept using the words "dairy products," yet he kept using the word "milk." He never once used the word "dairy."

I told him what I noticed and asked him whether the fact that he consistently used the word "milk" instead of "dairy products" had any significance. He looked puzzled and said, "What do you mean? Use the REAL MILK seal for dairy products? There is no way we'll do it. We are only willing to do it for pure milk and nothing else!" Now it was my turn to be puzzled. His response made no sense to me, and without the endorsement of the largest player in the industry, there was no way the program could be successfully launched.

He continued by providing an explanation, which did make logical sense. He said, "We have spent hundreds of millions of dollars over many years on marketing and advertising campaigns to convince the consumer that our brand-name cheeses, butter, and dairy products are better than our competitors' products, so that consumers will buy our products. If we, and our competitors, put the same REAL MILK seal on all our products, it will commoditize our products. It will give the consumer the impression that our products and our competitors' products are exactly the same. Milk is the only product that everybody knows to be the same. So, putting the seal on milk would be fine with us; it is already viewed as a commodity item. Putting it on all other dairy products is a nonstarter for us."

He then proceeded to tell me that all the "smaller" players in the industry—hundreds of them—would love nothing more than to commoditize all dairy products, thereby erasing the competitive advantage his company enjoyed.

I suddenly understood why the association's members showed 95 percent support in the surveys for this proposition. No one seemed to pay much attention to the 5 percent that didn't approve—apparently too few to worry about, even though they represented the largest players in the industry. I now saw that this program was going to be dead on arrival! Again, a small exception to (A) leads to (B), but a fatal one here!

I immediately interviewed the other large competitors, and sure enough they all confirmed the same point. I gathered the team and shared my findings. This time it was easy to convince them, and I became a "hero" again. Unfortunately, we now had no immediate solutions as to how to reverse the decline in milk consumption. We knew we had to come up with some new strategies.

As it turned out, I was also instrumental in conceiving and shaping the final recommendations because, again by happenstance, I also benefited from one additional coincidence. In the previous year, I was involved with a study that required quite a bit of travel to Europe. What I had happened to notice, particularly in France and Germany, triggered what I realized could be a solution for the dairy industry.

At the time, in the U.S., there was minimal selection of milk and cheeses, while in Europe the variety of cheeses was remarkable. So we recommended that the government no longer link subsidies to the fat content of milk. We then recommended that producers should be encouraged to bring to market new varieties of dairy products, starting with nonfat milk; 1 percent, 2 percent, and 3 percent milk and cheeses; and other dairy products in a multitude of varieties. We recommended that the Dairy Association be funded to manage a new R&D effort to help develop new varieties for dairy products. Booz Allen made a presentation to the U.S. Congress, which accepted all our recommendations and applied pressure on the association and the farmers to adopt the recommendations so that the government wouldn't have to purchase so much unsold milk. The rest, as they say, is history. In retrospect, we were right on with our observations, conclusions, and recommendations.

The "Incompetent Management" Example

Shortly after I started JK&B Capital in 1996, I saw a great opportunity to raise a new substantial fund. The venture capital industry had begun to grow exponentially, and new sources of institutional capital became available to venture capital funds. The institutional investors had little experience in evaluating fund managers because it was an emerging industry. The tendency for investors was to invest in funds that had a proven track record, and it was difficult to convince them to invest in new funds that didn't. I represented one of those new funds.

All funds, and in particular new funds, were competing for those institutional investors. Institutional investors primarily looked for three differentiating criteria in making their investment decisions: (i) previous track record; (ii) past experience of the fund's manager, which would imply that they possessed the kind of skills necessary to do well in this emerging industry; and (iii) the specific investment strategy that the fund would pursue.

To invest in a fund, the institutional investor would have to conclude that the experience of the fund manager and the investment strategy of the new fund would indeed yield superior returns. Since the hi-tech industry was just emerging, investors had to use their subjective judgment in ascertaining what was really critical for a hi-tech start-up to succeed in the marketplace against the few but dominant corporations. As a result, they would also have difficulties ascertaining whether fund managers indeed possessed the necessary skills to help lead the hi-tech start-ups to success. The challenge for the new fund managers was similar to the challenges that candidates face in a job interview. They are competing against many other potential candidates and need to differentiate themselves in a superior way. Also, any negative proxy was enough to result in rejection.

I devised what I believed was a unique and compelling strategy to attract investors. I knew that conceptually it would be very impressive, convincing and uniquely so, enough to significantly differentiate my fund from all other funds. I was certain that the industry was about to undergo major, radical changes, with significant implications for which funds and investment strategies would likely yield superior returns. I needed to explain it to investors in a persuasive way.

The challenge was that what I had to say would sound completely different from the common wisdom at the time. Also, investors had neither the context nor the expertise to confidently conclude whether I was right. I decided that I needed some way to make them believe that I was more insightful and knowledgeable about the industry than all other fund managers. In other words, I needed some way to influence their perception of me and get them to accept, up front, that my opinions, even if radically different, were credible. If I was able to do so, then the investors would be much more likely to accept my view about the future of hi-tech and what it would take to be successful as a fund manager.

I became preoccupied with this dilemma. After five days something suddenly clicked. I found a mini common wisdom that had a major fallacy, a situation where everybody believes that (A) leads to (B), but I could disprove it conceptually.

If one would have asked anybody in the venture industry to enumerate the three most important things in a hi-tech start-up's success, one would have consistently heard the same answer: management, management, management. The quality of the management team was critical to the success of the start-up. Having a poor management team invariably resulted in failure. As a result, all fund managers seeking to raise a new fund needed to convince investors that they had the strongest experience in evaluating managers and/or had a great network of contacts that would result in the identification and hiring of the best management talent for their portfolio companies.

I found a fallacy in this common wisdom, which I could use to help influence their mindset about my understanding and insightfulness of the industry. Most VCs in the early stages of our industry came from financial, banking, and insurance companies. These companies had capital, which they were routinely investing in a wide range of industries. As such, they were the first to invest in start-ups, thereby creating a new category of investments: venture capital. The early VCs came from within their ranks. They knew how the process worked and whom to contact to receive the funds for investments. Bankers were perceived to have the knowledge of how to evaluate investment risk because, presumably, they did it for a living when approving loans (even though evaluating risk associated with debt is completely different from risk associated with business success of technology start-ups—but few understood it at the time). Thus, financial investors within the insurance investment departments and bankers were the first to take advantage of this new and emerging VC industry.

Another important, well-known fact was the failure rate of hi-tech start-ups. The majority would either completely fail, or fail to reach a success level that enables exit with attractive returns on investments. The industry more than made up for this ratio because the few that succeeded provided more than enough profits to cover the high ratio of failures. I used both facts to help influence their mindset about my credibility.

At the beginning of the presentation, I made an "innocent" comment to the effect that the industry was new and that most VCs, even those with some experience, didn't really understand it all that well. Thus, as a result, they were prone to making major mistakes. My comment naturally caught the attention of the investors, followed by a request to elaborate.

I then said, "Well, a good example is the pervasive belief that the most important thing for success in the VC industry is 'management, management, management.' It couldn't be further from the truth."

I let that sink in for a couple of seconds and could see the puzzled expressions on their faces. I continued, "Well, if I am not right [I specifically didn't use the phrase "if I am wrong"], then how could you explain the high ratio of failures, when every fund manager claims that they are able to evaluate and hire superior managers? Either they don't know how to hire well, because they fail with over 50 percent of their companies, or the 'management, management, management' mantra is not the true differentiator."

I could see the logic sink in and their facial expressions become less quizzical and more curious. I continued, "Obviously, fund managers have the experience to know what to look for in management teams and hire well. So one cannot help but draw the conclusion that the management team is not the most important reason for success or failure. Let me be clear: I'm not disagreeing with the statement that bad management will yield failures. I am also not disagreeing with the statement that good management is needed to succeed. I am, however, saying that good management is not the most important thing in determining success or failure. There are other reasons that are more critical than management, without which even the best management team will fail. Understanding those factors is much more relevant and more important to achieving superior returns. This is the only rationale that explains the paradox I pointed out earlier."

The investors had warmed up and were ready for my knockout blow. "It is easy to fall into the trap and the misconception that the most important aspect is 'management, management, management.' Assume for a second that there are other reasons for a hi-tech start-up to fail, completely independent of the quality of the management team. I claim that in most cases it is the architecture of the technology of the start-up that is the most important element for success or failure." (You may safely surmise that one of my proposed fund's differentiated strategies centered around it being the most "technical" fund in the industry.)

"Let's say for the sake of argument that a start-up developed a great technology and has the best management team. Let's say that six months later a new start-up introduces a competitive product, with a great feature that the market liked. Clearly, our company now must change its technology to add this feature. Most VCs in the industry do not understand technology, because they all came from financial backgrounds and not technical backgrounds.

"One important thing to understand about technology development is that there is an underlying architecture, a kind of a blueprint of the technology. This blueprint represents many trade-offs that affect the features and cost of the technology. This architecture becomes the most important part of the ability to make changes in the future. If it is designed in a way that does not allow flexibility for potential future changes, then changes would be costly to accommodate. If the architecture didn't take into consideration the capability to adapt, and didn't appropriately plan for future requirements, then it could never incorporate those changes. If the architecture anticipated some future changes, but those changes didn't occur while other changes did, the architecture would not be able to accommodate them. In other words, predicting what the technology trends will be and having the capability to incorporate them in a sound, flexible architecture that would permit quick and easy changes in the future is critical for any new technology and start-up company.

"So, back to our example. A new feature due to a change in the technology needed to be added, but the architecture wasn't designed with this in mind. It is very easy to underestimate the efforts in accommodating changes, particularly when the architecture didn't anticipate them. So, management teams always believe that they can make the changes quickly. They then lean on the R&D engineers to make it happen quickly. But it is very difficult. The VCs make demands, the management teams say that it is 'right around the corner,' and again it doesn't happen and the cycle repeats. Because it is unable to make those adjustments in time, the company's technology becomes uncompetitive and the company begins to fail.

"From the perspective of a VC, all they see is that management kept promising change but never delivered, which is clearly the sign of incompetent management; thus the VCs conclude that management incompetence leads to the failures. Since the VCs don't understand technology, they never suspect, nor understand, that failure is a product of inflexible architecture and not the wrong management team."

I had everybody's full attention when I then proceeded with my formal presentation. Needless to say, the central theme of my differentiation was that we would assemble a team with senior technical expertise and would become an exceptionally strong technology-oriented fund. In fact, a prominent statement in my presentation describing my newly proposed fund was: **"We understand technology better than the chief technology officers of our portfolio companies."** I also plowed new ground with that vision. Until then, the common wisdom was that the most important value-added skills that VCs brought to the scientist inventor/founder were financial, M&A, fundraising, marketing, and deal negotiation skills—in short, MBA-type skills. I proposed to bring in technology people with no MBA skills whatsoever. The more established funds had technical experts on their advisory board who were relied upon for quick advice during the due diligence process to help with the judgment of whether there was a need for the proposed technology. What I proposed to do was to take what other funds had on their advisory board and bring them as full-time and fully functioning partners of the fund itself. My logic was that if indeed the understanding of the technology and how it needs to change over time becomes more important, then my fund will be able to provide such value-added skills to the start-up companies on a constant and ongoing basis. Additionally, I argued that all other funds had a weakness with their board members, since none understood the technology side of the business, so how could they provide effective board oversight on anything that dealt with technology issues? I also argued that because we would be able to provide unique value in that respect, we would be invited to join many more potential deals to complement what other funds lacked, and therefore would be in a better position to select the better deals to invest in. Nobody at the time believed that non-MBAs, or anyone without a deep understanding of finance, could be successful in the VC industry. Every time I was asked, my answer was: "I can teach a good engineer everything about finance in two, three years, but I can never teach a good financial guy everything about engineering!" I also had two "traditional" (MBA-skilled) partners with financial/transactional backgrounds (one was myself) and made sure that we worked as a team on all investments so that all the necessary skills were brought together at the same time on all our deals. Investors seemed to have accepted my logic. I successfully raised over $500 million from some of the top names of institutional investors. All I predicted in my presentation indeed did come to pass. The industry changed completely over the following decade, as I foresaw, and we were well positioned to take full advantage of it.

30

Dimension II: The Ways of Articulating Logic

A s mentioned, the second dimension in inferring your analytical skills lies in how you articulate your thoughts, logic, and reasoning. In this case, I am not referring to a high degree of fluency with language. Rather, it is the substance of what you communicate, the logic and reasoning you present. The previous "Incompetent Management" example demonstrates that such articulation indeed plays a role in how knowledge and analytical thinking are inferred. This chapter provides a broader, more detailed description of all the various ways to achieve such desired outcomes through more "effective" articulation.

There are various ways of articulating the logic of (A) leads to (B). For the sake of an example, let's assume that (A) leads to (B) is a mini common wisdom that everybody is likely to accept. One way to articulate it is simply to state that (A) leads to (B), note that everyone is in agreement, and stop there. Do so and you will be thought of as a solid thinker and one who is able to logically influence others. However, by taking a different approach and articulating the full, logical decision-tree, and using framing, priorities, alternatives, trade-offs, and so on to explain how you arrived at your conclusions, people will give you credit for being a deep, analytical, and insightful thinker. In other words: **The more you frame the total picture and then frame the specific issue within it, define the variables with more precise interpretations,** place boundaries, and describe the logic and decision-tree that led you to your conclusions, the more credit for analytical skills you'll receive.

Add to your conclusions how best to influence specific outcomes based on specific logical branches of the decision-tree, and you will be given even more credit and go even further in differentiating yourself. Add to this the third dimension of analytical skills—the methodology that leads to sound analyses (to which section VII: "A Sound Methodology for Business Analyses," is devoted)—and you will likely outshine most.

Here, too, there are simple "tricks" that can be used to achieve the desired outcome. Each of the tricks will influence how your analytical skills are perceived; in combination, they are even more powerful. The tricks are pretty straightforward to understand and use. They are not really "tricks," but rather part of a very sound logical thinking process. But, as with the simple statement of the (A) leads to (B) example, pointing out the full logic and analyses buys you much more than simply communicating the final conclusions. It is more impressive and, more importantly, will yield better outcomes. Following are the "tricks."

When possible and appropriate, show the trade-offs. Most, if not all, alternatives have some kind of trade-offs. Sometimes, the term "pros and cons" is used instead of "trade-offs." Evaluating these trade-offs is an intrinsic part of reaching conclusions and recommendations. Oftentimes, people communicate the conclusions and decide not to talk about the trade-offs. They might think the conclusions are obvious or believe that it is a waste of time to bring up any trade-offs.

What they lose is a great opportunity to impress others in the room. By skipping the analyses and trade-offs and only articulating the final conclusions, they will only receive credit for being solid thinkers. But adding the trade-off analyses will result in appreciation for their analytical skills, depth of thinking, and thoroughness of logic. In some cases, it might not be appropriate to discuss the trade-offs for one reason or another, so use your judgment.

Framing the problem or issue and describing the methodology to be used to reach conclusions is always impressive. This refers to the idea of restating the problem or issue that needs to be resolved in a way that helps give it more clarity and therefore points in a clearer way to the type of analyses or methodology that might be required to resolve it. It also happens to be an effective technique to help shape a discussion and convince people to accept your conclusions and recommendations. You will not just be more convincing and reduce the likelihood that others will disagree with you, you will also receive great credit for being very logical and a deep thinker.

Frame the complete picture before focusing on the relevant items for consideration. This is similar to framing the problem above, with the same logic and benefits, but is slightly different. Actually, framing the problem may be a subset of framing the complete picture.

You first elevate the perspective and describe the totality of the picture and how the specific problem you want to resolve fits within that picture. Then you zero in on the relevant parts that need to be addressed. The relevant parts could be the specific problem that needed to be resolved in the first place.

To illustrate the application of these tricks, I make use of the tough interview question I talked about earlier in the book that was presented to a friend, who told me he had no idea as to how to respond, and neither did I. The interviewer asked, "How would you go about determining how many manholes there are in the United States?" (Remember, in those days, there was no internet, no Google Earth, no accessible repository of any publicly available data.) Although at the time I had no idea how to properly respond to this question, I can think of numerous responses now. Please take a moment and think about how you would respond to the interviewer's question; it will help you better understand what I'm trying to point out to you in this chapter.

Now, one potential answer would be something like this: "Some federal government department such as a bureau of statistics might have the data, so all I need to do is call them to get the appropriate data. Should the federal government not have the data, then I will try state-level departments. If they, too, don't have the data, then I will call municipal-level offices. Asking enough questions of enough officials should lead to the right answer."

Here is another possible response: "I would use sampling and statistical analyses to determine the answer. We will probably need four different samplings: large and dense cities, smaller and less dense cities, suburban areas, and rural areas. We can canvas a block of 8 × 8 streets in a big city and count the manholes. We can count how many such blocks exist in the city. Then it becomes a matter of extrapolation. We can do the same for the small cities, suburban areas, and rural areas. Add them all up, and we get a decent estimate of the number of manholes in the United States."

One more potential answer could be: "I will use sampling and statistical analyses to determine the answer. I will first find a large architectural company specializing in city planning and find out from them which variables they use to calculate how many manholes there should be in big cities, smaller cities, suburban areas, and rural areas. Once I know the variables, I can then use the same variables in my sampling and extrapolate from there."

Which of the three answers is more logical in your view? How would you rate the different answers, if you were the interviewer? How would you rate the answers relative to one another?

Now, let's use the various "tricks" to see how different the answer may appear to be. Notice that I will not change any of the details from the answers provided above. All I'll do is give a broader perspective and frame the various options to create a methodology that enables me to narrow down the options, provide details when needed, and show some trade-offs. I will use the top-down approach and interweave the "tricks" as appropriate. Here is the resultant answer:

> Off the top of my head, I can think of four ways by which we might be able to determine the answer. The four alternatives are driven by whether the data are recorded somewhere within the governmental structure or not. If the data are not available, then we will need to generate it from scratch. The only way to do so is by using sampling and statistical analyses to arrive at a reasonable approximation.
>
> There are therefore four separate options that might be available to us to get the answer. They reflect four separate assumptions as to how the data on manholes can be obtained. The first assumption would

be that some department at the federal government has this data. The second assumption is based on the supposition that the federal government doesn't have this data, but each state does keep track of such data. The third assumption is that neither the federal nor state-level departments have data, but that municipalities might have the data. The fourth assumption is based on the supposition that nobody keeps track of the number of manholes, and the data do not exist or cannot be found.

Clearly, the fastest, the easiest, and perhaps the most accurate data would come from the federal government. The next fastest solution would come from the states. The municipalities would be more challenging because of how many phone calls may be involved and the complexity of collecting all of the data. The fourth option, which is using various sampling and statistical analyses, should also be relatively easy, but the accuracy of the answer may be suspect.

Under the first three assumptions, that the data are housed in a bureau at federal, state, or municipal departments, the methodology used in obtaining the answer is simple and straightforward, which is to make as many phone calls as you need to locate the data. Start at the federal level, because it might be the most efficient method. If the data are not available, next try the state level, and if unsuccessful there, try the municipalities. Assuming that none has the numbers, or that it would be impossible to track the number down, then we proceed with the fourth assumption, where we need to conduct sampling and statistical analyses.

At first glance, and using common sense, I can see four different geographies that will need to be sampled, representing four different population densities. Here I'm assuming that the number of manholes is correlated to the density of the population, which makes sense to me. The four population densities, in my mind, are big cities; smaller, secondary cities; suburban areas; and rural areas.

We can select a representative block of 8 × 8 streets and physically count the number of manholes. Then, based on the number of square miles of streets, we can extrapolate the number of manholes in the big cities. The assumption here is that all big cities are somewhat similar in the way they are planned. To the extent that they are not, then our results may be distorted. We can correct such a distortion, but the sampling will involve doing it for each city separately, thus making the whole process much more cumbersome and complex.

We can use the same kind of methodology for sampling and extrapolating in the secondary cities and suburban and rural areas. I would recommend we try various different variables to extrapolate from. One is based on the number of streets. Another potentially could be calculating the number of manholes per the population base in the sampling area and then extrapolating based on the total population. Another could be using the geographical size of the sampling area versus the geographical footprint of the city as a whole. We do the same for secondary cities, suburban, and rural areas.

Now, there might be a shortcut possible, as well as a way to get a better list of correlating variables, which I would try first. I'd contact civil engineering companies that specialize in urban planning. They should know exactly how they go about determining where and how many manholes to put in the blueprints. They can tell us which variables they use for their blueprints in each of the different population density areas. Clearly, the statistical analyses and extrapolations will be much more accurate if we use those variables in our own samplings.

Now assume you were the interviewer; how would you have reacted to this answer? I hope you would have been much more impressed. If so, I close my case!

You have probably noticed that the above "tricks" are used throughout the book. As I stated, they are not really "tricks," but rather part of a very sound, progressive, logical process. This process does influence others when you are making a case for something. There is one additional benefit.

When you frame the issue/problem and use either the top-down or the bottom-up approach, you ensure that you cover in a more logically methodical way all the elements that need to be considered when analyzing an issue/problem. In other words, you will end up with a thought process that is more well rounded and much deeper. This is the real reason why people are so impressed when exposed to it.

Back to the original topic of this section of how to interview well: We've just covered the analytical skills criteria and are ready to move on to the remainder of the factors, which are the "liabilities" that can kill a job offer, regardless of your analytical skills. As you will see next, there is a single piece of advice I give regarding such "liabilities"— avoid them as best you can! I will next discuss how to do so effectively.

31

Avoid All Liability Proxies: Be Careful with What You Say!

We have discussed the damage that can be caused by the wrong proxies. **It is best to avoid them altogether,** but sometimes it might be impossible. In those cases, there is a better language that one can use to avoid the potential of being a victim of wrong interpretations. To best describe how to do it, I thought that it would be appropriate to take the "wrong" language I used in the earlier example, and show how to use "better" language that is much less vulnerable to "wrong" inferences. Clearly, there are thousands of variations of the actual language that can be used, but the examples below will give you a directional idea. In general, they suggest using "softer" language, giving more of a hint, rather than stating something directly, avoiding being adamant, avoiding criticizing others, and so on.

"My coworkers were not as hardworking . . ." Use instead:

- The contribution by team members varied somewhat.

- The performance of the team members wasn't as even as I would have liked it to be.

"I didn't agree with my boss . . ." Use instead:

- Although I clearly understood my boss's logic, I had a somewhat different perspective.

"People working for that company are not very happy . . ." Use instead:

- It appeared to me that some employees might not have been as happy working there.

"I was trying to tell them, but they didn't listen to me . . ." Use instead:

- I wasn't completely convinced that the team reached the right conclusions. I had a somewhat different perspective and wanted to share it with the team. I was unable to change the team's convictions.

Using the word "I" too often.

- There is no alternative, so try to use "we," "the team," "the department," and so on when you can.

"I hear you, but I still think that I am right . . ." Use instead:

- You bring up some interesting points. All in all, though, I'm not convinced that my observation is completely invalid. It still appears to me to have some merit.

Maintaining an opinion even after a second challenge from the interviewer. Use instead:

- Again, you bring up very good points, but somehow I still feel that there is some merit in what I said.

Using definitive words such as "I know," "I'm sure," "always," "never," "absolutely," "definitely," "there is no way," "the best," "the greatest," "the most," "the least," "the worst," and so on. Use instead:

- "likely," "probably," "I would expect that," "may not be the best solution," "looks like something that will likely work," "it appears to me that," "doesn't sound as convincing to me," "in some cases," "in many cases," "in most cases," "seems a little better to me," "doesn't seem as bad to me," and so on.

Obvious self-promotion or self-compliments of any kind during an interview, without specifically being asked to make such a reference. Avoid it, but if you cannot, use instead:

- "I would hate to take credit, but it just so happened that . . ."

- "I believe that I am reasonably good at . . ."

- "I was told that I am reasonably good at . . ."

- "I've been told by managers that I am good at . . ."

Other Observations and Recommendations Regarding Potential "Liabilities"

- Never try to cover up or excuse mistakes or lack of knowledge.

I mentioned earlier in the book that there is nothing wrong with admitting mistakes or that you might not know something. It may likely be fatal if you don't follow this advice in an interview.

It is not only true in interviews, but at work as well. Mistakes are most likely to be forgiven, but a cover-up is never looked upon favorably. Don't ever guess at an answer and take the risk of making an incorrect guess. If you feel like you must take a guess, for whatever reason, make sure you explain that it is a guess, just in case you might be wrong. A good way to position it would be, "I'm not sure I know the answer, but if I had to take a guess, I would say that . . ."

- Be relaxed in interviews.

Being nervous or tense is generally taken as a sign of a lack of maturity, while a relaxed posture is taken for maturity and confidence. There is no need to show any deference to the interviewer, no matter what their title and position might be. I always recommend to candidates in an interview that they behave as if speaking with a friend or family member who is there to help with some good advice.

- **In an interview, be friendly and always smile, smile, smile.**
  First, being friendly and smiling makes you appear more relaxed, and that is always preferred. Second, people react more positively to people who smile, rather than always having a serious countenance.

We have covered all the important topics I wanted to discuss about how to interview well. There are only two things left to give you, which are a list of "smart" questions to ask interviewers and a list of the "typical" questions that you should expect to be asked in interviews so that you can be well prepared to answer them.

32

Recommended Questions to Ask and Expect in Interviews

You may ask as few or as many questions as time permits. Be sensitive to the body language of the interviewer as you ask the questions. Use your judgment to decide when to ask, and when not to, when to continue, and when to stop. These questions can be brought forward in any and all interviews, and even repeated in subsequent interviews within the same company. Each will be perceived as being a mature, sound, and reasonable question. None puts undue pressure on the interviewer, or runs the risk that the interviewer may not know the answers; this is what makes the questions so valuable. It will most likely be so different from the questions of other candidates, current and past, that it is sure to catch the interviewer's attention and differentiate you in a positive way.

I divide the kind of questions you should ask into two categories: (i) impression-related, which are the questions you ask to influence the interviewer and differentiate yourself in a positive way, and (ii) knowledge-related, which are legitimate questions that you might have about the job, department, and the company you are considering for employment.

You will rarely have the time, nor should you take too much time, to ask a lot of questions. So, you should pick and choose as you deem appropriate for the circumstances. As a general rule, I would suggest the following overall guidelines:

- Impression-related questions are more appropriate in the earlier stages of the interviewing cycle. Avoid asking them in the later stages, when it becomes more apparent that you are likely to receive an offer. The reverse is true for knowledge-related questions.

- Try to ask at least two questions from the first category, impression-related, to help your differentiation, and only then ask the knowledge-related questions.

- Impression-related questions can be safely asked of all interviewers, regardless of their position or title. They were specifically designed with that in mind.

- Match your knowledge-related questions to the specific interviewer. Make sure that the specific interviewer is in a good position to competently answer your questions, and avoid asking questions for which the interviewer may not have the knowledge to answer them properly.

- Be sensitive to the body language of the interviewer. Stop asking questions when you sense that the interviewer is not answering them with enthusiasm.

Impression-Related Questions

- Who in your opinion are your company's main competitors, and what do you consider to be your differentiation as a company?

- What kind of a person and what does it take, in your opinion, to be successful in this position (or company)?
    - o Use "position" if the interviewer works in the department or a related department that is offering the job. Use "company" if not.

- Should a candidate be fortunate enough to receive an offer, what do you believe they should look at or consider when making their decision?

- What, if any, in your opinion are the pitfalls a new employee should be aware of in the first one to two years?

- Would you mind sharing with me what led you to join this company and whether there were any "surprises" after you joined?

  o Ask this question only with interviewers closer to your age group and/or who have not been with the company for longer than five years.

Knowledge-Related Questions

There are many legitimate and appropriate knowledge-related questions. You may ask whichever you feel would be appropriate under the circumstances, but try to follow these rules:

- Only ask the questions that you are genuinely interested in understanding.

- Make sure you ask questions that the interviewers can competently answer.

- Never ask questions about compensation or benefits unless a job offer was already extended. Most likely that type of information will all be spelled out for you in a formal written letter when the offer is made.

Questions You Should Be Well Prepared to Answer

There is no real significance to the questions listed below. Some of them make sense, and others I found to be less reasonable. I am listing them below so that you have an opportunity to think about the answers in advance, as opposed to being surprised and struggling to make up an answer during an interview:

- Why do you want to be in this industry (or profession)?

- Why do you want to work in this company?

- What kind of a place would you like to work at?

- What kind of a job (or career) are you looking for?

- Tell me something about yourself.

- What would you like to do (or be) in the short term (five years)?

- What would you like to do (or be) in the long run (ten to fifteen years)?

- What are your strengths and weaknesses?

- What do you consider to be your greatest accomplishment?

- What do you consider to be your greatest failure?

Congratulations for staying the course throughout this section. However, just for the sake of thoroughness, I want to remind you again that, as I mentioned at the beginning of the section, I only covered very specific observations and recommendations, those that I believe will likely give you greater insight that will enable you to do well in interviews and differentiate yourself from other candidates. There are many more straightforward factors that are identified in books, academic articles, and journals, and passed along as advice by knowledgeable people. Don't dismiss them offhand just because I didn't cover them. As a closing comment, I would like to emphasize an observation I made in chapters three and eight, where I discussed how to write a good resume. I mentioned that there was one fatal negative that will most often yield an immediate rejection, so make sure you don't fall prey to it. **Make absolutely sure that your resume has no typos or grammatical mistakes!**

A SOUND METHODOLOGY FOR BUSINESS ANALYSES

33

Correct Analyses Require a Proper Framework and Methodology

An integral part of doing well as a business revolves around carrying out analyses, reaching correct conclusions, making right decisions, and taking the necessary and appropriate actions. Doing the analyses well is essential to the performance of practically every business enterprise. Do analyses better and the business will do better. Do analyses less well and the business will do less well. To do analyses well requires a proper framework and a methodology that yields correct results and accurate understanding. The professionals who can do it well not only help their companies, but also help differentiate themselves from others, and are greatly rewarded.

Unfortunately, it has been my observation that most analyses in the business world are somewhat deficient and leave much to be desired. Worse yet, neither those conducting the analyses nor their managements who use such analyses are aware of the deficiency. All believe that the analyses and conclusions are of the highest quality. This is so for two reasons. First, relatively few learn how to do it well, and even fewer know how to teach it well. Second, there is a huge gap between the theory and the practice. So, even if taught well, analyses could easily be poorly executed.

However, one can become much better at it. Therefore, and because of its importance, any incremental improvement would lead to better business results and concurrently advance one's career. My goal in this section is to teach you the proper way to conduct analyses and also to bridge the gap for you between theory and practice. **The first question that should come to mind is, How can it be possible that this activity is so essential in the business world, yet relatively few know how to do it well?**

The most important aspect to understand is that the theory is not very complicated. It is the application of the theory, in its practice, where deficiencies creep in. Thus, as you read this section, focus your attention on the application and where the practice can falter. Understand this dimension and you'll become much better at it.

There are two key reasons why, in practice, this activity and its methodology are not applied well. First, as stated already, few are taught and practice this methodology to the degree necessary to do it well. Second, but just as important, to do it well is often expensive and time-consuming—and money and time are two commodities not abundantly available to professionals working for corporations. In other words, oftentimes those conducting the analyses must resort to taking shortcuts. Those who may know how to do analyses well and are competent at it will likely be careful enough with the shortcuts to make sure that the overall quality of the analyses and results are not overly compromised. Those who are not as knowledgeable and as competent (which are many) will very likely end up with compromised and subpar results.

In my view, this is so because only the most critical issues a company faces would receive the resources required to apply the methodology well. Thus, most of the professionals working for a corporation rarely have an opportunity to learn how to do it properly. So, it is routinely applied poorly, but not recognized as such, because neither the one conducting the analyses nor their supervisors and management possess the necessary expertise to properly assess it, or if they do, they rarely check the competence behind the analyses. It is not their role to do so, and they mostly assume that such analyses were conducted competently. Such analyses are also generally presented to management in a summary form. In those presentations, the focus is on the conclusions and recommendations requiring management's attention and actions, and not on the veracity of the analyses. In such a summary form, it is impossible to decipher how well and competently the analyses were conducted.

This phenomenon is amplified with time. Since it is difficult to decipher the quality from a summary presentation, the feedback from management regarding the presentation (which assumes that the underlying analyses supporting the observations and conclusions were done well) is often positive, and promotions still occur, leading all to believe that the quality was solid. Those same analysts then train the next generation of up-and-comers and the cycle continues, a kind of "the blind leading the blind" phenomenon.

Fortuitously, my experience was different, and I learned how to do it properly. There were three factors that facilitated my learning. First, I was taught by the best teachers. Second, I applied what I learned for many years with the best quality control supervision one could have. Third, I had ample opportunities to compare and contrast the difference between proper and deficient analyses early on and throughout my career.

I learned all I know as a consultant at Booz Allen. The premier consulting firms were hired by boards of directors or top management to work on the most critical issues facing a company. For this very reason, clients were willing to pay the hefty fees and expenses to ensure the utmost quality of the analyses, conclusions, and recommendations.

It is for these reasons that those consulting firms hired those they felt had the best analytical skills and who adhered to the highest standards of performance. The outcome was of significant importance to the clients, and there was little room for substandard quality. At the same time, there was an even more compelling reason for the consulting firms' high standards—the survival of the consulting firms themselves depended on it.

Because of the nature of the projects and because they worked directly for a board of directors, these firms wielded a tremendous amount of power and influence. Their analyses and conclusions exposed poor past performance, mistakes, incompetence, poorly considered decisions, and so on. Their recommendations in many cases affected individual careers, some for the better and some for the worse. The executives whose careers were likely to be negatively impacted didn't just passively accept the inevitable. They had their subordinates go over every bit of the data, analyses, and conclusions with a fine-tooth comb in an attempt to find something that would discredit the conclusions. Thus, these consulting firms would have never survived had they made mistakes.

It is in this environment that I was schooled, where I practiced for many years, and where I became reasonably competent at it.

34

Data: The Key Element in the Overall Methodology to Resolving Problems and Assessing Opportunities

The overall methodology and process to assessing business situations comprises four steps:

1. Data collection

2. Analyses

3. Drawing conclusions

4. Making recommendations

Compromise could happen anywhere along this process. However, it is my experience that the majority of the compromise occurs in the data collection and analyses phases. They are interrelated, and many times it is very difficult to know what was compromised. To fully appreciate where and how compromises occur, it would be helpful to understand how data are collected and used in the analyses.

Data Collection and Analyses

Data collection is the most critical element of the overall methodology for reaching proper conclusions. Everything is based on the data. If the data are compromised, so is everything else that flows from them. Unfortunately, this is also where most of the shortfalls and shortcuts occur. Do this part well, and the probability of reaching better conclusions and recommendations increases measurably.

The most important observation and understanding regarding data is best captured in the adage "Garbage in, garbage out." This adage emerged when computers began to penetrate the business world. Computers didn't do any "thinking," nor were they capable of checking results for "reasonableness." Numbers were input, manipulated according to specific algorithms, and results were spilled out into reports.

When the data were wrong, the results were wrong. When business managers received reports based on incorrect data, it was obvious to them that the output made no sense. They would blame the computers and the IT department. The IT professionals would tell these managers that they were not at fault.

The managers had no concept as to how computers worked. So, for them, it must have been the fault of the computer, because no human would have allowed the dissemination of obviously erroneous reports. It would have been caught on sight and corrected. Thus, endless back-and-forth arguments would ensue.

The IT professionals then coined a memorable phrase that attempted to explain how computers worked and why the erroneous reports were not the fault of the IT professionals or the computers: "Garbage in, garbage out." End of argument!

So, unequivocally, the highest priority in regard to data is to make sure that data do not comprise "garbage." In my experience, most of the failings occur because the practitioners view the adequacy of data from a narrow perspective, **mostly whether it is accurate**. In my mind, data must be viewed from a **much broader perspective** in order to produce a quality result. **Data need to meet four criteria to pass the adequacy test:**

- Be most relevant

- Be complete

- Be accurate

- Be organized

Each and all of the criteria require sound thinking and critical judgment. In most situations, it is not a straightforward undertaking. The process is prone to mistakes and, indeed, mistakes are made frequently.

To understand how to do it well and how easy it is to err, one needs to look at the various sources of the data. The sources of data (listed below) can be categorized into eleven distinct categories representing various collection and aggregation methods, and each is prone to potential errors and inaccuracies.

1. **Internal, elementary, raw data:** The "smallest" and most "raw" data elements that are collected at the source that generates them. For example, sales slips for "sales"; expense receipts for "costs"; self-monitored machine diagnostics of all kinds; and so on. These types of data, in general, are *reasonably accurate* and present few potential pitfalls.

2. **Internally aggregated raw data:** The raw data are generally aggregated into categories in order to allow management to see the bigger picture and observe trends. The aggregation continues upward, so that each management layer can view it from their higher-level perspective. These data, too, are generally *reasonably accurate*.

3. **Internal, raw data with allocated overhead costs:** These data are generated to allow management to get the actual manufacturing costs for the various products, as well as the various business lines. Indirect and overhead manufacturing costs are added to the raw, direct costs of an activity. This activity is most often used to calculate the real cost of manufacturing or "cost of goods sold," thereby the gross margins (gross profits) of the various products. The same is done to calculate the true total costs

of the various business lines by allocating to them the costs of the various support functions like research and development, marketing and sales, finance and accounting, and so on. There are specific methodologies and algorithms that are used to determine how to allocate the different overhead costs properly across the organization and products. These allocation algorithms attempt to allocate the overhead costs so as to represent the actual costs of the various direct activities, or business entities. These algorithms are at best an attempt to estimate the real costs and therefore are vulnerable to compromised results. **The accuracy of the allocations should always be verified whenever important conclusions are drawn from analyses using these data categories.**

4. **External, private-sector aggregated data:** These are data that are aggregated to include broader information than for a specific company. They come with different levels of aggregations. For example, the most common are an industry association's data for its industry. These data are generally used for multi-year trend analyses and are collected and completed by the different member companies. Nobody is responsible for the accuracy or consistency of the data, **and as such these data should rarely be relied on in making important decisions without verification**. They are fine for general, big-picture trend analyses. At Booz Allen, we never relied on this type of data without verification. Every time I attempted to verify such data by studying how they were collected and aggregated, I found deficiencies that gave rise to compromised data and inaccuracies.

5. **External public-sector aggregated data:** These are data collected by different governmental agencies, from local agencies all the way up to the federal level. **Accuracy may be questionable, as some data are more accurate than others, and should rarely be relied on without verification in making important decisions.** They are fine for general, big-picture trend analyses.

6. **Statistically generated data:** These are data based on statistical principles from which broader information/data are extrapolated.

Quality depends on the sampling, but if done properly, this type of data should be fine. **Always verify the sampling methodology.**

7. **Survey-generated data:** These data are generally collected via questionnaires and other such means of data collection methods. This type of data may generate more "complete" data, or may be used to generate "sample" data to be used as input for statistically generated data. This category presents many pitfalls. The quality of this type of data depends heavily on the veracity of the questions being asked and the sampling of the respondents. I found in most cases that such data are not thorough. Participants are not asked all of the necessary questions to lead to a complete picture on all of the important variables. The worst data compromise happens when the questions have multiple-choice answers. I rarely found the multiple-choice answers to be specific or accurate enough to allow respondents a clear, unequivocal choice. Most of the answers are, therefore, a best guess of proximity to the truth, and not the truth itself. **Check such data thoroughly before relying on the results.**

8. **Focus group–generated data:** These data are collected verbally from groups, with the collection carried out in a methodical way. Such data generate much better-quality data than questionnaire surveys. However, here, too, the quality of results heavily depends on the moderator, the questions asked, how and when they are asked, and the people selected for the focus group. I personally have sat in on focus groups and was seldom impressed. The moderators were often too quickly satisfied with the first level of answers; didn't consider a gap between how a person articulated an answer versus what they meant to say; rarely paid attention to the conviction level of the answer; and mostly ignored group dynamics and its impact on the answers. **Check such data thoroughly before relying on the results.**

9. **Informal customer feedback data:** This consists of verbal feedback, done in an informal, non-methodical way. **Accuracy cannot be relied on. Never rely on them without a more formal methodology to collect data.** Unfortunately, many times companies heavily rely on them, particularly if feedback comes from important customers.

10. **"Expert" interviews:** These are generally verbal interviews. It is a very important part of the analysis process. However, no specific data are collected and aggregated. So, there is no issue of accuracy. Just be mindful of the 80-20 Rule.

11. **Salesforce feedback:** This is an important but informal source of constant feedback. Salespeople are out there fighting daily in the trenches. They have firsthand experience with all the competitive dynamics on the ground. They are generally thought of as the eyes and ears of the company. However, feedback from salespeople may be unreliable and needs to be studied in a formal way before any hard conclusions are drawn and changes implemented. (An in-depth case study is presented later that convincingly illustrates this point.) This process is very susceptible to the "squeaky wheel gets the grease" phenomenon. Also, salespeople might have the tendency, for reasons of self-preservation, to blame everything on a product's price or features. Take the feedback seriously, but do additional due diligence before drawing conclusions.

Data Relevancy, Completeness, and Accuracy

While everybody would agree that any data used must be relevant and complete, the problem is that thoroughness is often in the eyes of the beholder. As a result, it is easy to believe that the data are relevant and complete when in reality they might not be.

First, let's discuss relevance. Relevance is a relative measure, and in my way of thinking—and in our case—has a dual meaning. It is in the dual meaning wherein the potential for abuse of the data and compromised results lies. The dual meanings are the two ends of the stick; one can look at it from one end or the other. They represent two opposite directions of using data and logic. One way is to have *relevant data* justify the relevancy of a conclusion. The other is to have an *irrelevant conclusion* be derived from what *may appear* to be relevant data.

Conceptually, data only become relevant because they support some observation or conclusion. Without a specific observation or conclusion, data, by definition, have no relevancy. Do you see the nuance? Any data that support any observation or conclusion automatically become relevant to that conclusion. Yet, the observation or conclusion itself may or may not be important, relative to the issue or challenge at hand. Thus, **to decide whether the data are relevant, one needs to look at whether the observation or conclusion they support is relevant or not.** Placing judgment on that is not simple.

Oftentimes, people see a subset of the data that they believe leads to a logical and relevant conclusion. Yet there may be other data that could be even more important, and that may even negate the initial observation. This is a classic case of actually not seeing (or looking for) all the trees, yet believing we are clearly seeing the forest. This is why I said that data must also be complete (where you are looking at all the trees before you focus on the forest) to allow for proper analyses and conclusions. When data are not complete, compromised business decisions are likely to be made.

Thus, I define relevancy to acknowledge this potential pitfall. I define it to be relative to the **overall quality, importance,** and **correctness** of the **observations or conclusions they drive,** as opposed to data that drive relatively unimportant or even potentially misleading observations or conclusions. This leads to another logical point: The only way to place judgment on relevance is when one knows without doubt the correct observations and conclusions, which is rarely the case. Thus, a judgment call is made, and as such is rife with potential pitfalls and mistakes. The following is an example of just how easy it is to err with the relevancy and completeness of data.

Example: The Case of Airfone

In 1986, a few years after the breakup of the AT&T monopoly, the founder of Airfone approached Ameritech for a very large investment and a potential partnership agreement. Airfone was a company that was founded by the founder of MCI Communications, Inc., a few years earlier.

MCI was the first telecommunications company that began to compete directly with AT&T for its long-distance telephone business. For more than a decade, MCI fought AT&T in court until finally, in 1980, it won an antitrust lawsuit that subsequently led to the breakup of AT&T. It was the first and only organized competitor to AT&T for its long-distance telephone business and was able to offer substantially better prices for long-distance telephone calls. MCI grew rapidly to become the second-largest long-distance telephone company, behind AT&T. The founder of MCI shortly thereafter retired from the company and founded a number of start-up companies. One of those companies was Airfone, which was based in Chicago.

Airfone's vision was to become a main player in the newly emerging cellular telephone technology and industry. While the cellular industry was seeing some momentum, calls were expensive at thirty cents to fifty cents a minute for local calls, and double that cost for long-distance calls. Airfone was developing technology for the airline industry, wherein passengers would be able to make telephone calls in-flight. It was an ambitious and costly undertaking. The founder had already invested close to $30 million to develop the necessary technology. He approached Ameritech soon after Airfone had developed a working prototype. He had also secured, on an exclusive basis, service contracts with some of the largest airline companies to install the technology in their airplanes. Initially, the service would be available in the U.S. only, but with time it could expand internationally. Airfone estimated that it would require about $100 million of fresh capital to finish the development, commercialize the technology, and launch the business. Ameritech was their preferred strategic partner. Both were headquartered in Chicago, and Ameritech was the largest telephone company in the Midwest and rich in cash.

I met with the founder to evaluate this opportunity on behalf of Ameritech. Our initial meetings centered on the viability of the technology and the risk involved in finishing the development and commercializing the technology. Because of the substantial cost of installation in the airplane, the initial phase called for between two and six cordless phones per airplane, depending on the size of the plane. The phones would be placed in the galley, adjacent to the kitchen. They would be connected via wireless technology inside the plane, so that the passengers could pick them up and take them from their cradle by the galley to their seat for use. The calls would be transmitted from the airplane via radio communications equipment to a specialized network of receiving towers on the ground. Those towers would then need to be integrated into the existing cellular industry towers to complete the calls.

After extensive due diligence, we were convinced that the technology could indeed be successfully commercialized, albeit at a substantially greater cost than Airfone estimated. We subsequently began to discuss the business potential of the opportunity and negotiate the terms of the partnership.

Airfone presented its business case to us in detail, which was very impressive and looked promising at face value. They presented a logical plan that suggested the business would become successful and grow to billions of dollars in revenues. Based on their assumptions, they placed a pre-money valuation of $500 million on the company. The centerpiece of the data was an extensive survey of thousands of airline passengers from around the country, who were asked if they would make use of a telephone on an airplane. Ninety-five percent of the responders said they would, and 50 percent suggested that they would make multiple calls. With such a demand, the phones would be in constant use. Multiply the large number of airplanes by their average flight-time per flight, and then by the cost per minute charge for the call, and you easily get revenues into the billions of dollars.

I asked to see the questions used in the surveys and was given a list of fifteen questions. I studied them carefully and then said to the founder that we would not have any interest in pursuing partnership discussions with Airfone unless he was willing to accept a value of about $50 million, which was a little more than the cash he had invested in the company up to that point. Of course, I provided the logic of my position, but he strongly protested before leaving. He went to look for another partner and successfully reached an agreement with GTE, which was the largest independent telephone company in the United States, competing in both the local and long-distance telephone services.

What I saw, and based on what they told us in earlier discussions, was a fatal flaw in the questions of the survey. The questions overlooked a critical dimension. It was hard to accept that such a simple and obvious error would escape scrutiny.

As hard as it is to believe, Airfone never asked the passengers whether they would be willing to pay five dollars *per minute* for a call. Such a high price was needed to support the heavy cost of providing the service. Just to put it in perspective, five dollars of value in those days would be equivalent to about ten dollars to fifteen dollars in today's money. Nobody in their right mind would spend so much money per minute on a telephone call, unless it was an emergency. With such a steep price, I didn't think those phones would be used as often as Airfone thought they would.

This may have been a case of either complete incompetency or passive incompetency, but incompetency, nevertheless. The complete incompetency refers to those who drew up the questions for the survey, who may have been lower-level managers not concerned with price, and top management, who were not involved enough to notice it. The passive incompetency would have been an incompetency out of naivete. The survey was conducted before the technology was fully developed, and perhaps used to justify the investment in developing the technology in the first place. As such, Airfone may have believed, or assumed, that the cost to build its technology would have been comparable to the cost of existing cellular technology, and thus the price of a call would approximate the then current cellular rates. In either case, Airfone should have corrected the survey once it realized that the pricing would be completely out of whack with standard rates.

In retrospect, I was right. GTE subsequently invested in Airfone and lost hundreds of millions of dollars, and the business never took off.

Interestingly enough, there were two other major problems with the initial plans, which proved to be critical as well. Both problems could have been avoided and addressed with a smarter initial design of the technology/product had the data collection been more complete. One of the problems dealt with airline regulations, the other with human behavior.

The first was Airfone's assumption that the phones would be used throughout the entire flight. However, between ten to twenty minutes after takeoff and prior to landing, passengers are required to be in their seat, thus reducing the number of potential minutes of use by at least twenty to forty minutes per flight. The second problem was even worse. Passengers would pick up the phone at the galley by the kitchen, go back to their seat, and attempt to make a call. If they got a busy signal, which occurred often because the network coverage was not yet ubiquitous, they would not return the phone to the galley. Rather, they would keep it with them and redial a few minutes later, and so on, until they got through. Thus, phone use in reality became very limited. To solve these two problems, Airfone/GTE redesigned the technology to allow a telephone to be installed in each row of seats. It was massively expensive. I learned about those facts because two years later the company needed to secure another $200 million in funding and invited Ameritech to join their partnership. I turned it down again because I wasn't convinced that there would be any financial returns for many years to come.

As it turned out, the promise of Airfone/GTE never materialized. GTE was subsequently purchased by Verizon. Airfone operations lost hundreds of millions of dollars over the years and service was completely terminated in 2006. Some quotes from Wikipedia capture well the demise of Airfone:

- "The head of the Airfone division told *The New York Times* in 2004 that only two to three people use the Airfone service per flight."

- "On June 23, 2006, Verizon Communications, Airfone's parent company, announced that they would be discontinuing their Airfone service on all commercial flights by the end of 2006. They cited the declining use of the service."

- "On December 28, 2007, Airfone announced it would discontinue service effective December 31, 2008, unless it successfully concludes negotiations with LiveTV, an affiliate of JetBlue, to take over the business on that date."

A conversation on Aviation Stack Exchange, an online question and answer forum for aircraft enthusiasts, captures the essence of the demise:

Question: "Did AirFone ever make money?"

Answer: "I remember when the first AirFones were put into service in the 1990s and marveled at who would be rich enough to pay $7/min for air-to-ground phone service. Even though every seat eventually had an AirFone, I cannot once recall seeing one in use (except in movies) in twenty years of flying (in economy)."

Question: "I know they're being pulled out now, but did AirFones ever make a profit? Who paid for their installation? Was it the airlines or did GTE, etc., pay for everything?"

Answer: "Despite impressive technological achievements and great expectations all around, the service's business performance ultimately proved an **abject failure**. In the ten years before Verizon finally pulled the plug, Airfone generated only 50 million total calls, a fraction of the calls carried daily by cellular companies. While the Airfone service was heavily used when bad weather caused significant delays, the system's utilization at other times was extremely low. A typical plane was equipped with as many as 60 phones. From these, the average large jet generated fewer than 100 calls per day in about 16 hours of flying time. As a result, **the expensive system, with its heavy load of fixed costs, remained idle well over 99% of the time.**"

Data Organization

Simply collecting data is not all that is required before it can be analyzed. The data must be organized so that one can observe findings that lead to conclusions. Most data and trends are best portrayed via graphs and charts of all kinds.

We are now ready to proceed onto the next steps of the process.

35

The Methodology for Proper Analyses, Conclusions, and Recommendations

This phase of the process is where the heavy lifting takes place and where analytical skills and insightfulness rise to the forefront. This is the phase that counts most in making the correct observations and reaching the optimal solutions. It is also where potential flaws and deficiencies may come into play, resulting in subpar or even erroneous outcomes. Fortunately, there are ways to mitigate them.

First, I'll identify a generic conceptual methodology for you to follow, which will more likely lead you to higher-quality results. Then, I'll point out some insightful observations that should help elevate the quality of your work significantly. I will also point out where and how the most common mistakes are made so that you may be able to recognize and avoid them. Finally, I'll walk you through a detailed, step-by-step example to liven it all up for you.

The methodology is appropriate for most, if not all, the issues you may be called upon to deal with. Many of those issues will likely focus on the competitive dynamics and financial performance of a company or product. For this reason, I will tailor my comments and explanations to more specifically align with these kinds of analyses.

Before I get into the specifics, I would like to address a nuance, and as usual, one that is front and center in achieving optimal results. The nuance lies in the difference between the end results of shallow and simple perspectives versus deeper and more insightful analyses.

The following may appear to be an oxymoron, but it is not. It may appear to be insignificant, but it is not. It is an important observation to ensure that conclusions and recommendations are well communicated and understood by the decision makers. Otherwise, they will not be adopted and implemented:

> **Whereas most compromised conclusions and recommendations are a result of relatively shallow and simplified analyses and perspectives, deep and thorough analyses, conclusions, and recommendations must be conceptually simplified in order to be well communicated, understood, and properly adopted.**

In other words, it is difficult to tell compromised conclusions and recommendations apart from the correct ones, since they both appear simple and only give a "top of the wave" perspective when communicated to management. The real difference stems from the quality of the analyses that led to them, which is rarely communicated at higher management-level presentations. That is why, **when you are in a management position, you must understand the quality of the analyses behind any conclusions and recommendations before accepting them.**

Insight: The Key to Achieving Quality of Analysis

Analyzing competitive situations is never simple. There are many variables and interrelationships to consider. In most cases, significant insight is necessary to enable the best understanding of these variables and interrelationships, and therefore, the most accurate conclusions and recommendations. The professionals behind the analyses spend an inordinate amount of time and energy in the process. They become intimately involved and familiar with every aspect of it. They know the many inflection points and the different branches of the decision-tree that led them there. They know all the nuances and see all the details, without losing sight of the overall relevance and importance of each.

They understand exactly how the complex details led to the final conclusions and recommendations.

This is not the case for management or, for that matter, anybody else not involved with the actual analyses. Those people have limited time to absorb the essence and full details behind the analyses, conclusions, and recommendations. Thus, the challenge is to reduce the complexity inherent and embodied in the analysis phase into a simplified, clear, and convincing presentation that management can quickly comprehend and feel comfortable with when subsequently endorsing the necessary recommendations.

There are two parts to doing it properly. One deals with how to conceptually summarize and explain the actual findings, conclusions, and recommendations, without sacrificing the full picture and the essence of what is important. The other part deals with the actual writing of the presentation deck/report itself. The two involve different aspects and are reasonably independent activities, other than the fact that the conceptual simplification of the analyses and conclusions must occur first; otherwise, it would be impossible to simplify the writings. I am addressing only the former in this section and won't discuss how to compose and generate well-written presentations. (Recall how I emphasized the importance of the actual written reports/presentations at Booz Allen, which added about an extra one-third to the project time.)

The process of simplification is done through framing, defining, categorizing, and grouping variables with common logic that leads to the same outcome. Then, these groupings are further consolidated into still higher-level categories until the most macro-level, top-down perspective is achieved. To do so properly, the important must be separated from the trivial; the high-priority from the low; and the variables with the most impact from those with a lesser impact. The following three rules will help one do so properly:

1. **The groupings must be logically sound.** This means that, in the minimum, there is obvious logic for why the groupings are correct. **Variables grouped together would have either individually led to the same conclusion or would have had no impact on the final conclusion.**

This way, the new groupings continue to focus on and lead in the desired direction.

2. **The groupings must remain independent from each other.** In other words, all the important interrelationships should be fully captured within a single group and should not spill over into other groups.

3. **The groupings should represent and emphasize the more relevant and important variables that drive the final conclusions and recommendations.** In other words, the grouping is done so as to emphasize the most important aspects of the entire analyses that will maximize succinctness and comprehension while maintaining focus on the most important and relevant variables, conclusions, and recommendations.

This book is full of these kinds of simplifications. I define concepts and terms more precisely to help categorize them in more appropriate, logical ways. I frame and reframe issues to create better-defined groupings and a clearer focus on the higher-priority and more impactful variables. I also use top-down and bottom-up approaches to allow for the more convincing logical flows.

It is the exact same process that should be applied when it comes to simplifying any and all business analyses for the purpose of better defining and explaining the logic flow and reasoning of findings, conclusions, and recommendations. There are some common "tricks," which I will point out, that can make the process a bit easier to accomplish.

A quick side note: I mentioned in an earlier chapter that in job interviews one can score higher on the analytical skills by describing the methodology that can be used to resolve an issue or reach conclusions before diving into any specific conclusions. The methodology discussed in this section could be used in any case-study discussions to frame the approach you plan to take. Use it if you can. It sounds impressive and will further differentiate you from others.

The Methodology for Market and Competitive Analyses

This methodology comprises eight distinct steps and an iterative process that lead toward successful analyses, conclusions, and recommendations. The steps are:

1. General assessment of the current situation

2. Trend analyses and current competitive dynamics and segmentation

3. Development of key success factors

4. Evaluation of competitors and the company relative to the key success factors

5. Drawing primary conclusions

6. Devising alternative recommendations

7. Analyzing trade-offs of alternative recommendations

8. Reaching final conclusions and recommendations

Step 1: General Assessment of the Current Situation

In this step, background and performance-related information is assimilated for context. It defines the basic, big-picture competitive "lay of the land." It assesses recent industry dynamics and the company's performance, and identifies the issues and challenges that may need to be addressed. It may also include a description of the exact methodology that will be followed to address and resolve the identified issues and challenges. It is generally a straightforward undertaking.

Step 2: Trend Analyses and Current Competitive Dynamics and Segmentation

It is in this step where most of the basic analyses that lead to the more important observations are carried out. It builds the necessary foundation upon which the observations, conclusions, and recommendations will follow. This step identifies and explains the important market and competitive dynamics currently at play. The most important aspect of the analyses is to accurately define the segmentation of the market. It is in the definition of various segments where most of the insights occur, as well as where many of the compromised subpar conclusions take place.

Segmentation of the Business and Markets

Note: This topic regarding segmentation is reasonably complicated and represents a "Level 3" teaching (per the three levels I mentioned in the Author's Note). A reader without an MBA, and/or one not deeply involved in the analyses of competitive and corporate strategies, may find some parts regarding the theory somewhat confusing or unclear. However, it is not essential to fully understand the theories in order to gain the full benefits and insights I intend to share with all readers. The more important take-away observations from what follows are summarized toward the end of this segment.

Segmentation reflects the activity of dividing a broad consumer or commercial business market into subgroups based on some type of shared, common characteristics. Segmentation can be done along many different dimensions, such as different businesses, different product lines, different customers, different demographics of customers, different income levels, different geographies, different countries, different distribution channels, and so on. Each segmentation scheme or grouping of customers is generally designed for some specific objectives. For example, segmentation to help devise specific marketing and advertising campaigns may be done along demographics, age groups, income levels, product preferences, geographies, and so on. Segmentation for the purpose of financial reporting and measuring profitability can be done by product lines, geographies, distribution channels, and so on.

However, whereas most segmentations aid in the management of some specific objectives and/or activities, there is one category of segmentation that is most critical in determining overall competitive strategies. This category is referred to as Business and Market segmentation (as opposed to customer segmentation, geographic segmentation, demographic segmentation, product lines segmentation, financial segmentation, etc.). This Business and Market segmentation is specifically designed to capture the most important aspects of how to compete successfully and outperform other competitors. As such, this segmentation represents critical building blocks that help shape and differentiate overall competitive strategies, thereby representing the highest level of potential impact on the performance of a product, company, or enterprise. It is not a trivial undertaking and is mired with pitfalls. It requires competence and expertise to be done well. One can find many books and articles that address this topic and how to go about correctly defining Business and Market segments. In this section, I plan to cover only a specific aspect of it, one that is not well addressed elsewhere and that would be of benefit for you to understand. However, some background information is first needed for context.

About forty years ago, the concept of business segmentation changed dramatically. It evolved from straightforward segmentations generally along a single dimension like different customer groupings and/or product lines and/or geography to more complicated and sophisticated segmentations that were generally defined along multiple variables that fully captured and put boundaries around the most strategically important competitive dynamics. They were referred to and became known as *strategic business segments* (or, in short, strategic segments).

The proper, more complicated, and multidimensional strategic segmentation required a higher degree of specific analytical skill and expertise, which at the time few corporations possessed. It required a deep understanding of the competitive dynamics in the industry of all the players, including direct competitors, indirect competitors, supply-chain companies, distribution channels, sales activities, and customer behavior, to name a few. Segmentation was no longer a discrete, independent, automatic classification exercise, as was the practice before. It had been transformed to acknowledge many different, broader competitive forces that were at play in shaping the competitive landscape.

For example, before the introduction of the new business segmentation concept, a kitchen appliance company may have defined its segments by its various product lines; a competitor may have used a different segmentation, like different geographies; a third could have segmented along the various buyer categories, like direct sales, wholesalers, and retailers; a fourth may have segmented along the various distribution channels it used, like large specialized appliance stores, large general-purpose department stores, medium-size specialized appliance stores, medium general-purpose department stores, small general-purpose department stores, small retailers, and on and on. Yet, all those competitors essentially sold the same products to the same potential end users/customers. So how could different competitive strategies be effectively formulated when each competitor used an arbitrary, single segmentation scheme?

The new theory argued that there are definitive, common-to-all-competitors business segments that capture the real competitive dynamics in the marketplace and explain the relative success of the various competitors. Each of the segments represented different competitive dynamics and success factors. Thus, each competitor needed to devise different competitive strategies to compete in each of the segments, and competitors were not required to compete in all the segments. It also explained why competitors had varying degrees of success—they could be successful in some segments but not others. In other words, different competitors had different strategies that were better suited to compete in specific segments but not necessarily in others. Examples of such multidimensional business segments in the appliance industry could include large builders who bought direct from the manufacturers; large specialized appliance stores; small- to medium-size specialized appliance stores; large general-purpose department stores; and so on. There could even be additional and more refined segments; for example, a single segment like large builders who buy directly from the manufacturer could be broken up into multiple business segments, such as large builders in rural areas versus those in urban centers.

To determine the new strategic segmentation, one needed to understand everything about the competitive dynamics in the industry. Such deep and insightful understanding was not a trivial exercise. At Booz Allen, for example, we would read everything available about the industry, including information published by the different competitors. In addition, we would interview on average between thirty and sixty different executives who represented the various players in the industry to broaden our understanding. A commitment to an undertaking like this requires resources and expenses to a degree that are rarely available to internal corporate staff.

Furthermore, such preparation was just the legwork—the data collection phase for the analysis stage. One would think that after thirty to sixty interviews of high-level executives and other industry experts, a consistent picture of the actual competitive dynamics would easily emerge, but this is not true. The perspectives and opinions as to what is important vary substantially. Everybody has their own perspective based on their own individual experiences, and nobody has a handle on the correct overall picture and insightful understanding of the totality.

This reminds me of, and is analogous to, an observation I made while at Wharton. As part of our class material, we used case studies to learn how various theories can be applied in real situations. Generally, the case studies were based on companies that had experienced poor and deteriorating performance. We students were asked to analyze the case studies. This meant that we were to reach an understanding of the reasons for the deteriorating performance and come up with the proper recommendations that would either help the company to avoid the deteriorating performance or reverse the trend.

What I noticed fascinated me. In all of the case studies we were given, without a single exception, the problems were always and exclusively related to the subject of the class, and so were all the solutions. Meaning, if the case study was part of a finance class, all the problems that led to the company's deteriorating performance and the commensurate solutions were finance related. In the marketing class, they were marketing related; in the human resources class, they were human resources related; in the accounting class, they were accounting related; and so on. Most of the professors were not even cognizant that there may have been other factors involved, some perhaps even more important to understanding and solving the performance-related issues of the whole company. This is also how easy it is to have a narrow perspective in business and remain convinced that such a perspective is an accurate one. This is why developing a total and complete picture with real, deep, and insightful understanding is not a trivial task. **Proper strategic segmentation became the underpinning of such a complete and correct understanding.**

As stated, the concept of segmentation changed in a fundamental way about forty years ago. The Boston Consulting Group (BCG) was the main driver. This is what propelled the firm's initial reputation and success. Until that time, segmentation tended to focus on categorizing the various customers. The implicit assumption that underscored segmentation was that the better a company understood its various customers and their needs, the better it could address those needs with the right products and services. In turn, the more the customers' needs were met, the more products they would buy from the company, and thus the more financially successful a company would become. This changed dramatically with a new concept introduced by BCG. It coined and introduced the new concepts called strategic business units and strategic business segments.

The introduction of these concepts fundamentally changed a long-standing common wisdom that "customer segmentations lead to a better understanding of the customers and, therefore, better financial results." BCG suggested that it was fallacious and that there were completely different reasons for the relative performance of the different competitors. BCG claimed that those competitors that have the lowest overall cost structures stand the best opportunity to outperform others. The logic was simple: The lower the cost, the lower the price; the lower the price a competitor can offer to its customers, the higher the number of customers who will buy; the higher the number of customers who will buy, the more sales and thus the more successful the company.

Accompanying this new theory were a couple of other observations, which I alluded to earlier. The first was that the competitive dynamics in each of the strategic business segments were different and unique. Thus, each competitor needed to devise unique strategies for each of its strategic business segments. The second was that the overall cost structure of the company as a whole didn't matter much. Rather, the lowest cost structure theory applied for each of the strategic business segments, separately and independently. Thus, the cost structure associated with each of the strategic business segments needed to be understood and managed separately. BCG coined the term "cost to serve," meaning all the costs associated with competing and serving a specific strategic business segment. This required changing most of the allocated direct and indirect overhead costs so that they would more accurately reflect the real costs related to serving each of the different strategic business segments. This represented very complicated and complex analyses that could easily be applied incorrectly if done by a less-experienced person.

Another observation was that for each strategic business segment, the bigger a company's market share, the lower its costs relative to its competitors, and therefore the more successful they would be in that strategic business segment. This was explained by the theory of the "economies of scale." It suggested that the larger a competitor is in any strategic segment, the lower its costs to serve that segment. This led to a change in the strategic imperative for companies. They began to pursue strategies that would enable them to increase market share in each of their newly defined strategic business segments. If they deemed it impossible to increase market share, they would strongly consider exiting that particular segment, because the theory claimed they would likely lose money in that segment. In my view, the methodology used to define the various strategic business segments has since been somewhat corrupted and not well applied in practice, but the importance of market share within each of the segments is still considered a sound theory.

Since then and over the years, how companies defined such strategic segments got corrupted. There were many factors that influenced how and why the strategic business segments were corrupted over time. First, companies slowly transitioned back into "market/ customer-driven" segmentation, because those were easier to define, comprehend, and evaluate. At the same time, industry associations continued to use market-driven and/or distribution channel–driven segmentations, because those were the statistics that they had always aggregated. Financial research firms have their own segmentations to help create "comparables" for stock analyses, as well as help set valuations in merger and acquisition situations. The SEC requires its own accounting segmentations in financial statements, and so on. All these various segmentations, in one way or another, and over time, bleed into each other and modify the purity of what was intended to be the true strategic business segments, thereby diminishing one's ability to devise sharp and insightful competitive strategies. Perhaps a personal example will demonstrate just how widespread is the misapplication of the concept of proper strategic segmentation.

My daughter, Beth, worked as an analyst for one of the top investment banking firms in New York. These firms really work their analysts—about seventy to one hundred hours a week, every week, without a break. I knew the time pressures placed on her, so I coordinated a dinner with her months in advance. I would fly in from Chicago for the occasion. I asked her to make sure that her managers were aware of the dinner so that she would not be assigned a last-minute task that would preclude her from attending. She got approval and all was fine. On the morning of the dinner, I called to confirm that she would be able to have dinner with me that evening. She checked and reconfirmed that all was fine. I hopped on a plane and flew to New York. I called her upon landing, and in a despondent voice she said, "Daddy, I'm sorry. I got a last-minute assignment that will keep me up and working the whole night. I will be able to give you no more than twenty minutes." We decided to meet for pizza near her office. She didn't look all that well. In fact, she looked quite distressed.

I asked her what was wrong, and she told me that her manager assigned her a job that was due the very next morning. The team was supposed to make a presentation to a large logistics/trucking company the next day. Beth's manager gave her a list of data that she needed to collect and display in graphs, charts, and table forms the next morning. Most of the data she asked her to collect was not very common, and even peculiar. Beth couldn't find the needed information anywhere, not even a reference to it. (Remember, those were the days without internet and online data repositories everywhere.) Her firm had a senior managing director who was presumably an expert in the logistics business. Beth thought that he might know where she could find the data. She was hesitant to call him in the evening at home. She first told me her dilemma and asked if I thought it would be okay to call the senior partner, whom she didn't know personally. My answer was that she should. She said she would do so after our hasty dinner.

Beth knew that I was quite adept at data collection. She told me the specific data she was after. I told her that I had no idea where to find such data. I added that it appeared to me that the data were uncommon, and that I doubted they could easily be found. She almost started to cry. I then innocently asked her why she was looking for those specific data, since they looked so peculiar to me. She then told me how her manager was planning to use the data.

Investment bankers' presentations always included a breakdown of the industry and the competitive segmentation of all the players, along with commentary on the relative differentiation of the company they made the presentation to. Her manager gave her what she believed would be the proper segmentation in the trucking industry and needed Beth to collect the data for the graphs and charts she left with her, so that she could incorporate these in her presentation to the potential client. I said, "Beth, there is no way you will get the data you are looking for overnight. There might be another option for you. The segmentation your manager gave you makes no sense to me. I know what investment bankers' presentations generally contain. I recommend you provide a different segmentation scheme, one that would be much more accurate, and for which the data would be easily available. Why don't you submit that, instead of what you were asked to do?"

She looked at me, still distressed, and said, "But, Dad, she specifically asked me to complete the graphs and chart for that data and nothing else. Won't she be angry with me?"

I replied, "Beth, there is no way you can give her the data she asked for. This is your next best choice. What have you got to lose? Not just that, but I'll predict she will actually accept what you provide and will be happy with the result. Let me help you with the presentation and segmentation and show you what data you will need." She agreed.

In my previous life as a consultant, I was involved with a couple of projects that dealt with logistics and trucking companies, so I was familiar with the industry and its segmentation. We spent the next hour writing a presentation with all the charts and graphs hand-drawn. She only needed to fill in the numbers and properly display the various graphs and charts. She was still very nervous when we parted. I knew that she would spend the entire night collecting the data and preparing the presentation for the meeting.

The next afternoon, Beth called, and as soon as I picked up the phone, she repeated a favorite sentence of hers on such occasions: "Dad, you are a genius!" She proceeded to tell me that her manager was so impressed with what she gave her that she took the presentation and Beth directly to the managing director so that Beth could explain it to him as well. He loved it, too. She, in turn, had just made a name for herself.

I wrote this example to show how widespread and pervasive is the misconception about the role segmentation plays. **It is not a nice, informative display of a competitive mapping to be treated as an afterthought or as background information. Rather, it should be a potent tool and a driver in the foreground of formulating competitive strategies.** Unfortunately, if one of the premier firms on Wall Street can so offhandedly deal with segmentation and how it is used, what should be the expectation for the rest of corporate America?

I thought it might be of value to point out some telltale signs that segmentation might be corrupted, just in case you come across them. The telltale signs rely on the fact that in theory the different segments represent unique and different competitive dynamics. When this is not the case, segmentation may be improper. The telltale signs include the following:

- When the competitive dynamics within each segment appear not to be consistent, it might likely point to an inappropriately defined strategic business segment.

- When two separate segments appear to have similar, or undifferentiated, competitive dynamics, it may suggest that they might be a single segment, rather than two separate ones.

- When within a single segment there are substantially different reasons as to why customers purchase products or services, this may suggest an improperly defined segment.

- When within a single segment there are substantially different needs and service requirements by customers, this may suggest an improperly defined segment.

- When within a single segment there are substantially different salesforces required to reach the customers, this may suggest an improperly defined segment.

- When within a single segment there are substantially different and independent distribution channels required to reach the customers, this may suggest an improperly defined segment.

- When within a single segment there appear to be small competitors who perform well, and perhaps better than the larger ones, this may suggest that there are two separate segments, where one of them is defined by where the smaller competitor thrives.

A quick note to keep in mind: Unless you are a senior manager, do not criticize a segmentation scheme or claim it is wrong unless you can identify the correct scheme with convincing evidence to prove it.

To summarize, segmentations are used for different purposes. Of the highest importance is the strategic business segmentation. The main purpose of this segmentation is to explain the competitive dynamics facing the company in each of the segments so that effective competitive strategic plans can be developed. **The most important observation is that each of the segments, at least theoretically, has its own independent competitive dynamics and therefore should have its own specific competitive strategies.**

Although it is potentially somewhat corrupted in practice, you should be well aware of the concept and rationale of segmentation, because it still represents a very important theory. Also, as a business manager, and in job interviews, you would be expected to be well versed in it.

As I pointed out, there are some situations where segmentation has a more direct impact on performance, both on the positive and the negative side. Be cognizant of those situations, and perhaps one day you will be in a better position to add substantial value and differentiate yourself.

Before I leave the segmentation topic, I would like to make another pertinent observation. This book was written to make you aware of insight and being insightful, with the hope that it will allow you to become more insightful yourself. Did you notice that the invention of the concept of the strategic business segmentation is an illustration of creative and insightful thinking? It was indeed very insightful—different, logical, and quite convincing. Anyone could theoretically have thought of the idea. In fact, a story circulating at the time suggested that a summer intern at BCG came up with this concept. Maybe you can change the world, too!

Step 3: Development of Key Success Factors

The previous segmentation topic was very long, and so by now you may have forgotten that we were enumerating and explaining the eight-step methodology of conducting sound business analyses. The segmentation topic was step 2, and so we are on to step 3. This step is critical in formulating overall effective competitive strategies, but is often not done well. It starts with identifying the competitive strengths and weaknesses of a company. Once those have been determined, then a company can devise strategies that build on its strengths and take advantage of competitors' weaknesses. The mapping of the strengths and weaknesses is therefore a fundamental building block in the process of devising competitive strategies.

To do this step well, one must focus on the more relevant aspects of the business and competitive dynamics and ignore the trivial ones. Just as in the case of segmentation, the outcome of this step is also vulnerable to misjudgments. A poor or incorrect understanding of the various strengths and weaknesses will inevitably lead to less effective strategies. In my experience, just like in segmentation, it is not practiced all that well. Here, too, and for almost the same reasons, the implications are for the most part also inconsequential. However, in some cases they can be very consequential. The good news is that, unlike segmentation, which requires substantial analytical skills and time-consuming data collection and analyses, to do well in this step is relatively easy. The poor practice is not due to the difficulty level and the complexity required in the analyses. Rather, it is simply due to a poor understanding of how to apply it well. It is easy to correct by explaining a few nuances. These few nuances represent the difference between a pedestrian application with minimal positive or negative consequences and an insightful application with potentially substantive implications for strategy. It is these few nuances that I will bring to your attention. When you understand the nuances, you will be in a much better position to contribute more value and outperform others.

To demonstrate the difference in the way this is applied in practice, I'll start with an example. Assume a group of people is asked to list the strengths and weaknesses of a well-known person. Let's, for the sake of this example, use Arnold Schwarzenegger. Born in Austria, Arnold immigrated as a young adult to the U.S. He was a bodybuilder, about six foot two and 250 pounds, with nothing but muscles. He won the title of Mr. Universe in his twenties, which landed him an acting career. He became a popular star, despite a very strong accent. Years later, he was elected governor of California. Here is a list of characteristics any group is likely to observe:

Strengths	Weaknesses
Big	Thick accent
Strong	Not well educated
Handsome	Large ego
Wealthy	Not American born
Famous	
Intelligent	
Street-smart	
Speaks multiple languages	
Wants to help other people	
Loves the country	
Knows how to act	
Not nervous in front of cameras	
Has influential friends in Hollywood	
Persistent	
Ambitious	
Strong willpower	
Willing to work hard	
Charismatic	

Look at the list and ask yourself whether you would switch any of the descriptors to the other column. That is, would you consider an item listed under the strength category to be more of a weakness, and vice versa? My guess is probably not.

Herein lies the problem. People interpret certain things with a preconceived view based on a bias. For example, we all have a common conception of the difference between "good" and "bad," "attractive" and "unattractive," "good smell" and "bad smell," "happy" and "sad," and so on. The same is true for "strengths" and "weaknesses." It is why most readers would accept the items on the list. However, it is a mistake to apply a preconceived view to an exercise wherein one draws a list of strengths and weaknesses. **In reality, there is no such thing as absolute strengths and weaknesses. Strengths and weaknesses can only be defined relative to a specific situation, challenge, or task.**

Let's look at the list. Let's assume a group of people is stranded in a cave that is filling up with water, with apparently no way out. Without a way to escape, everybody is destined to drown. Somebody discovers an opening above that will save them. However, the opening will only permit small bodies to pass through. Now, list the strengths and weaknesses relative to this situation. Clearly, an earlier perceived strength of Schwarzenegger, of being strong and big, has just become a significant (even fatal) weakness.

Perhaps using another and more realistic example, a group of people, including Arnold Schwarzenegger, is being evaluated for an ambassadorship to another country. Schwarzenegger's heavy accent will be perceived as a real weakness and may likely disqualify him for such a position. However, if the country were Austria, where he speaks the language fluently and is a native, the previous weakness actually becomes a strength.

This insight has profound implications for devising competitive business strategies. **Before one can identify the true strengths and weaknesses of a company and its competitors, one must first well define the specific challenges, actions, or tasks that would apply or will need to be achieved to do as well as competitors.** In other words, define a list of factors that will enable a competitor to do well, which I call a list of *success factors*.

To put the importance of the above observation in its right perspective, notice that all the previous steps of the methodology—data collection, analyses, and segmentation—are done as precursors to enable us to accurately arrive at the success factors. **The success factors are the foundation upon which business strategies are developed.** To define the success factors well is likely to yield better, more precise, and effective strategies. Do it poorly and performance is likely to be compromised.

For example, a company erroneously classifies something as a strength, which in reality, given the challenges the company needs to overcome, is a weakness. It devises a strategy to play more aggressively on the perceived strength. Clearly, and unbeknownst to them, they will be making things worse, since this new strategy more heavily relies on what is perceived to be a strength, whereas in reality it is a weakness, thereby exacerbating a problem. The same poor outcome would be created in reverse, wherein the company perceives something a weakness when it is actually a strength. Situations like these offer a great opportunity for an insightful individual to have a more significant impact on the performance of a company. The above nuance, that of correctly classifying the strengths and weaknesses, was the first of five insightful observations. The other four will be discussed next.

Now that we understand what we are after, the key question becomes how we generate the list of proper success factors. How do we ensure that we identify the key ones that will lead to the correct strategies, as opposed to trivial ones, which would likely lead to the wrong strategies?

Clearly, **the "right" success factors should comprise a list that strategically represents the most important factors in determining potential competitive success.** I'll adopt the definition that Booz Allen used and refer to such a list as the *key success factors*—key as in "the most important" as opposed to more trivial, less determinative factors.

The list of the key success factors is one of the more important aspects of strategic analyses. All strategies should be devised to meet them; anything else, by definition, is less important or consequential. Compromised or erroneous key success factors will most certainly lead to compromised or erroneous strategies. After the fact, this list would look to be simple to generate, but simple it is not. Getting the correct list is a challenging undertaking. Ask the thirty to sixty higher-level executives whom we would interview in the course of studying an industry to generate such a list, and you can expect a huge variety of responses, with many success factors, and each "expert" is likely to have their own perception of the factors' relative importance. Reducing the list from the many success factors mentioned during interviews into the few most important key success factors is where the creativity, insight, perspective, and consulting expertise come into play. Once the list is determined, the subsequent challenge is to have everybody at the executive management level agree to, accept, and own the list—that is the way successful implementation of the resulting strategies will occur. It also follows that each of the strategic business segments should have its own key success factors and resulting strategies, reflecting the unique competitive dynamics in that segment. An example at the end of the section (chapter thirty-six) will clearly demonstrate everything mentioned above.

Most corporate staff professionals are not aware of the nuance and the need to generate the distinct list of the key success factors, nor its importance in the process of generating strategies. They do consider it, and are aware of it, in a roundabout way. It is implied in how they do the overall strategic analyses, and how they arrive at the recommended strategies. However, by not making it a distinct step that focuses all attention on prioritizing the many potential success factors into the very few that become the *key* success factors, it becomes an afterthought, just one of the many considerations when devising strategies, and not the centerpiece and driver of such strategies. This nuance is the difference between pedestrian strategies and insightful ones, between potentially compromised strategies and well-conceived ones.

The second nuance relates to the number and relative importance of factors that are identified as the key success factors. It is almost impossible to deal with a long list of success factors. If one doesn't understand the purpose of creating a list, then one's tendency is to list more rather than less, practically everything they can think of, and not be very sensitive to their relative importance, which is very often the case. First, **the list should be as short as possible, no more than three to five factors.** Second, the factors **must be properly prioritized**. The reason is simple. From a practical standpoint, it would be difficult to devise a strategy that needs to address and incorporate a long list of factors. It becomes even more difficult, or almost close to impossible, if some of them conflict with each other. For example, assume that three of the most important success factors are the price of the product (the lower, the more product people will buy), the features offered (the more features offered, the more attractive the product becomes to the buyers), and the perceived "quality" of the product (how durable it is, meaning if it is of poor quality, people won't buy it). Notice that the three factors conflict with one another to some degree. A strategy to increase the number of features, which addresses the second factor, will add to the cost of the product and therefore conflict with the lower price factor. A strategy to bring down the price, which addresses the first factor, can only be done by taking away some features or using cheaper components, thereby conflicting with the second and third factors. Clearly, the answer is in either addressing some factors while completely ignoring the others, or reaching some reasonable balance between them. Both would be difficult to do with a long and unprioritized list of success factors.

The third nuance relates to the interdependency (one can't be achieved without the other) between the success factors, as opposed to the potential conflict between them. If some are dependent on each other, then it is impossible to prioritize them separately and just as difficult to decide which to use in the strategy and which to potentially ignore. Any such interdependencies suggest that the items should be combined into a single factor.

To summarize: **The list of the key success factors must be very short, reflecting only the highest priority factors; they must be prioritized, and without interdependencies.** Note that they may be conflicting. But, when the conflicts become an issue when devising the corresponding strategy, the prioritizations of the factors should be used to deal with it properly; the higher the priority on the list, the more precedence that success factor should receive. In other words, the strategy needs to address first the highest priority success factors, even at a cost to a lower priority factor. **This makes it apparent why the judgment on the prioritization of the success factors is so important. It is not a trivial judgment, since all are considered critically important; otherwise, they would not be on the list in the first place. The judgment should be** based on real facts that emerge from the findings in the analyses step. Unfortunately, it is very easy to arrive at erroneous priorities. Worse, in some cases, it is almost impossible to discern whether the prioritization was well arrived at or not, yet the implications could be significant. This is so because all factors are very important, and the relative importance and prioritization requires refined judgments and discerning understanding that can only be achieved with skilled fact-findings and questions. This is where the skillful expert is separated from the pedestrian practitioner.

The fourth nuance is the most important one. It has to do with the difference between a pedestrian application of the list of the key success factors and an insightful one. The following observations are somewhat unique and based on my experience at Booz Allen. The concept I will cover here has broad implications beyond just dealing with the key success factors, in that it applies to many different aspects of the business world and is likely to be just as unique in those applications as well.

I touched on this concept in the context of getting experts' advice regarding job interviews. I suggested that most experts will provide advice they think is the most important, advice that would be at the top of their list. Indeed, the advice may contain their most important factors, but the experts tend to ignore the fact that there will be multiple candidates who will successfully meet those important criteria. At that point, different screening criteria will be applied, yet no expert is likely to point it out in the initial conversation. I referred to their initial advice as addressing only the factors related to how **to enter and stay in the game** (i.e., not failing before even getting an opportunity to play), but not at all addressing the issue of how to subsequently **compete and win the game.**

The exact same observation is applicable when generating the list for the key success factors. Everyone focuses on the most important elements in their minds, but those apply to a company's capability to stay in the game. Often, the secondary ones that apply to competing and winning are not well addressed. At Booz Allen, we referred to the initial list as the **"fatal flaw criteria,"** meaning that you must pass those criteria at an acceptable level to continue to stay in the game.

But a secondary list becomes critical to compete effectively and *win* the game. Under specific circumstances, I discovered that there could even be a third level of screening criteria that are mostly ignored when devising corporate strategies. In fairness, marketing departments may be aware of them for the purpose of trying to devise specific marketing programs, or in recommending specific changes to a product and its features. However, I discovered that oftentimes the professionals responsible for evaluating and formulating overall company strategy don't give them the necessary attention required.

To help understand why the fourth nuance is so easy to overlook, we only need to examine the methodology people use to arrive at the list of key success factors. Look back at the various ways data are collected, whether through direct interviews and feedback, or surveys and questionnaires, or focus groups, etc. The question asked of the respondents will always be the same: "What were the most important reasons for buying a product from any competitor?" Pay attention to the wording of the question, because here is where the mistake is made. When asked for the most important reasons, one will most likely get the fatal flaw reasons, since they would be top of mind for the respondent. Thus, everyone is convinced that they are the most important reasons because they came directly from the buyers.

The problem is that everyone in the industry would most likely arrive at and use the same list of factors. More often than not, those factors would reflect the price, features, reputation for quality, and (if applicable) warranty or return policy. They may assign different priorities to those factors, and formulate strategies that address those priorities. This is the pedestrian application of the methodology. Just think about it: They all work from the exact same list and devise strategies based on them. Assume multiple companies assign the same priority to this list and formulate their strategies accordingly. Logic would therefore suggest that their strategies would be almost identical. Herein lies the problem: How could strategies that do not address the differentiation from other competitors be of much value? Where would be their relative competitive advantage?

It goes without saying that all the competitors must meet the fatal flaw criteria; otherwise they would never survive as competitors. However, the fatal flaw criteria rarely explain the reasons why some competitors perform better than others. Hence, the need for the secondary criteria. At Booz Allen we always separated the fatal flaw criteria from the secondary criteria. I refer to them as *differentiating success factors*.

To arrive at these important secondary criteria, one must ask a different set of questions. The first in the series of questions would be, "Which of the competitors did you consider at the beginning of your purchasing process?" You will easily get a list of between two and six competitors. The next question would be, "Which of those competitors were still viable before making the final purchasing decision?" The list will be narrowed down to between one and three. The next question would be, "What criteria did you use to narrow it down to those specific competitors?" Then the last question should be, "What were your reasons for selecting your final choice?" Only when one has those answers can one really understand the true competitive dynamics and differentiations that affect the purchasing behavior and the actual competitive performance in the industry.

However, these answers are not easy to arrive at. Although the questions are reasonably straightforward, the answers rarely are. A respondent's first answer to each question would be to repeat the most important reasons they came up with in the first place—price, features, quality, and so on. This is so because these factors are the ones that are always the most important and overriding factors in their minds. They don't change, even when narrowing the number of competitors. What changes are the additional secondary criteria that they used to help narrow down the options. One needs to prod with leading questions and suggestions to let them know and understand that they should focus on the next level of reasons. This is what experienced consultants understand and learn how to do well. To put it in perspective, I had to spend between five and ten minutes prodding the customer before I was convinced that I had received the real reasons.

In one of my projects, I discovered that there could be, in some cases, yet another level of screening criteria, which I refer to as the *final purchasing decision criterion*.

The final purchasing decision criterion is mostly applicable in businesses that sell products to consumers (B2C) as opposed to companies that sell their products to other companies (B2B). The questions that lead to discovering the final purchasing decision criterion are rarely asked and prodded at the depth and thoroughness they require to get accurate and insightful answers. The questions are: "Was there anybody who influenced your decision in making your final choice?" or "Did somebody help you in reaching your final decision, when you were debating the final options?" or "What, or who, convinced you that you had made a wise choice at the very end?" Just like in the secondary differentiating criteria, these questions need to be asked in a variety of ways because the person from whom you are eliciting answers has likely never been asked to reflect on their decisions in this way. So, their first inclination is to give the first answer that comes to mind. It may or may not be an accurate answer. Asking more questions gives the responder an opportunity to reflect further. It is amazing what further reflection reveals. A whole new dimension may open up that nobody considered before. As stated, the professionals working in the marketing department might attempt to ask those questions, and may receive thoughtful responses that lead to a reasonable understanding of the dynamics, but these rarely get elevated to solve fundamental corporate strategies.

Just to make sure I am not misunderstood when I say that I "discovered" the third level of criteria, I don't mean to imply that nobody would get the right answers but me. In fact, I have no doubt that others could reach the correct understanding as well. What I mean to say is that I made it part of my formalized methodology so that it doesn't just become an accidental discovery, but the outcome of a deliberate search. I followed this practice over and over in my career. It always paid dividends. More importantly, it was always perceived as very insightful.

In summary, the fourth nuance is that **the key success factors must be understood on at least two levels, and at times three: the fatal flaw, the secondary differentiation, and the final purchasing decision.**

You are now ready to see how everything I mentioned in this section comes together in a real project situation. I will describe a project I was involved with that demonstrates it all. It will also show how the remaining steps of the overall methodology for market and competitive dynamics (steps 4–8) come into play. To make it a real, teachable example, I will lead you through my thoughts and observations as they progressed on the project. I plan to show you in detail how decisions are made and conclusions drawn, and how the theory is applied in practice. It will also serve as an example of how insightfulness is attained. It is not about a sudden discovery. It is a step-by-step logical analysis that leads one there. One just needs to constantly look for nuances and potential exceptions.

36

Applying the Methodology:
A Case Study in Consumer Products

bout four months into my tenure with Booz Allen, the firm was asked to help a large conglomerate solve a problem beleaguering one of its companies. That company had two separate divisions (companies), each selling major appliances. One sold washers and dryers and the other major kitchen appliances, such as stoves, ranges, ovens, microwave ovens, and so on. The company that sold washers and dryers was of a reasonably decent size and had good brand name recognition, particularly in the commercial marketplace, such as laundromats, hotels, and laundry service companies. The kitchen appliances company was relatively very small, with less than $70 million in annual sales. (Just to put it in perspective, General Electric, Sears/Kenmore, and Whirlpool brands had combined sales in the billions of dollars annually.)

Both companies were experiencing the same problems. Eight years earlier, the companies had begun a trend of high growth and commensurate profits. However, for the previous two years, growth and revenues had precipitously declined, especially for the kitchen appliances company. Performance deteriorated from a peak of $70 million in annual sales to only $30 million, resulting in serious losses. The CEO of the conglomerate was ready to shut down the operations of the kitchen appliances division; it was too small and losing too much money. However, the CEO wanted to find out if the washers and dryers division could be turned around.

The Booz Allen team was assembled with one analyst (myself), a newly promoted job manager, a junior partner, and a senior partner. The junior partner, with the day-to-day, hands-on responsibility for the job, decided to have two parallel efforts at the same time—one dedicated to the washer and dryer company, and the other to the kitchen appliances company. I was assigned to work on the kitchen appliances company. I was supposed to work independently, so as to allow the remainder of the team to focus without distractions on the washers and dryers company.

I told the partner that I didn't feel qualified to work independently without ongoing supervision and guidance. His response was, "You don't need to worry about it. There is no hope there, and all you need to do is to collect all the relevant data so that we can rationalize the closing of that division."

I pleaded, "What if there is an opportunity for turning it around? I may completely miss it."

He laughed and said, "Don't worry; there is no opportunity for a turnaround there."

I contested, "How do we know that, without analyzing the situation first?"

His answer was appropriate for an experienced consultant with many scars to show for it. He said, "When it looks like a duck, walks like a duck, and quacks like a duck, then it is a duck. So, when it looks like a turkey, walks like a turkey, and gobbles like a turkey, then it is a turkey. It is obvious the division is a turkey—nothing to save there."

When I arrived at the company's headquarters, the president and I spent the full first day together in his conference room. I got an overview on the product lines, customers, distribution channels, and differentiation in the marketplace. I asked the president about the segmentation of its market. He gave me two: (i) developers and builders of homes and (ii) department stores. (In those days there were no specialized stores that sold appliances. All appliances, big and small, were purchased at department stores. The largest department store chain was Sears, Roebuck and Co.; the next was J. C. Penney; and there were hundreds of other regional and local stores around the country.) I asked him to list what he perceived to be his company's strengths and weaknesses. He listed the strengths:

- Its high-end products had a reputation for quality.

- Products were known for their great features.

- Products were known for their attractive and appealing design.

He listed the weaknesses:

- Products were too highly priced.

- There were no low-end models.

- Some expensive features were not needed, making the products unnecessarily higher in price.

I then had the president give me his perspective on what had led to the steep decline in business. We finished by discussing whether he thought the performance of the division could be turned around. I needed him to agree with the view that it couldn't be turned around. If he agreed, then my report would be easy to put together. But if he didn't, then I'd have to prove him wrong with facts, data, and analyses, which would mean much more work for me. His response was that it would be unlikely to be able to turn performance around unless the company introduced a new low-end line. He then told me that his boss, the CEO of the conglomerate, was unwilling to undergo the substantial costs that would be required to change the features in the current lines and develop a whole new lower-end line. If the company could not do these things, he saw no hope of staying competitive in the marketplace. Following are some of the specific details I learned from him regarding the market and competitive dynamics.

The company manufactured a wide variety of high-end major kitchen appliances, both freestanding and built-in, with features and quality commensurate with high-end products. Prices were relatively high, reflecting the high quality of design and features. The company had one smaller competitor at the high-end level. The rest of the players in the industry, including the larger companies, were focused primarily on serving the mass market.

Developers and home builders accounted for about 70 percent of his company's sales, and department stores about 30 percent. The president attributed the precipitous decline in performance to the fact that the company didn't have a low-end line, and so their prices were no longer competitive, particularly for larger contracts with the larger home developers/builders. He emphasized that the larger developers, which built many homes at the same time, preferred to buy the various kitchen appliances from a single manufacturer. They would always solicit bids from the various competitors and would select the lowest-priced bid. He told me that his inability to offer lower prices alone was killing them and their ability to win the larger contracts. I asked him where he got the data to support his suppositions. He told me that it came from their salespeople and that he himself heard the same comment directly from many of their larger customers.

Over dinner I was thinking about what I heard and began planning my next steps. It appeared quite simple: I needed to focus on two issues. First, I needed to confirm what the president had told me. I needed to personally interview a handful of the company's larger customers to verify and document what the president had said. I decided to also interview two or three smaller home builders for balance purposes. Second, I needed to accurately calculate and estimate the research and development costs that would be involved in pursuit of the development of a lower-cost line, which was what the president had recommended, to affirm that it was unreasonable, as the CEO of the conglomerate believed. With those two analyses in hand, my job would essentially be done.

However, while I was planning and rationalizing everything in my head, a couple of nagging questions kept popping up. A nuanced inconsistency. Seemingly trivial, unimportant, and completely out-of-context questions, which I couldn't answer in my own mind. By now you also know how I react to nuances. I decided to resolve the nagging questions first.

The questions were so simple and innocent. The first was, How could they do so well with builders for five years or more prior to the decline? What suddenly happened? What had changed? The customers were still the same and doing the same things they had been doing for years. The product lines were exactly the same. The prices hadn't changed all that much. So, what had created a sudden upheaval in the market for this appliance company? The second question was this: If indeed the president was right and the company was losing business because it didn't have low-end models, then how come it didn't lose *most or all* of its builders and customers? How come many of them were still customers, but were buying fewer products than in previous years? I decided to get answers to these questions. I also decided, just to make sure that I had covered all the bases, to check to see whether the company's competitor was experiencing the same decline in performance.

I met with the president the following morning and asked him to set up in-person interviews with six larger builders and three smaller ones. I then asked him to give me the data and analyses that he used to estimate the cost and time to build and introduce a new low-end line, per his recommendation. The following three days, I was busy flying around the country conducting interviews. I also ordered, from a for-a-fee financial database service company, the estimated revenues and profits of the other high-end competitor for the previous seven years.

The initial findings led me to a different assessment of the market and competitive dynamics from that of the president. I asked him to provide the company's annual sales for the last seven years, broken down by each individual customer and summarized at three levels: (i) the smaller builders (those who built fewer than fifty homes a year), (ii) all other builders, and (iii) department stores. I meanwhile researched and got the previous seven-year trends of home construction in the U.S., broken down by the more expensive custom homes and the typical middle-market, mass-built tract homes. First, let's summarize my findings from the interviews. Below is a summary of the relevant things I was told:

- I found two distinct kinds of builders who were customers of my client: the larger home builders, who built hundreds and thousands of homes annually, and smaller builders, who tended to be custom home builders that built fewer than fifty homes a year.

- The two groups had completely different demands and requirements. They were clearly two separate strategic business segments, and not a single one, as the company viewed them. What I discovered in my interviews was an entirely different set of purchasing behaviors and decision making by the two groups. They each had completely different key success factors and "cost to serve" economics.

For the larger builders, the lowest price was very important and played a key role in their final purchasing decision. But there was an even larger factor involved that substantially overshadowed the price consideration. The lowest price was a secondary consideration. The primary fatal flaw criteria were completely different. I asked whether the quality and the features of the appliances were important to them. The answer was consistent. They all said that it would be nice to have a higher quality appliance, but they wouldn't be willing to pay that much more for it. In their own words, "Nobody buys a new home because of the appliances we install. We can install anything; it wouldn't make that much of a difference. Of course, if we can get a higher quality appliance for about the same price, we would buy it instead of the run-of-the-mill appliances, like G.E., Whirlpool, or Kenmore." That made a lot of sense to me, but the other finding, the one related to the fatal flaw, was a completely new discovery for me.

All the large builders had a single criterion that had to be met, with no exception. It was **just-in-time delivery of the appliances**. The builders explained that because they built tens and hundreds of tract homes at a time, projects followed a rigid schedule. Appliances for all the homes had to be delivered and installed in the same period. The builders signed contracts with subcontractors to install those appliances, way in advance of installation time. These subcontractors would show up on the day appliances were to be delivered and installed. If the appliances had not arrived, the builder was still obligated to pay the subcontractor's workers full wages for the day. Each day that went by without appliances to install was very costly. Therefore, no delay was tolerated. My client had issues with delivering on time. They were okay for smaller quantities, up to ten or so at a time, but seemed to have problems delivering larger quantities punctually. That is why builders would order only small quantities of appliances at a time. When I asked them what had changed, since they had been buying larger quantities from the company for five years previously and only stopped in the last two, the answer was almost laughable.

- The builders said that in the previous five years the industry had experienced a boom, and the market was growing at a high rate, and none of the appliance manufacturers, large or small, were able to keep up with the growing demands. The builders bought products from whoever was able to supply them. During that period, all the manufacturers had a problem with just-in-time delivery. The builders said, "We had to live with it. But times were good then, and we all made a lot of money and could afford the delivery problems. We couldn't correct them anyways, so we just had to ignore them for the time being."

  However, the industry had begun to slow down as the economy slipped into a recession and new home sales dropped substantially. Profits for the developers declined, and they became much less tolerant of delivery issues. The larger appliance companies were able to adhere to the contracted timing. My client could not make the necessary adjustments. I knew that there was no way my client could consistently and reliably deliver on large quantities. It was too small and had no ability to build large inventories for this purpose. There was no way it could compete with the large players on this specific requirement. In other words, they had fatal flaw disadvantages in this business segment and therefore would not likely enjoy success.

- The smaller custom home builders had completely different requirements. They were building custom homes to the exact specifications of the owners. Those homes were bigger, more expensive, and used only high-end products and finishes, including appliances. These builders purchased high-end, fully featured merchandise with a good brand reputation. They viewed both my client and the other high-end competitor as perfectly befitting their requirements.

I asked the builders how they selected which of the two to buy from. They said that they didn't. They would bring the two high-end choices to the home buyer and let them make the final choice. I asked them if they knew how the owners made such a choice. They said that it varied greatly and they hadn't noticed a pattern. I asked whether the builders would benefit from an introduction of lower-end models. They said no. Worse, if the company introduced a low-end line, they would stop recommending them to the buyers, since it would ruin their own reputation for being builders of high-end homes and high-end interiors. I asked what they thought of the expensive features and whether it would make a difference if they were eliminated. They said that those features make the appliance a high-end product. Eliminate the features and builders would stop recommending my client's products. I asked them whether their business had been hit by the recession. They said no. Their business had been thriving for seven years and did not appear to be vulnerable to the recession.

I looked at the industry trend for homes built in the U.S., and they were consistent with what I heard. A boom had started seven years earlier and lasted for five years. The recession had begun two years prior, affecting the building of tract homes. Custom home builders experienced no slowdown, but rather showed healthy growth.

I realized that the president had an inadequate grasp of the market. His segmentation was wrong, as well as what he thought were the success factors. Therefore, his recommendations for product changes were very wrong as well. The large tract builders wouldn't have cared whatsoever about those changes, and the custom home builders would have stopped buying from them.

With those findings, I asked the president for his specific sales numbers broken down by the two categories of builders to see if the numbers agreed with what I heard from the customers. I also asked him to give me the sales to the department stores as well, to see if something would jump out at me. I received all the numbers the next day and started looking at what they revealed.

Let's pause for a second and focus on a couple of things that I said in this section regarding the pedestrian application of the segmentation and analyses of the key success factors. This example is not atypical. It supports my observations and experience over the years with many companies.

You would have noticed how unreliable the salesforce feedback was. The large tract builders needed more competitive pricing, and that's all the salespeople heard. They either were not told or ignored the issue over delivery schedules. Management was not made aware of it either. The salesforce also completely missed on the requirements of the smaller custom home builders. Apparently, this segment was too small to pay much attention to.

So, the following morning, I studied the numbers and several revealing patterns emerged:

- There had been a definitive and severe decline in orders from the larger tract builders dating back three years. The average bid price per unit declined substantially during these three years, and therefore the margins for my client as well.

- The smaller custom home builders didn't show the same pattern. It was in fact the opposite. Over the same period, these builders increased their orders. The average price per unit for this group hadn't declined. The margins increased a bit.

- Department store sales stayed stable for the most part.

I wanted to know whether the president was the only one in the dark, or if the marketing and sales organization was just as clueless. I asked to interview the vice president of marketing and sales. He was as pedestrian a thinker as one can imagine. His focus was exclusively on the larger builders and how he could win their business back. According to him, he needed more salespeople to have better coverage and allow them to interact more frequently and closely with their more

important customers, the larger builders. This way they could anticipate their needs better and be on hand to deal with problems when they
occurred. He pointed out that his larger competitors had many more
salespeople working that segment. It didn't even cross his mind that
his company may not be able to afford more salespeople, as the larger
companies may. He was the one who had pushed to eliminate some
features as a way to reduce prices and become more competitive. He
also pushed to introduce a lower-end product line. I asked him what
the effect would be on the smaller builders should that happen. He dismissed the question out of hand. They were too small to worry about.
I knew that if the division survived, he would have to be replaced—he
didn't demonstrate the kind of thinking, understanding, and awareness
commensurate with his position.

I began to form some hypotheses and needed more data to confirm
them. The first hypothesis was that the larger builders were the main
reason for my client's losses over the last three years. Clearly it was
not because of declining sales and profitability with the custom home
builders. In fact, this aspect of the business had actually experienced
improved margins. The second hypothesis was that a major factor in
the increasing losses was due to hiring additional salespeople over the
last three years. The VP told me that he had hired additional salespeople because he believed it to be the only way to reverse the trend.
Yet sales continued to decline, and so the additional salespeople just
exacerbated and magnified the company's losses. The third hypothesis was that the just-in-time delivery demand from the larger builders
would introduce additional costs, because there was no way, in my
mind, that such a small company had the infrastructure capacity to
handle just-in-time delivery. For example, the company didn't have its
own delivery trucks. If a customer called a week before the scheduled
delivery and asked to delay delivery, my client would have to pay a
penalty to the trucking company. My client would also have to pay
extra costs for warehousing the shipment until the actual delivery date.
The larger competitors had no such issues, because they owned their
trucks and warehouses. The fourth hypothesis was that if we reduced
the focus on the large tract builders, and eliminated most of the direct
salesforce, we might bring the company quickly back to profitability,

thereby reducing the pressure to close the division down. The fifth hypothesis was that the custom home builder segment was a growing one and might support continued growth for my client. I needed to pay close attention to this segment, as well as the department store segment. (Just as a side note to further demonstrate the concept of the true "cost to serve" I discussed earlier in this chapter: It is clear that the two segments [large builders and the smaller custom home builders] had substantially different cost-to-serve economics. When allocating the true-cost-to-serve for the two different segments, the majority of the extra salespeople hired specifically to serve mostly the large builders should be allocated to that segment. Also, the extra costs associated with building and storing the larger inventories in advance of delivery, necessary to assure just-in-time delivery, would also need to be allocated mostly to that segment. It was also true for any extraordinary storage and transportation costs resulting from serving the just-in-time requirements of the large builders' segment.)

I asked the president to free up at least a half day for me. We met and I laid out all my findings and the observations from the numbers he provided me. I also gave him my conclusions and hypotheses. He was completely bewildered. The only words he uttered were, "I'll be damned!" He also immediately gave me another data point regarding my hypothesis about the losses attributable to the larger tract builders. He said that at times they had to work three shifts to meet larger orders with short delivery times. They had to pay substantial extra pay for overtime, which was not reflected in the pricing for the products. (These costs, too, needed to be mostly allocated to the large builders' segment when calculating the true-cost-to-serve.)

He immediately understood the implications of my findings and told me that he would take immediate steps to lessen the focus on large builders, eliminate salespeople and overtime shifts, and terminate the VP of marketing and sales. We worked very closely together from that point on. I asked him to have his people do an actual cost-to-serve analysis for all his customers. I explained the concept and we built the methodology on how to do it properly. We also agreed on how to allocate the various overhead and functional department costs to reflect true-costs-to-serve. He asked the accounting department to work on it. I also asked him to set up interviews with additional custom home builders and larger customers in the department stores. I spent the following week focusing on these tasks. Here is what I discovered:

- The additional custom home builders I spoke with confirmed what I had been told in previous interviews. This segment was growing at a healthy rate.

- During one of the interviews, the interviewee mentioned to me that he worked closely with kitchen remodelers who worked on remodeling existing homes. He mentioned that they also bought high-end products, and was a segment growing at a fast rate.

- I learned that the department stores sold many product lines, from low end to high end, and how the process worked internally for them. The majority of buyers were women. The management at the stores appeared to have little insight as to the way their salespeople interacted with the buyers.

I decided that I needed to study the customer interactions on the floor with the department store salespeople. I spent the next three days interviewing salespeople at various department stores, as well as women who happened to have been shopping for new appliances. I also interviewed kitchen remodelers. I asked the president to have his marketing staff collect whatever market data they could on this segment. At the end of the three days, I made the following observations:

- The kitchen remodelers were indeed a growing segment. Their needs, requirements, and purchasing decisions were almost identical to those of custom home builders. Both segments seemed to me to comprise a single segment from a strategic point of view.

- When asked how they decided between the two high-end competitors, all responded the same way. They work with their customers and let them make the final choice. I found out that these women almost always go to the department stores to inspect the products before making a final decision. (I thought that this

was an especially important finding and decided to follow up more
on this later.)

- The salespeople at the department stores were extremely important
  in influencing the final purchasing decision for these women.

- The women who came to the department stores could be
  categorized, from my perspective, into one of three groups: (i)
  those who came specifically to buy only a high-end product, (ii)
  those who didn't exactly know what they were looking for, and (iii)
  those who were very cost- and budget-sensitive. All three categories
  had little knowledge of appliances and didn't really know how
  to go about selecting the best. Most heavily relied on what the
  salesperson on the floor told them.

  Also, many came to the store with a preconceived idea of which
  brand might make the most sense for them. The preconceived ideas
  came from multiple sources, such as their own experience with
  appliances they had owned in the past, what their relatives and
  friends may have told them, and what a serviceperson may have
  told them in the past when their appliance needed servicing.

  The latter seemed to leave an unusually strong impression
  on their preference. These women viewed the serviceperson as a
  knowledgeable and credible expert. So, if the serviceperson told
  them that the brand that they came to fix was known for breaking
  down, the customer would not be very likely to buy that same
  brand again. Conversely, if the serviceperson mentioned a brand
  that they claimed had a great reputation for quality, they would be
  predisposed to that brand.

Everything began to fall into place and my hypotheses appeared to
have been confirmed. I understood that I found two important contrib-
utors in the final purchasing decision of these women: the salesperson at
the department store and the appliance servicepeople who made house
calls. I understood that I found two levels of success factors in the two
segments under consideration: custom home builders/kitchen remodelers and the department stores. The first success factor was the recommendation either from the custom home builder/kitchen remodeler

to their clients. Without such recommendations, my client wouldn't even be in the game. Thus, the requirements of the home builders/kitchen remodelers fell under the fatal flaw category. I prioritized these fatal flaw criteria as: (i) reputation as the best high-end products, (ii) top-of-the-line features, (iii) reputation for top-quality products (meaning they don't break down or need service very often), and (iv) actual experience to prove that it is a high-quality product (demonstrating the longevity of the product. If products were to break down, the reputation of my client's products would be damaged, and home builders would not trust the brand any longer, which would have a ripple effect).

Success also depended on finding out how store salespeople decided to recommend a specific brand to the customers, and whether they could be influenced to recommend my client's appliances. I spent the following week interviewing salespeople at the department stores, women who came to purchase appliances, and some independent servicepeople. My questions were more specific, more probing, more leading. They were exclusively focused on trying to understand why they recommended certain brands to these women.

I found what I was looking for. I found out exactly why the salespeople and servicepeople made their recommendations. It solved another layer of the puzzle. Here are my findings.

Servicepeople

These were small, independent, and local entrepreneurs who specialized in fixing appliances. The large companies, like G.E., had their own servicepeople based around the country. The independents mostly serviced the other brands and less populous areas where the larger manufacturers didn't serve with their own employees. They appeared to be straightforward, honest people. When customers asked for a recommendation, it came from their own experience and that of their colleagues. I tried to probe for the kinds of things that might influence their perception and I found something interesting.

I asked whether when they formed their opinion about the "quality" of a brand, they differentiated between whether they have encountered minor versus major service problems for that brand. They did! They tended to assign less importance to minor problems that were easy to fix. I then asked them to give me specific examples of brands with minor problems and those brands that had relatively more major problems. As the servicepeople walked me through the examples, I noticed a small nuance. For some brands, they discussed the technical reasons as to why the appliance didn't work properly. For other brands, they didn't. I also noticed a correlation between how technically familiar they were with the brands and the severity they assigned to a brand's poor performance. The more familiar, the less severity and the more "forgiveness." The less familiarity with the brand, the greater the severity they assigned to it. I logged this correlation in my mind to rethink later about how it could be used to advantage.

Department Store Salespeople

Here I found a more complex situation. I began by making three key observations regarding how they made their recommendations to these women. The first was not that surprising. They earned different commissions for different products they sold. Not surprisingly, they tended to recommend the products where they would earn the highest commissions. I followed up with their managers to see how those commissions were determined. The response was quite simple. It mostly depended on the margins the department stores made on the different product lines. The higher the profits for them, the more they tried to incentivize the salespeople with higher commissions to sell those brands. Another reason was to try to incentivize selling specific products that were sitting for too long in inventory.

The second observation regarding the recommendations of the salespeople on the floor was somewhat surprising to me. Many of the salespeople wouldn't allow the size of their commission to affect their recommendations. They didn't want to feel like they would sell their soul for money. They would give their honest opinion to the customer. I found out that these salespeople had a higher technical understanding of some brands and less of others. Not surprisingly, just as with the servicepeople, the more knowledgeable they were of the technology behind the features of a particular brand, the more they would recommend that brand, convinced that it offered more unique value. I continued to test this hypothesis with all the salespeople, and it proved to be correct. I also found out that salespeople, even within the same department store, recommended different brands but for the exact same reasons. Whatever brand they understood best, they recommended.

I asked all interviewees how they acquired their specific technical understanding about the different brands. I got two consistent responses. The first and most important source was technical classes given by the manufacturers about their products. The other was the general marketing literature and product brochures that the manufacturers provided as point-of-sale material.

I also accidentally found out that the turnover of salespeople was very high in department stores. The average tenure of a salesperson was about three months. First, those are not the highest-paying jobs and so the general tenure was short, until they found another, more lucrative job. Second, if they were not generating enough sales, they would be moved to another department. Training classes for salespeople by the appliance companies were conducted infrequently, about once every couple of years, if not longer. Thus, most salespeople at any given time were without the added knowledge that such training classes tended to provide. That clearly suggested that more frequent training classes could be used by my client to impart technical knowledge and thereby likely influence salespeople's recommendations.

I was convinced I had all the information I needed to form my key success factors. As you saw from the above, I discovered three levels instead of two.

Key Success Factors

Fatal Flaw (required to pass the screening of the high-end builders/ remodelers):

- Top-of-the-line features

- Reputation for top-quality products (meaning they don't break down or need service often)

- Real experience to prove that a product is of the highest quality (if the product would break down, brand loyalty would be lost)

Secondary Differentiation (related to who influences the majority of buyers)

- Positive recommendations from salespeople

- Positive recommendations from servicepeople

Final Purchasing Decision (related to how salespeople and servicepeople make recommendations)

- Highest payout of commissions/bonuses

- Deeper understanding of features and technology for product/ features differentiation

- Frequent training of all salespeople to ensure they have the necessary product knowledge

Note, unlike what common sense might have suggested, none of the key success factors reflect on specific preferences that women may have had regarding specific physical attributes of the appliances, like features, color, size, and so on. It is not because in some cases these attributes didn't help influence a final decision; rather, it was because of two specific factors. First, the specific physical preferences were really secondary considerations and completely subjugated to the above-mentioned key success factors. Second, all the competitors had a large selection in inventory, and nobody really had anything from a features or appearance standpoint that others didn't have as well (other than the high-end models). Thus, the physical attributes and features would be determined more by the marketing department to make sure that the product lines offered what women wanted and preferred, rather than be elevated to become part of the overall corporate competitive strategies.

I now needed to complete the data collection and analyses to make sure that I could build a solidly substantiated case for my recommendations. When I had all the data and facts, I met with the president and showed him the results. He agreed with my findings, conclusions, and recommendations, which were:

- Reduce marketing focus on large tract builders.

- Increase marketing focus on custom home builders and kitchen remodelers. They should be the highest-priority market segment.

- Increase marketing focus on department stores, but as a secondary focus.

- Reduce the direct salesforce significantly to reflect the new strategy.

- Eliminate third shifts at the manufacturing plant, and try to reduce the need for second shift as well. (This was possible because the need for just-in-time delivery of the larger builders was no longer as relevant, and the custom home builders were not as sensitive about delivery schedules.)

- Create a new department within the marketing organization with the following responsibilities:

  o Establish training programs and generate informative brochures for salespeople in the department stores and for the independent servicepeople. Make sure to provide "technical" facts explaining the reasons for the uniqueness of their products.

  o Training for salespeople in department stores should be held at least once a quarter.

  o Formalize a process to follow up with independent servicepeople on a regular basis. They should call the various service firms no less than at least once every six months. Actual training classes for servicepeople on location should be considered as dictated by conditions on the ground.

o   Actively manage the commissions/bonuses rewards for salespeople in department stores. Try to ensure that commissions/bonuses are relatively high, and at least higher than the other direct high-end competitor. If need be, sacrifice margin to achieve the above goal. Consider topping up the stores' commissions as added incentive.

I called the junior partner at Booz Allen and asked to meet him. I presented my findings with all the exhibits and rationale, as if he were the client. I had all the accompanying numbers to show the immediate impact on the revenues and losses/profits. The analyses showed an almost immediate return to a positive cash flow, with a growing business over time and great margins. When I was done, the junior partner looked at me pensively and asked one question: "Is the president in agreement with you?" My answer was, "Every inch of it, every number in it, every finding and conclusion, every single recommendation. In fact, we worked on everything together as a team." He then said, "I'll be a son of a gun!"

A while later, we met with the CEO and the executive level management of the conglomerate. Present in the meeting were the two presidents of the divisions we worked on. I started the presentation with the situation regarding the appliance division. I spoke for almost thirty minutes and didn't have a single question, which is extremely unusual. When I was finished, the CEO said nothing at first and then turned to the president I had been working with and asked him if he agreed with my analyses and recommendations. The president responded, "One hundred percent."

To complete the story, what we predicted happened, just as if we had scripted it. Sales in the custom home and kitchen remodeler segment continued to grow, and sales in department stores increased dramatically. Profitability was achieved almost immediately. The company grew from $30 million back to the peak of $70 million within three years. I did not keep up with what happened subsequently.

Perhaps another example will serve to demonstrate how mediocrity can exist even within an organization of smart people, and how easy it is to arrive at the wrong strategic conclusions.

37

My Last Hurrah at Ameritech:
A Case Study of Strategic Analyses
and Recommendations

Five years after I joined Ameritech, I gave the company notice that I planned to resign to join an independent venture group. I promised to stay for another six months to help find my replacement and ensure a smooth transition. At about the same time, Ameritech decided to embark on an ambitious plan to acquire four companies. I was asked to complete the acquisitions before I departed. What transpired made me postpone my departure for an additional full year.

Six years earlier, before I joined Ameritech, the company acquired an up-and-coming database management software (DBMS) company called ADR. DBMS refers to a software program or utility used for creating, editing, and maintaining computer database files and records. This type of software allows users to store data in the form of structured fields, tables, and columns, which can then be retrieved directly and/or through programmatic access.

Nowadays practically all data stored on computers—large and small—use DBMS. In those days, however, most data was stored in a "linear" manner, without any structure and "linkages." Thus, when needing to search for specific data, the computer had to search each piece of data linearly, until it found a match. Large databases would require significant amounts of time to do such searches. The DBMS organized and linked the data with a special organizational structure and tags. When specific data was needed, the DBMS would look for the tag and link, zeroing in on the data immediately and thus shortening the search time significantly. Such DBMS capability had just started to emerge in those days.

Ameritech paid $200 million for the acquisition, which in those days was a large acquisition with an expensive price tag. The rationale was to expand into new growth industries with proprietary technologies. Ameritech, being a large corporation, was a large user of software and databases. However, the company knew little about how software products were sold and the competitive dynamics in the software industry. The company was naïve enough to think that just because it knew how to use the software, it could easily and successfully manage a software company in a highly competitive industry.

At that time, IBM was the only company that offered large commercial database software. ADR and a number of new start-up companies began to offer competitive products with some new technical capabilities and attractive features. ADR developed a DBMS product to compete with IBM's offering, and it began to show promise for commercial success. ADR grew from zero to about $100 million in revenues during the first five years, all the while competing against IBM. Just to put it in perspective, IBM's database business was in the billions of dollars annually. So, Ameritech expected that it could grow ADR substantially and reasonably quickly. Ameritech assumed that since ADR showed early success with limited cash resources, then it could aggressively invest additional funds in this business and grow it even faster.

Coincidently, a number of years earlier, at the dawn of the mobile telephone industry, Ameritech had launched its own mobile company, called Ameritech Mobile Corporation. The industry was growing quickly. From a strategic point of view, all the competitors had the same technology, so their success depended on the efficacy of their marketing and sales strategies to reach consumers. Hundreds of agents were hired, and retail stores opened to allow registrations of new customers. Ameritech had the best brand-name recognition in its region, since it was the local telephone landline provider of telephone services, and thus it had a competitive advantage that contributed to strong growth in the mobile market. The president of Ameritech Mobile Corporation, a rising star, was asked to head up ADR to replicate his marketing and sales success at Ameritech Mobile. The first thing the newly appointed president of ADR did was to replicate the marketing and sales strategies that contributed to Ameritech Mobile's success. It worked great there; it should work well with ADR as well was the thinking.

The company immediately started growing the marketing and sales organization. Within a single year, the salesforce grew from 40 to 180. Additionally, ADR adopted Ameritech's corporate structure with layers of management. Within a single year, the payroll cost of ADR grew from about $50 million to over $100 million annually. ADR viewed it as an investment for growth—that revenue growth would make up for the additional costs.

Unfortunately, expected revenue growth didn't materialize, and the company started losing millions of dollars a year. Four years later it brought in a software consulting firm to study what had gone wrong and how to correct it.

The consulting firm spent a full year on the project and made a number of fundamental recommendations. The recommendations were first presented to the president of ADR, who endorsed all the findings, conclusions, and recommendations. They were then presented to the president of Ameritech, to whom the president of ADR reported, and the executive vice president of corporate strategy for Ameritech. Both approved the consultant's recommendations. They then presented all the findings and recommendations to the chairman and CEO and the board of directors. The recommendation called for an additional $200 million to acquire four start-up software technology companies, which they believed would reverse the trends and losses at ADR. That's when I was called in. I was responsible for mergers and acquisitions, and so I was asked to acquire the four companies.

I needed to understand the logic for the acquisitions, so the consulting firm was asked to present its findings and recommendations to me and my staff. The consulting firm was small and specialized in what was then called computers and data processing. It was a relatively new firm, and one I was not familiar with, and I wondered why such a small consulting firm was selected for such a challenging assignment.

When I greeted the senior partner of the consulting team, my jaw dropped. I had worked with him at Booz Allen, where he was the senior partner responsible for the practice related to computers and data processing. His stellar reputation explained the rationale for the firm's selection for this assignment. He was as surprised to see me as I was him. We exchanged warm greetings. He led the presentation to my group.

I need to digress a bit to put some things into perspective. Booz Allen had a number of primary overall organizational practices. They included the corporate strategy practice, which dealt with all corporate marketing and competitive strategic issues, and which was the organization where I worked; the compensation and organizational practice, which dealt with board-level corporate organizational structures and executive compensation strategies; the operations group, which dealt with corporations' operational issues, such as manufacturing, distributions, warehousing, etc.; the banking group that dealt with banks and financial institutions; the government group; and the computers & data processing group.

In those days, companies built and managed their own data centers to house their computer technology. The IT department of each corporation had two distinct groups that oversaw computers and related software: the computer operations group and the systems and development group.

The computer operations group was responsible for the hardware and the management of the data centers. The systems and development group maintained the applications software that ran on the computers, such as payroll, accounting, human resources, financial processing, inventory, distribution, manufacturing, and so on. The computer operations group was comprised mostly of technical computer people, while the systems and development group was comprised mostly of software designers, software developers, and programmers.

The two practices had little in common. Each had a unique set of skills and expertise. One group was responsible for deciding what kind of computers to buy, how many of them, how many data centers to build and where to build them, how to connect them in a network, and everything else associated with the efficient and cost-effective operation of those computers.

The other group was strictly a user of those computers and maintained the application programs. The application programs, at the time, were written mostly by IBM. They were generic in nature and were sold as such. Customizing those generic application programs and subsequently maintaining them and changing them as the need arose was the responsibility of the corporation's internal systems and development staff. The Booz Allen practice exclusively dealt with the computer operations side.

Every now and then, Booz Allen was called to do work where computer operations were a critical element in the overall corporate strategy. When that was the case, Booz Allen assembled a team that comprised people from the strategy group and the computer operations group. The strategy group devised the strategies, while the computer operations group assessed the effectiveness of how computers were deployed in terms of cost efficiency and their overall capabilities. Because of my previous EDS background, I was one of the few people at Booz Allen who worked for the strategy group and who also understood computers. Thus, often when a combined team was needed, I was assigned to it. That is how I worked with and got to know the senior partner who made the presentation to us at Ameritech.

The above elaboration was necessary to make a nuanced point. The issues that faced ADR were strategic in nature, and dealt with marketing and competitive dynamics. They had nothing to do with computer operations. The Ameritech executives who hired the small consulting firm and the ex-senior Booz Allen partner, like most management at the time, had no inkling of the above nuance. My former colleague at Booz Allen was involved with enough combined teams, and sat in on enough "combined" presentations, that he became familiar with the overall concepts of corporate and competitive strategies. He knew the top-of-the-wave lingo and concepts, but never practiced the nuances of analyzing and formulating competitive corporate strategies. I knew the difference and I knew his experience, so I listened to his presentation with a high degree of skepticism.

The presentation lasted close to two hours, and it was true to the quality of one produced at Booz Allen. Findings and recommendations were supported with graphs, charts, and detailed data. Here are the key observations and conclusions:

- ADR had a very large marketing and sales organization that came with a huge price tag. Almost 80 percent of the losses attributed to ADR stemmed from the cost of that department.

- Dividing ADR's revenues by the number of salespeople, which was 180, yielded a "revenue-per-salesperson" number.

- The consulting firm compared the revenue-per-salesperson with many other software companies. The comparison revealed that ADR's ratio was five times smaller than the norm for the industry. The consultants concluded that the sales organization was therefore not operating at the same sales efficiency as its competitors, leading to ADR not being competitive on a cost basis. This is also what contributed to the huge losses experienced by ADR in the last few years. They therefore also concluded that to correct the above, ADR needed to increase product sales significantly so as to bring the revenue-per-salesperson ratio in line with industry competitive norms.

- The product that ADR sold unfortunately experienced slower growth than expected. Other competitors in the same market segment also showed slower growth. Thus, ADR needed to look elsewhere to find additional revenue growth opportunities.

- The consulting firm identified an emerging technology called artificial intelligence (AI) software. It was the new buzzword in the industry, and the market for AI products promised unlimited potential.

- Four start-up companies had built a reputation and name recognition in this new field. Because they were start-ups, their technologies had not yet been fully developed and therefore were not fully commercialized and had no revenues to this point.

- As a result, ADR could purchase the four companies at a reasonable price and establish a dominant leadership position in this field. ADR would therefore be the only benefactor of the expected growth.

- The consulting firm forecasted performance for the combined company. The numbers were huge. Forecasted revenues would improve ADR's revenue-to-salesperson ratio to competitive levels. They would also stimulate and ensure continued new growth that would last for many years to come.

- To purchase the four start-ups would cost Ameritech about $200 million. This was a tremendous amount of money in those days, in excess of a billion dollars today.

- Ameritech was a very large company and could easily afford such a price, and the acquisition of the four companies would be one way to take advantage of its cash-rich position. However, it was made clear that the strategy would only work if ADR purchased all four companies; otherwise, a preeminent position without competition could not be guaranteed.

As I mentioned, these analyses and recommendations were endorsed by the president of ADR and approved by the president of Ameritech and the EVP of corporate strategy. They presented the same package to the chairman and CEO of Ameritech and then to the board of directors. The recommendations were formally approved by the board. I was called upon to execute on the approved strategy—to buy the four start-ups.

At the conclusion of the presentation, I asked to meet with the EVP of corporate strategy, whom I worked with closely before and who was one of my strongest supporters at Ameritech. I went up to his office and said the following: "I have a real dilemma I need to share with you, and I need you to make a decision for me." He looked surprised and asked me to continue.

I said, "I listened to the presentation by the consulting firm regarding ADR. My job is not to critique the presentation, nor to challenge the conclusions. My organizational responsibility is to execute on the approved recommendations. However, as you well know, I was a strategic consultant for many years. I saw four major potential flaws in the presentation that lead me to believe that the overall recommendations may be wrong for Ameritech. I can investigate it with my own people and confirm the recommendations or refute them. I have my suspicions about this, and I understand that if my suspicions are confirmed, you may lose face personally. This is the last thing I would care to bring onto you. However, I felt compelled to let you know. If you tell me to ignore my suspicions and just go ahead and buy the companies, I will do so, and I will speak to nobody else about this matter again. What would you like me to do?"

He picked up the phone and asked the president of Ameritech to come to his office. He did, and I restated my views. Both were people of high professional integrity, and both knew me well enough to take my suspicions seriously. Without hesitation, they asked me to conduct my own independent study to either confirm or refute my suspicions.

I pretty much knew that they were not just suspicions. I was very sure that I was right. I only needed to collect all the data to prove them beyond any reasonable doubt. Too much was at stake and too many people stood to be embarrassed. I asked for one thing—that they direct the president of ADR to work with me and meet all my data requests. I knew that I had to convince him first. They agreed.

I picked nine of my best people for the team, which included a number of ex-consultants, including four from Booz Allen. I instructed them to drop all of their work and be dedicated to this project. I gave ourselves a three-week deadline, and we worked nonstop for the next three weeks.

We indeed worked hard and long hours. The president of ADR, while he had the most face to lose, worked with us to find the truth. Three weeks later, I wrote the final report and presented it to the president and EVP, corporate strategy, of Ameritech. It took about an hour to make the presentation.

My analyses and recommendations were not questioned. The EVP said he would take my findings to the chairman and board. Below is a summary of what I presented in my report with supporting data. It confirmed my suspicions that the consultant's presentation was flawed in its logic.

The biggest flaw stemmed from the very first strategic observation that the consulting firm made. It concluded that the revenue-per-salesperson ratio was way too low, which made ADR extremely uncompetitive in the marketplace from a cost structure standpoint. There are two major flaws with the logic. First, revenue-per-salesperson is not a strategic imperative that drives any competitive decisions. It is a mathematically calculated ratio that at best shows a problem, but nothing that should be relied upon to reach a conclusion. It is a symptom of something larger, and fixing it is in no way a cure. Second, the idea that having that ratio increase by adding revenues is a mathematically correct observation, but doesn't lead to any strategic resolutions. The most likely conclusion is that there are too many salespeople. If the number of salespeople had not been increased so dramatically, that ratio would have been competitive. This should have been the consulting firm's first conclusion. Then the firm should have studied why the product was not selling as expected. Had it become somehow uncompetitive?

The idea that the new AI software companies would affect that ratio was nonsensical. It was a completely different product and represented a completely different strategic market segment. The purchasers were different; the purchase decision was different; and the marketing and sales team required completely different expertise. It would require its own independent marketing and sales organization to effectively sell the product. The current ADR salespeople would not be able to sell it. Only a naïve person who sees all software products as similar would draw such a conclusion.

The assumption that purchasing four start-ups would give Ameritech a preeminent position in the artificial intelligence segment, at a cost of $200 million, was also naïve, because this figure was just the estimated acquisition price of the companies. These start-ups had no revenues, and the products still needed to be fully developed. Finishing the development and commercialization of the products would cost Ameritech an additional $50 million per company, or $200 million, with a very high-risk profile, since there were no guarantees that the technology would be successfully developed and subsequently find widespread acceptance in the marketplace.

Since this was a new field, Ameritech would need to assume that other start-up technologies would emerge, sooner or later. To continue to maintain a preeminent position, Ameritech would need to stand ready to purchase all these new companies that would find early success as well. This may cost another $200 million to $500 million.

The assumption that entry into the AI field via the four acquisitions would change the revenue-per-salesperson ratio did not make any sense from another perspective, too. The product was under development, and time to market was an unknown. It would take years before the product would be fully developed and commercially available. Even if there would be commercial success realized, it would take a minimum of five years. By then, ADR would lose another $200 to $300 million. It would most likely go out of business before then.

Worse yet, artificial intelligence was a new concept. The likelihood that the concept would somehow be translated into a specific product with well-defined functionality and features to be purchased as an independent software to solve commercial problems was quite remote and very unlikely to yield commercial success in the foreseeable future.

The consultant's study was completely silent on why ADR's previous success had slowed down. This question was never raised or studied. We conducted our own study and concluded that the reason for the slowdown was because of fundamental changes in the marketplace. First, IBM changed its product to be more competitive with ADR's. Also, there were a number of new start-up companies that entered the database market. Some had very interesting features and were beginning to make commercial inroads. One of them was called Oracle (yes, the currently famous Oracle, which became the largest in this space over the years).

Thus, our conclusion was that ADR's subpar performance was a result of losing competitive position. Ameritech would be much better off selling ADR. Should Ameritech decide to accept the consultant's acquisition strategy, it should be prepared to invest close to an additional $500 million to $1 billion over the following five years and accept a high degree of risk.

My recommendations were accepted, and I was then tasked with selling ADR. The president of ADR and I worked together for nine months to find a buyer. We traveled the world together. It was a challenging sale since ADR had substantial operational losses. The bad news was that the sale of ADR postponed my departure from Ameritech and my start date with my new independent venture group.

The good news is that I sold ADR to Computer Associates (CA). I dealt directly with the founder, chairman, and CEO, Charles Wang. He took a liking to me and we became friends, for reasons I have yet to understand; he was a kingmaker, and I was a nobody. He invested half-a-million dollars in the fund my new partners and I raised after I left Ameritech. We stayed in close touch and had dinner at least twice a year in New York. Four years later, he encouraged me to start my own independent venture fund. He committed to invest a substantial amount of personal money in the fund himself, and called on some of his friends to do the same. I raised $100 million within two weeks. That was a reasonably large fund in those days. Just to put it in perspective, the fund that I had previously shared with three other partners was a $25 million fund. Charles had two daughters at the time, Jasmine and Kimberly. We decided to name my fund after our daughters—Jasmine, Kimberly & Beth—JK&B Capital. The rest is history.

Just to close the story, the anticipated commercial success in AI never materialized, and as a result the four companies targeted for acquisition went bankrupt. The president of ADR left Ameritech about a year later and joined another Baby Bell company, Bell Atlantic, based in New Jersey, to head up its mobile company. Many of the Baby Bells, including Ameritech, Bell Atlantic, Bell South, and GTE, subsequently merged into a single company called Verizon Communications, Inc., one of the largest communications companies next to AT&T. He rose in the ranks and years later became the president and COO of Verizon.

Before I conclude this section, and as a final example, I thought that it might be interesting for you to see how I used the methodology described in this section VII to help me raise my last fund at JK&B. You can see an exact copy of the presentation in appendix III. It serves to demonstrate how many of the principles of the methodology I offered in this section come into play. Pay particular attention to how the trend analysis supports the key success factors and thus the differentiation of my fund, JK&B Capital. Next, competitive analyses relative to the key success factors and other factual data are presented that support other important differentiation aspects.

Also observe that the presentation is succinct, but each page is easily and fully understood so that a presenter is not required to explain every single detail. The graphs and charts also serve the same purpose.

I hope that you will also notice all the "little things" that are in the presentation to help influence perception and convince a potential investor that JK&B is indeed unique and worthy of their investment.

Congratulations! You endured, and we have reached the end of what I intended to bring to your attention. I've given you all the ammunition you need to go out there and "conquer the world" (the business world, that is). I wish you the best of luck!

The remainder of the book comprises three appendices, which I believe offer significant value and are worth reading. Appendix I deals with how to avoid becoming a "talker" and a "loser" and instead becoming a "doer" and a "winner." It was specifically written to target teenagers and young adults. The goal is to allow you to gain a perspective that should aid in your ability to positively influence teenagers and young adults you care about, such as family members, friends, acquaintances, neighbors, students, and so on. You might consider letting them read appendix I.

Appendix II illuminates important aspects about my personal journey to success and some of the ups and downs I've encountered along the way and how I overcame them. I believe that a glimpse into my personal journey and who I am as a person will give you a better, more complete perspective on how to reflect on the content of this book. I also believe that, in addition to enhancing your own perspective, it could be of substantial value to teenagers and "foreigners" (people raised in different countries and cultures) who wish to develop a successful career in the United States. Thus, you may consider also sharing appendix II alongside appendix I with teenagers you care about, and potentially any "foreigners" in your circle of friends and acquaintances.

Appendix III, as mentioned at the conclusion of this last section, provides a real-life illustration of what was taught in section VII and the art of translating the concepts into a real-life summary presentation deck.

Now that we have reached the end, just as with any good show, I thought that a "grand finale" would be appropriate before finally closing the curtain on this book. I debated and struggled quite a bit with what might be an appropriate grand finale. Since I have already presented all the important things I wanted to share with you, how can there be a grand finale that will surpass it? It appears to be an oxymoron! However, two things occurred to me, which I believe would be appropriate to address at this juncture.

This book focuses solely on a single dimension—*insights*—and how to become more insightful. As a result, it may not have properly emphasized an obvious observation. The book strongly emphasized that attaining insights is mostly achieved through an iterative process of dissecting and analyzing situations, utilizing some sound conceptual "methodologies," paying closer attention to nuances and potential exceptions, and "thinking out of the box." It also reasonably well emphasized another dimension: that insights are simple to arrive at and that they are driven by pure, simple *logic*. However, *insightfulness* (aka, insights with a high degree of consistency) requires two additional dimensions that constantly interplay with the "insights" and "logic" dimensions. The two additional dimensions reflect what I refer to in the book as *perspective* (wisdom that comes through experience) and *pragmatism*.

The importance of this simple observation is to drive home a point I made earlier in the book—that one need not be a genius to achieve insightfulness. It takes a combination of four factors to achieve insightfulness, and only one—logic—may reflect "brainpower." (Although even that one requires only simple logic and not that of a rocket scientist.) This is exactly why I claimed in the Author's Note that **"anybody and everybody who reads and puts to practice what the book teaches will most likely increase greatly their probability for success in business. Just how much so will depend on you as an individual."** So, if by any chance you might have felt overwhelmed by the amount of insightfulness in this book and may have begun to wonder whether it even is within your reach, then to you I say: Yes, indeed it is! Just remember the acronym **LIPP** (Logic, Insights, Perspectives, and Pragmatism) should you ever begin to wonder again.

The second thing I realized is that this book imparts hundreds of "teaching" moments, nuanced observations, concepts, recommendations, methodologies, etc., with the single purpose of enabling you to become more insightful. There are so many of them that it is inevitable that you may not remember some of them. It is for this reason that I recommended in the introduction to this book that you will benefit from reading and rereading it, and practicing and re-practicing what it teaches. However, under the assumption that it would still be impractical to assume that a reader will not forget some of the many insightful things the book teaches, I decided that the grand finale should reflect and highlight the single most important and practical (as opposed to conceptual) element for achieving insightfulness.

So, if you happen to forget everything else, you should at least remember this one single, most important, and overarching insight—the one that trumps all other observations, lessons, and recommendations. I had a hard time isolating such an element, but then the proverbial lightning struck, and I found it! It comprises a visual image and an insightful observation already mentioned in the book, but being one of the plethora of many other observations made in this book, it may have gotten lost in the shuffle and may not have struck the necessary chord and recognition.

The Grand Finale

Henceforth, I would like you to equate the process of achieving insightfulness to an image of an inverted four-sided pyramid (the tip at the bottom and the wide base at the top) perfectly balanced on its tip (see page 384). The tip at the bottom represents the beginning of the insightfulness process, which grows, widens, and spreads upward, as the four **LIPP** dimensions and numerous analyses lead through the various branches of the decision-trees, and result in the broader set of conclusions and recommendations that surface and emerge at the top.

In my mind, this image depicts the essence of how insightfulness is achieved. First, it is not easy to guide the inverted pyramid into perfect balance. Second, a seemingly minor push will likely tilt it to fall out of balance. Third, the strength and width of the tip is the most critical element in being able to get the pyramid into a balanced position. The same holds true for insightfulness; it is not easy, nor trivial, to get it to "perfectly balance." It requires an iterative process in trying to help "guide" and achieve the ultimate balance. Yet any minor "push" in the wrong direction, as the book so vividly demonstrated can easily occur in "pedestrian" business analyses, will easily cause it to lose balance and tilt over. And, because as stated, the most important element of achieving the balance lies in the strength and width of the tip, the question is whether there exists a single element that is the most critical in the process of achieving insightfulness—the one single element that could justifiably represent the tip of this pyramid. Indeed there is, and if you remember anything from this book, then do remember this image of the inverted pyramid and the importance of this one element in reaching insightfulness. More importantly, make sure to remember what it really means and comprises.

As suggested, this element was already discussed in the book. So, for added emphasis, allow me as a grand finale to refresh your memory and repeat verbatim what I wrote when I first addressed it in section VII, so it will forever be front and center in your mind's eye and ingrained in your brain. I introduced the adage "garbage in, garbage out," reflecting the importance of data as a basis for achieving correct analyses. Indeed: **The data represent the most important, most critical element in any analysis aspiring to reach correct conclusions. Any compromise in the data used will, unquestionably, compromise the quality of the outcome. Conversely, ensuring that the data meet all the requirements I enumerated in the book will substantially increase the probability of reaching correct and insightful results.** With that in mind, below is how it was described in section VII:

> So, unequivocally, the highest priority in regard to data is to make sure that data do not comprise "garbage." In my experience, most of the failings occur because the practitioners view the adequacy of data from

a narrow perspective, **mostly whether it is accurate**. In my mind, data must be viewed from a **much broader perspective** in order to produce a quality result. **Data need to meet four criteria to pass the adequacy test:**

- Be most relevant

- Be complete

- Be accurate

- Be organized

Each and all of the criteria require sound thinking and critical judgment. In most situations, it is not a straightforward undertaking. The process is prone to mistakes and, indeed, mistakes are made frequently.

So, from this point forward, if you remember one thing, remember the image of the inverted balanced pyramid as representing insightfulness, which will remind you of the importance of the tip, which will remind you of the importance of the data, and that adequate data comprise the four elements above.

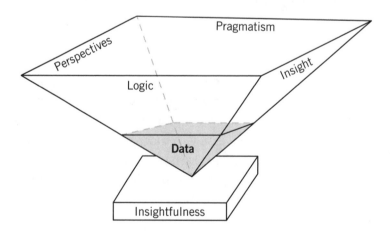

Always be mindful of the above, both as a practitioner as well as a manager who is presented with the analyses, and you will significantly increase the probability of attaining insightfulness. This observation holds true not just in business but life in general.

And now for the final closing of the curtain, I would like to repeat what I said a few paragraphs ago: I've given you all the ammunition you need to go out there and "conquer" the business world. I wish you the best of luck!

APPENDIX I

ADVICE FOR TEENAGERS
AND YOUNG ADULTS

How to Build a Platform for a Successful Career

Part I: Thinking Ahead, Commitment, Perseverance, and Success

Success in life, at the most fundamental level, can be attributed to the difference between "talkers" and "doers" or "winners" and "losers." I believe that a single critical attribute, *perseverance*, separates the achievers from the non-achievers. The road to success is not an easy one. It is full of commitments, sacrifice, and pain. It is a roller coaster of emotions, and there are many temptations and obstacles that stand in the way. Only perseverance, or what is more commonly referred to as willpower, can see a person through the ups and downs of the journey to success.

Based on my personal experience and observing others, I believe that how much willpower a person has later in life is acquired at an early age and mostly through the teenage years and the early twenties. What I noticed with many of my friends and acquaintances is that the weakening of willpower happens gradually and inconspicuously. However, at some point, a person crosses over a critical juncture beyond which it would be difficult to revert, and the person would most likely have weakened willpower as an adult. There are two telltale signs of a weakening willpower. Be aware of them, so you may recognize and avert them before they get rooted deep inside your psyche, before it becomes too late.

Sign 1—The "Talker's" Habit

Because "talker's" habits generally form over time, they are somewhat incremental and therefore may be hard to detect. However, with some self-awareness they are easy to spot and correct. A talker's habit starts and then intensifies with the passage of time by producing psychological self-gratification, despite not accomplishing anything.

When one makes a mental commitment to do something they consider a challenge, and in their mind intend to follow through, one generally experiences a sense of gratification and accomplishment that goes along with such a mental commitment. One feels a jolt of energy, empowerment, and a sense of accomplishment. It is also often accompanied by daydreaming of the benefits to come. All very psychologically gratifying.

Unfortunately, the fact that subsequently we might have not followed through doesn't take away from having felt gratified and accomplished in the first place. Clearly, the level of gratification is not as intense, nor as long-lasting, as the level felt after actually having accomplished something. Nevertheless, it is still gratification, albeit short lived. Because it is short lived, and because nobody wants to feel that they are "failures," they re-commit again, feel gratified again, and the cycle repeats itself. Over time, and before one realizes, it becomes a habit. One has just crossed over to become a "talker"!

So, my advice to you, particularly the younger reader, is very simple: **Don't allow yourself to feel gratification for making the decision, but only when you have achieved actual accomplishments.** Never be fooled into thinking that committing to overcome a challenge is the same as putting in the effort to accomplish it. If you fall into this habit, your potential success in life and career would likely be handicapped and falter. However, this advice is simpler said than done! It takes quite a bit of self-discipline and honest self-criticism to successfully adhere to it. Every time you feel gratification, you need to consciously ask yourself whether it is well earned or not. Is it a result of actual accomplishments? Ask yourself that question, and over time it will become second nature, and you'll avoid becoming a talker or loser, and will be well on your way to becoming a lifelong doer and winner.

Sign 2—Making Excuses

Over the years, I have also observed another phenomenon, which occurs simultaneously with the first sign of a lessening willpower. People find a way to absolve themselves and excuse away inaction. In their mind, they believe that indeed a subsequent inaction was somehow justified and doesn't reflect a personal failure to persevere. They find reasons as to why it is okay and/or not so bad after all. Sometimes, they even convince themselves that it actually is for the better—the "silver lining on the cloud" phenomenon. In all cases, such excuses shield them from thinking of themselves as having failed. The most common reasons those people use tend to fall into one of five categories: (i) it is not their fault; (ii) they can't fight the whole world; (iii) the odds were stacked against them; (iv) it is just a convenient "pause," or perhaps a bit of procrastination on their part, but for sure they will return to the original plan; or (v) in retrospect, they decided, or realized, that the "gain" was not really worth the "pain."

I don't call them reasons; rather, I call them *excuses*! So, the lesson to take away is simple. Rarely accept reasons for failing to persevere; they are in most cases excuses, whether you came up with them or somebody else offers excuses on your behalf. Stated differently: **There are rarely good reasons for failing. And you should rarely accept excuses. Persevere until you succeed. There is no substitute!**

Note that I said **there are rarely good reasons for failing**. This implies that there are a few good reasons, too. Indeed, there are. If we aim way beyond our natural capabilities to accomplish something, and recognize it down the line, it is a legitimate reason to stop and redefine another path to success, perhaps one more within our natural capabilities. Also, it may not be a limitation of our natural capabilities, but rather, circumstantial conditions that are truly outside of our control. This, too, would become a legitimate reason.

In other words, "legitimate" failures can and will happen. If they don't, it probably means that we didn't aim high enough to begin with. We should embrace and accept failures and expect them. There is nothing wrong with failure, so long as one doesn't give up completely but gets up to fight another day. This is what separates winners from losers.

Simply stated: **Don't fear failures. Learn from them, adjust, restart, and persevere.**

As I stated, the road to success is not an easy one. Perseverance, willpower, and sacrifice are the keys to overcoming the obstacles that may come one's way. I'd like to share a personal story of perseverance. Should you ever experience despair and be at the brink of faltering, please remember this example. If I was able to persevere, you can, too!

A New Immigrant's Challenge

I grew up in Israel in a family with little in the way of economic resources. Attaining a successful career was a thought far from my mind as I was growing up. Some personal dramatic events led me to understand that a good education is fundamental to enjoying a more fulfilling and successful future. (I discuss them in appendix II: "Personal Reflections.")

I decided to major in engineering, specifically electrical engineering and computer science. I saw opportunity in this area. I was fourteen years old when I committed to make it happen, no matter what.

There was only one school of engineering in Israel at the time, called the Technion. The odds of getting into the school were low. One had to do exceptionally well in high school and pass very difficult pre-admittance tests that were used as a primary tool to screen the various applicants. It required complete dedication of time and commitment. One couldn't falter and succeed. At the age of twenty-two, after three years of military service, I had about three weeks to brush up on all I had learned in high school and prepare for the entrance examinations. I studied day and night with no more than about three or four hours of sleep. I was fortunate enough to do well in the entrance exams and was admitted to the Technion.

Before I started my first year at the Technion, I got married. My wife (now ex-wife) was American. During my first year at the Technion, we decided to complete my education in the United States. Clearly, one contributing factor was that my wife was American and she wanted to be close to her family. Another was that I would have more career opportunities upon graduating, as the computer field was new and commercially almost nonexistent in Israel. I applied to U.S. engineering schools as a sophomore student and was accepted by several. I chose to go to Stevens Institute of Technology in New Jersey, not too far from where my in-laws resided. I was very excited about moving to the U.S. and completing my education there. However, I didn't anticipate what followed. I didn't appreciate the difficulties of studying in a language in which my vocabulary was very limited, and I was not familiar with any engineering or technical terms.

On my first day, I had five lectures, each delivered by a different professor who had accents foreign to my ear, which made comprehension almost impossible for me. I realized that to understand the lectures and the material, I'd have to focus on learning from the textbooks. As soon as I got back to my room, I dove into the textbooks and started reading. I understood maybe 10 percent of the words; I looked up the rest in the dictionary. It was unbelievably laborious, and sometimes it took an hour just to read through one page of text. It took many hours to cover all the material for a single lecture. To study this way was not practical; I would not be able to keep up. I purchased a cassette tape recorder and took it to my classes. With my wife's help, I thought I could learn more quickly by going over the recorded lectures at home.

Unfortunately, recording had limited capabilities in those days. The microphone had to be close to the professors to capture their voices, and was attached by a cord to the tape recorder. Imagine this scene: I arrive early at classes to sit in the closest proximity to the professors. I hold out my hand, gripping the microphone, aiming it at the professors as they walk back and forth.

At the end of the day, my wife and I would listen to a sentence, stop and rewind the tape, and then listen again, over and over. We still had to look up technical words in the dictionary. This took even more time than just trying to read the textbooks. I suddenly realized that this was not a viable option either. I could not see a solution that would allow me to continue there. I became desperate and depressed.

It is hard to describe the desperation I felt, the deep feeling of defeat. All of my dreams and aspirations suddenly became impossible to reach. I continued to try, but every day the cycle repeated itself and the desperation grew stronger. The stress became enormous; I became an emotional wreck. I couldn't sleep at night and felt completely lost.

I was sure that there was no longer any hope for me to complete my education. However, in the back of my mind, I realized that quitting was not an option and that my only hope of getting an education was to somehow keep going, no matter what. So I kept going and going and going!

In about three weeks, I became more attuned to the accents of the professors, and I learned enough additional words to comprehend the lectures better and understand most of what was said. My level of comprehension improved and, as they say, the rest is history. In the following three years, I ended up pursuing two parallel degrees and earned a bachelor's in electrical engineering and a master's in computer science. I also managed to graduate as one of the top students at the school.

Part II: A Good Education Gives You Options and Opportunities

As stated in the introduction to the book, this specific chapter was meant for the younger reader. It is meant to illuminate the importance of quality education and serve as a complement to what parents may give as advice to their children. You might want to bring it to the attention of a younger member of your family and their friends.

In life, we are constantly called upon to make trade-off decisions, balancing between conflicting considerations. How we end up resolving such conflicts and the actual decisions we make along the way may at times determine the trajectory of our lives. This is certainly true with respect to one's career and business success. However, for the younger reader, one overriding, critical factor needs to be considered before committing to longer-term plans. **Thinking longer term is essential as it gives one a general direction to follow. However, the younger the age, the more one needs to incorporate the likelihood that they might change their perspectives and priorities over time.** This is so because, although we always, at all ages, have dreams and aspirations, the younger we are, the less perfect is our understanding of what is out there in the world. As we grow older and wiser, we gain new understandings, which change our perspectives, and, accordingly, our aspirations and goals. So, it follows that **when it comes to career decisions earlier in your life, you must incorporate a strong likelihood that your definition for success in life and business may change over time.** The only way to accommodate such changes over time is to put oneself in the best position to make necessary adjustments when the time comes. To do so, one must take, in advance, appropriate actions that will allow such future flexibility. I refer to it as building a foundation or platform that is wide, strong, and flexible, one that will enable you to make career changes as required. How well you are able to do this is related to the quality of education you pursue.

Education is the most important and predictable factor that you control and that can influence your career opportunities and choices. Think about it in the extreme. If for whatever reason you decide early in your life that education is not a high priority for you, then you are unlikely to retain the flexibility of pursuing a professional career in business. I was brought up in challenging circumstances, where pursuit of a higher education was of little priority, if any. In the neighborhood where I grew up, everybody—my family, relatives, friends, and neighbors—all shared the same sentiments. We just didn't know enough to understand the value a good education could bring about. I was the only one who pursued a higher education. I can now tell you with absolute certainty that all those same people will tell you unequivocally that they were wrong and that they wish they would have pursued education instead on focusing on shorter-term considerations, which at the time appeared more gratifying and wiser to them.

At the same time, I can now also tell you that education just for the sake of education is not enough. There is another factor that directly impacts your future success and flexibility to pursue opportunities. This factor reflects on the "quality" of your education and how well you did in school in terms of your grade point average (GPA). The quality of your education and grades will forever be used to compare you to other potential applicants vying for the same opportunities. Absent knowing you well beforehand, those in a position to make these opportunities a reality for you will use those criteria to evaluate and place judgment on your smarts, dedication, perseverance, reasoning, judgments, and added value you might bring to their organization. The better the quality of your education and your grades, the greater the likelihood you will be selected and benefit from such opportunities. The quality of education in this context will be measured by what you majored in, as well as the reputation of the school you attended. Thus, my advice is almost self-evident, and you have probably heard it many times before: **Quality education is very important. Commit to doing the best you can and attend a reputable school. There is no substitute for it.**

Committing to your education is a longer-term decision, while doing well in school is the shorter-term action required. I would like to reemphasize the importance of the second part, but cast it in a more general way, one that will be applicable throughout your career and an important aspect for you to remember.

You may have heard the following adage, and if you haven't, you will: "In business, you are as good as the last thing you did." Another proverb that attempts to communicate the same idea is, "In business, one cannot rest on past laurels." These sayings are full of wisdom and apply in all facets of life. It is also true for your accomplishments in school.

I already stated that the quality of one's grades plays an important role in the selection process from among multiple candidates vying for the same opportunities. So, at the risk of being overly repetitious, but in an attempt to reemphasize its importance, allow me to again state what you may have heard many times before: **In school, always do your best, regardless of the cost or personal sacrifice. Any slipup in grades may be hard to overcome!** Remember, any personal "costs" and sacrifices at school are only short term, while the potential gains will last a lifetime. Also, short-term slippage in grades will affect your overall GPA and likely be hard to rectify later on. Commitment and perseverance would be the key. Allow me to bring, by way of an example, a personal story to demonstrate just how much one person was willing to endure in pursuit of this advice. It involves my daughter, Beth.

As you can imagine, from the time Beth was a youngster, I tried to instill in her the importance of excelling in school. She was a very serious student and did exceptionally well. Right before her junior year of high school, Beth and her mother joined a couple of friends who drove to New York on a holiday. Beth's mother and I were divorced at this point, and I was living on my own. On the way back, they left New York early in the morning and attempted to drive nonstop through the night back to Illinois. Before the night was over, at around five in the morning, my phone rang. The caller was a trooper with the Indiana State Police. He informed me that there was a serious accident involving the car that Beth and her mother were riding in.

Apparently, the driver of the car had fallen asleep and the car veered off the road at a high speed. It rolled a number of times. A truck driver who saw the accident called the police. Beth had been thrown from the vehicle. She was in the hospital in stable condition, with a broken left ankle and broken left wrist. Her mother was hospitalized for about three weeks. The driver and other passengers suffered various degrees of injuries.

I rushed to the hospital. Beth's left leg and arm were in casts. She appeared to be in great pain. She was discharged into my care and I took her to my apartment. As a father, it was one of the most difficult experiences I ever faced, seeing her feel pain every time she had to move. She stayed at my place for three weeks until her mother was released from the hospital for continued care at home. By that time, Beth's pain had subsided, but she could not bear weight on her leg and was unable to use her left hand. She would require a wheelchair for at least another three weeks. At about that time, she was to start the school term.

Her school gave her permission to stay at home until she fully recovered and told her that she would be able to catch up later on the missed classes. They also promised to give her passing grades, so that she could graduate with her classmates.

Beth was concerned that missing school and trying to rush through making up for the missed classes would inevitably detract from her overall GPA. She believed that, in turn, it would impair her longer-term academic plans and, by extension, her future probability of a successful career.

I told her not to worry about it, that her health was more important. I pointed out that she would not be penalized because of a lower GPA, given the circumstances. "Everybody will understand and be sympathetic," I said. But Beth would not accept it and insisted on attending school, no matter what. She would be in a wheelchair for eight hours or more, making her way around campus in that chair, and be unable to get up for any momentary reprieve.

She called several friends who volunteered to wheel her around school from class to class. Imagine the pain and discomfort she had to endure. She never complained. She persevered. She finished that semester with one B and three As.

She subsequently graduated high school among the top students and decided to attend Vassar College. It was the only school she wanted to attend, and the only school she applied to. She was an honor student there, and upon graduation joined Morgan Stanley's investment banking practice in New York. Six years later, she received an MBA from The Wharton School and again proved her mettle as an honor student.

Be wise, be committed. Perseverance and willpower will take you a long way!

APPENDIX II

PERSONAL REFLECTIONS

This book was written primarily to share observations, lessons, tools, and techniques to enable you to become more insightful, and thereby accelerate your career. I thought that it would be of value to now share some additional personal stories about myself so as to give you a more complete perspective on not just the advice I offer, but also about me as a person.

My Early Education

When I was young, I did not like school. As a grammar school student (first through eighth grade), I rarely did much homework. I loved playing soccer, though, which I did constantly. I became skilled at the game and was selected to play on a little league sports team affiliated with the professional soccer team in the city. Whatever I learned academically was limited to what I retained in the classroom. I would cram for an exam, but never for more than a day. Yet, I always managed to get good grades.

When we were about to graduate from grammar school, we were given some exams to see if we would qualify to enter high school. At the time, high school was not mandatory in Israel. The city of Tel Aviv, where I grew up, was divided into eleven districts. Each district had one municipal public high school. This school accepted only the top students who passed the qualifying exams. That meant most kids had the choice of attending a private vocational school or going to work. I passed those exams and was accepted to attend my district's high school. Tuition was relatively affordable, but still a hefty burden for my parents. However, two very unfortunate things happened to me in high school. One was fully my fault; the other partially so.

The outcome I accept full responsibility for was a result of my poor study habits. I did the minimum to prepare for exams. I was playing soccer for the youth team, which consumed most of my free time. At the same time, I had just become of age and so I spent most evenings and weekends with a group of friends, which included girls. School was not a priority. I assumed that I would still achieve good grades, just as I had at grammar school. I didn't grasp that the standards had changed. We started learning algebra, geometry, physics, and chemistry at a demanding level. We also took four humanities classes: grammar, literature, geography, and history.

The other thing that happened, which was not really my fault, I attribute to just the luck of the draw—unfortunately, a very unlucky and bad draw for me. The teacher of all of the science classes taught in such a boring and muddled way that I could not understand a single thing. Students resorted to private tutoring and were diligent about their homework. I did none of these. At the end of the first semester, I did well in the humanities courses but failed the science subjects. My parents were very upset. I was not used to failure and vowed to do better in the following semester.

I started applying myself more to schoolwork. Not all that much, but more than I had done before. There were two exams during the semester in each of the subjects. I studied for at least one week before each exam. My older brother spent day and night teaching me and preparing me for those exams.

My older brother was a senior at one of two decent semi-vocational private schools. He was also very good in all the science subjects. With his help, I really applied myself. We carefully went through the chapters in the textbooks and solved every question. I felt confident, as did my brother, that I understood the material. However, I continued to fail the exams for all the science subjects. Four mid-semester tests—four failing grades! The story repeated itself for the final exams!

My parents were beside themselves. I couldn't understand how I had failed, but fail I did. I promised my parents that I would do better in the third and final semester. I studied even harder with my brother's help. A week before each exam, my brother helped me to learn, and again I felt I clearly understood everything he taught me. Again, I had eight science tests for the last semester, and I received eight failing grades—although I did very well in the other subjects. I would be expelled. The conclusion I drew was that I was not smart enough. I had tried hard, yet I failed time and time again. This feeling of failure and not being very smart was to stay with me for many years.

What I didn't understand at the time was that, without learning the basics of science first, there was no way I or any other student could ever subsequently succeed in more advanced subject matters. My brother and I always concentrated on the very topics I had to face in an exam, but I still lacked the basics. I never learned those well and never made up for the deficiency. So, for example, in algebra, I never learned what we studied in the first semester, like the four operations with positive and negative numbers and how to deal with multi-level parentheses. So, while I understood the more complicated topics at hand, when it came to answering the exam questions, I would fail to reach the correct final answer because of making basic mistakes in simple math operations and the unraveling of parentheses. In my mind, I failed in spite of trying so hard, so I concluded that I was stupid.

But I did very well in soccer. Each high school had a soccer team; however, the players weren't very good. I loved the game and was skilled at it. That year, my school ended up in the finals against a good team from a vocational school. The finals were played in a big stadium. We won the championship because of my skillful play. I was everywhere on the field, helping the defense, leading the offense, and creating the opportunities for the goals we scored. Never in the history of the country had one of the public high schools won the country's championship. Public high school students were mostly considered to be "nerds" and non-athletic. I was a hero to my classmates.

After failing the final semester, the principal invited me to his office. He told me that he thought I was very smart but didn't apply myself well in the science classes. I still remember what he said: "David, it is obvious that you are very smart. You did very well in all the non-science classes. You probably didn't apply yourself correctly in the science classes. You know that a failing student is always expelled. But we are willing to make an exception in your case. You may stay, if you wish, but you will need to repeat the freshman year again." I was certain at the time that the invitation to stay was based on my soccer ability. However, now I am not so sure that he didn't mean what he actually said. I turned his offer down, as by then I had thought up other plans, which are elaborated on next.

Four Defining Moments in Childhood That Turned My Life Around

In hindsight, while growing up, I was definitely on the wrong track for a successful career, but I didn't know any better. The implications of education were not something I understood nor appreciated. I was no different from anybody I saw around me—friends, neighbors, and relatives. There was nobody to make me understand that higher education would offer a new path for a career and my life.

However, I became determined to do financially better than most of those around me and formed other plans. Those plans were shaped by three specific events, which had major impacts on me in the shorter term. A fourth had a major impact for the longer term. All four events happened within months of each other, and each left a strong impression and affected my life in fundamental ways.

The First Event

The first event happened when I was around twelve or thirteen years old. My best friend, who was my neighbor, met somebody from a different neighborhood and was invited to a party. In those days, teenagers would form a circle of about twenty to thirty friends who would hang out together. On weekends they would host parties on a rotating basis. If a party wasn't happening, they would get together in a park or on a busy street corner. You needed an invitation to join such a group, and my friend invited me to this party, which was my first. I met girls and danced, and liked it. I became part of that group.

On days when there were no parties, we would walk together as a group to the center of the city and hang around there until it was time to go home. It was about a fifteen-minute walk. We would all go to a popular falafel kiosk. Everybody bought falafel—everybody but me. I didn't have money to buy falafel, which cost about the equivalent of a dollar today. I had a small weekly allowance but spent it on bus fare to get to and from school. I wouldn't even think about asking my parents for more money.

I found a way to hide this embarrassment from the rest of the group. When the group started our walk, I slowed down my pace until the group was ahead of me. My friends would arrive at the falafel kiosk as I watched from a distance, waiting until they finished eating before rejoining them. Nobody seemed to notice.

I felt terrible. All my friends worked and had money. They spent it on clothes, movies, and other fun activities. I had to forgo all those. I later became close to a girl in the group. We tended to spend more time together. I still found a way to separate from her on the walks to the falafel kiosk. I became very self-conscious about it. I was the only boy without money. I didn't really see the value of going to school. Besides, I wasn't doing all that well in school anyway. The thought of perhaps going to work and starting to enjoy life instead of attending school started to grow in my mind.

The Second Event

A couple of months later, I needed new shoes. We used to buy cheap shoes, and it was fine then. But now I was going out with girls and my friends. They were more into fashion and looks. I wanted to wear better, more modern-looking shoes.

Unlike in the big shopping malls in the U.S., buying items in Israel at the time was mostly done in small stores or flea markets/bazaars. There were no fixed prices, and every purchase was haggled over. I told my mother that I wanted more modern, fashionable shoes, and she agreed to look for those. We walked from store to store until we found a store that had more fashionable shoes. I would pick a pair, and then the store owner and my mother would negotiate the price. An agreement on price was not reached, and we moved on to find the next store that sold shoes. We must have spent about two hours walking to different shops with no success.

Then we came to a store and I saw a pair of shoes that I instantly wanted. I put them on, and they fit well. My mother asked for the price and the owner said sixteen dollars. Shoes we were used to wearing cost between eight and ten dollars. My mother refused and offered eight dollars. They went through the back-and-forth ritual that lasted about ten minutes. He came down to fifteen dollars, but my mother would pay no more than eight dollars. After about another five minutes, he was down to twelve dollars and twenty-five cents. My mother offered twelve. They started haggling over the last twenty-five cents for at least five minutes. Neither budged. I wanted the shoes so badly, but couldn't say a word. The owner would not accept twelve dollars. We left to look elsewhere. We ended up buying shoes for ten dollars, ones that I didn't really like.

I didn't blame my mother. I understood her. This was not the first time I witnessed walking away from a purchase for even less than twenty-five cents. This was, however, the first time I wanted something so badly. I was so affected that I made a lifelong decision: I would never, ever be satisfied with a life where I had to worry about twenty-five cents. Making money, more money than all my friends and neighbors at the time, would forever become one of my strongest motivations. I would do whatever it took to get there. I had no idea what it meant and how to get there, but my motivation and willpower were cemented at that moment. It wouldn't matter to me how; all I knew was that I would never waver from this commitment, whatever the challenges, whatever the obstacles.

The Third Event

About a month before the end of the school year, I fortuitously helped a neighbor with his work. He was a TV repairman and had studied at a vocational school. Most of his work involved installing antennas on roofs. From time to time he would also have to fix TVs.

TVs were a new phenomenon, and everybody saved to purchase one. Work was plentiful for my neighbor. When his regular apprentice fell ill, he asked me to help him on one of his jobs. I soon learned that he was making very good money as a TV technician and had little competition, since few people went to school to earn an electronic technician diploma.

He made about double what I knew to be average wages for a typical worker. I asked him what it would take to get a diploma, and he said I would need to go to a vocational school. I was surprised and told him that I thought that vocational schools were for "idiots" and that the schools taught little of value. He agreed but said, "There is one school that is an exception. It has a full curriculum and teaches at very high standards. I went to that school and got my diploma there." I asked how long it would take to get the diploma. He said that I could do it in two years as a full-time student, or four years in the night program. He said he went to the night program, and that's how he was able to afford the tuition.

I had found a solution to both of my problems. I could work full-time during the day and go to school at night. I would have money to enjoy life with my friends, while at the same time attending school to become a TV technician, like my neighbor. I was committed. He told me that registration began at the end of the summer. I couldn't wait to register. I was looking forward to the next stage in my life. I had found new bearings. I felt like a new person.

At that time, the girl I mentioned became my formal girlfriend. We celebrated the occasion with a kiss. It was my first kiss! We spent as much time together as possible. The school year came to an end and, as I mentioned earlier, I turned down the offer to repeat my freshman year at high school. I had a month before registration in the vocational school for the electronic technician diploma. I was carefree and happy.

The Fourth Event

I was a creative thinker. I was efficiency minded. I was always looking for ways to find shortcuts. I was, at the same time, I thought, a great bullshit artist. Thus, the next idea came naturally to me. I would try to convince the principal at the vocational school that during the summer

I had restudied the classes I failed and would ask to start at the vocational school as a sophomore. I had nothing to lose and a year to gain.

My girlfriend started working during the day. She told me that she was planning to go to night school and that the public high school in her district offered a nighttime program. The teachers who taught in the daytime also taught at night. The standards were equally as high for daytime and nighttime courses. She said that it was the best night program in the city. She also said that we would not be able to see each other during the week once the summer was over.

I remembered that her older brother attended another private night school in the area. She had told me at an earlier time that her brother's school had the best reputation in the city. But she also said the school she was going to attend was the best. I asked her about the "conflict" between how she characterized her intended school and her brother's school. She said that indeed the private school that her brother attended was the best private school, but it wouldn't be better than the public school, which had a night program identical to what it offered during the day—the same curriculum, teachers, and facilities. I didn't pay much attention to this conversation at the time, but it became pivotal just a month later.

A month before registering at the vocational school, I went to visit my neighbor and told him that I wanted to register as a sophomore, not a freshman. I gave him the story line, and he said that it sounded reasonable to him. He knew the principal and said he'd call to arrange a meeting with him so that I could explain my special situation. The meeting was set up for the following week.

I spent the week agonizing over whether I was doing the right thing. I might have set myself up for failure, never having restudied the subjects I had failed. On the one hand, the idea of finding a way to cheat the system and save a full year was appealing. On the other hand, the fear of failing my classes because I wasn't really ready for sophomore math weighed heavily on my mind. An hour before my meeting with the principal, I decided to go ahead and give it a try.

I met the principal and told him that I was committed to going to his school and doing well there. I had only one issue, which I hoped he would understand and help me with. I proceeded to tell him the story

I had prepared. His body language wasn't very encouraging. He said that I was asking for something that was impossible to accommodate. He asked me, "By the way, which school did you go to?" I had forgotten to mention it before.

I told him I had attended Ironit Z (Municipal Z). His response was immediate, and he appeared surprised. "You went to Ironit Z?" I answered in the affirmative. His expression changed and he said, "If you went as a freshman to Ironit Z, then you can register here as a sophomore. It will be fine."

The school year began about two weeks later than the public schools. Class began at 6:00 PM and ended at 9:00 PM. There were about twenty-five students in my class. My first class was engineering drawings and was uneventful. My second class was math. I started getting nervous and could feel my heartbeat accelerating. I dreaded what was to come. Would my claims of having studied to make up for my failing grades be exposed?

The math teacher walked in and announced that he needed to see how well the students knew math so that he could adjust his lessons to reflect the proficiency of the students in the class. He said that, to that end, he would call each student, alphabetically, to the blackboard to answer math questions. He looked at his roster and called the first student on the list.

My worst fears had just materialized. I started shaking. I was frozen from fear. In the Hebrew alphabet, K is toward the end, so I would be one of the last students to be called to answer questions.

The teacher asked the first student to write the number two million, twenty thousand and two on the blackboard. The student got confused over the number of zeros and could not write the number. The teacher asked the next student to write thirty-seven million, thirty-seven thousand and seven. The student couldn't write it correctly, either. Eight out of the first ten students failed to write a correct answer.

I went from a state of being close to a mental breakdown to complete surprise. These guys—sophomores, no less—*didn't even know how to write numbers*! I had known how to do that since fifth grade.

I so vividly remember those moments. I started looking around at the students and focused on a few. There was only one thought on my mind: *What am I doing here, among people who don't know how to write numbers? There is no way that I can be one of them or be like them. What am I doing to myself?*

The transformation from complete state of fear to complete shock and surprise was more than I could handle. I started to cry, silently. I couldn't stop the tears. I was in a daze. I faintly heard something familiar: "Kronfeld." A pause. "Kronfeld." The teacher was calling me to the board. "Is Kronfeld here?" I still didn't respond. "Is Kronfeld here?" At that point I understood that the teacher was calling my name.

My face wet with tears, half dazed, as if I were in a slow-motion movie, I got up from my chair, said nothing, left my books on the desk, and walked out of the classroom. I must have looked like a zombie. I walked home, which was about a twenty-minute walk. I continued to cry. I realized what I had unintentionally done. I realized that I wanted something very different. If students like them would become TV technicians, I for sure didn't want to be one of them. On the walk home, I decided to repeat the year in high school. This time I would not fail. I understood at that moment that I had to find a way out of my environment, and a good education was the key.

I got home around 8:00 PM. My father was still working, bent down over his sewing machine. My mother was there, too. A scene I'd seen a thousand times before. My father looked at me and saw that I was crying. He asked, "What happened?"

I said, "I want to go back to Ironit Z."

"What do you mean, you want to go back there?" he asked.

I said, "I made a big mistake. I want to repeat the year. I want to go back and study again."

"But you failed there," my father said.

I said, "Yes, but I will study this time, I promise. I will not fail again."

"You promised three times before, and each time it amounted to nothing. You promised and didn't deliver. We don't believe you anymore."

I became panicky. "I know, I know, but this time it is different. I understand that I have to do so to succeed in life. I really do."

My father said, "This school is expensive. We can't afford it and take the risk with you failing again. We paid for the new school and now you are walking away from this one, too. We don't believe any of your promises any longer." I was devastated.

I wasn't angry with my parents. I didn't blame them; I blamed myself. I now had to pay my own way for an education, and Ironit Z was no longer an option. I remembered what my girlfriend had told me about her night school. She went to Ironit A. It was out of my district, but that was the only option I had left. The only good school with a night program. I could work during the day and pay for the tuition myself. There was no other option. The next day, at 3:30 PM, I got on my bike and rode to Ironit A. What happened next was a series of completely unexpected events.

Scene One

I went to the administration office. It was quiet and, I thought, deserted. Then I saw an older gray-haired man sitting at the secretary's desk. It was an unusual sight in those days, as men didn't hold secretarial positions. I approached him, and he looked at me and asked how he could help. I told him that I needed to see the principal. He asked me why. I told him I wanted to register for classes. He said that it would be impossible, because the admission period had closed a month earlier. There were at least twenty-five students on the waiting list who could not be admitted. Also, classes had started two weeks ago.

I didn't even consider that there was a possibility of not being able to get in. What did I know about admission periods, waiting lists, and the like? I looked at him and said, "No, you don't understand. I must get in here." I proceeded to tell him that I went to Ironit Z and failed, because I didn't apply myself at school; that I had gone to a vocational school the day before, and that solution was not for me, which I now realized; and that I could go back to Ironit Z, but my parents were poor and couldn't afford the tuition. This school was my only option. I had to get into this school. He looked at me and asked a couple of questions, which I don't even remember now. Five minutes later, he said, "I told you that I don't think it is possible, but I'll let you talk to the principal." He walked into the principal's office, and within the minute, they both came out.

The principal looked at me and asked how he could help. I said that I wanted to register. He repeated what the secretary had told me. I told my story again and promised to become the best student in the school.

He said, "I'm really sorry, but we have no room for additional students, not even a single one. However, there is another very good night school, which teaches at high standards. They are private and they will have room. I know the principal there. I will write a letter of recommendation and I'm sure that he'll let you in."

The name of the school he mentioned was the school that my girl-friend's older brother went to. I nodded and thanked the principal. He asked me to wait. He went back inside his office and within minutes handed me a handwritten letter. He asked me to go to the school immediately, because every day counted, and give the letter to the principal. I rode there in about ten minutes.

Scene Two

I found the principal's office and gave the secretary the letter. A couple of minutes later, the principal came out and told me to follow him to class. On the way, he told me that it was a very nice letter of recommendation and that I could officially register the following day. He introduced me to the teacher, and I sat down. During the class, I listened to the teacher and students. I looked at each student. I did the same in the following class. I wasn't very impressed. This school was still not even close to what I expected. I had been around smart students in Ironit Z. I knew the difference already. I decided that this was not my solution. The next day, at 4:00 PM, I was back at the other school.

Scene Three

The secretary saw me and asked, "What happened? Did they not accept you?" I said that they did, but after two classes I realized that they were not of the right caliber. I needed to get into his school. He looked at me momentarily and said, "Wait here. I'll get the principal."

The principal looked at me and asked what had happened. I repeated my experience. I pleaded with him. He kept saying that it was impossible. I kept pleading but his response was always the same. After about the fifth iteration, he used different words. Instead of saying that it was impossible, he said, "I'm unable to do it."

I was a thirteen-year-old kid. I didn't understand he was saying it was still impossible, but in different words. To me it was a different reason. I responded, "If you are unable, then who is?" He started laughing and repeated my question twice while laughing very hard. He finally said, still laughing, "Well, there is only one person that is able to do it, and that is the Minister of Education of the country of Israel." I had no idea who the Minister of Education was, so I asked where I could I find him. He burst into laughter, repeating the question a number of times, while walking back to his office. I didn't understand what was so funny.

When the principal entered his office, his secretary looked at me and in a serious but quiet tone said to me, "The Minister of Education is responsible for everything involving education in the country. He is the commander of all the schools and all the principals. His office is in Jerusalem, where all the government offices are. But I know that tomorrow the minister will be in his branch office in Tel Aviv. Here is the address and his office number. You can catch him there." I thanked him and went out.

It didn't even dawn on me that the whole interaction was so strange. First, an older male secretary, which was very unusual. Second, he walked into the principal's office and the principal came out within the minute—not once, but twice. Third, he knew where the Minister of Education would be the very next day and the exact address and office number. I was too young to even think about it.

Scene Four

Next morning, I took my bike and rode to the address I was given. It took a good forty-five minutes. I went to the office. I was a kid, and nobody stopped me. The secretary looked at me and asked politely how she could help me. I said that I needed to talk to the Minister of Education. She smiled and asked, "Do you have an appointment?" I asked, "What is an appointment? What do you mean?"

She explained what an appointment was and asked me again, "Do you have one?" I said that I didn't, but that it was urgent that I see the Minister of Education. She said that she was very sorry, but that nobody could see the minister without an appointment. I told her the reason why it was so important. She said again that she was sorry, but I couldn't see the minister. I walked away.

As soon as I turned the corner, I stopped and waited. About twenty minutes passed when she got up and walked away from her desk. I dashed to the office, opened the door, and walked in.

The office was huge, with fancy furniture, a big desk, chairs all around, and a sofa. I had never seen anything like it. I stopped in my tracks. I suddenly realized the importance of the man and the enormity of the moment.

I stared at him. He looked startled and confused. He just looked at me. I was dumbfounded; I couldn't say a word. Words just wouldn't come out. He asked me whether I was the messenger boy (in those days, kids like me were often used as messenger boys). The words wouldn't come. I nodded my head from side to side, gesturing "no." Still patient, he asked, "Are you lost? What are you doing here?"

My emotions exploded. I started crying and talking at the same time. I repeated my story, from beginning to end—my failing in Ironit Z; my vocational school experience; my trying to get in to Ironit A for night classes; my trying the other school; my conviction that Ironit A was the only viable choice; that I promised that I would be the best student; that the principal said that he was unable to admit me.

When I was done, he asked, "I understand, but what are you doing here, in my office?"

I told him, "The principal said that he was unable to admit me. When I asked the principal who would, he said that only the Minister of Education could do so, and that's why I'm here."

He started laughing. With a bemused expression on his face, he said, "Go back to the principal and tell him that I said that he should admit you."

I looked at the minister and said, "I could have told him that yesterday. Why would he believe me?"

The minister burst into loud laughter. He picked up a pen, wrote something on paper, placed it in an envelope, and sealed it. He handed the envelope to me and said, "Give this to the principal." I thanked him and reached to get the letter. He handed me the letter and said, "I believe you. I know you'll do well. Good luck."

Scene Five

At 4:00 PM that afternoon, I got back to Ironit A and walked over to the principal's office. The secretary saw me approaching, and he asked, "Did you get it?"

I said, "Yes."

He said, "Wait here," and entered the principal's office. The principal came out. He looked annoyed and said, "I thought I already told you that I can't help you." I said nothing, just handed him the letter. He took it and with a puzzled expression said, "What is this?" I said nothing. He opened the letter, read it, and said, "I'll be damned. Follow me." He took me to a classroom and said, "This is your classroom. Come in tomorrow early and formally register."

Scene Six

The first class was a geometry class. The teacher started explaining the material. He was the best teacher I'd ever had. He used colored chalks and explained everything in such a clear and logical way. Everything was so logically simple. Now I understood and fell in love with the subject. The same teacher taught the next two classes, algebra and physics. He taught these subjects so logically and clearly, too. I fell in love with the logic. I never again earned anything other than "A" and "A+" in all quantitative and science classes.

The Closing of the Curtain

A month later, I learned that the male secretary was not an ordinary secretary. That was his second job. He had a full-time day job as a high-ranking person in the Ministry of Education. He was at a higher level than the principal. I then understood why he was able to walk so freely into the principal's office and get his attention so quickly. It also explained how he knew where the minister would be the following day. He followed my progress closely. We became very friendly. He was very pleased with me and my performance in school. I was the second-best student there. The best student was a damned genius, unfortunately for me. It was obvious to me that he was very smart, much smarter than me. What I concluded stayed with me for a long time, which was that I wasn't as smart. I just knew how to study well for exams.

My girlfriend didn't finish night school. She left after two semesters. I was committed to school, and we couldn't see each other much. The relationship cooled off. She met another boy, and I told her she should become his girlfriend. She ended up marrying him a number of years later.

Four years later, I was more mature and more understanding of what happened during that fateful period. Right before the graduation ceremony, I stopped by the principal's office and asked the secretary why he did what he did on that day. He looked at me and said, "I've never seen anything like this in my life. A thirteen-year-old kid doing what you did. I looked at you and realized immediately that you are special. I knew you would do well. I knew that you were determined. I felt instinctively that I had to help. If anybody deserved to be helped, it was you." He smiled and said, "I never regretted it."

I never had an opportunity to visit him and thank him again. It actually never crossed my mind. I wish it had. I wish I had visited and thanked him, after I became successful.

My Early Education in Business

All my life, people kept telling me that I was extraordinarily smart. I never thought so myself. In fact, until the age of thirty, I was convinced that I wasn't that smart at all. Instead, I thought that I was a great "bullshit artist." I believed that I was exceptionally good at using logic and getting people to see whatever point of view I cared to leave with them, including that I was smart. Even an extraordinary academic achievement hadn't convinced me otherwise. I just believed that I knew how to study hard and prepare well for exams.

At the age of thirty, I experienced an unbelievably odd event that caused me to change my self-perception. Still, even then, I didn't give myself that much credit. Rather, I accepted that I was just as smart as many other people, but not extraordinarily so. At this point of my life, and with all my experiences, I still don't believe that I am extraordinarily smart. However, I do believe now that I possess four different talents that in combination make me an extraordinary thinker. The four elements are *logic, insights, perceptiveness*, and *pragmatism*—four very important elements in being able to out-think and out-analyze situations, whether in life or business, in an extraordinary way and better than most people. In the combination of those four elements, I may be somewhat extraordinary. As stated above, my first transformation occurred at the age of thirty, but not before experiencing substantial angst along the way.

When I graduated from Wharton and got a job offer with Booz Allen, I was sick with anxiety for the whole three months from the time the offer was made until my first day at work. I was convinced that I had fooled everybody during the interviews into believing that I was smart. But the judgment day would soon arrive when I started working there. My ability to bullshit would not carry the day. I would have to produce. Then the truth about me would be discovered. In addition, I had another experience during the recruiting cycle that hadn't helped much.

Before Booz Allen extended offers, I and fifteen other candidates were flown to the Chicago office for a day of final interviews. We were told that eight offers would be made. We met the evening before with the senior HR person who was responsible for managing the process. I was the only student from Wharton; the rest were from Harvard and Stanford. The conversation centered around school, business, and careers. I was impressed with every single one of the candidates. Some had CPA certification in addition to an MBA. They were smart, articulate, and well-versed in all business topics. I began to feel desperate. I thought that if it were up to me, I would hire every single one of them before I would hire myself.

We spent the entire next day in interviews. I felt that I had no chance. I was discouraged and disheartened. Then, two days later, I got a call from Booz Allen and received an offer. It felt unbelievable to me!

When I arrived that first day, I learned that Booz Allen hadn't hired eight of the candidates. The company had only extended an offer to two of us. It made no sense to me to have been chosen. The other new employee and I shared an office.

For the first five months, I appeared to do well and received strong positive feedback. However, from my perspective, I thought I was exceptionally lucky because I got assigned to projects that were not very demanding. We were aware of all the projects that the office was working on and encouraged to read "progress" and "final" presentations of ongoing and completed projects.

In those early months, I must have read about a dozen different such presentations written by other teams. Every time I read a report, I felt sick. I thought to myself that if I were assigned to one of those projects, I would have never been able to come up with those analyses as portrayed in the reports. I felt very lucky not to have been assigned to them. I remained anxious, knowing that one day I would be assigned to a difficult project.

The analysts like me did data collection and analyses. We created graphs and charts to illustrate the observations and conclusions. Our job managers managed us on a day-to-day basis. They would write up the presentation, incorporating our graphs and charts and oftentimes changing them, visually, not numerically, to better fit the presentation flow. They then handed the presentation to the partners and together they would create a new draft. When they were finished, the senior partner took over and would often rewrite the report. The reports were impressive. The analyses were well presented and very compelling.

About seven months into the job, I picked up a report, and as I flipped through the pages, I felt sick to my stomach. It contained absolutely unbelievable analyses. I thought there was no way whatsoever that I would have survived that project. I kept reading the report with total fascination, and getting sicker and sicker with each page. Then, about a quarter of the way through the report, I felt that it looked familiar. Usually when I read reports I primarily looked at the graphs and charts and how they were done, or focused on the conclusions. I never read the reports in full. This time, being so impressed with the creativity of what I saw in the analyses, I looked to identify the client to see which study it belonged to. *It was the job I had worked on. All the analyses were mine.* I know it is hard to believe, but please believe me that not a word of this is an exaggeration. That was the first time I thought to myself, *Wow, maybe I'm actually not as stupid as I thought.*

To finish the story, a while later I asked a junior partner, who ultimately became my mentor, why the company hadn't hired more than two analysts when we were told that eight would be hired. He said that the rest weren't all that impressive. The other person who was hired along with me, and with whom I was exceptionally impressed, was asked to leave after six months. The firm judged him to be very smart, but too much of a linear and pedestrian thinker.

Dealing with My Poor English and Accent

Another sense of inferiority I felt had to do with my poor English skills and thick accent. I was sure these would be a major impediment to my career. I couldn't be as articulate as everybody else, and my accent made it difficult for people to understand me, at least initially, until they got more used to the accent.

One day, while working with the kitchen appliances company I wrote about in chapter thirty-six, the president and I had lunch. We worked together closely, and he thought the world of me. He complimented me over lunch and said I should do very well at Booz Allen.

I told him that my tenure was likely to be short-lived. He looked surprised and asked why I thought so. I told him that a partner had to be extremely articulate, and because of my accent and poor English, I could not measure up to that, and so I would never advance to a partner level. I meant it completely.

He looked at me for a while and pensively said, "I think you are wrong; the accent should work in your favor."

I looked at him, believing that he was just trying to be polite and make me feel a little better. But he wasn't; he looked very serious. I asked, "How so?"

He responded, "For two reasons. First, because your accent is different, when you speak, people wake up and really pay attention to you, and concentrate on what you are saying in order to understand your accent. That is a real advantage. Second, they figure that if a person like you with poor English and a strong accent was hired by Booz

Allen, you must be much, much smarter than their average employee, and so they listen to you even more attentively."

I thought about what he had said, and it actually made sense to me. I still would have preferred not to speak with a thick accent, but I wasn't as paranoid about it after that.

My Learning and Awareness of Cultural Differences

People Always Thought That I Was Stubborn, but I Never Did

I have had a habit, ever since childhood, that I still find hard to control. I am driven by logic. I see nuances all the time. I see people connecting dots prematurely. I see people drawing conclusions that are based on incomplete logic (even if the conclusion may have been correct). I always saw the exceptions. My problem was that I felt compelled to correct the person, or the conclusion, or both. I can't stand incomplete logic; it drives me crazy.

Sometimes I would correct logic that in the scheme of things was irrelevant. But I couldn't help myself. I suppose I felt I was helping people to understand how to apply proper logic. But those on the receiving end rarely viewed it that way.

I also always made it a practice to listen to people very carefully. I wanted to understand exactly what people meant to say. That is, I would listen carefully until I heard flaws in their logic, and then, sure enough, I interrupted them.

While I could quickly find flaws in logic, I never drew quick conclusions myself. By the time I decided on a position, of any kind, I'd have evaluated it from a hundred different perspectives, taking into consideration all the nuances and implications. I was thorough in my initial thinking, which made me often "more right" than others.

So, as you can see, often finding flaws in other people's logic, interrupting them in mid-speech, and believing that I was right most of the time led people to think that I was argumentative and stubborn. How frustrating. I would say to others that I wasn't stubborn, which always drew a chuckle or a laugh.

Here is my own conclusion after all these years. I define a person to be argumentative and stubborn when they continue to argue even though they know that they might be wrong and refuse to accept another position. (I've seen hundreds and hundreds of such situations.) So, what do you call a person who puts a point across, or defends one, and is *right*?

I am probably the least stubborn person you'll meet. I can argue for hours, but as soon as you show me a better logic, or that my logic is faulty, I'll change my position immediately. I take no pride in having to be right. I am, therefore, not stubborn in my own mind. However, as a dear friend made me aware recently, even if right, one can be "stubborn" when one continually tries to change the other person's mind. As my friend stated, the non-stubborn person would not try as hard and would chalk it up to a lost cause unworthy of trying to continue to argue about.

I've learned over the years to try to correct people less and to accept logic that is not perfect when it really doesn't matter all that much. People now claim that I have mellowed quite a bit from when I was young. I guess everything is in the eye of the beholder, although I must admit that this kind of behavior did get me into trouble every once in a while.

I was into my sixth month at Booz Allen, and my command of English was still not very good. A senior partner agreed to do a "small" project for a large client. The budget didn't allow for a full team. He asked me to be the acting job manager and work directly for him. No associate would be working for me, and no junior partner would act as an intermediary between the senior partner and me. I had done some good work for him on a previous job, and he liked me a lot.

It was time for a final report, which he asked me to write. I gave him my first draft. I was sitting at his desk when he read it, page by page, and made small corrections and offered comments for me to incorporate in the next draft. All in all, he seemed very pleased. So was I. He did stop at one point and asked questions about a concept I had advanced in the report. I gave him my logic. He said he was not sure and asked me to think it over.

Three days later, he asked to see the next draft presentation. I took it to his office and left. About an hour later, he called me, obviously upset.

As soon as I set foot in his office, he threw the presentation on the desk, slapped it hard, and said, "David, I told you to take this page out. What the f*** is it doing here?"

I replied, "No, you didn't say that."

He got even angrier. With a raised voice he said, "What do you mean that I didn't ask for the page to be removed? I specifically asked you to take this page out."

I responded, not knowing better that in situations like these, one should just accept the criticism, apologize, and move on. Instead, I said, "No, you didn't. I have a great memory for things like that. I remember exactly what you said. You said, 'David, I'm not sure about this page. Why don't you think it over?' I thought it over, and decided that it was fine and should stay here." He almost fell off his chair laughing.

I was completely confused. I had no idea what was going on. He relaxed and said, "David, when somebody in America tells you, 'I'm not sure about this page; why don't you think it over,' he means to say, 'This is a piece of crap. Get it the hell out of here!'"

People Thought I Was "Pushy"—Indeed I Was; I Wish I Weren't!

I have always thought of myself as a perfectionist. I was a perfectionist with logic. I was a perfectionist with doing things efficiently and as quickly as possible. I just didn't know another way. Although at face value it sounds like a positive attribute, it is not necessarily so. In retrospect, it was not one of my strengths.

Had I been a perfectionist with "gentle" and "smart" interpersonal skills, then it might have been fine. But I was short on good interpersonal skills, but not by intention or out of disrespect for others. I just couldn't help it. There were three reasons for this.

First, as I mentioned earlier, when I listen to people, I concentrate very hard on what they say. When I concentrate, I become entirely focused. I stare at the other person and forget to smile and be friendly. I ask short and terse questions, and because of the intense focus, my voice tends to get louder. In short, I look like I'm a judge about to decide whether to send somebody to death row for a minor shoplifting offense. This was the topic the psychologist I mentioned earlier (see chapter fifteen) wanted to talk to me about.

When I arrived for the second appointment, he set up a video camera that focused on me and started a conversation. He asked questions I found interesting, that required me to think and then respond. We went back and forth for about ten minutes and then he stopped the recording. He replayed the video and asked me to detect anything wrong or strange about it. I watched the video and listened carefully to our exchange. At the end of it, he asked the same question: "Did you notice anything wrong or strange?" I repeated again that I didn't. Everything sounded very logical to me.

He looked at me and said, "I thought so. I have never seen a video like this. In fact, this is the strangest video I've ever watched. You are the one that makes it so strange." I had no idea what he was talking about. Everything I said in the video was perfectly logical. I told him so. He said, "That is not what was strange. You are strange. I have never seen anybody like you, ever. Throughout the entire ten minutes of conversation, your body was frozen. You didn't move. You didn't shift in your seat. You didn't move your head to the right or left. You looked intense and stared at me for the whole time. You didn't shift your eyes, not even for a second. That is not normal; it is extraordinarily strange. I want you to look at the video again and observe what I just said."

He replayed the video. He was so right. I started laughing. It did look strange even to me now that I paid attention to it. I was indeed like a statue. He proceeded to tell me that he had observed that in our previous session and that was the reason he wanted me to come back. He said, "When you concentrate, everything in your body freezes. You stare at people intensely. The color of your eyes is striking to people. This leaves people very uncomfortable. They are not used to this kind of intensity. You make people feel that you are constantly judging them, and this will make everybody nervous. This will not help you in your career. Here is what I recommend you do. Whenever you talk to somebody, pause, shift your eyes away, move your body a bit, shift in your chair, and try to smile a little. But most important of all, you must shift your eyes, as they can be very intimidating." I immediately took it all to heart. I have followed his advice ever since. But my manner of communicating remains far from perfect. Old habits die hard!

My body language and perfectionist drive are but a few reasons for my poor interpersonal skills; there is another. When I listen to someone and draw any conclusions, particularly negative conclusions, I have a tendency to check and recheck to make sure that I'm right and making no errors in judgment or am misunderstanding something. I do so by digging and asking the questions in different ways until I'm satisfied that I am right and understand the person correctly. As I kept pressing people for more information, understandably this would make them feel very uncomfortable.

To add to this, there is a cultural element as well. I grew up in Israel, in a culture that doesn't have the words "politically correct" in its lexicon. Individuals are not sensitive to the words they use. Please understand that nobody gets insulted, unless one really means to insult. "Arguments" and "insulting" language are commonplace. Nobody takes it as a personal affront; forceful arguments are just another, typical way to show the strength of one's position or disagreement with another point of view. This happens for serious matters as well as minor ones. Here are examples of the difference in language between "American-speak" and "Israeli-speak":

American-speak: I understand what you are saying, but I am not quite as convinced.

Israeli equivalent: That was a stupid thing to say.

American-speak: Yes, I heard your answer, but I'm still not 100 percent convinced.

Israeli equivalent: Now that was a dumb response. Why would you say that?

American-speak: Yes, okay, but you might not be considering that . . .

Israeli equivalent: That was the most stupid thing I've heard in my life. How could you be so stupid? Complete idiocy!

You get the idea? Should Israelis want to be more "appropriate," they may use a more polite language, but one will still hear a lot of "You don't understand"; "It doesn't make much sense"; "You are not explaining it clearly"; "Did you really mean to say that?"; and so on. Now, it is possible that the culture may have changed, since Israelis travel more and interact much more with people from other countries. So, perhaps the culture is no longer as insensitive as when I grew up. It actually reminds me of a cute story.

My daughter, Beth, wanted to have her Bat-Mitzvah in Israel. That was her first visit to the country, and I prepared her on what to expect there. We met a friend, and during the conversation he jokingly suggested that she should marry an Israeli man when she had grown up. I jokingly responded that there is no way she, as an American girl, would be able to be married to an Israeli. Only God knows just how many cultural issues I had with my American ex-wife. He dismissed my comment offhandedly. He looked at Beth with a smile and said, "Nah, that was the first generation: Gen 1.0. We now have Gen 2.0, and they are completely different." That's the background I come from, Generation 1.0.

Additionally, Israelis are not very polite in terms of American and European standards. They will interrupt, argue, and interject questions at will. Nobody takes offense at it. If one wants to be heard, one will just try harder to outdo the other person. Lectures at school are a sight to behold. Students will interrupt and argue with the professors and use the same insensitive language: "It doesn't make any sense"; "No, it is wrong"; "The logic here doesn't make sense"; and so on.

When I arrived in the U.S. and went to school, I couldn't understand why American students rarely asked questions of professors at lectures. Consistent with my culture, I did all the time, and not just because I had difficulty reading the textbooks and had to ask questions. No, that wasn't the main reason. I would've done it regardless, since that's what I was used to from my culture. I would ask anywhere from five to fifteen questions in any given class. My American classmates rarely asked a single one. I just couldn't understand why not.

I remember being concerned about it and went to one of the professors after the class was over. I asked him whether I was asking too many questions in class and therefore being disruptive. His answer was, "No, not at all. Ask as many questions as you wish. I know one thing for sure. You are the best student in the class, and if you don't understand, I'm sure many other students don't either." Thank God for his reply. I don't know how I would have been able to comprehend everything from classroom lectures had he discouraged my questions. Although much later, I became aware that the way I asked questions left a lot to be desired.

After I graduated from Stevens Institute of Technology, I joined EDS. The company sent every new employee through three intensive months of internal schooling to teach us all we needed to know about computer programming and computer systems design. Again, I was the one asking most of the questions.

About two weeks into the course, our instructor, who was a senior vice president in the company, asked me to stay behind after he dismissed the class. He told me that he wanted to make me aware of something. He said, "David, I would appreciate it very much, if when you ask questions, you stop using sentences like, 'No, it is wrong,' or 'It doesn't make sense.' You are my best student in class, and everybody in class knows it. So when you use those sentences, they believe it and it undermines my authority as an expert." Believe it or not, but I had been in the country for three years by then, and it was the first time I heard and became aware of the fact that there was a difference in cultural communications between what I was used to and those in the U.S. This brings another cute story to mind.

Twenty years later, as an established venture capitalist, I was frequently invited as a guest speaker to lecture in MBA classes. I gave a number of those guest lectures at Northwestern University, Kellogg School, in Chicago. I got to know the dean of the business school, who had just been promoted to the role. He had a strong affinity to Israel and had visited the country many times. He was a guest speaker at Israeli universities and thought highly of the educational system.

Kellogg had three visiting Israeli professors teaching MBA classes at the time. He invited them to join us for lunch, and we had a wonderful and fun time together. We mostly talked about the difference in styles between the two countries. He proceeded to tell a really funny story that stuck with me.

He told a story about going to a convention in Israel with the former dean, who was his boss. It was his boss's first time in Israel, and he was there to give a guest lecture at one of the universities. The room was packed with students. At the end of the lecture, the dean was fuming. He left the lecture hall, visibly upset. He said to the people around him that he would never again accept an invitation as a guest speaker in Israel.

When asked why, he answered that he had never been so insulted in his life. He had never seen such rude students! The new dean explained to us that he tried to calm him down and told him not to take it personally. It was just a cultural difference and the students were not being disrespectful. He said to his boss, "Let me explain to you what it is. You see, when I go to Japan, I give *lectures* to students. In the U.S., we have *discussions* with the students. In Israel, we have *arguments* with the students!" I thought it was hilarious!

I am fully aware of how people must have felt when they interacted with me, due to my poor interpersonal skills. Some perhaps understood that it was only a cultural difference and that I meant no disrespect. Others, I'm sure, felt very uncomfortable with me. I guess that this is what my mentor at Booz Allen meant when he said, "To know David is to love David."

As I look back at my past, it looks to me that those who were more interested with "substance" tended to like me and were forgiving of my poor interpersonal skills. Those who were sensitive to "form" tended to dislike me. The only consolation I have, and not by way of an excuse, is that whether people liked me because of "substance" or disliked me because of "form," most respected me for what I said and what I stood for.

All knew that I meant to always do my best. My motivations were pure. I was always straightforward and called it the way I saw it. I always kept my promises. I never went back on my word. My word was better than any written contract; once I promised to do something, I would always deliver. I thought my substance was enough to forgive my poor form. But it wasn't, and it shouldn't have. Not too long ago, I found out that I even intimidated my own daughter.

On that day, Beth and I were reminiscing about some experiences when she was young. I reminded her of a nasty habit she had, which used to make me angry with her, and we'd get into an argument. Just to put it in proper perspective, Beth and I had (and have) a very special relationship and we almost never argued. We had disagreements, but we handled these without getting angry or upset, albeit with raised voices at times (not because of anger, but reflective of my Israeli culture at play). The only exception was that one nasty habit she had as she grew up.

She was around nine or ten years old, and it was a time when the phrase "I don't know" entered common usage and younger children adopted it as well. Their first response would be, "I don't know," regardless of the question. I was trying to teach Beth how to think logically. So, I would raise topics that she knew little about and asked for her opinion. I intended to use her answer as a way to discuss her logic and teach her how to think "properly." I had been doing it ever since she was able to think.

At about the age of ten, she acquired the same habit as all of her friends. "I don't know" was the first thing that came out of her mouth whenever I asked a question. I would get agitated and tell her in no uncertain way that "I don't know" was not an option. I would say, "When I ask you a question, even if you don't know the answer, think about potential answers—guess if necessary, but answer you must." Nevertheless, she would not desist from responding, "I don't know," and over time I got angrier and angrier with that reply.

This is what I reminded her of when we were reminiscing, and I told her how angry that made me at the time. She looked at me with a surprised expression on her face and asked, "Dad, you still don't know why I did it?"

I said, "What do you mean?"

She responded, "Dad, I knew exactly what I was doing. I knew perfectly well that you didn't like it, and that you would become angry with me and start scolding me. But I preferred to get you angry that way and avoid giving you an answer. I knew that once I answered, I would be totally intimidated by you trying to explain how proper logic worked. Once we got to that point, it became a never-ending lecture from you."

I started laughing hard. I really had no idea that she purposefully did it for that reason. I had no idea that my own daughter was so intimidated when I entered my "logical" frame of mind. (A side note that I think is cute and perhaps carries another powerful lesson for all to learn from: I had my niece, who also has had a successful career, review this part of the book for comments, before finalizing the content. She placed the following "note" at this point: "*Genius!!* ☺ ☺ *Sometimes to know is not to know—Love it!!*")

I realize now that over the years I may have used the cliché "substance over form" as an excuse—an excuse not to try as hard as I should have to change. I am fully aware of it now. I've mellowed significantly. Unfortunately, some of the old habits still haven't completely died away. Fortunately, many have. Talking about old habits brings to mind another humorous story.

When Beth visited Israel, my cousin took us on a tour around the country. It is a very small country and one can tour it in a day or two. We went to visit the Golan Heights. I wanted her to understand why it was so strategically important to Israel and what happened there during the Six-Day War.

I was a tank commander in the Six-Day War.

Remnants of the war, including disabled tanks, were still visible. She asked me a lot of questions about my military days and my experiences, which had occurred twenty-five years earlier. Three stories stood out: two about old habits that don't die, and a third about the fact that sometimes they *do* die.

We were walking on a barren, steep hill, full of loose rocks and pebbles. One had to be very careful navigating the slope. We had to walk up and down some of the hills to visit points of interest. Beth was very nervous and careful with her footing.

Since we talked about my military experiences, I told her that we learned how to run down such slopes as part of our training routine. She didn't believe it was possible. I said, "Sure, let me show you," and got ready to dash down a hill. She was fearful and exclaimed, "No,

Dad, are you crazy?" I replied, "No worries; old habits don't die," and ran down the hill, fast. I didn't stumble; she was extremely impressed.

Next, we arrived at a disabled tank. We climbed on the tank to the top of the turret. I looked at her and asked whether she would jump off the turret onto the ground. She said no way. It was a jump of about fifteen feet. I told her that as part of our training we had to jump off the turret. She said, "No way, that's suicide." I told her that if your tank got hit and caught on fire, it would be suicide not to jump! She didn't believe that anybody would dare jump. I volunteered to demonstrate it. She said, "I believe you. Please, Dad, don't." I gave her a reassuring smile and made the leap.

About fifteen minutes later, walking in those deserted hills, Beth asked where a toilet was in the area. I started laughing and said, "What toilet? You are in army territory now. You need to relieve yourself; you just go behind those bushes." She was surprised, but had no other choice and very reluctantly and hesitantly walked over behind the bushes. When she came back, I excused myself and walked over there, too. A minute later, I was done and came back laughing my heart out, as loudly as you ever heard a person laugh—I was roaring with laughter, holding onto my belly. It was already hurting. Beth looked at me and said, "Why are you laughing? What happened?" I responded, "I remembered all the old military habits and rules of engagements, but forgot the most important one. I forgot the rule that says that you never, ever piss into the wind!" I was wet from my waist down. Some old habits may indeed die!

APPENDIX III

JK&B CAPITAL V, L.L.C.—FUNDRAISING PRESENTATION

Private and ConfidentialPrivate and Confidential

Overall Profile

- **Based In Chicago, Over $900 Million Under Management**
  - Three Funds - - 1996, JK&B I/II - $112 Million
                    1999, JK&B III - $485 Million
                    2001, JK&B IV - $320 Million
- **Highly "Technical" Fund**
- **Focus On Communications And Information Technologies**
- **Early-To-Mid Stage Investor**
- **Proactive Lead Investor Requiring Board Seats**
- **International Reach And "Top-Tier" Reputation**

Private and Confidential
2

The Genesis Of JK&B Is The Conviction That Deep Technical Expertise Has Become More Critical

1970 – 1990s VC Environment		Current VC Environment
• Smaller VC Industry - - $100s millions		• Huge VC Industry - - Billions of dollars
• Total funding requirement per deal $3-10M - Mistakes have manageable financial damage		• Total funding requirement per deal $30-100M - Mistakes very costly
• Entrepreneurs were scientists with minimal knowledge of marketing/sales/financing	**SHIFT**	• Entrepreneurs bring broader skill set and are more savvy
• Product life cycle 7-10 years		• Product life cycle 1-3 years with **intense, complex** and **rapidly** changing competitive/technical environment
• Delayed product commercialization was **not fatal** in an environment of long life cycle and reasonable development cost		• Delayed product commercialization is **fatal** in an environment of short life cycle, intense competition and costly development

VC's in-house technical expertise not as critical. VC's critical value-added skills were in areas entrepreneurs lacked - - marketing, sales, financing and management of growth.

VC's TECHNICAL EXPERTISE MORE CRITICAL PARTICULARLY FOR INITIAL INVESTMENT DECISIONS AND ONGOING BOARD SUPERVISION.

Private and Confidential
3

JK&B -- Highly Technical, Uniquely Differentiated

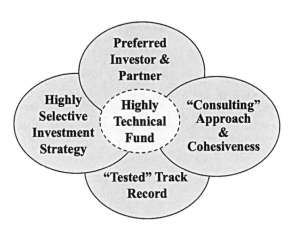

JK&B CAPITAL

Highly Technical Fund

Technology Assessment And Subsequent Product Commercialization Is JK&B's Key Differentiation

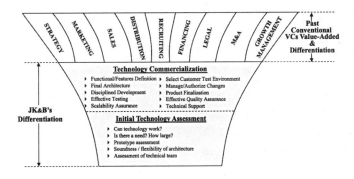

JK&B CAPITAL

Highly Technical Fund (continued)

Often, JK&B Has Broader Technical Expertise Than The CTOs Of Portfolio Companies

Selected Examples:

Robert Humes, *Partner – Communications*

- 10 years in Venture Capital, **35** years in the Communications Industry
- **Vice President of Engineering and Technology** at **Ameritech**
  - Ameritech's highest level "technical" executive, headed an organization of 9,000 people
  - Responsible for all aspects of corporate-wide network engineering, technology development and implementation
  - **Board of Directors** of **BellCore**
  - At divestiture, responsible for allocating **AT&T's** technical and network operations functions between newly created RBOCs
  - Responsible for consolidating all technical functions for Ameritech post-divestiture
- **Vice President, Operations** for **Michigan Bell**, responsible for 20,000 employees
- Began career at **Bell Labs** – on original design team of cellular telephony; still holds patent for cellular mobile design; involved in original Chicago trial, which was the first trial of cellular telephony in the United States
- B.S.E.E. from Purdue University and M.S.E.E. from Polytechnic Institute of Brooklyn

---

Selected Examples (continued)

Ali Shadman, *Partner – Communications*

- 6 years in Venture Capital, **25** years in the Communications Industry
- **Vice President of Technology Development** at **Ameritech/SBC**, responsible for evaluation and introduction of all new technologies into the **Ameritech's** network
- **CTO, Ameritech New Media** and **President, Ameritech New Media,** broadband services to over 250,000 subscribers
  - Developed next generation of interactive video services for **Americast** (*joint venture between **Walt Disney, Ameritech, GTE** and **Bell South***)
- **Senior Vice President, Corporate Strategy** at **Ameritech/SBC**, responsible for all M&A activities. Led the $72 billion **SBC / Ameritech** merger, one of the 10 largest in US history
- **Director of Technology Development** at **MCI Telecommunications**, responsible for the evaluation and introduction of all new technology platforms, including the implementation of MCI's fiber optics network
- Ph.D. in Electrical Engineering and Computer Engineering, M.S.E.E. and B.S.E.E. from Oregon State University

Selected Examples (continued)

Albert DaValle, Jr., *Partner – Communications*

- 6 years in Venture Capital, **23 years** in the Communications Industry
- **Vice President, Engineering and Construction** for **Ameritech**, responsible for $2 billion capital budget and led **Ameritech's** 7,000 person engineering, technology development and network construction groups
  - Various engineering and operations positions within **Ameritech** all involving the specification, selection and implementation of new technologies (ISDN, SS7, IN, AIN)
- **Chief Technology Officer (CTO)** at **Belgacom**, Brussels, led the company's technology development and marketing organizations, responsible for network planning/engineering/design, technology/product selection
- **Senior Architecture Planner** at **Sprint** – one of 5 member team that designed the architecture and topology for the **Sprint** fiber network, the first nationwide fiber optics network
- B.S.E.E. from Purdue University and Masters in Management from Northwestern University's Kellogg School of Management

Selected Examples (continued)

Marc Sokol, *Partner – Software*

- 6 years in Venture Capital, **25 years** in Enterprise Software
- **Vice President Engineering** at **Computer Associates (CA)**, responsible for product development
- **Senior VP of Business Development** for **CA**, involved with merger and acquisition activities, including investments in technology ventures
- **Senior VP of Advanced Technology** for **CA**, involved with technical evaluation of strategic new business initiatives, including database management, enterprise management, security
- **Senior Vice President and General Manager**, Global Marketing for **CA**
- Authority on Internet and infrastructure technology – testified before U.S. Congress and addressed United Nations
- **Co-Founder and Executive Vice President, Realia Inc.**, sold to **Pansophic Systems**, which was acquired by **CA**
  - Co-authored COBOL compiler, runtime, and various utilities
- **Software Developer** at **NASA's** Goddard Space Flight Center

Preferred Investor & Partner

Unique Insights Make JK&B A Preferred Partner To Entrepreneurs And Other Top-Tier VC Funds

JK&B's Unique Attributes

- *Understand key customers/vendors purchasing decisions*
- *Senior contacts in Engineering Departments*
  - *Relationships forged over a long period of peer relationships*
  - *Hired and mentored many of them*
  - *Understand and talk their "language"*
- *Insights on customers/vendors' shorter and longer term business/technology challenges and priorities*
- *Can properly translate these insights into technology developments*
- *Can introduce portfolio companies to key customers and get critical technical feedback*
- *Can attract strategic investors*

Results

Enhanced ability to make wise investment decisions

Preferred investor with entrepreneurs

Preferred partner with VCs

Private and Confidential
10

JK&B CAPITAL

Preferred Investor & Partner (continued)

JK&B Leads Investments, Requires A Board Seat And Works Closely With Portfolio Companies

Lead/Co-Lead Investor

Lead 70%

Co-Lead 14%

16%

Board Participation

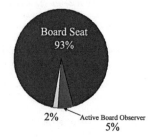

Board Seat 93%

2%   Active Board Observer 5%

Funds III and IV - - 58 companies

Private and Confidential
11

JK&B CAPITAL

Preferred Investor & Partner (continued)

Able To Bring Together Strong Syndicates Including Key Strategic Investors

VENTURE CAPITAL FIRMS			
3i Ventures	Citicorp Venture Capital	Metropolitan Ventures	TH Lee Putnam
Accel Partners	Commonwealth Capital	Mohr, Davidow	Trinity Fund
Adams Street Capital	Cordova Intellimedia	Morgan Stanley	US Venture Partners
Advanced Technology Ventures	Crescendo Ventures	Neurone-Platinum Ventures	Vanguard Ventures
Advent	Crosspoint Ventures	New Enterprise Associates (NEA)	VenGrowth Capital
AKN Technology	Diamondhead Ventures	Norwest Partners	Vesbridge Partners
Alliance Ventures	Draper Fisher Jurvetson	Novak Biddle	Walden International
Alta Vista	Emergence Capital	Oak Investment Partners	Walker Ventures
Apax Partners	Evergreen Ventures	Paladin Capital	Worldview Technology Partners
Ascend Technology	Financial Technology Ventures	Polaris Ventures	
Atlas Venture	Flagship Ventures	Prelude Ventures	STRATEGIC INVESTORS
Austin Ventures	Foundation Capital	Prism Ventures	
August Capital	Gemini Israel	Providence Equity Partners	3Com · Mitsubishi
B & M Ventures	Greylock	QTV Capital	Alcatel · Motorola
Bank of America Venture Partners	Grotech Capital	Redwood Ventures	AT&T · NEC
Battery Ventures	HIG Ventures	Ridgewood Capital	Bell South · Nokia
BDC Ventures	Hummer Winblad	Saturn Ventures	Cisco · Oki Electronics
Benchmark Capital	Industry Ventures	Satwik Ventures	Computer Associates · Samsung
Bessemer Ventures	Investor AB	Seed Capital	Converse Tech. · SBC
BV Capital	Kinetic Ventures	Selby Ventures	Dell · Seagate Technologies
Canaan Partners	Labrador Ventures	Sevin Rosen	Deloitte & Touche · Siemens
CapVest Venture	Madison Dearborn	Sigma Partners	Goldman Sachs · Sun Microsystems
Celtic House	Magnum Communication	Soros Fund Management	IBM · Symantec
Charles River	Matrix Partners	Spectrum Equity	Intel
	Mellon Ventures	Sutter Hill Ventures	JDS Uniphase
			Juniper Networks
			Microsoft

Preferred Investor & Partner (continued)

Acknowledged Value-Added Investor And Partner

Testimonials:

"JK&B Capital delivers the deep technology knowledge we look for in a co-investor. They bring substantial value added to our companies with strategic advice in product positioning and commercialization of the technology."

John Thornton, General Partner
Austin Ventures

" JK&B Capital brings a unique knowledge of technology and markets making them a sought after, value-added syndicate partner. They are great to work with, bond easily with technical founders and are a great match for the investing we do here at Hummer Winblad."

John Hummer, Co-founder and General Partner
Hummer Winbald

"JK&B Capital has the extensive understanding and the experience working with technology that we look for in a co-investor. As an investor, they bring insightful strategic advice and leadership to their companies. As co-investors, they are excellent and dependable partners."

Bob Fleming, Founding Partner
Prism Ventures

"JK&B Capital partners combine technology expertise with significant operational experience and personal relationships with key market makers. They are able to guide young companies across the hurdles that await them and add genuine business value along their trajectories."

Eric Benhamou
Ex-Chairman & CEO, 3Com
Co-investor & Board Member, Atrica

"JK&B Capital brings an uncommon combination of technical expertise and industry knowledge making them a uniquely valuable co-investor."

Mort Topfer
Ex-Vice Chairman, Dell, Inc.
Co-investor, Sheer Networks

"JK&B Capital brings a unique level of technical and operational expertise to young companies and they are valued partners to have on the board as co-investors."

Deepak Kamra, General Partner
Canaan Partners

Investment Philosophy

Highly Selective Investment Criteria – Targeted At "Unlimited" Upside And "Protected" Downside

Investment Criteria

- "Must Have" Technologies Only - - Avoid "Nice-To-Have" Technologies

- Major Trend Enablers - - "Order Of Magnitude" Impact

Ex.) Phone.com/Openwave Systems	--	Enabled data/Internet communication for cellphones
Interwoven	--	1st platform to enable large-scale Internet website development and maintenance
CoreTek	--	Order of magnitude cost reduction through tunable lasers enabling "broadband" to the last mile
Zone Labs, FaceTime	--	Internet security companies beyond "firewalls"

- "Best Of Breed" Technologies

- Other Conventional VC Screening Criteria

  - Management, Markets, Barriers To Entry, Competitive Dynamics, Deal Structure, etc.

- Investment Criteria Remained Consistent Over The Years

  - No "knee-jerk" change in investment strategy after "bubble burst"

JK&B CAPITAL

Investment Philosophy (continued)

Many Deals Self-Generated In Advance Of Companies' Requirements For VC Funding

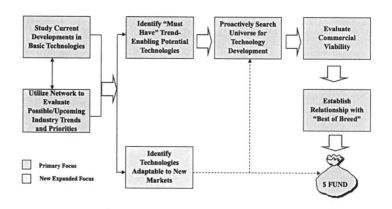

JK&B CAPITAL

Investment Philosophy (continued)

Investment Strategy Requires A Wide Geographical Reach – Chicago Is A Great Base Location

Chicago/Midwest - - Utmost Flexibility In Travel And
Pre-eminence In A Growing Startup Market

Number of Deals

Canada 3
Europe 6
Israel 4

Private and Confidential
16

Consulting Approach & Cohesiveness

JK&B Uses The "Consulting" Approach To Due Diligence And Investment Decisions

- Partners Only - - No Junior Professionals!
- Long Experience Of Working Together
- Two Teams - "Communications" Team
           - "Software" Team
- Shared Due Diligence - - Entire Team Involved With Every Deal
- Team Must Agree Unanimously On All Investments
- Partnership Must Agree Unanimously To Make Investment

Private and Confidential
17

Track Record

Summary Observations

Private and Confidential
18

All Funds Expected To Show Superior Top-Tier Performance

Summary Performance
(As of March, 2007)

Fund	Capital Committed	Capital Called	% Distributed*	Total Value/Paid In*	Best Estimate Multiple Return	Key Observations
			(Net to LPs)	(Net to LPs)	(Net to LPs)	• Proven **superior** track record
I/II (1996)	$112M	100%	566%	5.7x	5.6 – 6.0x	– One of the best in the industry
III (1999)	$482M	96%	35%	0.73x	0.8 – 1.1x	• **Disciplined** investments - - No dot.com Cos • Proven **value preservation** under challenging "post-bubble" conditions – Sold 13 "bubble" companies at profit – Currently **15 active** portfolio companies – Return of principle expected
IV (2001)	$313M	69%	7%	0.92x	3 – 5x	• **Disciplined** and **conservative** investments in **down markets** – Called only **17%** of capital in first 3 years – Started heavy investment in 2004 – 2001 Vintage, but profile of a "young" fund

 * On capital called through December 31, 2006

Private and Confidential
19

Track Record (continued)

Broad Appeal Of Our Companies Validates JK&B's Investment Philosophy And Technical Judgment

- **Many Current Portfolio Companies With "Best Of Products" Awards**
- **Successes/"Exits" Pervasive - - Not Just Luck!**
  - **Even some failing businesses acquired for technologies**

IPOs	M&A Above Cost	M&A Below Cost
Commerce One	21st Century	EmWare
Daleen	Ab Initio	Gloss.com
Exodus	Andromedia	Paragon
Interwoven	CoreTek	PointBase
Intrado	Entercept	Seaway
Mpower	ESI Software	
Openwave	ICON Solutions	
Selectica	Jareva	
SilverStream	Knightsbridge	
Ubiquity	Reactivity	
	Sheer Networks	
	Synchrologic	
	UniSite	
	Zone Labs	
	XOsoft	

	IPOs	M&A Above Cost	M&A Below Cost
Cost	$59.3M	$89.0M	$38.6M
Exit	$694.1M	$251.9M	$11.4M

Private and Confidential
20

New Fund

Private and Confidential
21

New Fund

- JK&B Capital V, L.P.
- Target $250 Million
- 2.5% Management Fee
- Had a First Close - - $200 Million
- Key investors include
  - *Paul Capital*
  - *ATP, Denmark*
  - *Northrop Grumman*
  - *Partners Group*
  - *Pantheon Ventures*

  - *Charles Wang*
  - *Permal Capital*
  - *Illinois State Treasury/Northern Trust*

Private and Confidential
22

Appendix

- Detailed, Comparative Fund Performance
  - JK&B Capital I/II - - Vintage 1996
  - JK&B Capital III - - Vintage 1999
  - JK&B Capital IV - - Vintage 2001
- The Story of XOsoft

Private and Confidential
23

Detailed, Comparative Funds' Performance

The comparative analyses/data in this section reflects data available as of 9/30/06

Private and Confidential
24

JK&B I/II - - Vintage 1996

Superior Returns, Outperforming Many Top-Tier Funds

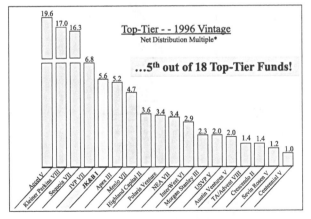

*Net to LPs, based on available public information.
Private Equity Intelligence, data available as of 9/30/06

Private and Confidential
25

JK&B III - - Vintage 1999

Strong Performance - - Better Than Many Recognized Top-Tier Funds In IRR...

Top-Tier Funds - - Net IRR Performance*

Fund Name 1999	% IRR	Fund Name 2000	% IRR
Alta California Partners II	-5.0	Accel – KKR Company	0.9
Ampersand IV	5.7	Accel VIII	-26.8
Apex Fund IV	-35.9	Alta California Partners III	-6.2
Austin Ventures VII	-6.3	Baker Communications II	-10.3
Battery Ventures V	7.0	Battery Ventures VI	-3.2
Benchmark Capital Partners IV	-2.7	Benchmark Founders Fund IV	23.8
Kleiner Perkins Caufield & Byers IX-A	-23.3	Charles River XI	2.3
Mayfield X	n/a	Crescendo IV	-22.1
Menlo Ventures VIII	-18.9	Draper Fisher Jurvetson VII	-4.6
Morgan Stanley Venture Partners IV	-17.0	Kleiner Perkins Caufield & Byers X-A	-17.5
New Enterprise Associates IX	-13.2	Matrix Partners VI	-11.4
Oak Investment Partners IX	-16.5	Mayfield XI	-11.5
Prism Venture Partners II	-7.3	Menlo Ventures IX	-5.2
Sequoia Capital Franchise Fund	-17.0	Morgenthaler Venture Partners VI	-4.5
Sequoia Capital IX	-6.1	Oak Investment Partners X	-6.2
Sevin Rosen Fund VII	-25.8	Polaris Venture Partners III	-6.5
Sierra Ventures VII	-16.9	Prism Venture Partners III	-29.1
SOFTBANK Capital Partners	n/a	Sequoia Capital X	-31.0
Summit Accelerator	-3.9	Sevin Rosen Fund VIII	-15.4
		Spectrum Equity Investors IV	10.2
		Summit Ventures VI	14.5
		TA Associates / Advent IX	13.6
		Technology Crossover Ventures IV	4.4
		US Venture Partners VII	-20.1
		US Venture Partners VIII	-8.8
		Vanguard VII	-26.9
	-11.95%		**-10.74%**

JK&B III | **-8.58%**   **Total Average** | **-11.29%**

*Net to LPs, based on available public information.
Private Equity Intelligence, data available as of 9/30/06

JK&B CAPITAL

JK&B III Performance (continued)

... And 10th Out Of 46 In Actual Cash Distributions

Top-Tier Funds - - % Distributed*

Fund Name 1999	% Distributed	Fund Name 2000	% Distributed
Alta California Partners II	33.5	Accel – KKR Company	0.0
Ampersand IV	100.0	Accel VIII	0.0
Apex Fund IV	1.0	Alta California Partners III	5.5
Austin Ventures VII	22.9	Baker Communications II	21.7
Battery Ventures V	100.2	Battery Ventures VI	31.2
Benchmark Capital Partners IV	28.9	Benchmark Founders Fund IV	0.0
Kleiner Perkins Caufield & Byers IX-A	0.0	Charles River XI	8.5
Mayfield X	4.1	Crescendo IV	4.1
Menlo Ventures VIII	30.0	Draper Fisher Jurvetson VII	6.5
Morgan Stanley Venture Partners IV	7.8	Kleiner Perkins Caufield & Byers X-A	0.0
New Enterprise Associates IX	11.9	Matrix Partners VI	11.8
Oak Investment Partners IX	14.8	Mayfield XI	7.6
Prism Venture Partners II	46.8	Menlo Ventures IX	2.2
Sequoia Capital Franchise Fund	36.7	Morgenthaler Venture Partners VI	52.3
Sequoia Capital IX	60.4	Oak Investment Partners X	15.5
Sevin Rosen Fund VII	4.3	Polaris Venture Partners III	16.8
Sierra Ventures VII	5.0	Prism Venture Partners III	4.4
SOFTBANK Capital Partners	9.8	Sequoia Capital X	2.2
Summit Accelerator	45.2	Sevin Rosen Fund VIII	0.0
		Spectrum Equity Investors IV	42.3
		Summit Ventures VI	26.0
		TA Associates / Advent IX	31.7
		Technology Crossover Ventures IV	50.0
		US Venture Partners VII	3.0
		US Venture Partners VIII	2.5
		Vanguard VII	2.5
	29.65%		**12.82%**

JK&B III | **34.96%**   **Total Average** | **21.02%**

*Net to LPs ,based on available public information.
Private Equity Intelligence, data available as of 9/30/2006

JK&B CAPITAL

JK&B III Performance (continued)

JK&B III Performed Well To Date Even With High-Valuation, "Bubble-Era" Portfolio Companies...

- Cash Distributions To Date About Equal To Write-Offs
- Sold Eleven Bubble Companies <u>After</u> The Burst, Not At A Loss But Rather An Overall Positive Return!

<u>M&A After December 2000 ("Bubble Burst")</u>
(As of March, 2007)

Company	Investment	Return Multiple	$ Return
Entercept	$10.0M	1.9	$19.0M
Gloss.com	2.5	0.5	1.3
Jareva	3.3	3.1	10.3
Point Base	12.0	0.1	1.0
Synchrologic	8.0	1.5	12.0
ZoneLabs	11.0	2.0	22.0
emWare	10.0	0.2	2.0
Sheer	11.5	1.4	16.3
Seaway	4.2	0.8	3.3
Ubiquity	10.7	1.3	14.2
XOsoft	13.0	2.4	31.7
Total	**$96.3M**	**1.4**	**$133.1M**

JK&B CAPITAL

JK&B III Performance (continued)

...And Still Has An Attractive Portfolio, Well Positioned To Greatly Improve Overall Performance

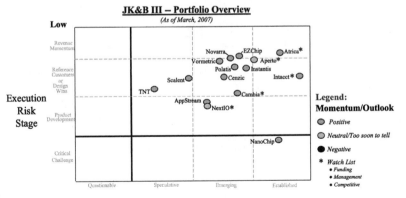

JK&B III – Portfolio Overview
(As of March, 2007)

JK&B CAPITAL

JK&B III Performance (continued)

Strong Revenue Growth, A Key Indicator Of Traction And Value Creation, Despite Depressed Markets

JK&B III
Revenues for Current Portfolio Companies
($ Millions)

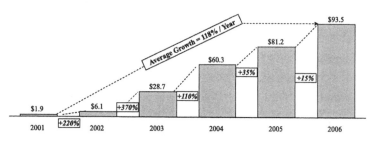

JK&B III Performance (continued)

Revenue Growth Enjoyed By All Vintage Year Companies

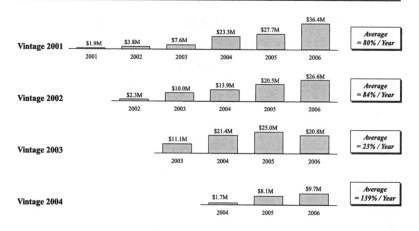

JK&B III Performance (continued)

Superior Competitive Position Recognized By A Plethora Of Industry Awards

Industry Best of Product Awards & Special Partnerships

Company Name	Description of Award/Special Partnerships
AlterPoint, Inc.	•Named finalist in *Network World's* "Best of the Test 2005" •Partnerships with **Cisco, Hewlett-Packard, BMC, Concord**
Aperto Networks, Inc.	•Named one of *The Fierce 15* Top Wireless Startups of the Year (2004) •Partnerships with **Motorola, Nortel**
AppStream, Inc.	•*Codie Award Finalist* for "2005 Best Distributed Computing Solution" •"Best of Silicon Valley Entrepreneurship" by the *Indus Entrepreneurs* (TIE, 2004) •Recognized as *Red Herring* "10 Top Companies to Watch" (May 2000) •Received two "Best of Show" awards at the 2000 Network+Interop. •Twice selected as the "Most Likely To Succeed Startup" by the San Francisco Bay Start Biz Conference (1999, 2000)
Atrica, Inc.	•*Light Readings* "Top 10 Private Companies" (2005) •*Light Readings* "Top IPO or M&A Candidate" (2004) •*Red Herring* "100 Most Promising Startups" (2004)

BlueFire Security Technologies, Inc.	•*Software & Information Industry Association Codie Award* for:
	  - "Best Security Product/ Service" (2004)
	  - "Corporate Newcomer of the Year" (2004)

Cambia Security, Inc.	•Selected "Top Ten Technology Innovator" by the Technology Association of Georgia (2005)
Cenzic, Inc.	•*Codie Award Finalist* for "2005 Software Newcomer of the Year" •Named "Award Winner in Security Category" by Network+Interlop (2002)
ClearPoint Metrics, Inc.	•Partnership with **Symantec**
Cranite Systems, Inc.	•Named Winner in category of "Control Access to Wireless Access" *eWeek* (2003) •Partnership with **Symbol Technologies**

Private and Confidential
32

Company Name	Description of Award/Special Partnerships
EZchip Technologies, Inc.	•*Red Herring* "Top European Companies List" (2005) •*The Linley Group, A Guide to Network Processors* named EZchip as the Leading Next Generation Technology (2004) •Winner of the prestigious *Microprocessor Report Analyst Choice Award*, for "Best Network Processor" (2003)
FaceTime Communications, Inc.	•Partnerships and interoperability with **AOL, Microsoft, Yahoo, IBM, Google, Bloomberg, Jabber and Reuters** •Winner of the prestigious *SC Magazine* "Best Buy Award" (2005) •Key Labs certified FaceTime's IMAuditor™ as "The First in the Industry to Scale to 100,000+ Users" •*Lotus Advisor Magazine Award* for two consecutive years (2004, 2005) •*IDC* named FaceTime "Leader in Instant Messaging Management Market" for two consecutive years (2004, 2005)
Intact Corporation	•Named *Codie Award Finalist* for "Best Financial Product/Service three consecutive years (2003, 2004, 2005) •"Top Ranked Web-Based Solution" in the *CPA Technology Advisor's Review* (2005) •Partnerships with **IBM, Salesforce.com, ADP** and **PayMaxx**
Novarra, Inc.	• Selected finalist for "BREW 2005 Developer Award" by Qualcomm
Reactivity, Inc.	•Named one of the "2004 *Red Herring* 100 Companies Most Likely to Change the World" •Named one of the "Always on Top 100 Private Companies for 2004" •Named Finalist in "The Best of Interlop Award" for Network+*Interlop* (2005) •Named one of five "Cool Vendors in Enterprise Networking Solutions 2005" by Gartner •Partnership with **Computer Associates (CA)**
TenXc, Inc.	•Partnership with **Nortel, Nokia, Ericsson** for the T-Mobile account
Trusted Network Technologies, Inc.	•Named "Top 50 Technology Innovator" by *IT Week* •Voted "Most Likely to Succeed in Identity Management Category" at *IBDNetworks Under the Radar* event (2005)
Vormetric, Inc.	•Received *Computerworld's* "Annual Innovative Technology Award" (2004)
Xosoft, Inc.	•"Gold Product of the Year Award" in the Backup and Disaster Recovery Category (2005) •"Clear Choice Award" from *Network World Magazine* (2004) •"Best Practices in Storage Award" from *Storage Networking World Magazine* (2003) •Partnerships with **IBM, BMC** and **Computer Associates (CA)**

Private and Confidential
33

JK&B IV - - Vintage 2001

Too Young For Meaningful Overall Performance Evaluation, But Compares Well With Top-Tier Funds

Top-Tier 2001 Vintage - - Net IRR Performance*

Fund Name	2001	% IRR
Accel IV – S		-5.8
Ampersand V		-11.2
Austin Ventures VIII		-2.3
Centennial Fund VII		-13.0
Enterprise Partners VI		-9.9
Matrix Partners VII		1.4
Mesirow Capital Partners VIII		22.0
Morgenthaler Venture Partners VII		-4.9
New Enterprise Associates VIIIA		-6.8
New Enterprise Associates X		5.3
Polaris Venture Partners		-4.2
Prism Venture Partners IV		-23.4

JK&B IV	-6.66%

*Net to LPs, based on available public information.
Private Equity Intelligence, data available as of 9/30/06

Private and Confidential
34

JK&B IV (continued)

Portfolio Doing Well - - Revenues Steadily Growing At A Healthy Pace Despite Depressed Markets

JK&B IV
Revenues for Current Portfolio Companies
($ Millions)

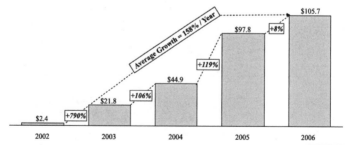

Private and Confidential
35

JK&B IV (continued)

Revenue Growth Enjoyed By All Vintage Year Companies

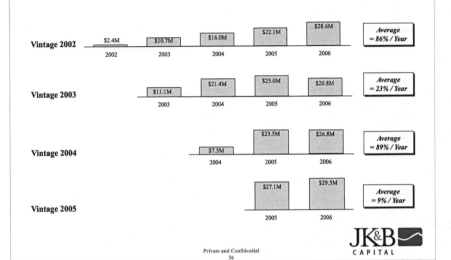

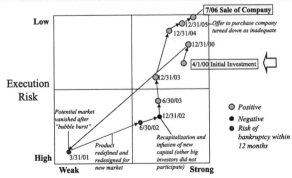

The Story of XOsoft

Conviction And Hands-On Involvement

Technical Competence And Market Insight Allowed JK&B To Turn Around A Failing/Displaced Technology Into A Success Story

Note: The chart placement of company and dates taken from formal presentations to JK&B LPs over the years.